Colloquial
Panjabi

The Colloquial Series

The following languages are available in the Colloquial series:

* Albanian
* Amharic
* Arabic of Egypt
* Arabic (Levantine)
* Arabic of the Gulf
  and Saudi Arabia
* Bulgarian
* Cambodian
* Cantonese
* Chinese
* Czech
* Danish
* Dutch
* English
* Estonian
* French
  German
* Greek
* Gujarati
* Hungarian
* Indonesian

* Italian
* Japanese
* Malay
* Norwegian
* Panjabi
* Persian
* Polish
* Portuguese
* Romanian
* Russian
* Serbo-Croat
* Spanish
* Spanish of Latin
  America
* Swedish
* Thai
* Turkish
* Ukrainian
* Vietnamese
* Welsh

* Accompanying cassette(s) available

Colloquial
Panjabi

A Complete Language Course

Mangat Rai Bhardwaj

London and New York

First published 1995
by Routledge
11 New Fetter Lane, London EC4P 4EE

Simultaneously published in the USA and Canada
by Routledge
29 West 35th Street, New York, NY 10001

© 1995 Mangat Rai Bhardwaj

Typeset in Times by Thomson Press (India) Ltd, New Delhi, India

Printed and bound in Great Britain by Clays Ltd, St Ives plc

British Library Cataloguing in Publication Data
A catalogue record for this book is available from the British Library

Library of Congress Cataloguing in Publication Data
A catalogue record for this book has been requested

ISBN 0-415-10191-3 (book)

ISBN 0-415-10192-1 (cassettes)

ISBN 0-415-10193-X (book and cassettes course)

Contents

Acknowledgements   vii
A word to the learner   1
Panjabi pronunciation and writing system   6

Conversation units

1 ਕੀ ਹਾਲ ਹੈ?   22
How are you?

2 ਮਿਲਕੇ ਬੜੀ ਖ਼ੁਸ਼ੀ ਹੋਈ   34
Pleased to meet you

3 ਕੀ ਚਾਹੀਦਾ ਹੈ?   47
What would you like to have?

4 ਕੀ ਤੁਹਾਨੂੰ ਸੰਗੀਤ ਪਸੰਦ ਹੈ?   64
Do you like music?

5 ਕੱਲ੍ਹ ਨੂੰ ਤੁਸੀਂ ਕੀ ਕਰਨਾ ਹੈ?   83
What are you going to do tomorrow?

6 ਕੱਲ੍ਹ ਤੁਸੀਂ ਕੀ ਕੀਤਾ?   99
What did you do yesterday?

7 ਕੀ ਤੁਸੀਂ ਪੰਜਾਬੀ ਬੋਲ ਸਕਦੇ ਹੋ?   120
Do you speak Panjabi?

8 ਇੱਥੇ ਕੀ ਕੀਤਾ ਜਾਂਦਾ ਹੈ?   138
What is done here?

9 ਮੈਨੂੰ ਕੁਝ ਹੋਰ ਵੀ ਕਹਿਣ ਦਿਓ   **157**
Let me say something else as well

10 ਯਾਦਾਂ 'ਚ ਤਾਜ਼ਾ ਨੇ ਸਭ   **166**
They're all still fresh in the memory

Script units

1 ਪਹਿਲਾ ਪਾਠ - ਪੜ੍ਹਾਈ ਲਿਖਾਈ   **176**
Script unit 1

2 ਦੂਸਰਾ ਪਾਠ - ਪੜ੍ਹਾਈ ਲਿਖਾਈ   **179**
Script unit 2

3 ਤੀਸਰਾ ਪਾਠ - ਪੜ੍ਹਾਈ ਲਿਖਾਈ   **183**
Script unit 3

4 ਚੌਥਾ ਪਾਠ - ਪੜ੍ਹਾਈ ਲਿਖਾਈ   **192**
Script unit 4

5 ਪੰਜਵਾਂ ਪਾਠ - ਪੜ੍ਹਾਈ ਲਿਖਾਈ   **198**
Script unit 5

6 ਛੇਵਾਂ ਪਾਠ - ਪੜ੍ਹਾਈ ਲਿਖਾਈ   **208**
Script unit 6

Grammatical summary   **220**
Word groups   **242**
Panjabi–English glossary   **261**
Key to exercises   **283**
Listening exercises transcripts   **289**
Index   **294**

Acknowledgements

The author and the publishers wish to thank the following for permission to reproduce extracts from their published writings:

Mr Surinder Delhavi for an extract from the short story *Makaan*;
Mr Amarjit Chandan for the poem '*Is Vele*';
Dr Mohinder Gill for extracts from the poem '*Shaam*'.

Several friends and colleagues read whole or parts of the first typescript of the book and offered valuable suggestions for improvement. The author is especially grateful to Narinder Singh, Susan Escribano, Gordon Wells and Dr Tej Bhatia (author of the sister volume *Colloquial Hindi*).

A word to the learner

Welcome to *Colloquial Panjabi*. The course, as the cover of this book clearly specifies, is a complete language course which aims at helping you learn the colloquial variety of Panjabi. As a complete language course for beginners, *Colloquial Panjabi* deals with all the four traditionally recognised linguistic skills:

	Receptive	*Productive*
Aural–oral	Listening comprehension	Speaking
Visual	Reading comprehension	Writing

But, more importantly, it attempts to do something else as well. One of its major objectives is to help the learner take her/his linguistic skills to the level from where she or he is able to take charge of her/his own learning, become her/his own language teacher and attain higher levels without anybody's help.

This course has been designed in such a way that you do not have to learn reading and writing at the same time as spoken Panjabi. So it does not 'force' the script upon those who do not wish to learn it. It is, of course, ideal to learn a language through its own native script. But you can learn its spoken variety through phonetic transcript as well. If you wish to learn reading and writing, you can start it at any time you like. If you already speak the language well, you can use this course to learn the Panjabi script.

You have learnt a language well if you are able to understand the new utterances you have never heard before and are able to produce new utterances you have not produced (or even heard) before. Life is always full of new and novel situations and challenges, which demand that you use your existing linguistic skills creatively to understand new and novel utterances and to produce new and novel utterances, both in speech and reading and writing. If your linguistic skills can deal with such situations satisfactorily, you have learnt your language well. A basic-level complete language course like this one cannot attain the impossible goal of imparting to you a complete mastery of the language. Rather, it ought to set you on the right course towards attaining it.

Clearly, this course is not a phrase book. A phrase book simply gives you ready-made utterances for different occasions. You simply memorise them and use them on appropriate occasions (and understand their purpose when others use them). Such books obviously can be helpful. But *Colloquial Panjabi* has a different set of aims and objectives. It is intended for adult learners who would like to learn how to understand and produce all sorts of utterances in all sorts of situations.

Methods and styles of learning

Each adult learner of a second language has his or her own style of learning. Some learners like to learn the alphabet of the language first. Some like to learn the rules of grammar, while others like to 'extract' from the spoken and/or printed sentences the relevant rules of grammar, and then check their 'discovery' against the rules given by the author. Some learners like to listen to the recording without looking at the printed dialogues (for example, when they are driving), while others like to read while listening. Some like to devote half a day once a week to language learning, while others like to do some practice every day. In short, there can be numerous styles of learning, and you can use the one (or a combination of the ones) that best suits you.

But all successful adult learners of a second (or third, or fourth, or ...) language agree that there is only one good method of learning: intelligent and creative practice. The structure of this course assumes that you will be using this method of learning. An intelligent and creative adult mind is a questioning mind. It needs to know why it is doing what it is doing. Accordingly, you will find in this book many explanations of why the Panjabi grammatical and writing systems work in the ways they do and how they differ from those of English. Word-for-word English glosses under the Panjabi sentences along with natural English translation are meant to highlight these differences. You should keep in mind these explanations and differences when you start practising these structures. In other words, your practice must be intelligent. Then move on to make your practice creative. There is a section called 'Word groups' at the end of this book. It gives you some Panjabi words used in different fields of everyday life. There is also a list of important Panjabi verbs at the end of the section called 'Grammatical summary'. After you have successfully done the exercises at the end of a 'Conversation unit', choose some new nouns, adjectives and verbs from the above-mentioned sections, imagine some new situation and try to construct new utterances, using the grammatical structures you have already mastered. Be bold and do not let the fear of making mistakes deter you. Do not always try to construct so-called 'full' sentences. You are learning *colloquial* Panjabi, which is full of utterances which are grammatically 'incomplete' but convey 'full' meaning in real-life situations. It is this colloquial variety of Panjabi which this course attempts to teach from the very beginning. Remember that it is ultimately by practice that you are going to learn the language. You can start by consciously applying the rules of grammar. But then a lot of practice should make the use of those rules habitual and automatic. Only then can you be really creative in your use of the language.

Cassette recordings

A comprehensive 'input' of authentic Panjabi speech into your mind is the first and most important prerequisite. So if you do not get an opportunity to hear a native Panjabi speaker regularly (and even if you do), the use of the cassette recordings is highly recommended. In speech, proper intonation and stressing of words is as important as correct pronunciation of vowels and consonants. This you can learn only by intensive and careful listening. The cassette symbol ▣ marks the passages which have been recorded on the cassettes.

These recordings also have brief explanations and comments in English, so that you need not look at the printed page every time you listen to a recording. You can use the recordings while you are driving!

The book

The book (the one you are now reading) is divided into sections. It starts with the introductory chapter 'Panjabi pronunciation and writing system'. This chapter is essential reading for every learner, whether or not he or she is learning the Panjabi script. It gives a concise but comprehensive description of the salient features of Panjabi pronunciation. Examples are recorded on the cassettes. The letters and symbols of the Panjabi script are introduced and the conventions used for the phonetic transcription of Panjabi are also described here.

The book has separate 'Conversation units' and 'Script units'. It is not necessary (but it is extremely useful) to learn spoken Panjabi through the Panjabi script. So you can start learning the Panjabi script (if you wish to) at any time. The phonetic transcription of Panjabi has been devised in such a way that for most words there is a one-to-one correspondence between phonetic symbols and Panjabi letters and symbols. All that you have to do is to substitute the correct Panjabi letters and symbols for the phonetic symbols.

Each of the first eight conversation units consists of the following parts:

(a) dialogues with English translation,
(b) vocabulary,
(c) language points, which give details of pronunciation, grammar and usage,
(d) exercises.

The vocabulary or the new words used in the dialogues are given both in the phonetic transcription and the Panjabi script. Panjabi nouns are marked either as masculine (*m*) or feminine (*f*). But the dialogues themselves are in the phonetic transcription only. If you wish to read them in the Panjabi script, you will find them in Script unit 6. The language points, which give details of pronunciation, grammar and usage, are quite detailed. But you do not need to memorise all the rules of Panjabi grammar. However, a proper understanding of these rules is necessary for your practice to be intelligent. In some exercises from Conversation unit 5 onwards, you will be asked to make use of the Panjabi vocabulary given in the section Word groups. You will need to first search for and then use the appropriate word or words. This will help you make your practice creative. Some of the exercises require you to listen to the recordings. If you do not have the cassette recordings, you can refer to the 'Listening exercises transcripts' at the end of the book.

Conversation unit 9 presents some important Panjabi grammatical structures with examples, which, for reasons of simplicity, could not be incorporated into the dialogues in the earlier units. Conversation unit 10 presents, with notes and explanations, some poetry and prose passages from published British Panjabi literature. You are, however, not expected to be able to write prose or poetry of comparable standards immediately after completing this course. (But there is no reason why you shouldn't be able to attain this capability in a few years' time.)

Five of the six script units explain in detail the principles underlying the Panjabi writing system. This book deals only with the Panjabi (Gurmukhi) script used for writing Panjabi in India and by people of Indian origin. All the major Panjabi dictionaries and newspapers use this script. In Pakistan, however, Panjabi is written in the Perso–Arabic script. But considerations of space did not permit the inclusion of this script in the course. Script unit 6 gives the dialogues of the conversation units in the Panjabi (Gurmukhi) script.

Since Conversation unit 10 and Script unit 5 are meant for those learners who wish to carry on learning Panjabi after completing this course, they are somewhat technical. Linguists interested in the grammatical and phonological structure of Panjabi may also find them informative. But those who wish to acquire simply a working knowledge of Panjabi may ignore them.

The Grammatical summary gives an overview of the Panjabi grammatical system. You should keep referring to the relevant parts of this section while you read the language points in the conversation units in order to have a better and more comprehensive knowledge of the relevant points of grammar.

Answers to the exercise can be found in the 'Key to exercises'.

The Glossary gives all the Panjabi words used in the dialogues. The words are listed alphabetically.

The 'Word groups' section gives some Panjabi words divided into areas of meaning. This is an extremely important section of the book, and you will need to refer to it not only while doing some of the exercises but also for some time after you have completed the course and mastered the grrammatical system of the language. Then, if you wish to go further, you will need a good Panjabi dictionary and a grammar book. Language learning is a life-long process!

ਸ਼ੁਭ ਕਾਮਨਾਵਾਂ
Best wishes!

Panjabi pronunciation and writing system

Introduction

This introductory chapter briefly describes the Panjabi pronunciation and writing system. Read this chapter again and again even if you are not learning the Panjabi script. If you are learning the Panjabi script, you will need to refer to the table on p. 9 again and again until you have learnt the shapes of all the letters (which takes quite some time).

Listen to and repeat the pronunciation of Panjabi vowels, consonants and tones recorded on the cassettes accompanying this book (with the book lying open before you, for the first few weeks at least).

Panjabi writing system

The Panjabi writing system (also known as the Gurmukhi script) is one of the simplest and most consistent writing systems. But the assertions often made by Panjabi chauvinists that 'Panjabi is a phonetic language' or that 'in Panjabi you speak exactly as you write and write exactly as you speak' are completely absurd. However, the Panjabi writing system is consistent in the way the German writing system is and the English writing system is not. Most letters and symbols in the Panjabi script have a fixed pronunciation. Only a few (seven out of fifty-five, to be precise) have variable pronunciation, depending on their position in the word. But even these letters and symbols have consistent pronunciation relative to their position.

In this book we use the phonetic transcription to teach you not only Panjabi pronunciation but also the Panjabi script. The phonetic symbols we use are taken from the International Phonetic Alphabet (IPA). Most of the time, these symbols represent both spelling and pronunciation when the relation between the two is direct. But when the pronunciation is different from what the spelling suggests, we give pronunciation in square brackets. For example, the Panjabi word meaning 'that' is written as ਉਹ in Panjabi. But its pronunciation is different from what the spelling suggests. Our transcription will follow the Panjabi spelling in such cases and transcribe it as **úfì**. But the pronunciation will also be given in square brackets, as [**ó**]. The relation between spelling and pronunciation is rule-governed, and the rules are very simple. But, as in any other language, some words defy all rules. Luckily for you, Panjabi has only a few 'trouble-makers' of this type.

In our system of phonetic transcription, as in the Panjabi script, there are seven symbols whose pronunciation will vary according to their position in the word. Those who know German or Italian or Spanish will already be familiar with this positional variation in the pronunciation of a letter. You can easily learn it in a few days. This will make the learning of the Panjabi script very easy: you will mostly be substituting Panjabi letters and symbols for the phonetic characters and observing a few rules of Panjabi spelling.

The Panjabi script does not have separate sets of lower case and upper case (or capital) letters. Only three of the forty letters of the alphabet change their shape relative to their position. Like all other modern scripts of Indian origin, the Panjabi script is a descendent of the Brahmi script used in ancient India. All these scripts have the same underlying system of organisation and only the shapes of their letters and symbols differ. If you learn one of these scripts, the learning of the other dozen or so used in India becomes quite easy. The people who developed the Brahmi script more than two thousand years ago are regarded even today as some of the finest linguists the world has ever seen. So the Panjabi script (or any other sister script) is not just a random collection of letters and symbols. It is an extremely ingenious system organised on phonological principles, as we shall see.

In this system, consonant sounds are represented by letters grouped on phonological principles. Vowel sounds are represented by symbols which are added to the letters. Some letters do not stand for consonant sounds and in fact have no pronunciation of their own. They are called vowel bearers to which vowel symbols are added when they cannot be added to consonant letters. Panjabi has three such vowel bearers. As you will learn later on, the system is thoroughly logical and consistent and hence very easy to learn.

Tones in Panjabi

Panjabi is a tone language like Swedish, Norwegian and Chinese. Very often the meaning of a sound sequence depends on the pitch of voice or tone used in pronouncing it. For example, if the Panjabi word **mɑ̄:** 'mother' is pronounced with a high tone as **mɑ̄:**, it becomes a different word meaning 'black lentils'. Similarly, **pɛ** 'to fall' becomes 'fear' if it is pronounced with a low pitch or tone as **pɛ̀**. A woman using the Panjabi word **mɛ̃** 'I' has to be extremely careful with the use of tone. If she pronounces the word with a high tone as **mɛ̃́**, she will be calling herself a buffalo!

Interestingly enough, tones are not represented by any letters or symbols in the Panjabi script. They started developing in the language about three or four centuries ago, long after the origin of the Panjabi writing system. But any intelligent student of the language can see that a Panjabi tone word nearly always has one of the six letters ਘ, ਝ, ਢ, ਧ, ਭ, ਹ which we transcribe as **gʱ**, **jʱ**, **ɖʱ**, **dʱ**, **bʱ**, **ɦ** respectively. In the Central variety of Panjabi, which this course aims to teach you, these letters used to be pronounced with a breathy voice. (These consonants are also recorded with a breathy voice on the cassettes accompanying this book.) Now the pronunciation of these letters except **ɦ** has changed. They have lost their breathy voice, and have given either a high tone or a low tone to the words in which they occurred. But in some Western Panjabi dialects spoken in Pakistan, these letters are still spoken with a breathy voice like their equivalents in other North Indian languages.

You can pronounce these consonants with a breathy voice if you like. Then your Panjabi will sound like the Western Panjabi dialects, which are respectable members of the Panjabi language family. Most speakers of Panjabi (including the author of this course) are not purists and do not care which dialect you speak as long as you are understood. You may also want to learn some other North Indian or Pakistani language which has breathy voiced consonants. Or you may already be speaking such a language. If that is the case, feel free to pronounce these consonants with a breathy voice. But do not forget to add the Panjabi tones. You may have noticed that we have chosen **ɦ** and **ʱ** with a peculiar 'hooked' shape to symbolise these consonants. This peculiar letter is an International Phonetic Alphabet (IPA) symbol used to indicate breathy voice. If you wish to sound like speakers of the Central variety of Panjabi, this 'hooked' letter should serve as a reminder that the word is most likely to have tone. But we shall also mark the tone in our transcription.

The Panjabi Consonants chart below shows the Panjabi consonant sounds and the Panjabi letters and the phonetic symbols used for representing them in writing. Do not worry about the technical terms like 'voiced', 'aspirated', 'tone', etc. They are fully explained later on in this chapter and examples are recorded on the cassettes.

Panjabi consonants

ੳ	ਅ	ੲ	ਸ	ਹ
	Vowel bearers		s	ɦ

The consonant square

	Voiceless unaspirated	Voiceless aspirated	Voiced unaspirated	Voiced aspirated	Nasal
k-group	ਕ	ਖ	ਗ	ਘ	ਙ
	k	k^h	g	$g^{ɦ}$	ŋ
c-group	ਚ	ਛ	ਜ	ਝ	ਞ
	c	c^h	j	$j^{ɦ}$	ɲ
ṭ-group	ਟ	ਠ	ਡ	ਢ	ਣ
	ṭ	$ṭ^h$	ḍ	$ḍ^{ɦ}$	ɳ
t-group	ਤ	ਥ	ਦ	ਧ	ਨ
	t	t^h	d	$d^{ɦ}$	n
p-group	ਪ	ਫ	ਬ	ਭ	ਮ
	p	p^h	b	$b^{ɦ}$	m
	ਯ	ਰ	ਲ	ਵ	ੜ
	y	r	l	v	ɽ
	ਸ਼	ਖ਼	ਗ਼	ਜ਼	ਫ਼
	ʃ	x	ɣ	z	f

Notes on the Panjabi consonants

Some of the rather outlandish-looking phonetic symbols on the chart (ŋ, ɲ, ɣ) and the Panjabi letters they stand for – ਙ, ਞ, ਗ਼ respectively – are hardly ever used in modern Panjabi. They have been included in this chapter simply because they are a part of the system. But we shall not be using them in this course.

The Consonant square

All the consonants within the Consonant square are pronounced by stopping the outgoing breath completely in the mouth and then releasing it. In the case of nasal consonants, breath goes on escaping through the nose during the 'hold phase' in the mouth. It is important to remember the grouping of these twenty-five consonants into five groups because some rules of Panjabi spelling take this grouping into account.

Place of articulation

All the consonants within a group (i.e. in a row in the square) have the same place of articulation. They are also called homorganic consonants because the same vocal organs are involved in the pronunciation of all the five consonants of a group, as described below.

k-*group*

ਕ	ਖ	ਗ	ਘ	ਙ
k	k^h	g	g^ɦ	ŋ

The back of the tongue touches the soft palate, as for the English 'k'.

c-*group*

ਚ	ਛ	ਜ	ਝ	ਞ
c	c^h	j	j^ɦ	ɲ

The front part of the tongue touches the hard palate behind the upper gum ridge, as for the English sound 'ch' in 'church'.

ṭ-*group (the 'tailed group')*

ਟ	ਠ	ਡ	ਢ	ਣ
ṭ	ṭ^h	ḍ	ḍ^ɦ	ɳ

The tongue curls back and the underside of the tongue touches the part of the palate behind the gum ridge. There are no equivalent sounds in English. It is important to use the *underside* of the tongue for all the sounds of this group and also for ṛ. The curled tails of the symbols for these consonants should serve as a reminder that the tongue should be curled when you pronounce them. The following diagram can be helpful.

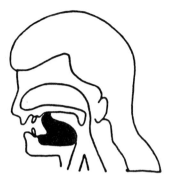

Diagram 1   Position of the tongue for the Panjabi [ʈ, ʈʰ, ɖ, ɖʱ, ɳ, ɽ]

t-group

ਤ	ਥ	ਦ	ਧ	ਨ
t	tʰ	d	dʱ	n

The tip of the tongue touches the teeth. Do not try to pronounce the sounds of this group by touching the gum ridge as you do for the pronunciation of the English 't' or 'd'. If you pronounce the Panjabi sounds of this group like the English sounds, you will not be able to maintain the distinction between these sounds and those of the ʈ-group.

Study the following diagrams very carefully.

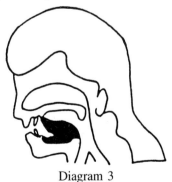

Diagram 2
Position of the tongue
for the Panjabi [t, tʰ, d, dʱ, n]

Diagram 3
Position of the tongue for the
English [t, d]
Avoid this tongue position if
you wish to keep Panjabi [ʈ, ʈʰ, ɖ,
ɖʱ, ɳ] and [t, tʰ, d, dʱ, n] series
distinct.

p-*group*

ਪ	ਫ	ਬ	ਭ	ਮ
p	pʰ	b	bɦ	m

The upper and the lower lip join, as for the English 'p'.

Manner of articulation ◖◗

All the consonants in a column in the Consonant square have the same manner of articulation.

Voiceless unaspirated

ਕ	ਚ	ਟ	ਤ	ਪ
k̲	c	t̲	t	p

The English 'p' and 'k' consonants are lightly aspirated. They are pronounced with a light puff of air. But the Panjabi sounds in this row are unaspirated. You have to control the force of your breath carefully. The stream of breath passes through the throat without creating any 'voice' or the buzzing sound made by the vibrating vocal cords.

Voiceless aspirated

ਖ	ਛ	ਠ	ਥ	ਫ
kʰ	cʰ	t̲ʰ	tʰ	pʰ

Consonants in this column are strongly aspirated and voiceless. If your aspiration is light, as in English, you can be misunderstood. The little symbol ʰ in the phonetic transcription is meant to remind you of strong aspiration. Remember that the sounds in this row are single consonants. For example, pʰ is a single consonant, not a sequence of 'p' and 'h'.

Voiced unaspirated

ਗ	ਜ	ਡ	ਦ	ਬ
g	j	d̲	d	b

Vocal cords vibrate and make a buzzing sound called 'voice'. The force of breath is light and the sounds are not aspirated.

Breathy voiced (or voiced aspirated)

ਘ	ਝ	ਢ	ਧ	ਭ
g^h	j^h	d^h	d^h	b^h

Breathy voice is a combination of voice and aspiration. While aspiration need not be very strong here, it should be clearly audible. The IPA symbol ^{h} marks breathy voice or the presence of a tone, depending on which variety of Panjabi you wish to choose as your model of pronunciation. As we have mentioned above, these breathy voiced consonants are used only in the Western dialects of Panjabi spoken in Pakistan. The Central and the Eastern varieties have lost them. They have been replaced by homorganic voiceless unaspirated consonants in some positions and by homorganic voiced unaspirated consonants in other positions. In addition, the words formerly having these consonants are now pronounced with tones. We shall fully explain all this later on in the book. This course teaches the Central (the so-called Standard) variety of Panjabi. But since the Panjabi letters for these consonants are still in use, we shall use their phonetic equivalents in our transcription. But our transcription also shows tones, which are not marked in the Panjabi script. You can choose either the Western or the Central pronunciation in your Panjabi speech. If you choose the latter, rest assured that the rules for 'translating' the Panjabi spelling and our phonetic transcription into pronunciation are extremely simple. We discuss them later on in the book.

Nasals

ਙ	ਞ	ਣ	ਨ	ਮ
ŋ	ɲ	ɳ	n	m

Outgoing breath is stopped in the mouth, but it goes on escaping through the nose during this hold phase. All these consonants are voiced.

Consonants outside the square

More or less English-like

ਸ	ਹ	ਯ	ਰ	ਲ
s	ɦ	y	r	l

ਵ	ਸ਼	ਜ਼	ਫ਼
v	ʃ	z	f

You can pronounce these consonants like their English equivalents. ਸ ʃ is pronounced like 'sh' in 'ship'. Panjabi ਹ is breathy voiced. So we transcribe it as ɦ. But you can safely pronounce it like the English 'h'. Panjabi ਵ can be pronounced either like the English 'v' or 'w'. Both are equally acceptable. Try to make your Panjabi ਲ sound like the English 'l' in 'light' and not like that in 'bull'.

No English equivalents

The 'tail' of the phonetic symbol ɽ for ੜ indicates that this consonant is pronounced by curling the tongue, as for the sounds of the ʈ-group. ɽ is simply a quick and rapid ɖ pronounced by flapping the underside of the tongue against the palate. ਖ x is pronounced like 'ch' in the Scottish word 'loch', and ਗ ɣ the voiced counterpart of x.

Panjabi vowels

Panjabi has ten distinct vowel sounds, which can be pronounced either orally (through the mouth only) or can be nasalised (pronounced through the mouth and the nose at the same time). Six of these vowels can be grouped into short-long pairs. The remaining four are long.

All these vowels are pure. The position of the tongue does not change during the pronunciation of the vowel, as it does in the case of the vowel sounds in English words like 'boy', 'try', 'go', etc. The Panjabi and the phonetic symbols for these vowels are:

Vowel	Panjabi symbol	Length
a	invisible	short
aː	ਾ	long
i	ਿ	short
iː	ੀ	long
u	ੁ	short
uː	ੂ	long
e	ੇ	long
ɛ	ੈ	long
o	ੋ	long
ɔ	ੌ	long

Remember, we have said that the symbol for the Panjabi vowel is invisible. We have not said that this vowel has no symbol. The distinction between 'invisible symbol' and 'no symbol' will become clear when we deal with the Panjabi letters known as the vowel-bearers.

Nasalisation

A vowel sound is said to be nasalised if it is pronounced through the mouth and the nose at the same time. In our transcription, we show nasalisation by placing the symbol ˜ above the vowel symbol, as in ɑ̃ː, ũ, ẽ etc.

Tones

Tones are not marked in the Panjabi script. But in our phonetic transcription we mark the low tone by the symbol ˋ and the high tone by the symbol ˊ placed above the vowel symbol, as in à and έ.

[kaɽiː]	link
[kàɽiː]	clock
[káɽiː]	curry
[koɽaː]	whip
[kòɽaː]	horse
[kóɽaː]	leper

Other symbols

To complete the list, we mention the remaining symbols used in the Panjabi script.

˘	marker of a long or 'double' consonant
ⁿ	marker of a homorganic nasal consonant or nasalisation of a vowel
˙	marker of nasalisation of a vowel
ˏ	**r** in some positions
ˌ	**ɦ** in some positions
˛	**v** in some positions

Do not worry about these symbols. They will be dealt with later on in the book.

Pronunciation practice

Listen to the cassettes if you have them, and repeat.

Vowels

Oral vowels

The English near-equivalents of Panjabi vowels given below are those of
the standard Southern English unless otherwise specified.

Vowel	Example	Length	English near-equivalent
a	amar	short	like 'a' in 'about'
aː	aːp	long	like 'a' in 'arm'
i	kir	short	like 'i' in 'sit'
iː	biː	long	like 'ee' 'seed'
u	tur	short	like 'oo' in 'book'
uː	ruːs	long	like 'oo' in 'food'
e	seb	long	like Scottish 'a' in 'gate'
ɛ	ɛʃ	long	like 'a' in 'bad', but slightly longer
o	ɦo	long	like Scottish 'o' in 'home'
ɔ	sɔkʰ	long	like 'o' in 'God', but slightly longer

Nasalised vowels

You need to practise the nasalised varieties of long vowels only.

ãː	mãːj	ɛ̃	gɛ̃ɖaː
ĩː	nĩːd	õ	gõd
ũː	bũːd	ɔ̃	nɔ̃
ẽ	gẽd		

Consonants

We do not include the 'breathy voiced' consonants **gʱ** ਘ, **jʱ** ਝ, **ɖʱ** ਢ, **dʱ** ਧ,
bʱ ਭ and nasals **ŋ** ਙ, **ɲ** ਞ in this list. We shall deal with these sounds

separately as special consonants. Listen to and repeat the following words.
Take care that you do not omit the 'r' sound in these words.

Consonant		*Example*
k	ਕ	kɑr
kʰ	ਖ	kʰɑː
g	ਗ	gɑː
c	ਚ	cɑl
cʰ	ਛ	cʰe
j	ਜ	jɑːg
ʈ	ਟ	ʈok
ʈʰ	ਠ	ʈʰok
ḍ	ਡ	ḍɑːk
ɳ	ਣ	sɑɳ
t	ਤ	tɑːʃ
tʰ	ਥ	tʰɑːn
d	ਦ	din
n	ਨ	nɑːp
p	ਪ	puːjɑː
pʰ	ਫ	pʰir
b	ਬ	biː
m	ਮ	mɑːp
y	ਯ	yɑːr
r	ਰ	rɑːs
l	ਲ	lɑːl
v	ਵ	vɑːriː
ɽ	ੜ	sɑːɽ
ʃ	ਸ਼	ʃɑːm
x	ਖ਼	xɑːs
ɣ	ਗ਼	ɣɑlat
z	ਜ਼	zɑxm
f	ਫ਼	fɑrz

'Breathy voiced' consonants and Panjabi tones

In our transcription, a 'breathy voiced' consonant is marked with the superscript 'hooked' ^fi symbol. There are (or were) five such consonants in Panjabi.

g^fi	j^fi	$\d^fi$	d^fi	b^fi
ਘ	ਝ	ਢ	ਧ	ਭ

These consonants occur (or occurred some centuries ago) in all the major North Indian languages. In most of these languages, they are pronounced with a breathy voice, which is a combination of voice and aspiration (symbolised in our transcription by the 'hooked' ^fi). But in the Central and the Eastern varieties of Panjabi, they are no longer used. In some positions they have become voiceless unaspirated and in some other positions they have become voiced unaspirated. Additionally, the words which originally had these consonants are pronounced with a tone now. You can pronounce them with a breathy voice if you wish to sound like speakers of the Western dialects of Panjabi. But even the Western dialects have tones. So you can either pronounce them as

Consonant		Low tone	High tone
g^fi	ਘ	g^fiàr	bá:g^fi
j^fi	ਝ	j^fià:ɽu:	sá̃:j^fi
$\d^fi$	ਢ	$\d^fi$òl	ká:$\d^fi$
d^fi	ਧ	d^fià:ga:	sá:d^fi
b^fi	ਭ	b^fià:n	lá:b^fi

or you can pronounce the same words in the following way. Note that in words having low tone the '4th consonant of the group' (the breathy voiced one) becomes the '1st consonant' (voiceless unaspirate). In words with the high tone the '4th consonant' becomes the '3rd consonant' (voiced unaspirate). We shall deal with the rules (which are really quite simple) governing these changes when we discuss Panjabi spelling. But you may practise these consonants and tones right now.

The low tone

Listen to these words:

Consonant		Low tone
g^fi	ਘ	[kàr]
j^fi	ਝ	[cà:ɽu:]
$\d^fi$	ਢ	[tòl]

| **dʱ** | प | [tàːgɑː] |
| **bʱ** | ज | [pàːn] |

Listen very carefully to these five words again. You will notice that the movement of the pitch of voice is like this:

↘↗

The pitch falls and then rises. There is also some constriction in the throat, but you can ignore this because it is not very important at this stage. Once you have learnt how to manage the pitch movement properly, the constriction will come automatically.

The movement of the pitch in the word **gʱàr** [kàr] can be graphically represented as below:

The high tone

Listen to these words:

Consonant		*Low tone*
gʱ	ब	[báːg]
jʱ	झ	[sáːj]
ɖʱ	ड	[káːɖ]
dʱ	द	[sáːd]
bʱ	भ	[láːb]

Listen to these words again. You will notice that the movement of the pitch of voice is like this:

↗↘

The pitch first rises and then falls. So the word **sáːdʱ** [sáːd] can be graphically represented as below:

It is recommended that for the first few weeks you keep returning to this introductory chapter and this stretch of the cassette. At first listen carefully. Then listen and repeat. Your ears and vocal cords should get used to the pitch movement of the Panjabi tones. If you are not careful here, you may misunderstand others or may be misunderstood by them.

Remember that all the words having the smaller 'hooked' ˁ symbol and many words having the bigger 'hooked' ਲ਼ symbol have either of the two tones. Fortunately, you cannot have both these tones in a single word.

The consonants ŋ (ਙ) and ɲ (ਞ)

These consonants hardly ever occur as independent consonants in modern Panjabi. So you will probably never use them in your writing. We shall deal with independent and dependent consonants later on (in Script unit 4) when we deal with Panjabi spelling rules.

The 'new' consonants

ʃ	x	ɣ	z	f
ਸ਼	ਖ਼	ਗ਼	ਜ਼	ਫ਼

These consonant sounds were not there originally in Panjabi. They came from other languages through borrowed words. Many speakers of Panjabi do not use them and substitute the closest-sounding native Panjabi sounds for them. In their speech

ʃ	ਸ਼	becomes	s	ਸ
x	ਖ਼	becomes	k^h	ਖ
ɣ	ਗ਼	becomes	g	ਗ
z	ਜ਼	becomes	j	ਜ
f	ਫ਼	becomes	p^h	ਫ

You can easily see that the Panjabi letters for these sounds have been prepared by adding dots to the letters for the closest-sounding native sounds. The Panjabi alphabet is also called **pɛ̃ti:**, which means 'thirty-five', because it originally had thirty-five letters.

Some useful tips about Panjabi pronunciation

(a) Panjabi ਰ **r** in spelling is meant to be pronounced, not omitted. Pronounce it in all the positions; otherwise you can be misunderstood.

(b) Aspirated and unaspirated consonants should be kept distinct in pronunciation. Aspiration in Panjabi must be very (repeat, very) strong.

(c) Consonants of the **ṭ**-group (the 'tailed ones') and those of the **t**-group must be kept distinct in pronunciation. The English-like 'middle' pronunciation applied to both groups won't do. Look at the diagrams on p. 11 again.

(d) The speech rhythm of Panjabi is more like that of French than that of English. While practising, speak steadily, lightly and evenly, stressing all the words. Keep in check the English habit of stressing some words or syllables strongly and going through the others quickly, and thus weakening and shortening their vowels.

(e) Panjabi is a vigorous language spoken by vigorous people and involving vigorous movements of the lungs and the jaw. You may be able to speak English while holding a smoking pipe between your teeth. But you certainly cannot speak intelligible Panjabi in this way!

1 ਕੀ ਹਾਲ ਹੈ?

How are you?

In this unit you will learn to:
- use simple greetings
- use expressions for leave-taking
- ask simple questions
- make simple requests
- use personal pronouns (e.g. 'I', 'you', 'we', 'he', etc.)
- use some adjectives with nouns

ਗੱਲ ਬਾਤ   Dialogues

Panjabi greetings vary according to the religion of the speakers, not according to the time of day.

Dialogue 1: Sikh greetings

Darshan Singh and Sohan Singh know each other well but are not close friends. They meet in a Sikh temple in Birmingham

SOHAN:	sat sri: aka:l ji:.
DARSHAN:	sat sri: aka:l ji:. ki: ɦa:l ɦɛ?
SOHAN:	tʰi:k ɦɛ ji:, tusĩ: dasso.
DARSHAN:	tʰi:k ɦɛ.
	(The conversation continues for some time)
DARSHAN:	accʰa: ji:. sat sri: aka:l.
SOHAN:	sat sri: aka:l.
SOHAN:	*Greetings.*
DARSHAN:	*Greetings. How are you? (Lit.: What is (your) condition?)*

SOHAN:	*Fine. How are you?* (Lit.: *You please say.*)
DARSHAN:	*Fine.*
	(The conversation continues for some time)
DARSHAN:	*OK. Goodbye.*
SOHAN:	*Goodbye.*

Vocabulary

sat sri: aka:l	ਸਤਿ ਸ੍ਰੀ ਅਕਾਲ	Sikh greeting and reply to the greeting
fia:l (*m*)	ਹਾਲ	condition
ki:	ਕੀ	What?
tʰi:k	ਠੀਕ	fine, OK
tusĩ:	ਤੁਸੀਂ	you (*pl*)
dasso	ਦੱਸੋ	please say/tell
accʰa: ji:	ਅੱਛਾ ਜੀ	well, OK (used to indicate the end of the conversation)

Colloquial pronunciation

Colloquial pronunciation of the Panjabi **fiɛ** differs from region to region. But we recommend the pronunciation [ɛ], which we have recorded on the cassettes. We shall use square brackets to enclose pronunciation when it differs from what the spelling suggests.

The Sikh greeting

sat sri: aka:l (*lit.:* 'God is true' or 'Truth is immortal') is the most commonly used Sikh greeting. It is also used for leave-taking. **ji:** is often added to Panjabi utterances to show respect. **sat sri: aka:l** is usually said with hands folded in front of the chest and the head bowed down slightly.

Word-for-word translation

Where a Panjabi expression differs literally from its English equivalent, we shall use, where possible, a word-for-word translation to show this difference. For example, the Panjabi equivalent of 'How are you?' is

ki:	**fia:l**	**fiɛ?**
what	condition	is

And the reply

t̪ʰiː k	fiɛ
fine	is

is also different.

Position of the verb in a Panjabi sentence

In Panjabi, the verb (the equivalent of 'is', 'am', 'are', etc. in the above examples) usually comes at the end.

'Respectful plural' in Panjabi

The plural form of 'you' (**tusı̃ː**) and grammatical forms related to this plural form of 'you' are used to show respect even to one addressee. The singular form **tũː** of 'you' is used to show intimacy or disrespect or for addressing God. In the following Units, **tũː** will be used in the situations where speakers of Panjabi use it. But since being respectful is of paramount importance, it is recommended that *you* use **tusı̃ː** (unless you wish to address God in Panjabi!).

Dialogue 2: Hindu greetings

Baldev Yadav, who is fighting a council election in Coventry, goes to see Anil Sharma and to request support in the election. The two men know each other well, but their relations are rather formal

YADAV:	namaste *Sharma* jiː.
SHARMA:	namaste *Yadav* sáːfiab. bet̪ʰo.
YADAV:	ʃukriːa jiː.
SHARMA:	kiː fiaːl fiɛ?
YADAV:	t̪ʰiːk fiɛ. tusı̃ː suṇaːo. tufiaːɖa kiː fiaːl fiɛ?
SHARMA:	mera fiaːl vi t̪ʰiːk fiɛ. fiukam karo.
YADAV:	fiukam náfĩ̃ː jiː. benti fiɛ.
	(The conversation continues for some time)
YADAV:	canga *Sharma* jiː. ijaːzat̪ dio. namaste.
SHARMA:	namaste jiː.

YADAV:	*Greetings, Mr Sharma.*
SHARMA:	*Greetings, Mr Yadav. Please sit down.*
YADAV:	*Thanks.*

SHARMA:	*How are you?*	
YADAV:	*I'm fine. How are you?*	
SHARMA:	*I'm fine too. What can I do for you?* (Lit.: *Please order*)	
YADAV:	*I wish to make a request.* (Lit.: *It's not an order;* *it's a request*)	
	(The conversation continues for some time)	
YADAV:	*OK, Mr Sharma. Now please allow me to go. Goodbye.*	
SHARMA:	*Goodbye.*	

Vocabulary

namaste (ji:)	ਨਮਸਤੇ (ਜੀ)	greeting
sá:fiab (*m*)	ਸਾਹਬ	Mr (but put after the name)
mera:	ਮੇਰਾ	my
tufia:ɖa:	ਤੁਹਾਡਾ	your (*pl*)
bɛtʰo	ਬੈਠੋ	please sit down
ʃukri:a:	ਸ਼ੁਕਰੀਆ	thanks
suŋa:o	ਸੁਣਾਓ	please tell
fiukam (*m*)	ਹੁਕਮ	order
karo	ਕਰੋ	please do
náfii:	ਨਹੀਂ	not
benti: (*f*)	ਬੇਨਤੀ	request
canga:	ਚੰਗਾ	Well! (same as **accʰa:**)
ija:zat (*f*)	ਇਜਾਜ਼ਤ	permission
dio	ਦਿਓ	please give
vi:	ਵੀ	also

Colloquial pronunciation

sá:fiab is informally pronounced as [**sá:b**] and **náfii:** as [**nái:**], both with the high tone. You will learn later that **fi** is not pronounced in many words having the high tone. The rules of pronunciation are quite simple and are dealt with in Conversation unit 4 and Script unit 5.

The Hindu greeting

Like the Sikh greeting **sat sri: aka:l**, **namaste (ji:)** is used both as a greeting and a leave-taking expression and is said in the same way, i.e. with hands folded in front of the chest and the head slightly bowed down. **namaste** literally means 'I bow to you respectfully.'

The 'politeness game'

fiukam	**karo**
order	please do

is a rather formal way of saying 'What can I do for you?' Good manners demand the response

fiukam	**náfii:**	**ji:**	**benti:**	**fiɛ**
order	not	(respect)	request	is

It's not an order; it's a request.

The Persian word **arz** is often used in place of **benti:**. The two words have exactly the same meaning.

If someone takes the initiative in this 'politeness game' by saying

arz	**fiɛ**
request	is

You are expected to say

náfii:	**ji:,**	**fiukam**	**karo**
no	(respect)	order	please do

No please. Give me an order.

or simply

fiukam	**karo**
order	please do

All this may sound over-formal. But it is a part of the Panjabi culture. Do not feel that you must be so formal in your own Panjabi speech. Just be aware of the existence of such expressions and try to use them in order to practise your grammar.

Dialogue 3: Muslim greetings ●●

Panjabi-speaking Muslims often use some Arabic and Persian expressions or Panjabi expressions containing words borrowed from these languages. At this stage, you do not need to analyse these expressions. Just learn to use them as they are.

Nazir Haq and Khalid Rahman come across each other in a public library in Bradford

NAZIR:	assala:m alɛkam, *Khalid* sá:ɦab.
KHALID:	va: lɛkam assala:m, *Nazir* bʰà:i:. ki: ɦa:l ɦɛ?
NAZIR:	alla: da: ʃukar ɦɛ. sábʰ xɛri:at ɦɛ?
KHALID:	ji: ɦã:, alla: da: ʃukar ɦɛ. taʃri:f rakʰo.
NAZIR:	ji: náɦĩ:, ʃukri:a:. xuda: ɦa:fiz.
KHALID:	xuda: ɦa:fiz.

NAZIR:	*Greetings, Mr Khalid.*
KHALID:	*Greetings, brother Nazir. How are you?*
NAZIR:	*I'm fine. Is everything fine with you?*
	(Lit.: 'Thank God'.)
KHALID:	*Yes, I'm fine. Please sit down.*
NAZIR:	*No, thanks. Goodbye.*
KHALID:	*Goodbye.*

Vocabulary

ɦã:	ਹਾਂ	yes
bʰà:i: (*m*)	ਭਾਈ	brother

The Muslim greeting

Note that the greeting and the reply to the greeting are different. The expressions literally mean

assala:m alɛkam	Peace be on you!
va: lɛkam assala:m	Peace be on you too!
xuda: ɦa:fiz	God protect you!

You don't need to fold your hands while using these expressions, but bowing the head slightly is regarded as polite behaviour.

When people of different religions greet each other

There is no rule regarding which greeting should be used when people of different religions greet each other. Very often, the person who speaks first generally uses the greeting of the other person's religion (see Conversation unit 8). To respect other people's religious feelings is one of the ways of being polite. A completely 'secular' greeting **ɦɛlo ji:** ('hello to you') is also used these days, particularly by some Westernised Panjabis.

ਭਾਸ਼ਾ ਬਾਰੇ   Language points

The grammatical system of Panjabi (which, with a few minor differences, is shared by all the major North Indian and Pakistani languages) is not very complicated. In this section we briefly describe some salient features of Panjabi grammar. You do not have to memorise or intensively practise all of them in this unit. Do not feel that you have to 'master' everything in this lesson before you move on to the next! Just be aware of the existence of these features. We shall go on elaborating and using them throughout this course.

Word order in Panjabi

The order of words in a Panjabi sentence is not rigidly fixed as in English (or as some books on Panjabi grammar would like to make you believe). A Panjabi speaker or writer enjoys considerable freedom in placing words in an utterance (often to achieve stylistic effects). But this does not mean that you can 'put anything anywhere' in a Panjabi utterance. We shall discuss all this in later units. For the purpose of this lesson, just note that a verb in a Panjabi utterance is usually (but not invariably) placed at the end. Adjectives usually precede the nouns they qualify (as in English). For examples:

ki:	**fia:l**	**fiɛ?**	
what	condition	is	

mera:	**fia:l**	**tʰi:k**	**fiɛ.**
my	condition	fine	is

Yes/No questions

In spoken Panjabi, you can form a yes/no question simply by changing your intonation. You do not have to put the verb before the subject, as you do in English. In Dialogue 3 above, Nazir asks

sábⁿ	**xeri:at**	**fiɛ?**
everything	fine	is

How are you? (*Lit.:* Is everything OK?)

simply by using the the 'question intonation' (the pitch of the voice rising towards the end of the utterance). The same sentence with a 'statement intonation' (pitch falling at the end) would mean 'I'm fine'.

Pronouns

The Panjabi pronouns are

mḛ	ਮੈਂ	I
asi̇ː	ਅਸੀਂ	we
tṵː	ਤੂੰ	you (*sg*)
tusi̇ː	ਤੁਸੀਂ	you (*pl*)
iɦ [é]	ਇਹ	he, she, it, they
úɦ [ó]	ਉਹ	he, she, it, they

The plural form **tusi̇ː** is used to show respect even when the addressee is one person. **iɦ**, pronounced as [é] with a high tone and without the [ɦ] sound, is used when the person or persons referred to are present or are in proximity. **úɦ**, pronounced as [ó], is used to refer to a person or persons who are absent or at a distance. There is no gender distinction in Panjabi pronouns. (For other forms of Panjabi pronouns, see the tables in the Grammatical summary, pages 222–224.)

Some of you may have started suspecting that **iɦ** [é] and **úɦ** [ó] also (and primarily) mean '*this/these*' and '*that/those*' respectively. Your suspicion is indeed correct. If, like the author of this book, you relish grammatical technicalities, it may be of some interest to you that **iɦ** is called a 'proximate demonstrative pronoun' and **úɦ** is called a 'remote demonstrative pronoun' or a 'distal demonstrative pronoun' for reasons anybody can guess.

Number and gender

Panjabi nouns (like French, Italian and Spanish nouns) are marked for both number (singular or plural) and gender (masculine or feminine). Adjectives and most verb-forms agree with nouns in number and gender. This means that most verb-forms and about 50 per cent of the adjectives in Panjabi carry one of the following number–gender affixes.

	Singular	*Plural*
Masculine	-aː	-e
Feminine	-iː	-iːãː

We shall call this box the 'Magic square'. Memorise these four affixes. You will be using them with about 90 per cent of the verb-forms. (So you will not need to memorise a large number of conjugation tables!) About 50 per cent of Panjabi adjectives also take them. The rest do not take anything at all!

Remember that these affixes are added to verbs and adjectives only. Nouns (which force verbs and adjectives to 'agree' with them in number and gender by having these affixes) may or may not have them. Moreover, the form or meaning of a noun in Panjabi does not always indicate its gender. Male living creatures are nearly always masculine, and female living creatures are nearly always feminine. But sometimes the sex of a creature cannot be known or is unimportant. In such cases grammatical gender is assigned arbitrarily. **kā̃:** 'crow' and **maccʰar** 'mosquito' are masculine but **ka:ʈo** 'squirrel' and **jū̃:** 'louse' are feminine. The gender of nouns denoting inanimate objects and abstract ideas can be either masculine or feminine. There is no rule except 'Do as the Panjabis do.' So when you learn a new noun word, also learn its gender. If you have experience of learning a language like French or German or Spanish, you have already done this in the past.

Most, but not all, Panjabi nouns ending in **-a:** are masculine, and most nouns ending in **-i:** are feminine. But this is not the rule and there can be glaring exceptions. **ma:li:** '(male) gardener' is masculine and **ma:la:** 'garland' is feminine! A look at the following representative list of Panjabi nouns can be instructive.

Masculine			*Feminine*		
billa:	ਬਿੱਲਾ	tom cat	**billi:**	ਬਿੱਲੀ	female cat
gʰòɽa:	ਘੋੜਾ	horse	**gʰòɽi:**	ਘੋੜੀ	mare
munɖa:	ਮੁੰਡਾ	boy	**kuɽi:**	ਕੁੜੀ	girl
kamra:	ਕਮਰਾ	room	**kursi:**	ਕੁਰਸੀ	chair
bú:ɦa:	ਬੂਹਾ	door	**kʰiɽki:**	ਖਿੜਕੀ	window
dúddʰ	ਦੁੱਧ	milk	**cá:ɦ**	ਚਾਹ	tea
a:lu:	ਆਲੂ	potato	**ga:jar**	ਗਾਜਰ	carrot
sir	ਸਿਰ	head	**akkʰ**	ਅੱਖ	eye
safa:	ਸਫ਼ਾ	page	**kita:b**	ਕਿਤਾਬ	book
landan	ਲੰਡਨ	London	**dilli:**	ਦਿੱਲੀ	Delhi

dá:ɦɽi: 'beard' and **muccʰ** 'moustache', symbols of masculinity since time immemorial, are feminine in Panjabi.

Possessive adjectives

The Panjabi equivalents of the English 'my', 'our', 'your', etc. are

merɑ:	ਮੇਰਾ	my
sa:ɖɑ:	ਸਾਡਾ	our
terɑ:	ਤੇਰਾ	your (singular)
tuɦà:ɖɑ:	ਤੁਹਾਡਾ	your (plural)
íɦdɑ: [éda:]	ਇਹਦਾ	his, her, its (proximate)
úɦdɑ: [óda:]	ਉਹਦਾ	his, her, its (remote)

Since these adjectives end in **-ɑ:**, they are in the masculine singular form (see the Magic square on p. 29). By replacing this **-ɑ:** with one of the other affixes in the Magic square, we can make other forms. For example:

úɦdɑ: gʰòɽɑ:	**úɦde gʰòɽe**
his/her horse	his/her horses
úɦdi: gʰòɽi:	**úɦdi:ã: gʰòɽi:ã:**
his/her mare	his/her mares

For other forms of Panjabi adjectives, see the Grammatical summary, page 224.

The Panjabi rules for such agreement between nouns and adjectives must be learnt (and practised) very carefully to avoid a potential pitfall.

The pitfall

In English expressions like 'his horse', 'her dog', etc., it is the gender of the possessor that is marked on the adjective. In Panjabi, on the other hand, it is the gender of the possessed that is marked on the adjective.

úɦdɑ: gʰòɽɑ: means both 'his horse' and 'her horse'. Since **gʰòɽɑ:** 'horse' is masculine, the adjective **úɦdɑ:** also has the masculine form. Whether the owner is a man or a woman is not grammatically significant here.

Similarly, **úɦdi: gʰòɽi:** can mean both 'his mare' and 'her mare'. It is the feminine gender of the word **gʰòɽi:** 'mare' that is marked on the adjective **úɦdi:** as well.

Orders and requests

As in English, the bare stem of the verb can be used to make an order. In order to make a request, you add the suffix **-o** to the stem. This **-o** is the equivalent of the English 'please'. Actually, it indicates that the subject of the verb is plural. But, as you know fully well by now, using the plural form for a single person is a grammatical way of showing respect in Panjabi. For example:

kar	do	beʈʰ	sit down
karo	please do	beʈʰo	please sit down

There is another verb form of Panjabi which is used for requests which are made in the form of a suggestion. (See the Grammatical summary, page 229.)

Note that we use the expression 'stem of the verb', and not 'root of the verb'. This distinction is important in Panjabi and is discussed in a later chapter.

ਅਭਿਆਸ   Exercises

1   If you have the cassettes, listen to the recording. Are the speakers Sikhs, Hindus or Muslims? What are their names?   ▣

2   How would you reply to someone who said this to you?   ▣

(a)   sat sri: aka:l.
(b)   xuda: ɦa:fiz.
(c)   ki: ɦa:l ɦɛ?
(d)   assala:m alɛkam.
(e)   ɦukam karo.
(f)   canga: ji:, namaste.
(g)   arz ɦɛ ji:.

3   Match the replies in column B with the questions or greetings or requests in column A.

A	B
(1) namaste ji:.	(a) va: lɛkam assala:m.
(2) ki: ɦa:l ɦɛ?	(b) náɦi: ji:, benti: ɦɛ.
(3) taʃri:f rakʰo.	(c) ji: ʃukri:a:.
(4) assala:m alɛkam.	(d) tʰi:k ɦɛ ji:, ʃukri:a:.
(5) ɦukam karo.	(e) namaste.

4   Fill in the gaps in the two conversations given below:

Conversation 1

Man: _____
Woman: namaste ji:.

Man:	kiː fiaːl fiɛ?
Woman:	_____ tʰiːk fiɛ. _____ dasso. _____ kiː fiaːl fiɛ?
Man:	_____ fiaːl viː tʰiːk fiɛ.

Conversation 2

Man 1:	assalaːm alɛkam.
Man 2:	_____
Man 1:	k i ː_____ fiɛ?
Man 2:	allaː ._____
Man 1:	_____ rakʰo.
Man 2:	jiː ʃukriːaː.

5 Making use of the list of possessive adjectives on p. 31 and of nouns on p. 30, how would you translate the following into Panjabi? (Always use the respectful plural form of the Panjabi 'you'.)

my head	our tom cat
her room	our room
his chair	my horse
your book	your eye

2 ਮਿਲਕੇ ਬੜੀ ਖ਼ੁਸ਼ੀ ਹੋਈ
Pleased to meet you

In this unit you will learn to
- introduce yourself and others
- say and ask what you and others do
- say and ask where you and others work
- give simple information about your family
- talk about habitual and ongoing actions and events
- use the imperfective verb form

ਗੱਲ ਬਾਤ   Dialogues

Educated speakers of Panjabi, whether living in the Punjab or elsewhere, use many English words in their Panjabi speech. Their pronunciation of these words is often slightly 'Panjabi-ised'. But you do not need to modify your own natural pronunciation of these words while speaking Panjabi. In the following dialogues, these words and English and Panjabi names are not transcribed and are printed in italic type.

Dialogue 1 🔲

Ramesh Varma, a young accountant, is at a party given by his client and friend Ranjit Singh Bains. He sees a scholarly-looking man standing alone in a corner with a cup of tea and asks Bains who the man is. On learning that his name is Dr Joginder Singh, Varma approaches him

Varma:	maːf karnaː. tufiaːɖaː nãː ɖaːkṭar *Joginder Singh* fiɛ naː?
Singh:	fiãː jiː. meraː nãː *Joginder Singh* fiɛ.
Varma:	meraː nãː *Ramesh* fiɛ.

SINGH:	milke baɽiː xuʃıː fioiː. tufiaːɖaː puːraː nã̃ː kiː fiɛ?
VARMA:	*Ramesh Varma.*
SINGH:	tusĩː kiː kamm karde fio?
VARMA:	mɛ̃ *accountant* fiã̃ː. tusĩː *GP* fio jã̃ː *consultant*?
SINGH:	jiː nǎfiĩ̌ː, mɛ̃ *medical* ɖaːkʈar nǎfiĩ̌ː. mɛ̃ *PhD* fiã̃ː.

VARMA:	*Excuse me. You are Dr Joginder Singh, aren't you?*
SINGH:	*Yes. My name is Joginder Singh.*
VARMA:	*My name is Ramesh.*
SINGH:	*Pleased to meet you. What's your full name?*
VARMA:	*Ramesh Varma.*
SINGH:	*What do you do?*
	(Lit.: *What work are you doing?*)
VARMA:	*I'm an accountant. Are you a GP or a consultant?*
SINGH:	*No. I'm not a medical doctor. I have a PhD.*
	(*Lit.: I'm a PhD.*)

Vocabulary

maːf karnaː	ਮਾਫ਼ ਕਰਨਾ	Excuse me!
daːkʈar	ਡਾਕਟਰ	doctor
nã̃ː (*m*)	ਨਾਂ	name
milke baɽiː xuʃıː fioiː	ਮਿਲਕੇ ਬੜੀ ਖ਼ੁਸ਼ੀ ਹੋਈ	Pleased to meet you
puːraː	ਪੂਰਾ	full
kamm (*m*)	ਕੰਮ	work
karde	ਕਰਦੇ	doing

Formulas

Panjabi, like English and most other languages, has 'formulaic expressions' or 'formulas' which are spoken in certain situations. You learn a formula as an unbroken and unanalysed whole. 'Excuse me' and 'Pleased to meet you' and their Panjabi equivalents are formulas. We shall come across many such formulas in this book. Just memorise them and use them on appropriate occasions without worrying too much about their internal grammatical structure or meanings of individual words. We shall analyse and explain them later on.

Word order

mera:	**nã:**	**jogindar**	**síng$^\text{fl}$**	**fiɛ**
my	name	Joginder	Singh	is

My name is Joginder Singh.

tusĩ:	**ki:**	**kamm**	**karde**	**fio?**
you	what	work	doing	are

What do you do? *or* What's your job?

The position of a question word (**ki:**, for example) in a Panjabi sentence is quite flexible. It is not necessary to have it at the beginning of the sentence. If possible, try to avoid putting it there (except in the formula **ki: fia:l fiɛ?**) because you may sound abrupt, authoritative and less polite if you do this. Keep the question word close to the word or words it is connected with, as in

tufia:ɖa:	**nã:**	**ki:**	**fiɛ?**
your	name	what	is

What is your name?

You can also say

tufia:ɖa:	**ki:**	**nã:**	**fiɛ?**
your	what	name	is

As you will learn later, a yes/no question also sometimes starts with **ki:**. But this **ki:** is a different word and does not mean 'what'.

Tag questions

A tag question is a statement with a little question 'tagged' to it. The Panjabi equivalent of

You are Dr Joginder Singh, aren't you?

is simple. You simply add **na:** at the end. However, while the English sentence has two intonation contours, the Panjabi sentence has only one. Speak the English sentence aloud. You will notice a very short pause after the word 'Singh'. So the first intonation contour ends here, and the second begins with the word 'aren't'. But if you listen carefully to the Panjabi sentence, you will find that there is no pause within the sentence.

The English-type tag question is also there in Panjabi. It has a tag **ɦɛ nɑː** (*lit.:* 'Isn't it?') pronounced with a rising intonation. We shall deal with it in a later unit.

The Panjabi equivalent of the verb 'to be' – *ɦɛ*

It is wrong to say 'I are' or 'you am' or 'we is' in English. The English verb 'to be' has different forms, depending upon the person with which it is used. The same applies to Panjabi. The Panjabi counterpart of the English 'to be' **ɦɛ** has the following forms:

	Singular	*Plural*
First person	**ɦɑ̃ː** (I) am	**ɦɑ̃ː** (We) are
Second person	**ɦɛ̃** (You) are (singular)	**ɦo** (You) are (plural)
Third person	**ɦɛ** (He/she/it) is	**ɦɑn [ne]** (They) are

The endings given in the Magic square are not added to this verb.

The verb forms given above are the ones used in writing and/or formal speech. The more colloquial variants differ from region to region. In informal and colloquial speech

ɦɑ̃ː	becomes	**ɑ̃ː** *or* **vɑ̃ː**
ɦɛ̃	becomes	**ẽ** *or* **ɛ̃** *or* **ɑ̃ː**
ɦo	becomes	**o**
ɦɛ	becomes	**e** *or* **ɛ** *or* **vɑː** *or* **ɑː** *or* **je**
ne	becomes	**ɑː** *or* **vɑː**

You can use the variants recorded on the cassettes or you can choose the ones used by the Panjabi-speaking people you come into contact with. But you should use the chosen variants consistently.

The variety of Panjabi you will mostly hear outside the Panjab uses **ɑː** in place of **ne**. But we shall use **ne** in this book. Since this is a colloquial Panjabi course, we shall use **ne** in our dialogues as well. But when you write Panjabi, you should use **ɦɑn** ਹਨ in place of **ne**.

The Panjabi forms of the verb 'to be' given above are the present tense forms (see also the Grammatical summary, page 228).

Referring to habitual actions in Panjabi

The Panjabi equivalent of 'What do you do?' is

tusĩ:	ki:	kamm	karde	fio?
you	what	work	doing	are

This is closer in form to 'What are you doing?', which, in English, refers to an ongoing activity, and not to a habitual or repeated activity.

We can break up the verb-form **karde** into three parts

kar	+	d		+	e
stem	+	aspect marker	+	number–gender marker	

The aspect marker simply indicates whether the situation is viewed as completed or uncompleted/ongoing or as potential. Do not confuse an aspect marker with a tense marker. The aspect marker **-d-** (like the English aspect marker '-ing') indicates an uncompleted or ongoing or habitual activity or situation, without giving any indication of the time (past, present or future) of the activity or situation in relation to the time of speaking. It is a form of the verb 'to be' (see above) that indicates the time of the activity. The number–gender marker **-e** in **karde**, as you know, is masculine plural (see the Magic square in Conversation unit 1, if you have forgotten).This plural form can be used even for a single person to show respect. (Tense and aspect are also dealt with in the Grammatical summary, page 227.)

In the case of most verbs, you simply add **-d-** without any other change in the pronunciation or spelling of the stem. But if a verb ends in a vowel sound, you nasalise the final vowel of the stem. For example,

kar + d + a:	becomes	**karda:**

because **kar** ends in a consonant sound. But

pi: + d + i:	becomes	**pĩ:di:**
ja: + d + e	becomes	**jã:de**

Since **pi:** and **ja:** end in vowel sounds, the final vowel sounds are nasalised when **-d-** is added. With some verb stems ending in **a:**, the nasalised vowel **ũ** is inserted between the stem and the affix **-d-**. Examples are **pa:ũda:** (**pa: + ũ + d + a:**) and **suṇa:ũdi:** (**suṇa: + ũ + d + i:**).

The technical name for this verb-form is the imperfect participle form. But we shall use the simpler name imperfective form. The Panjabi imperfective form is a close equivalent of the English '-ing' form. Both these forms can be used as adjectives as well.

Dialogue 2 🔘

In another corner, Mrs Varma and Mrs Singh, having been introduced by the hostess, are busy eating and chatting

MRS SINGH:	ka:fi: pi:o.
MRS VARMA:	ji: náfĩ:, ʃukri:a:. mɛ̃ ka:fi: náfĩ: pĩ:di:.
MRS SINGH:	tã: cá:fi pi:o.
MRS VARMA:	ʃukri:a:.
MRS SINGH:	tufia:ɖe kinne bacce ne?
MRS VARMA:	mere do bacce ne. munɖe. te tufia:ɖe?
MRS SINGH:	tinn. do kuɽi:ã: te ikk munɖa:. tufia:ɖe bacce kamm karde ne?
MRS VARMA:	ji: náfĩ:. úfi páɽᵑde ne. ikk *high school* jã:da: fiɛ, te ikk *primary school.*
MRS SINGH:	*Have some coffee.*
MRS VARMA:	*No, thanks. I don't drink coffee.*
MRS SINGH:	*Then have tea.*
MRS VARMA:	*Thanks.*
MRS SINGH:	*How many children do you have?*
MRS VARMA:	*I have two children. Boys. And you?* *(Lit.: My two children are. Boys. And yours?)*
MRS SINGH:	*Three. Two boys and a girl. Do your children work?*
MRS VARMA:	*No. They are studying. One goes to high school, and one to primary school.*

Vocabulary

ka:fi: (*f*)	ਕਾਫ਼ੀ	coffee
mɛ̃	ਮੈਂ	I
tã:	ਤਾਂ	then, in that case
cá:fi (*f*)	ਚਾਹ	tea
pi:o	ਪੀਓ	please drink
bacce (*m*)	ਬੱਚੇ	children

te	ਤੇ	and
munḍa: (*m*)	ਮੁੰਡਾ	boy
munḍe (*m*)	ਮੁੰਡੇ	boys
kuɽi: (*f*)	ਕੁੜੀ	girl
kuɽi:ã: (*f*)	ਕੁੜੀਆਂ	girls
páɽ^ɦde	ਪੜ੍ਹਦੇ	studying, reading
jã:de	ਜਾਂਦੇ	going
kinne	ਕਿੰਨੇ	how many?
ikk	ਇੱਕ	one
do	ਦੋ	two
tinn	ਤਿੰਨ	three

Colloquial pronunciation

cá:fi is pronounced as [**cá:**]. **fi** is not pronounced at the end of a word in modern Panjabi. Since it has been retained in Panjabi spelling (like 'k' at the beginning of the word 'know' in English), we use it in our transcription.

Word order (Panjabi as an SOV language)

| **mɛ̃** | **ka:fi:** | **náfi:** | **pĭ:di:** |
| I | coffee | drinking | not |

I don't drink coffee.

You can put **náfi:** anywhere in the utterance after the subject **mɛ̃**.

In a Panjabi sentence the subject normally (but not invariably) comes at the beginning and the verb at the end. Everything else is sandwiched between the two. So linguists describe Panjabi and other major Indian languages as SOV (Subject Object Verb) languages. English and other European languages are described as SVO languages. This distinction is useful if we keep the qualifying word 'normally' in mind. A speaker or writer can deviate from the norm and manipulate word order to emphasise and focus on some part of the information or to achieve stylistic effects.

Inseparable possessions

Note the Panjabi expression for 'How many children do you have?'

| **tufia:ḍe** | **kinne** | **bacce** | **ne?** |
| your | how many | children | are |

Panjabi (like the vast majority of world languages) has no single word which is an exact equivalent of the English verb 'to have'. When in Panjabi you speak about possessions regarded as inseparable or non-transferable (such as relatives, parts of the body or dearly held material possessions) you use this grammatical construction. A different type of construction (to be dealt with later on) is used in the case of transferable possessions.

Singular and plural forms of nouns

Note the forms

munɖaː	boy	**munɖe**	boys
kuɽiː	girl	**kuɽiːãː**	girls

The rules for deriving plural forms from singular forms of nouns in Panjabi are given on pages 221–222 in the Grammatical summary section of the book.

Omission of *ɦɛ* in a negative sentence

The present tense form (but not the past tense form) of the Panjabi **ɦɛ** can optionally be omitted from a negative sentence in Panjabi, as in

mɛ̃	medical **ɖaːkʈar**	**náɦiː**
I	medical doctor	not

I am not a medical doctor

mɛ̃	**kaːfiː**	**náɦiː**	**pĩːdiː**
I	coffee	not	drinking

I don't drink coffee.

Dialogue 3 🔘🔘

Varma and Singh are talking about their work now

SINGH: Varma sáːɦab, tusĩː kittʰe kamm karde ɦo?

VARMA: *Birmingham* c. saːɖiː aːpɳiː *accountancy firm* ɦɛ, *Varma Accountants, Hagley Road* te. asĩː tinn sã̃ːjʰiːdaːr ɦã̃ː, mere baɽe bʰàːii sáːɦab, mɛ̃, te mera: cʰoʈaː bʰaràː. saːɖiː ikk bʰɛ̀ɳ viː ɦɛ. úɦi ɖaːkʈar ɦɛ, *medical* ɖaːkʈar, *PhD.* náɦĩː. tusĩː kittʰe kamm karde ɦo?

SINGH:	*Aston University* **c.**
SINGH:	*Mr Varma, where do you work?*
VARMA:	*In Birmingham. We have our own accountancy firm, Varma Accountants, on Hagley Road. We are three partners, my older brother, myself and my younger brother. We also have a sister. She is a doctor, a medical doctor, not a PhD. Where do you work?*
SINGH:	*In Aston University.*

Vocabulary

ɑːpɳiː	ਆਪਣੀ	own
sã́ːjʱiːdɑːr *(m/f)*	ਸਾਂਝੀਦਾਰ	partner
bʱarɑ̀ː *(m)*	ਭਰਾ	brother
bʱɛ̀ɳ *(f)*	ਭੈਣ	sister
viː	ਵੀ	also
te (ate)	’ਤੇ	and
te (utte)	’ਤੇ	on
c	’ਚ	in, inside

Colloquial pronunciation

Note that Central Panjabi has no breathy voiced consonants, although we have retained them in our transcription because they are there in Panjabi spelling. Listen to the recording again and note the pronunciation of the following words having ʱ in the transcription.

> sã́ːjʱiːdɑːr [sã́ːjiːdɑːr]
> bʱà̀ːiː [pà̀ːiː]
> bʱarɑ̀ː [parɑ̀ː]
> bʱɛ̀ɳ [pɛ̀ɳ]

Rules of pronunciation (which are really quite simple) will be explained later on. (You may already have discovered them by then!) Look at the table of consonants and see which consonant is replaced by which and look at the type and position of the tone in relation to the type and position of the breathy voiced consonant. However, you can pronounce these words with the breathy voice if you like. But do not forget to use the correct Panjabi tone. (See the introductory chapter 'Panjabi pronunciation and writing system'.)

In colloquial pronunciation, some words are weakened and shortened. You may think that Panjabi has the same word **te** for 'and' and 'on'. But this is not the case. **te** 'and' is actually a contraction of the word **ate** and **te** 'on' is a contraction of the word **utte**. This shortening of words in colloquial speech happens in many languages including English. In fluent English speech 'on', 'in' and 'an' often sound very similar. In Panjabi spelling most writers use an apostrophe in such shortened words as 'ਤੇ, 'ਚ, etc.

Word order

Hagley Road	**te**
Hagley Road	on
On Hagley Road	

Aston University	**c**
Aston University	in
In Aston University	

Note the position of **te** and **c**, the Panjabi equivalent of the English prepositions 'on' and 'in' respectively. **te** is called a postposition because it follows the noun.

The Panjabi social hierarchy

Varma refers to his older brother as **mere baṛe bʰàːi sáːfiab**. He uses the more 'polite' and 'learned' word **bʰàːi** for 'brother', adds the plural form of the adjective **baṛe** 'older' and also the title **sáːfiab**. But he refers to his younger brother simply as **meraː cʰoṭaː bʰaràː**, using the more colloquial word **bʰaràː** 'brother' and the singular form of the adjective **cʰoṭaː** 'younger'. Varma is not being disrespectful to his younger brother. He is simply following the standards of Panjabi social behaviour.

The hierarchical culture of the traditional Panjabi society shows itself in the use of the language as well.

Dialogue 4 🔘🔘

The ladies are busy doing justice to tea and samosas and also getting information about each other's families

Mrs Varma: tusĩ kinne bʰɛ̀ɳ bʰaràː fio?

Mrs Singh:	asĩ: panj bʰèṇ bʰarà: fiã:. tinn bʰèṇã: te do bʰarà:. tusĩ:?
Mrs Varma:	asĩ: caːr fiã:. mere tinn baṛe bʰarà: ne.

Mrs Varma:	*How many brothers and sisters are you?*
Mrs Singh:	*We are five brothers and sisters. Three brothers and two sisters. And you?*
Mrs Varma:	*We are four. I have three older brothers.*

Word order

tusĩ:	kinne	bʰèṇ	bʰarà:	fio?
you	how many	sister	brothers	are

How many brothers and sisters are you?

asĩ:	panj	bʰèṇ		bʰarà:	fiã̃:.
we	five	sister	brothers	are

We are five brothers and sisters.

ਅਭਿਆਸ Exercises

You have learnt a language well when you are able to understand sentences you have never come across before and are able to produce sentences you have never produced before. There is no mystery in this. When you have the building blocks of the language (words), know how they are shaped correctly for use in sentences (such as adding number and gender endings), and also know how they are arranged in sentences to express desired meaning in various types of situations, you have learnt the language. In other words, as you progress, you should go on building up your vocabulary and learning grammar. These exercises are meant to help you in both these processes. Read carefully what we have done so far and then attempt these exercises. After each exercise, check your answers with the Key given at the end of the book. Carefully note down and analyse your mistakes and attempt the exercise again next week.

As you progress, keep returning to earlier chapters and exercises again and again until you have mastered them. More and more practice will help you remember more and more. Remember that

Correct, intelligent and persistent practice is the method used by most successful language learners.

1 An official from the local Social Services Department comes to your neighbour's house to get some information. But your neighbour does not speak English. Can you act as an interpreter?

Official:	*What's your name?*
You:	_____ ?
Neighbour:	ɑnvɑr ɑliː.
Official:	*What's your job?*
You:	_____ ?
Neighbour:	mɛ̃ kɑmm náfiː kɑrdɑː.
You:	_____ .
Official:	*How many children do you have?*
You:	_____ .
Neighbour:	mere cɑːr bɑcce ne.
You:	_____ ?
Official:	*Boys or girls?*
You:	_____ ?
Neighbour:	tinn munɖe, ikk kuɽiː.
You:	_____ .
Official:	*Do they go to school?*
You:	_____ ?
Neighbour:	munɖe *school* jã̀ːde ne. kuɽiː cʰoʈiː fiɛ. úfi *nursery* jã̀ːdiː fiɛ.
You:	_____ .

2 If you have the cassette recordings, listen to them and then enter information about the second speaker on the following form.

Surname _____

First name(s) _____

Home address _____

_____

Occupation _____

Work address _____

_____

Mode of travel to work _____

3 When the following paragraphs were being typed, our computer was infected by a mysterious and nameless virus. This virus ate up some grammatical endings and forms of the verb **fiɛ** and then (to add insult to injury!) left a 'Victory sign' where it had done the damage. Can you restore what the virus has gobbled up?

asĩː caːr bʱaràː ✌. mẽ *number* do ✌. merᵇ baʈᵇ bʱàːi sáːfiab daːkʈar ✌. úfi laŋɖan c kamm karᵇ ✌. mẽ bas *inspector* ✌, te *Birmingham* c kamm karᵇ ✌. merᵇ do cʰoʈᵇ bʱaràː ✌. ikk *school teacher* ✌, te ikk bas *driver* ✌. merᵇ do cʰoʈᵇ bʱaràː *Coventry* c kamm karᵇ ✌. saːɖᵇ ikk cʰoʈᵇ bʱèɳ viː ✌. úfi *Manchester University* vic páʈʱᵇ ✌.

mere tinn baccᵇ ✌, ikk munɖᵇ, te do kuɽiː ✌. merᵇ baccᵇ *school* jãː ✌. baʈᵇ kuɽi *A Level* karᵇ ✌, te cʰoʈᵇ *GCSE*. munɖaː *primary school* jãːdᵇ ✌.

3 ਕੀ ਚਾਹੀਦਾ ਹੈ?

What would you like to have?

In this unit you will learn to:
- tell a shopkeeper what you wish to buy, using the verb **cá:ɦi:da:**
- describe locations and where you wish things to be put, using simple and compound postpositions
- refer to your own and other people's possessions
- use changeable ('black') and unchangeable ('red') adjectives

---

ਗੱਲ ਬਾਤ Dialogues

Dialogue 1 🔲🔲

Kulwant Kaur goes to a corner shop to buy some vegetables. Since she is a regular customer, the shopkeeper, Mohan Singh, greets her first

MOHAN: sat sri: aka:l, bʰɛ̀ɳ ji:.

KULWANT: sat sri: aka:l, bʰarà: ji:. ki: ɦa:l ɦɛ?

MOHAN: va:ɦiguru: di: kirpa: ɦɛ. dasso, ki: cá:ɦi:da: ɦɛ?

KULWANT: tuɦa:ɖe kol bʰìnɖi: ɦɛgi: ɛ?

MOHAN: ɦɑ̃: ji:, ɦɛgi: ɛ. kinni: cá:ɦi:di: ɦɛ?

KULWANT: tinn pɔ̃ɖ.

MOHAN: ɦor kújʰ cá:ɦi:da: ɦɛ?

KULWANT: ikk pɔ̃ɖ ga:jarã̀:, do pɔ̃ɖ bɛ̃gaɳ, do pɔ̃ɖ ʈama:ʈar.

MOHAN: ajj sa:ɖe kol ʈama:ʈar náɦĩ:.

KULWANT: koi: gall náɦĩ:. mɛnũ ɦara: dʰàni:a: vi: cá:ɦi:da: ɦɛ.

MOHAN: ɦari:ã̀: mircã̀: vi: cá:ɦi:di:ã̀: ne?

KULWANT: ji: náɦĩ:.

MOHAN: *Greetings, sister.*

KULWANT:	*Greetings, brother. How are you?*
MOHAN:	*I'm fine. What would you like to have?*
	(Lit.: God's kindness is.)
KULWANT:	*Do you have okra?*
MOHAN:	*Yes. How much do you want?*
KULWANT:	*Three pounds.*
MOHAN:	*Do you want anything else?*
KULWANT:	*A pound of carrots, two pounds of aubergines, two pounds of tomatoes.*
MOHAN:	*We don't have tomatoes today.*
KULWANT:	*It's okay. I want green coriander too.*
MOHAN:	*Do you want green chillies as well?*
KULWANT:	*No.*

Vocabulary

va:ɦiguru: (*m*)	ਵਾਹਿਗੁਰੂ	God (used by Sikhs)
kirpa: (*f*)	ਕਿਰਪਾ	kindness, grace
cá:ɦi:da: [**cá:i:da:**]	ਚਾਹੀਦਾ	desirable, desired
bʰìnɖi: [**pìnɖi:**] (*f*)	ਭਿੰਡੀ	okra
ɦɛga:	ਹੈਗਾ	definitely is
ɦor	ਹੋਰ	else, more
kújʰ [**kúj**]	ਕੁਝ	something, anything
kinna:	ਕਿੰਨਾ	how much
ga:jar (*f*)	ਗਾਜਰ	carrot
bɛ̃gaṇ (*m*)	ਬੈਂਗਣ	aubergine
ṭama:ṭar (*m*)	ਟਮਾਟਰ	tomato
ajj (*m*)	ਅੱਜ	today
koi: gall náɦi:	ਕੋਈ ਗੱਲ ਨਹੀਂ	It doesn't matter
ɦara:	ਹਰਾ	green
dʰàni:a: [**tàni:a:**] (*m*)	ਧਨੀਆ	coriander
mirc (*f*)	ਮਿਰਚ	chilli

Colloquial pronunciation

Most speakers of Panjabi pronounce **cá:ɦi:da:** as [**cá:i:da:**], i.e. without the **ɦ** sound but with a high tone.

You are likely to come across different pronunciations of [**tuɦa:ɖa:**] – such as [**tʰua:ɖa:**], [**tʰoɖa:**], [**tuà:ɖa:**], depending upon the dialect of the speaker. Similarly, **tufia:nũ:** ('to you'), is pronounced as [**tuà:nũ:**], [**tià:nũ:**], [**tʰua:nũ:**], [**tʰonũ:**] and even [**sonũ:**] by speakers of Panjabi coming from different areas. But you are absolutely safe with the pronunciation used in this book. Just be aware of the differences which exist.

While listening to the recording of the dialogue you may have noticed that the l sound in **kol** is different from the l sound in **aka:l**. Some dialects of Panjabi (including the one used in this course) have two varieties of l. In addition to the ordinary l sound, they use a strange-sounding (to Western ears) variety of l in words like **kol**. You pronounce it by curling the tongue backward, as you do for ʈ, ɖ and ɽ. Linguists write this sound as ɭ and call it retroflex ɭ. They would transcribe **kol** as koɭ. But we will not be using the symbol ɭ in our transcription, and the Panjabi alphabet has no special letter for the ɭ sound either. It uses the letter ਲ for both l and ɭ. But if you find this sound hard, do not use it and stick to l. Many speakers of Panjabi do not use it either.

Brothers and sisters

Mohan addresses Kulwant as **bʱɛ̀ɳ ji:** ('sister') and Kulwant responds by addressing him as **bʱarà: ji:** ('brother'). **bʱà: ji:** [**pà: ji:**] is also used and is considered less formal. Addressing unrelated people in this way is a part of the culture of the Indian subcontinent.

'What is desirable to you?'

In English 'What do you want?' is considered less polite than 'What would you like to have?' Similarly in Panjabi

tusĩ:	ki:	cá:ɦũde	ɦo?
you	what	desiring	are

would be considered less polite, like the English 'What do you want?' The polite Panjabi expression is

tuɦa:nũ:	ki:	cá:ɦi:da:	ɦɛ?
you-to	what	desirable	is

What is desirable to you? *or* What is desired by you?

Note that the the 'object of desire' is the grammatical subject in such constructions. So the verb carries the number–gender affix according to the desired object, and not according to the desiring person. If the person wants two pounds of carrots, she would say

menū:	do	pɔ̃ɖ	gɑːjɑrã:	cáfiːːdiːã:	ne
me-to	two	pounds	carrots	desirable	are

Note the feminine plural affix **-iːã:** in **cáfiːːdiːã:** because the 'object of desire' (**gɑːjɑrã:** – 'carrots') is feminine and plural.

menū: is clearly **mẽ** ('I') plus the postposition **nū:** ('to'). So we glossed it as 'me-to'. **tufiɑːnū:** is actually **tusĩ:** ('you') plus **nū:**. But changes in pronunciation do take place when postpositions are added to pronouns. These changes are discussed in the Grammatical summary, pages 222–224.

fiega: and subjectless sentences

The verb forms **fiega:**, **fiege**, **fiegi:**, **fiegi:ã:** (see the Magic square for the number–gender affixes) are very common in colloquial Panjabi speech but are rarely used in formal written Panjabi. As you can see, these forms are derived by adding **g** + number–gender affix to the verb stem **fie**. We shall deal with **g** + number–gender affix in a later unit. But the combination **g** + number–gender affix indicates emphasis or definiteness. When Kulwant asks

tufiɑːɖe kol bʰinɖi: fiegi: ɛ?

she emphasises her desire to buy okra. A more meaningful (but odd-sounding) translation would be 'I presume that you have okra. Am I right?' Mohan's answer

fiã: jiː, fiegi: ɛ.

amounts to saying 'Yes, I definitely have it.'

ɛ is a reduced form of the verb **fie**. Since this verb combination is nearly always used in spoken Panjabi, only the reduced form of **fie** is used. Some speakers pronounce **fie** as **ɑ:** or **vɑ:** or **ɛ** or **e**.

It is also notable that the grammatical subject is missing in the reply **fiegi: ɛ**. In Panjabi and many other languages, the subject of the sentence is omitted if it is clear from the situational context what we are talking about.

Separable or transferable possessions

In Conversation unit 2 we came across

mere	do	bʰarà:	ne
my	two	brothers	are

I have two brothers.

It was pointed out that this grammatical construction is used to indicate inseparable or non-transferable possessions such as relatives. But vegetables in a shop are meant to be transferable possessions. So we have

tufia:ɖe	kol	bʰɪnɖi:	fiɛgi: ɛ?
your	near	okra	(definitely) is

Do you have okra?

Similarly 'I have two cars' would be

mere	kol	do	ka:rã:	ne
my	near	two	cars	are

Note that **ka:r** ('car') is feminine in Panjabi. So the feminine plural ending **ã:** has been added.

Dialogue 2 🔲

bʰà:i:a:, generally pronounced as [**pà:i:a:**] has different meanings in different regions and communities. It can mean 'older brother', 'brother-in-law' (sister's husband), 'father', 'grandfather', 'old man' and many other things. In this dialogue, it is used informally to address an old man. As you can imagine, this word is difficult to translate. Here we use the makeshift translation 'gentleman'.

Avtar Bassi, a physiotherapist, is with the patient Bishan Das, a pensioner in his early eighties, who is also slightly hard of hearing

BASSI: kiddã: bʰà:i:a: ji:? t̪ʰi:k fio na:?
DAS: t̪ʰi:k ká:fida:? lattã: bã:fiã: caldi:ã: náfĩ:.
BASSI: caldi:ã: náfĩ:? bilkul t̪ʰi:k caldi:ã: ne. soʈi: ɔt̪ʰe
   rakʰo ... fiã: ji:. fiuɳ ɛt̪ʰe leʈo. gadde te.
DAS: kitt̪ʰe?

BASSI:	ɛtʰe, gadde de utte ... fiã: ʃaːbaːʃ. sajjaː pɛr utte cukko ...
	fiã: jiː ... t̪ʰiːk. fiuɳ kʰabbaː pɛr cukko ... báfiut accʰaː ...
	fior cukko ... fior ... fior ... ʃaːbaːʃ ... báfiut accʰaː ... fiuɳ
	dovẽ pɛr fiet̪ʰã: karo ... ʃaːbaːʃ ... dovẽ baːfiã: utte cukko.
DAS:	kʰabbiː bã́ːfi dukʰdi: fiɛ.
BASSI:	koiː gall náfiĩ:. utte cukko ... fior utte ... fior utte ...
	ʃaːbaːʃ ... báfiut accʰaː ... tusĩ: bilkul t̪ʰiːk fio, bʰã́ːiːaː
	jiː.

BASSI:	*How are you, gentleman? Are you alright?*
DAS:	*How can I be alright? My legs and arms are not working.*
BASSI:	*Not working? They are fine. Put your stick there ... Yes.*
	Now lie down here. On the cushion.
DAS:	*Where?*
BASSI:	*Here, on the cushion ... Yes. Well done! Raise your right*
	foot ... Yes ... Fine. Now raise your left foot ... Very good ...
	Now bring both your feet down ... Well done! ... Raise both
	your arms.
DAS:	*The left arm aches.*
BASSI:	*Don't worry. Raise them ... Higher ... Higher ... Well*
	done! ... Very good ... You are perfectly okay, gentleman.

Vocabulary

kiddã́:?	ਕਿੱਦਾਂ	How are you? (*informal*)
ká:fida:? [ká:da:]	ਕਾਹਦਾ	what sort of?
latt (*f*)	ਲੱਤ	leg
bã́:fi [bã́:] (*f*)	ਬਾਂਹ	arm
cal	ਚਲ	to move
bilkul	ਬਿਲਕੁਲ	completely
soʈi: (*f*)	ਸੋਟੀ	stick
utʰe/otʰe/ɔtʰe	ਉੱਥੇ	there
itʰe/etʰe/ɛtʰe	ਇੱਥੇ	here
leʈ	ਲੇਟ	to lie down
gadda: (*m*)	ਗੱਦਾ	cushion
kittʰe	ਕਿੱਥੇ	where
ʃa:ba:ʃ	ਸ਼ਾਬਾਸ਼	Well done!
sajja:	ਸੱਜਾ	right
kʰabba:	ਖੱਬਾ	left

pɛr (*m*)	ਪੈਰ	foot
cukk	ਚੁੱਕ	to lift
ɦor	ਹੋਰ	more
ɦuɳ	ਹੁਣ	now
dovẽ	ਦੋਵੇਂ	both
ɦeʈʰã:	ਹੇਠਾਂ	down, below
dukʰ	ਦੁਖ	to ache

itʰe/etʰe/ɛtʰe and *utʰe/otʰe /ɔtʰe*

Each speaker of Panjabi uses the variants **itʰe/etʰe/ɛtʰe** (meaning 'here') and **utʰe/otʰe/ɔtʰe** (meaning 'there') in his or her own way. In this book **itʰe** and **utʰe** are used as unstressed forms and **etʰe** and **otʰe** as stressed forms. **ɛtʰe** and **ɔtʰe** are used when these words are accompanied by the gesture of pointing. But this is not a standard rule, so you can make your own choice. You can even use only one variant of each of these two words if you like.

Strong and weak forms of postpositions and adverbs of place

Some postpositions in Panjabi can be used in both strong and weak forms. For example, the postposition **utte** is used in its unemphatic form **te** in

gadde	**te**
cushion	on

in fluent speech. But you can use the strong form and say **gadde utte** if you wish lay stress on **utte**. You can also say **gadde de utte** if you want to lay extra emphasis. **de utte** is actually a compound postposition. Compound postpositions are discussed below. (See also the Grammatical summary, page 226.)

Dialogue 3 🔲

Dr Joginder Singh has bought a new house and wants to convert one of the bedrooms into a study room. He is discussing his plan with Mr Saggoo, the carpenter

SINGH: *Saggoo sá:ɦab, tuɦa:ɖa: ki: xia:l ɦɛ? computer* kittʰe cá:ɦi:da: ɦɛ?

SAGGOO:	mere xia:l c *computer* kʰiɽki: de sá:ɦmaɳe t̪ʰi:k náfĩ:.
SINGH:	par íɦ *radiator* de kol vi: t̪ʰi:k náfĩ:.
SAGGOO:	tuɦa:ɖi: gall vi: t̪ʰi:k ɦɛ. mera: xia:l ɦɛ ki tusĩ: *buk-ʃɛlfã:* kánd̪ʱã: de na:l la:o.
SINGH:	te *computer*?
SAGGOO:	*computer* kamre de gábbʱe rakʰo, mez te.
SINGH:	˙bú:ɦe de kol t̪ʰi:k náfĩ:?
SAGGOO:	ji: náfĩ:.
SINGH:	te *filing cabinet*?
SAGGOO:	kʰabbe pa:se.
SINGH:	mere kʰabbe pa:se?
SAGGOO:	ji: náfĩ. *mere* kʰabbe pa:se, tuɦa:ɖe sajje pa:se.

SINGH:	*Mr Saggoo, what's your opinion? Where should the computer be placed?*
SAGGOO:	*I think that the computer shouldn't be facing the window.*
SINGH:	*But it shoudn't be near the radiator either.*
SAGGOO:	*That's right too. I think that you should have the book-shelves along the walls.*
SINGH:	*And the computer?*
SAGGOO:	*Have the computer in the middle of the room, on a table.*
SINGH:	*Won't it be okay near the door?*
SAGGOO:	*No.*
SINGH:	*And the filing cabinet?*
SAGGOO:	*On the left.*
SINGH:	*On my left?*
SAGGOO:	*No, my left, and your right.*

Vocabulary

xia:l (*m*)	ਖ਼ਿਆਲ	opinion, idea
kʰiɽki: (*f*)	ਖਿੜਕੀ	window
sáɦmaɳe [sámaɳe]	ਸਾਹਮਣੇ	in front of; facing
gall (*f*)	ਗੱਲ	talk, saying
kol	ਕੋਲ	near
kánd̪ʱ [kánd̪] (*f*)	ਕੰਧ	wall
na:l	ਨਾਲ	along, with
ki	ਕਿ	that (*conj.*)
la:	ਲਾ	to fix

kɑmrɑ: (*m*)	ਕਮਰਾ	room
dɑ:/de	ਦਾ/ਦੇ	of
gábbʰe [gábbe]	ਗੱਭੇ	in the centre
bú:ɦɑ: (*m*)	ਬੂਹਾ	door
neɽe	ਨੇੜੇ	near
pɑ:sɑ: (*m*)	ਪਾਸਾ	side
pɑ:se	ਪਾਸੇ	on the side

cá:ɦi:dɑ: revisited

The verb form **cá:ɦi:dɑ:** can be used in all sorts of situations. Dr Singh uses

computer	**kittʰe**	**cá:ɦi:dɑ:**	**ɦɛ?**
computer	where	desirable	is

to ask 'Where should the computer be kept?'

Oblique form

Do not let this technical term of grammar frighten you. The Panjabi form it refers to is really quite simple to use. In the English expressions 'from me', 'to him' and 'with them', the English pronouns 'I', 'he' and 'they' become 'me', 'him' and 'them' respectively because each of them is preceded by a preposition in these examples. The same thing happens in Panjabi as well, with the difference that Panjabi has postpositions, and many nouns, adjectives and two postpositions (**dɑ:** and **vɑ:lɑ:**) are also affected in this way. The changed forms of nouns, pronouns, adjectives and the two postpositions are called oblique forms. The ordinary (i.e. non-oblique) forms are called direct forms. In

mere	**xiɑ:l**	**c**
my	opinion	in
In my opinion		

the adjective **mere** appears to have the masculine plural ending **-e**. But this is not really the case. It is still masculine singular. **mere**, in this particular case, is the oblique form of **merɑ:**.

In expressions like

kʰiɽki:	**de**	**sá:ɦmaɳe**
window	of	front
In front of the window *or* facing the window		

radiator	**de**	**kol**
radiator	of	near

near the radiator

kɑmre	**de**	**gábbʰe**
room	of	middle/centre

in the middle of the room

de is the oblique form of the Panjabi postposition **dɑ:** ('of'). **dɑ:** and **vɑ:lɑ:** are the only postpositions in Panjabi which can have an oblique form. Also note the order of words, which is the exact opposite of the English word order and can initially confuse the learner.

It is extremely important to use the direct and oblique forms of Panjabi nouns and pronouns correctly. They are fully described on pages 221–224 in the Grammatical summary of the book. (You may need to refer to these tables when you do the exercise at the end of this unit.)

Postpositions, compound postpositions and adverbs

In Panjabi some words function both as adverbs of place and postpositions. (An adverb of place indicates a location.) Similar examples in English are words like 'below', which can be used either as prepositions, as in 'below the surface' or as adverbs, as in 'the examples given below'. All the Panjabi postpositions except **nũ:** ('to'), **tõ** ('from') and **dɑ:** ('of') are really adverbs of place.

In English, expressions like 'in front of', 'in the middle of', 'on top of,' etc. act like single prepositions. Such expressions may be called compound prepositions. The structure of a compound preposition is generally

preposition	+	*adverb of place*	+	*of*	*(noun)*
in		the middle		of	(the room)
in		front		of	(the building)

Panjabi follows a similar pattern except, of course, that it has postpositions, and not prepositions. The structure of a typical compound postposition in Panjabi is

(noun)	*de* + *adverb of place*	
(gɑdde)	**de** + **utte**	
cushion	of above	('on the cushion')

(kánd^ɦãː)	de + nɑl		
walls	of	along	('along the walls')

(kamre)	de + gább^ɦe		
room	of	in-middle	('in the middle of the room')

Compound postpositions are generally used for emphasis. **de** in such expressions is the oblique form of the Panjabi postposition **daː**.

The Panjabi equivalent of the English preposition 'of' is **daː**, which, of course, is a postposition. **daː** and **vɑːlɑː** behave like other possessive adjectives of Panjabi, such as **merɑː** ('my'), **tufiaːɖɑː** ('your'), etc. They are 'black adjectives' discussed below.

buk-ʃɛlfãː

Some English words have become so common in Panjabi that Panjabi grammatical endings are given to them now. Examples include **buk-ʃɛlfãː**, **bɑssã:** and **kɑːrɑ̃ː**.

Dialogue 4 🔘🔘

Mohammad Shafi comes home from the office and asks his wife Zubaida to make a cup of tea for him

SHAFI:	*Zubaida*, cáːfi daː kapp liaː. te ikk do *aspirin* viː.
ZUBAIDA:	kiː gall fiɛ? tufiaːɖi tabiːat t^hiːk fiɛ?
SHAFI:	fiã:, tabiːat t^hiːk fiɛ. maːmuːli sir dard fiɛ.
ZUBAIDA:	fiaːe allaː! sir dard kiũ?
SHAFI:	dard allaː de sir c náfiĩː, mere sir c fiɛ. ja: cáːfi liaː.

(Zubaida makes a cup of tea).

SHAFI:	*Zubaida,* meraː *pen* kitt^he fiɛ?
ZUBAIDA:	jeb c.
SHAFI:	par jeb c fiɛ náfiĩː.
ZUBAIDA:	kamiːz di: jeb c náfiĩː, *coat* di: jeb c.
SHAFI:	*coat* kitt^he fiɛ?
ZUBAIDA:	utte, *bedroom* c. fiuɳ pucc^ho *bedroom* kitt^he fiɛ. janaːb, *bedroom* g^ɦàr c fiɛ, g^ɦàr laɳɖan c fiɛ, laɳɖan, *England* c fiɛ.
SHAFI:	ífi kiː mazaːk fiɛ?

SHAFI:	Zubaida, bring a cup of tea. And one or two aspirins as well.
ZUBAIDA:	What's the matter? Are you alright? (Lit.: Is your health alright?)
SHAFI:	Yes, I'm fine. Just a little headache.
ZUBAIDA:	Oh God! Why headache?
SHAFI:	I have the headache; God hasn't. Go and bring a cup of tea. (Lit.: The ache is in my head, not in God's head.)
	(Zubaida makes a cup of tea)
SHAFI:	Zubaida, where is my pen?
ZUBAIDA:	In the pocket.
SHAFI:	But it's not there.
ZUBAIDA:	It's not in the pocket of the shirt. It's in the pocket of the coat.
SHAFI:	Where's the coat.
ZUBAIDA:	Upstairs. In the bedroom. Now ask me where the bedroom is. Sir, the bedroom is in the house; the house is in London; London is in England.
SHAFI:	What's this joke?

Vocabulary

kapp (m)	ਕੱਪ	cup
lia:	ਲਿਆ	to bring
gall (f)	ਗੱਲ	matter
tabi:at (f)	ਤਬੀਅਤ	health
ma:mu:li:	ਮਾਮੂਲੀ	slight, ordinary
sir (m)	ਸਿਰ	head
dard (f)	ਦਰਦ	ache, pain
ɦa:e alla:!	ਹਾਏ ਅੱਲਾ!	Oh God! (Muslim)
kiũ	ਕਿਉਂ	why
jeb (f)	ਜੇਬ	pocket
kami:z (f)	ਕਮੀਜ਼	shirt
pucc^h	ਪੁੱਛ	to ask
jana:b (m)	ਜਨਾਬ	sir
gʰàr [kàr] (m)	ਘਰ	house, home
maza:k (m)	ਮਜ਼ਾਕ	joke

Panjabi men do respect their wives!

Well, most of them certainly do! When Shafi asks his wife to bring a cup
of tea, he says

jɑː	**cɑ́fɦ**	**liɑː**
go	tea	bring

He does not add the 'polite' request marker -o to the verbs **jɑː** and **liɑː**. But
that does not mean that he is ordering her or is showing disrespect to her.
If he had used **jɑːo** and **liɑːo** instead, she would have interpreted it as
sarcasm. Zubaida, on the other hand, has to use the 'respectful plural'
forms to her husband (even when she makes a joke about his being
forgetful!). Such linguistic usage simply reflects the social conventions of
the traditionally male-dominated Panjabi society.

fɦɑːe ɑllɑː!

This exclamation expressing a mild surprise (listen to the recording again
for intonation) is used almost exclusively by Muslim women.

Chained postpositional phrases

In English, you can combine prepositional phrases like 'in the pocket' and
'of the shirt' to create chained prepositional phrases like 'in the pocket of
the shirt'. A similar process exists in Panjabi too, but you have to be
careful about the order of words. In Panjabi, we have

kɑmiːz	**diː**	**jeb**	**c**
shirt	of	pocket	in

Black and red adjectives

These 'colourful' grammatical terms are applicable to adjectives in all the
North Indian languages. The associated grammatical rules are

(a) red adjectives never change their form;
(b) black adjectives change their form according to the number and
the gender of the nouns they are used with;
(c) only black adjectives have differing oblique forms.

The words 'black' and 'red' are used because the Panjabi adjective **kɑːlɑː**
('black') is a typical black adjective and **lɑːl** ('red') is a typical red
adjective. The postpositions **dɑː** and **vɑːlɑː** are also black adjectives.

It is not difficult to determine the 'colour' of a Panjabi adjective. If it ends in **-aː**, it is black; otherwise, it is red.

(a) Direct forms of black adjectives

kaːlaː gʱòɽaː
black horse

kaːle gʱòɽe
black horses

kaːliː gʱòɽiː
black mare

kaːliːãː gʱòɽiːãː
black mares

(b) Oblique forms of black adjectives

kaːle gʱòɽe (nũː)
(to) black horse

kaːliãː gʱòɽiãː (nũː)
(to) black horses

kaːliː gʱòɽiː (nũː)
(to) black mare

kaːliːãː gʱòɽiːãː (nũː)
(to) black mares

You can see that in these examples the black adjective **kaːlaː** gets the same ending as the noun it is used with.

(c) Direct forms of red adjectives

laːl gʱòɽaː
red horse

laːl gʱòɽe
red horses

laːl gʱòɽiː
red mare

laːl gʱòɽiːãː
red mares

(d) Oblique forms of red adjectives

laːl gʱòɽe (nũː)
(to) red horse

laːl gʱòɽiãː (nũː)
(to) red horses

laːl gʱòɽiː (nũː)
(to) red mare

laːl gʱòɽiːãː (nũː)
(to) red mares

The red adjective **laːl** does not change its form at all, whatever ending the noun may have.

It should always be remembered that when a black adjective is added to a masculine noun, it behaves like a masculine noun ending in **-aː**.

You have come across

gadde	**de**	**utte**
cushion	of	above
(*m*)		

kamre	**de**	**gábbⁿe**
room	of	at-centre
(*m*)		

bú:ɧe	**de**	**kol**
door	of	near
(*m*)		

gadda: ('cushion'), **kamra:** ('room') and **bú:ɧa:** ('door') are masculine nouns ending in **-a:**. So because of the presence of the postposition **da:**, they get their oblique form and **a:** is replaced by **e**. But since **da:** itself is a black adjective used with a masculine noun and is followed by another postposition, its final **-a:** is replaced by **e**. So **da:** changes into **de**. In the following example

kʰiɽki:	**de**	**sá:ɧimaɳe**
window	of	in-front
(*f*)		

the feminine noun **kʰiɽki:** does not change its form, but **da:** becomes **de**. In

mere	**xia:l**	**c**
my	opinion	in
	(*m*)	

the possessive adjective **mera:** ('my') is used with the masculine noun **xia:l**. So it is also masculine. Since it ends in **a:**, this **a:** should change into **e** because of the presence of the postposition **c**. The noun **xia:l** does not end in **a:**. So its form does not change.

Possessive adjectives like **mera:** ('my') and **tuɧa:ɖa:** ('your') are black adjectives. For direct and oblique forms of other possessive adjectives see the Grammatical summary, page 225.

ਅਭਿਆਸ Exercises

1 If you have the cassettes, listen to them. Then mark the following statements as T (true) or F (false). You are advised to listen to the recording a second time (or even a third time) with these statements in mind before you mark them as T or F. ▮▮

T or F?

(a) Mr Malik wants to buy a very large house.
(b) He does not want a terrace house.
(c) He wants a house with a garage and a garden.
(d) He is very particular about a nice bathroom.
(e) He would prefer a house with four bedrooms.
(f) He would prefer a house with a rear garden.

2 Fill in the blanks with **meraː, mere, meriː, meriːã̃ː** or **mere kol**.

(a) _____ gʱàr vic caːr kamare ɦan.
(b) _____ do vaɖɖe bʱarà: ɦan te ikk cʰoṭaː.
(c) _____ do kaːrã̃ː ɦan.
(d) _____ kuṛiːã̃ː *school* jã̃ːdiːã̃ː ne.
(e) _____ munɖe nũː *computer* cá:ɦiːda: ɦɛ.
(f) _____ tabiːat ajj tʰiːk náɦĩ̃ː.
(g) _____ baṛe bʱàːi: sá:ɦab *solicitor* ne.
(h) _____ ɦaːl bilkul tʰiːk ɦɛ. tusĩ̃ː dasso.

3 Translate the following sentences, using the model given. Since Panjabi has no articles (the equivalents of the English 'a', 'an' and 'the'), you do not normally translate the English articles into Panjabi. (Also, do not translate 'car', 'hotel' and 'radiator'. They have been adopted by Panjabi.)

(a) I want a car. mɛnũ̃ː kaːr cá:ɦiːdi: ɦɛ.
(b) I want two pounds of carrots.
(c) I want a house.
(d) I want a cup of tea.
(e) I wish to have a daughter, not a son.
(f) But my brother would like to have a son.
(g) I want two rooms in a hotel.
(h) What do you want?
(i) I want a radiator under the window.

4 In the following description of Mr Malik's room, some word endings are missing. Can you supply them, remembering to choose between direct and oblique forms?

malik sá:ɦab da: gʰàr sa:ɖ _____ gʰàr d _____ sá:ɦmaɳe ɦɛ. gʰàr d
_____ vic tinn vaɖɖ _____ kamr _____ ɦan, te ikk cʰoṭ _____ kamr
_____ ɦɛ. cʰoṭ_____ kamr _____ vic malik sá:ɦab páʈʰde ɦan, te a:pɳ
_____ computer te kamm vi: karde ɦan. íɦ computer kʰiʈki: d_____ kol
ɦɛ. kamr _____ vic ikk vaɖɖ_____ mez ɦɛ te tinn kursi: _____ ɦan. do
kándʰ _____ na:l do vaɖɖ_____ buk-ʃelf _____ ɦan. íɦ _____ buk-ʃelf
_____ vic malik sá:ɦab d _____ kita:b _____ ɦan.

5 This is a role-play exercise. You are going to play the role of a customer at a greengrocer's shop. Your teacher or a classmate or some Panjabi-speaking friend can play the shopkeeper. If you cannot find anybody to play the shopkeeper, you can play both roles, in which case you should speak aloud both parts.

The shopkeeper starts the conversation and what (s)he says is given below in the phonetic transcript. Your part of the conversation is given in English.

Shopkeeper:	namaste ji:. ki: ɦa:l ɦɛ?
You:	(Reply to the greeting). I'm fine. How are you?
Shopkeeper:	dasso. ki: cá:ɦii:da: ɦɛ?
You:	Do you have green chillies today?
Shopkeeper:	ɦã ji:. kinni:ã: cá:ɦii:di:ã: ne?
You:	One pound. I want two pounds of tomatoes as well.
Shopkeeper:	éɦ ne ṭama:ṭar.
You:	But these tomatoes are not red.
Shopkeeper:	íɦ ṭama:ṭar ṭʰi:k ne.
You:	No, I want red tomatoes.
Shopkeeper:	ajj sa:ɖe kol la:l ṭama:ṭar náɦĩ:.
You:	It's OK.
Shopkeeper:	ɦara: dʰàni:a lao.
You:	No, thanks. I don't want coriander today.
Shopkeeper:	kújʰ ɦor vi: cá:ɦii:da: ɦɛ?
You:	Yes, I want some okra as well.

4 ਕੀ ਤੁਹਾਨੂੰ ਸੰਗੀਤ ਪਸੰਦ ਹੈ?
Do you like music?

In this unit you will learn to:
- talk about your and others' hobbies and interests
- talk about your and others' preferences, likes and dislikes
- talk about your and others' health and ailments
- talk about food and drink
- use the 'experiencer'-type constructions

ਗੱਲ ਬਾਤ Dialogues

Dialogue 1

Avtar Mahal and Prem Sharma were born and brought up in the same village in the Panjab and went to the same school in their village. After school, Avtar went to Canada and set up a business in Toronto. He also presents Asian programmes on a Canadian TV channel. Prem stayed on in India, learnt music and became a composer with Doordrashan, the Indian television company. During Prem's concert tour of Canada, the two friends met after thirty years. Avtar, after presenting Prem's concert on the TV, is now interviewing him. The interview is conducted in the usual manner, and neither of them gives any hint of their old friendship

AVTAR: acchʰa: *Sharma* ji:, sa:nū: ífi dasso ki tufia:ɖe ki: ki: ʃɔk ne? sangi:t tõ ila:va:.

PREM: *Mahal* sá:fiab, sangi:t mera: ʃɔk náfiĩ:, kamm fiɛ, ka:roba:r fiɛ. vɛse, mere kai: ʃɔk fiɛn. mɛnū: páɽʰan da: ʃɔk fiɛ, kavita: te gi:t likʰaṇ da: ʃɔk fiɛ, kʰa:ṇa: paka:uṇ da: ʃɔk fiɛ.

AVTAR: kʰa:ṇa: paka:uṇ da:?

PREM:	ɦɑ̃: ji:.
AVTAR:	pʰer tɑ̃: tuɦɑ:ɖi: patni: baɽi: xuʃkismat ɦɛ.
PREM:	íɦ mɛnũ: pata: náɦĩ:. úɦɪnũ: mera: kʰɑ:ɳa: báɦut pasand ɦɛ, mera: sangi:t bilkul pasand náɦĩ:.
AVTAR:	ki: tuɦɑ:ɖe dʰĩ:ɑ̃: puttarɑ̃: nũ: tuɦɑ:ɖa: sangi:t pasand ɦɛ?
PREM:	dʰĩ:ɑ̃: nũ: ɦɛ, puttarɑ̃: nũ: náɦĩ:.
AVTAR:	*Well, Mr Sharma, please tell us what your hobbies are. Besides music.*
PREM:	*Mr Mahal, music is not my hobby. It's my profession, my business. But I do have a number of hobbies. I'm fond of reading, writing poetry and songs, and cooking.*
AVTAR:	*Cooking?*
PREM:	*Yes.*
AVTAR:	*Then your wife is very lucky.*
PREM:	*That I don't know. She likes my food a lot, but my music not at all.*
AVTAR:	*Do your daughters and sons like your music?*
PREM:	*Daughters, yes; sons, no.*

Vocabulary

ʃɔk (*m*)	ਸ਼ੋਕ	hobby, interest
sangi:t (*m*)	ਸੰਗੀਤ	music
tõ ilɑ:va:	ਤੋਂ ਇਲਾਵਾ	besides, in addition to
vɛse	ਵੈਸੇ	otherwise
kɑ:robɑ:r (*m*)	ਕਾਰੋਬਾਰ	business
ɦɛn	ਹੈਨ	are (emphatic form)
páɽʰ [páɽ]	ਪੜ੍ਹ	to read
kavita: (*f*)	ਕਵਿਤਾ	poetry, poem
gi:t (*m*)	ਗੀਤ	song
likʰ	ਲਿਖ	to write
kʰɑ:ɳa: (*m*)	ਖਾਣਾ	food, meal
paka:	ਪਕਾ	to cook
pʰer tɑ̃:	ਫੇਰ ਤਾਂ	then, in that case
xuʃkismat	ਖ਼ੁਸ਼ਕਿਸਮਤ	fortunate, lucky
patni: (*f*)	ਪਤਨੀ	wife
pata: (*m*)	ਪਤਾ	knowledge, information

pasand	ਪਸੰਦ	liking
dʰiː [ûː] (f)	ਧੀ	daughter
puttar (m)	ਪੁੱਤਰ	son

Repetition of words

Avtar asks Prem

tufiaːɖe	**kiː**	**kiː**	**ʃɔk**	**ne?**
your	what	what	hobbies	are

What are your hobbies or interests?

He assumes that Prem has more than one hobby or interest. Repetition of words to emphasise number or quantity or intensity is very common in Panjabi and other South Asian languages.

The experiencer

mɛnũː	**páɽʰan**	**daː**	**ʃɔk**	**fiɛ**
me-to	reading	of	fondness	is

I am fond of reading.

The main reason why we are giving word-for-word English glosses below the Panjabi sentences should be clear to you by now. Languages can represent the 'same' reality in different ways. What is the subject of the sentence in English may not be the subject in the corresponding Panjabi sentence. For example, in the English sentence

I   have   a   temperature

the pronoun 'I' is clearly the subject. But in the Panjabi equivalent

mɛnũː	**buxaːr**	**fiɛ**
me-to	temperature	is

it is **buxaːr** that is the grammatical subject. Having a temperature, hunger, thirst, confidence, faith, doubt, likes and dislikes, etc. are very often not under the conscious control of a person. In Panjabi, you don't literally have them; rather, they are to you or they happen to you. You are simply an experiencer. So the experiencing person in such sentences is not the grammatical subject. The sentence starts with **mɛnũ** not because **mɛ̃** or 'I' is the subject but because it is more common to have human beings as focus of attention. Since word order in Panjabi sentences is very free, you can put any word anywhere in this particular sentence. By doing this you change emphasis and focus of attention, but the sentence will remain grammatically correct. If you say

buxɑːr mɛnũː fiɛ

with stress on **mɛnũː** you mean something like 'The high temperature is to *me*'. You can also say

fiɛ buxɑːr mɛnũː *or* **fiɛ mɛnũː buxɑːr**

with stress on **fiɛ** to mean 'I certainly have a high temperature.'

Now you can understand the grammatical structure of

ífi	**mɛnũː**	**pɑtɑː**	**náfiːː**
this	to-me	information	not

This I don't know.

Some linguists use the term 'dative subject' to refer to the experiencer in such sentences. But it is better to avoid this confusing term and use the term experiencer.

Gerund or verbal noun

In the English sentence

I am fond of reading

the word 'reading' functions as a noun. You could substitute a noun for it and say 'I am fond of books.' A noun formed by adding '-ing' to a verb in English is called a gerund or a verbal noun. In Panjabi, you form a gerund by adding **-ɳ/-aɳ** or **-ɳɑː** to the stem of a verb. The form with **-ɳ/-aɳ** is used before a postposition. Study the following examples carefully.

mɛnũː	**páɽʰan**	**dɑː**	**ʃɔk**	**fiɛ**
me-to	reading	-of	fondness/interest	is
I am fond of reading				

mɛnũː	**páɽʰnɑː**	**pasand**	**fiɛ**
me-to	reading	liking	is
I like reading			

tufiɑːnũː	**kʰɑːɳɑː**	**pakɑːuɳ**	**dɑː**	**ʃɔk**	**fiɛ**
you-to	food	cooking	-of	fondness/interest	is
You are fond of cooking					

tufia:nũ:	kʰa:ŋa:	paka:uŋa:	pasand	fiɛ
you-to	food	cooking	liking	is

You like cooking.

You may have noticed that in the gerund, ŋ sometimes becomes **n**, and sometimes a **u** is inserted between the verb stem and ŋ. The choice of ŋ or **n** is quite simple. You use ŋ except with verb stems ending in ŋ, **r** or ɽ. You insert an **u** between the stem and the affix if the stem ends in **a:** (except the verb stems **ja:** and **kʰa:**). For example:

kʰa:ŋa: (kʰa: + ŋa:)	eating
karna: (kar + na:)	doing
paka:uŋa: (paka: + u + ŋa:)	cooking
ja:ŋa: (ja: + ŋa:)	going
kʰa:ŋa: (kʰa: + ŋa:)	eating

See also the Grammatical summary, page 235.

Yes/No questions with *ki:*

In Panjabi, you can change a statement sentence into a question simply by changing intonation or tone of voice. You can also start such a question with **ki:**. But you still have to use the question intonation. The use of **ki:** is more common in writing. Remember that **ki:** does not mean 'what' when it is used in this way.

Dialogue 2

After the interview, Avtar is taking Prem home for a dinner. Away from the formal interview situation and TV cameras, the two friends resume their older manners of boyhood days

AVTAR: *Prem, ya:r teri: bansari: mɛnũ: baɽi: cangi: lagdi: fiɛ.*

PREM: éfi lɛ, pʰaɽ bansari.

AVTAR: mere káfiiŋ da: matlab fiɛ, mɛnũ: ífidi: a:va:z baɽi: mittʰi: lagdi: fiɛ. pata: náfiĩ: kiũ. mɛnũ: lagda: fiɛ ki ífi a:va:z bansari: ra:fiĩ: tere dil cõ a:ũdi: fiɛ.

PREM: bilkul sacc fiɛ. tɛnũ: sangi:t di: cangi: sámajfi fiɛ. par ki: tɛnũ: paccʰami: sangi:t pasand náfiĩ:?

AVTAR: *Classical* sangi:t tʰi:k fiɛ, par mɛnũ: *pop music* báfiut bura: lagda: fiɛ.

PREM: kiũ?

AVTAR: mɛ̃ ʃor ʃaraːbaː pasand náfiĩː kardaː. mɛ̃ fialkaː bʰàːratiː
        sangiːt pasand kardaː fiã̀ː, te panjaːbiː lok giːt viː.

AVTAR: *Prem, my friend, I like your flute very much.*
        [Lit.: Your flute strikes very good to me.]
PREM: *Here is the flute. Have it.*
AVTAR: *I mean it sounds very sweet to me. I don't know why. It*
        appears to me that the sound comes from your heart
        through the flute.
PREM: *Perfectly true. You have a good understanding of music.*
        But don't you like Western music?
AVTAR: *The classical music is okay. But I abhor pop music.*
PREM: *Why?*
AVTAR: *I don't like noise. I like light Indian music, and also*
        Panjabi folk songs.

Vocabulary

yaːr (*m*)	ਯਾਰ	very close friend
bansariː (*f*)	ਬੰਸਰੀ	flute
lag	ਲਗ	to appear, strike, attach
lɛ	ਲੈ	to take
pʰaṛ	ਫੜ	to catch, grasp
káfii [kɛ́]	ਕਹਿ	to say
káfiiŋ [kɛ́ŋ]	ਕਹਿਣ	saying
matlab (*m*)	ਮਤਲਬ	meaning
aːvaːz (*f*)	ਆਵਾਜ਼	sound, voice
mittʰaː	ਮਿੱਠਾ	sweet
raːfiiː	ਰਾਹੀਂ	through
dil (*m*)	ਦਿਲ	heart
cõ	'ਚੋਂ	from inside
aː	ਆ	come
aːũdiː	ਆਉਂਦੀ	coming
sacc (*m*)	ਸੱਚ	true, truth
sámajʰ [sámaj] (*f*)	ਸਮਝ	understanding
paccʰami:	ਪੱਛਮੀ	Western
báfiut [bɔ́t]	ਬਹੁਤ	very much, highly
buraː	ਬੁਰਾ	bad, evil, unpleasant
ʃor ʃaraːbaː (*m*)	ਸ਼ੋਰ ਸ਼ਰਾਬਾ	noise, din, hullabaloo

ɦalka:	ਹਲਕਾ	light
bʰà:rati: [pàrati:]	ਭਾਰਤੀ	Indian
lok (*m/pl*)	ਲੋਕ	folk, people

Colloquial pronunciation

The word we transcribe as **káɦi** (and in Panjabi written as ਕਹਿ) is pronounced as [**ké**]. Also, **káɦiɳ** (written as ਕਹਿਣ in Panjabi) is pronounced as [**kéɳ**]. The language points in this unit deal with the rules of spelling and pronunciation of such words.

Whether we like it or not, all languages change over time, and Panjabi is no exception. The Panjabi verb meaning 'tell' or 'say', which we transcribe as **káɦi** and pronounce as [**ké**] was actually pronounced as [**kaɦi**] some centuries ago. The older phonetic spelling ਕਹਿ is retained in modern Panjabi. As pointed out earlier, our transcription exactly reflects the modern Panjabi spelling. The rule of pronunciation is quite simple:

If you find **-ɦi** or -ਹਿ in the middle or at the end of a word in Panjabi, pronounce it as [**έ**].

In other words, do not pronounce the **ɦ** sound in such cases and use the vowel **έ** with a high tone.

A similar problem is exemplified by **baɦut** ਬਹੁਤ which is pronounced as [**bɔ́t**]. The rule of pronunciation in this case is

If you find **-ɦu** or -ਹੁ in the middle or at the end of a word in Panjabi, pronounce it as [**ɔ́**].

Don't pronounce the **ɦ** sound in such cases and use the vowel **ɔ́** with a high tone. Study the following examples carefully.

kaɦi	ਕਹਿ	[**ké**]	say
raɦi	ਰਹਿ	[**ré**]	stay, live
baɦi	ਬਹਿ	[**bé**]	sit
ʃaɦir	ਸ਼ਹਿਰ	[**ʃér**]	city
paɦila:	ਪਹਿਲਾ	[**péla:**]	first
saɦura:	ਸਹੁਰਾ	[**sɔ́ra:**]	father-in-law
paɦũc	ਪਹੁੰਚ	[**pɔ́̃c**]	approach, reach
gaɦu	ਗਹੁ	[**gɔ́**]	great care

See also page 203 of Script unit 5 even if you are not learning the Panjabi script. If you have the cassettes, listen to the pronunciation of the words on that page.

Word order

tenū:	sangi:t	di:	cangi:	sámaj^{fi}	fiɛ
you-to	music	of	good	understanding	is

You have a good understanding of music

mere	káfiiŋ	da:	matlab	fiɛ ...
my	saying	-of	meaning	is

I mean ... / What I really mean is ....

Note that **mere** is in the oblique form because of the postpositon **da:**.

The verb *lag*

teri:	bansari:	menū:	baɽi:	cangi:	lagdi:	fiɛ
your	flute	me-to	very	good	striking	is

I like your flute very much

menū:	ífidi:	a:va:z	baɽi:	mitt^hi:	lagdi:	fiɛ
me-to	its	sound	very	sweet	striking	is

It sounds very sweet to me.

The verb **lag** literally means 'to strike', 'to attach', 'to stick to', 'to touch', etc. But it can be used metaphorically in experiencer sentences as well.

pasand fiɛ and *pasand kar*

In Panjabi, you can say 'I like Western music' in two ways:

(1)	menū:	pacc^hami:	sangi:t	pasand	fiɛ
	me-to	Western	music	liking	is

(2)	mẽ	pacc^hami:	sangi:t	pasand	karda:	fiã:
	I	Western	music	liking	doing	am

There is a subtle difference of focus. (1) focuses on music and (2) focuses on the experiencer. But you do not need to bother about such subtleties at this stage.

From inside your heart

You already know that the Panjabi postposition/adverb **vic** means 'in' or 'inside'. You also know that in fluent speech, it is often shortened to **c**. In the following sentence, **-õ** is added to **c**.

ífi	ɑːvɑːz	bansari:	raːfiː :	tere
this	sound	flute	-through	your
dil	cõ	ɑːũdi:	fiɛ	
heart	from inside	coming	is	

Through the flute, this sound comes from the inside of your heart.

You can easily guess that the suffix **-õ** means 'from'. So you can also have

gʰàrõ	ਘਰੋਂ	from home
dilõ	ਦਿਲੋਂ	from the heart (i.e. honestly)
fiattʰõ	ਹੱਥੋਂ	from the hand
viccõ	ਵਿੱਚੋਂ	from inside
uttõ	ਉੱਤੋਂ	from above
fieṭʰõ	ਹੇਠੋਂ	from below
kolõ	ਕੋਲੋਂ	from near

The following interesting Panjabi proverb is used to describe hypocritical people.

uttõ	bi:bi:ã	dáfiɽiːãː,	viccõ	kaːle	kã:
from above	gentle	beards	from inside	black	crows

Omission of the experiencer

When Avtar says

pata:	náfiiː :	kiũ
knowledge	not	why
I don't know why		

he omits **menū:** 'to me' because it is clear from the situational context that he is talking about his own knowledge. Similarly, if he were to ask 'Do you know why?' he would most probably say

pata:	fiɛ	kiũ?
knowledge	is	why?

without using **tɛnū:** or **tufiaːnū:** 'to you' because the question is clearly addressed to the listener.

ífi/éfi/ɛ́fi and úfi/ófi/ɔ́fi

Different speakers of Panjabi use these variants in different ways. (As is the case with the variants **itʰe, etʰe, ɛtʰe**, etc. – see Conversation unit 3.)

This book uses **íﬁ** and **úﬁ** as unstressed forms, **éﬁ** and **óﬁ** as stressed forms, and **éﬁ** and **ɔ́ﬁ** with the gesture of pointing.

Dialogue 3 🔘🔘

Satwant, Avtar's wife, has prepared a special dinner for Prem

SATWANT:	viːr jiː, éﬁ lao *Avtar* jiː diː xaːs pasand.
PREM:	íﬁ kiː ﬁɛ, bʱàːbi jiː?
SATWANT:	*chicken* biriaːniː.
PREM:	náﬁ̃ː jiː, ʃukriːaː. mɛ̃ *vegetarian* ﬁã̃ː.
AVTAR:	*Satwant,* íﬁ bandaː sáːdʱuː ﬁɛ. *Meat* náﬁ̃ː kʰã̃ːdaː, ʃaraːb náﬁ̃ː pĩːdaː, sigriṭ náﬁ̃ː pĩːdaː.
SATWANT:	báﬁut cangi: gall ﬁɛ.
AVTAR:	ﬁɛ̃? sáːdʱuː ﬁoɳa: cangi: gall ﬁɛ?
SATWANT:	sigriṭ naː piːɳaː cangi: gall ﬁɛ. báﬁutaː naː bolɳa: vi: cangi: gall ﬁɛ. mū̃ːﬁ nũː kʰaːɳa: kʰaːɳ lai: ziaːda: varto, te bolaɳ lai gʱàṭṭ.
SATWANT:	*Brother, have this. It's Avtar's special favourite.*
PREM:	*What's this, sister-in-law?*
SATWANT:	*Chicken biriyani.*
PREM:	*No thanks. I'm a vegetarian.*
AVTAR:	*Satwant, this man is a saint. He doesn't eat meat, doesn't drink alcohol, doesn't smoke.*
SATWANT:	*That's very good.*
AVTAR:	*What? Is it good to be a saint?*
SATWANT:	*It's good not to smoke. It's also good not to talk too much. Use your mouth more for eating and less for talking.*

Vocabulary

viːr (*m*)	ਵੀਰ	brother (a term of affection)
lao	ਲਓ	please take (request form of **lɛ**)
xaːs	ਖ਼ਾਸ	special
bʱàːbi: [**pàːbiː**] (*f*)	ਭਾਬੀ	brother's wife, sister-in-law
biriaːniː (*f*)	ਬਿਰਿਆਨੀ	a rice dish
bandaː (*m*)	ਬੰਦਾ	man
sáːdʱuː [**sáːduː**] (*m*)	ਸਾਧੂ	saint, holy man

ʃigriʈ (*m*)	ਸਿਗਰਿਟ	cigarette
ʃara:b (*f*)	ਸ਼ਰਾਬ	alcoholic drink
ɦo	ਹੋ	to be, to become
ɦoɳa:	ਹੋਣਾ	being, becoming
báɦuta: [bóta:]	ਬਹੁਤਾ	too much
mṹ:ɦ [mṹ:] (*m*)	ਮੂੰਹ	mouth
kʰa:ɳ	ਖਾਣ	eating
zia:da:	ਜ਼ਿਆਦਾ	more
gʱàʈʈ [kàʈʈ]	ਘੱਟ	less
varat	ਵਰਤ	to use
bolaɳ	ਬੋਲਣ	speaking

'Drinking' a cigarette

Languages can refer to the same situation in interesting ways. Satwant says

sigriʈ	na:	pi:ɳa:	cangi:	gall	ɦɛ
cigarette	not	drinking	good	matter	is

It's good not to smoke.

Also note that she uses the form **pi:ɳa:**, and not **pi:ɳ**, because there is no postposition following the verbal noun. But when a postposition follows, she uses the verbal noun without **-a:**, as in

mṹ:ɦ	nū:	kʰa:ɳa:	kʰa:ɳ	lai:	zia:da:	varto ...
mouth	-to	food	eating	for	more	use

Use the mouth more for eating ...

na: and *náɦĩ:* are not interchangeable

It would be wrong to translate one of them as 'no' and the other as 'not'. But like 'no' and 'not', **na:** and **náɦĩ:** are not interchangeable. You will learn later that **náɦĩ:** is actually an emphatic form of **na:**, and we shall deal with the distinction in Conversation unit 8.

Definite object

Panjabi has no articles (the equivalents of the English 'a', 'an' and 'the'). But it has its own ways and means of doing what articles do in English. You may have noticed the postposition **nū:** after the object **mṹ:ɦ** in the sentence analysed above. It does the work of the definite article 'the'. It makes the noun **mṹ:fi** 'definite', so that it means 'this particular mouth', and not just any mouth. In Panjabi, one of the ways of making an object definite is to add the postposition **nū:** to it. You will see in Conversation unit 5 that this **nū:** is accompanied by some other significant grammatical differences as well.

Dialogue 4

Satwant offers Prem a special vegetarian dish

SATWANT:	vi:r ji:, ɛ́fi pa:lak pani:r kofta: lao.
PREM:	ífide vic ki: fiɛ?
SATWANT:	pa:lak, pani:r, gꜰꜱo, mɛda:, pia:z, adrak, dꜰàni:a:, metʰi:, mirc, masa:la:.
AVTAR:	te ik gupt ci:z vi:.
PREM:	gupt ci:z ki: fiɛ, bꜰà:bi: ji:?
SATWANT:	kújꜰ náfiĩ:, ífi ɛvẽ cʰeʈde ne.
PREM:	kiũ bai:? tenũ: ki: fiakk fiɛ meri: bꜰarjà:i: nū: cʰeʈan da:?
AVTAR:	mɛ̃ kadõ cʰeʈda: fiã:? kʰa:ŋe vic ik gupt ci:z fiɛgi: ɛ – prem.
PREM:	mɛ̃? kʰa:ŋe vic?
AVTAR:	náfiĩ:, mere káfiiŋ da: matlab fiɛ – pia:r.
SATWANT:	canga: fiuŋ bolŋa: band karo, te prem na:l kʰa:ŋa: kʰa:o.

SATWANT:	*Brother, have these spinach and cheese balls.*
PREM:	*What's in them, sister-in-law?*
SATWANT:	*Spinach, Indian soft cheese, clarified butter, plain flour, onion, fresh ginger, coriander, fenugreek, chilli and mixed spices.*
AVTAR:	*And also a secret thing.*
PREM:	*What's the secret thing, sister-in-law?*
SATWANT:	*Nothing. He's just teasing.*
PREM:	*Why man? What right have you got to tease my sister-in-law?*
AVTAR:	*I'm not teasing. There is a secret thing in the food -* **prem** *(love). (Lit.: When do I tease?)*
PREM:	*Me? In the food?*
AVTAR:	*I mean* **pia:r** *(love).*

SATWANT: *Well. Now stop talking and eat your meal with **prem** (love).*

Vocabulary

pa:lak (*f*)	ਪਾਲਕ	spinach
pani:r (*m*)	ਪਨੀਰ	Indian soft cheese
kofta: (*m*)	ਕੋਫ਼ਤਾ	meat or vegetable balls
gʰio (*m*)	ਘਿਓ	ghee (clarified butter)
mɛda: (*m*)	ਮੈਦਾ	plain flour
pia:z (*m*)	ਪਿਆਜ਼	onion
adrak (*m*)	ਅਦਰਕ	fresh ginger
metʰi: (*f*)	ਮੇਥੀ	fenugreek
masa:la: (*m*)	ਮਸਾਲਾ	mixed spices
gupt	ਗੁਪਤ	secret
ci:z (*f*)	ਚੀਜ਼	thing
kújʰ náfii:	ਕੁਝ ਨਹੀਂ	nothing
ɛvẽ	ਐਵੇਂ	simply, just
cʰeɽ	ਛੇੜ	to tease
bai:	ਬਈ	informal form of address
fiakk (*m*)	ਹੱਕ	right
bʰarjà:i: (*f*)	ਭਰਜਾਈ	brother's wife, sister-in-law
kadõ	ਕਦੋਂ	when
prem (*m*)	ਪ੍ਰੇਮ	love
pia:r (*m*)	ਪਿਆਰ	love
band kar	ਬੰਦ ਕਰ	to stop

Dialogue 5 ●●

Prem stays with Avtar. Next morning, he does not feel very well. Avtar takes him to his family doctor, Dr Qureshi, a Panjabi-speaking Muslim doctor, originally from Lahore, Pakistan. It is notable that in the presence of the doctor, Avtar refers to his friend formally by using the 'respectful plural' forms for him

AVTAR: ífi ne ɖa:kʈar *Qureshi*, te ífi ne mere dost *Prem Sharma.*
DR QURESHI: mɛ̃ ja:ṇda: fiã:. milke baɽi: xuʃi: fioi:, *Sharma* sá:fiab.
PREM: ɖa:kʈar sá:fiab, tusi: mɛnũ: kivẽ ja:ṇde fio?

DR QURESHI:	*TV programme* tõ. tufiɑːɖiː mosiːkiː kɑmɑːl diː fiɛ. vɑ́ːfi!
PREM:	jiː ʃukriːɑː.
DR QURESHI:	mere lɑːik koiː xidmat fiɛ tɑ̃ː fiukɑm kɑro.
AVTAR:	ɑjj ífiɑ̃ː diː tɑbiːɑt t̪ʰiːk nɑ́fiĩː.
DR QURESHI:	kiː gɑll fiɛ?
PREM:	mɛnũ̀ː t̪ʰoɽɑː buxɑːr fiɛ, sir dɑrd viː fiɛ.
DR QURESHI:	gɑlɑː t̪ʰiːk fiɛ?
PREM:	jiː nɑ́fiĩː, gɑlɑː viː xɑrɑːb fiɛ, peʈ dɑrd viː fiɛ.
AVTAR:	ɖɑːkʈɑr sɑ́ːfiɑb, mɛnũ̀ː fikɑr fiɛ. ɑgle fiɑfte ífiɑ̃ː dɑː ik fior *TV programme* fiɛ. *(Dr Qureshi examines Prem)*
DR QURESHI:	fikɑr diː koiː gɑll nɑ́fiĩː. mɑːmuːliː *flu* fiɛ. *Sharma* sɑ́ːfiɑb, tufiɑːnũ̀ː ɑːrɑːm diː loɽ fiɛ, dɑvɑːiː diː nɑ́fiĩː.
AVTAR:	*This is Dr Qureshi, and this is my friend Prem Sharma.*
DR QURESHI:	*I know. Very pleased to meet you, Mr Sharma.*
PREM:	*How do you know me, doctor?*
DR QURESHI:	*From the TV programme. Your music is wonderful! Great!*
PREM:	*Thanks.*
DR QURESHI:	*What can I do for you? (Lit.: If there is a service befitting me, please order.)*
AVTAR:	*He's not well today.*
DR QURESHI:	*What's the matter?*
PREM:	*I've got a slight temperature. Also a headache.*
DR QURESHI:	*Is your throat alright?*
PREM:	*No. I also have a sore throat and a stomach ache. (Lit.: Throat is also bad.)*
AVTAR:	*Doctor, I'm worried. He has another TV programme next week.* *(Dr Qureshi examines Prem)*
DR QURESHI:	*There is nothing to worry about. It's a little bit of flu. Mr Sharma, you need rest, not medicine.*

Vocabulary

dost (*m/f*)	ਦੋਸਤ	friend
jɑːṇ	ਜਾਣ	to know

kivẽ	ਕਿਵੇਂ	how
mosi:ki: (*f*)	ਮੋਸੀਕੀ	music
kama:l (*m*)	ਕਮਾਲ	wonder
vá:ɦi	ਵਾਹ!	Great!
la:ik	ਲਾਇਕ	capable, befitting
koi:	ਕੋਈ	any
xidmat (*f*)	ਖ਼ਿਦਮਤ	service
tʰoɽa:	ਥੋੜਾ	a little
buxa:r (*m*)	ਬੁਖ਼ਾਰ	high temperature, fever
gala: (*m*)	ਗਲਾ	throat
xara:b	ਖ਼ਰਾਬ	bad
peʈ (*m*)	ਪੇਟ	stomach
fikar (*m*)	ਫ਼ਿਕਰ	worry
agla:	ਅਗਲਾ	next
ɦafta: (*m*)	ਹਫ਼ਤਾ	week
agle ɦafte (*adverbial*)	ਅਗਲੇ ਹਫ਼ਤੇ	next week
loɽ (*f*)	ਲੋੜ	need
dava:i: (*f*)	ਦਵਾਈ	medicine
a:ra:m (*m*)	ਆਰਾਮ	rest

The sound of music

Dr Qureshi uses the word **mosi:ki:**, and not **sangi:t**, for 'music'. He also uses **xidmat** 'service' where a Hindu or a Sikh would use **seva:**. As was pointed out in Conversation unit 1, Panjabi-speaking Muslims use many Arabic and Persian words in their Panjabi speech.

Word order

mɛnũ:	**fikar**	**ɦɛ**				
me-to	worry	is				
I'm worried						

tuɦia:nũ:	**a:ra:m**	**di:**	**loɽ**	**ɦɛ,**	**dava:i**	**di:**	**náɦi:**
you-to	rest	-of	need	is	medicine	-of	not
You need rest, not medicine							

Possessive adjectives

ɑjj	ífinã:	di:	tɑbi:ɑt	t̪ʰi:k	náfii:
today	he	-of	health	good	not

He's not well today

ífinã: di: literally means 'they-of'. In a formal situation, a plural form has been used to show respect to one person. A table of Panjabi possessive adjectives appears on page 225 in the Grammatical summary.

A case of ambiguity

An ambiguous sentence has two or more meanings. Cases of ambiguity result not only from words having multiple meanings but also (and more interestingly) from their having multiple grammatical functions. An interesting example from English is 'I kissed her back.'

Ambiguous sentences occur (and are often deliberately constructed!) in all languages. Study the following Panjabi sentence.

	menũ:	fiuɳ	kújⁿ	kʰa:ɳa:	cá:fii:da:	fie
(1)	me-to	now	some	food	desirable	is
(2)			something	eating		

The first interpretation is 'I want some food now.' It regards **kújⁿ** as an adjective meaning 'some' and **kʰa:ɳa:** as an ordinary masculine noun meaning 'food'. But **kʰa:ɳa:** can also be a verbal noun derived from the verb **kʰa:** 'to eat', and **kújⁿ** can also be used as a noun or pronoun meaning 'something'. So the second interpretation is 'I should eat something now'.

ਅਭਿਆਸ Exercises

1 Answer the following questions, starting your answer with **fiã: ji:** or **náfii ji:** (as appropriate) and then saying whether you like or dislike the thing. The symbol ☺ means 'like' and ☹ means 'dislike'. If possible, match the grammatical form of your answer to that of the question. Remember that you don't need to use a form of **fie** in a negative sentence. The first question is answered for you.

(a) *Question:*   ki: tusĩ: ʃarɑ:b pi:ɳa: pasɑnd karde fio?

   Answer: ☹. I'm a teetotaller

náfĩ: ji:, mẽ ʃara:b pi:ɳa: pasand náfĩ: karda:. mẽ
teetotaller fĩã:.

(b) *Question:*   ki: tufia:nũ: *classical* sangi:t canga: lagda: fiɛ?
    Answer: ☺

(c) *Question:*   ki: tufia:nũ: kʰa:ɳe vic mirc masa:la: canga: lagda:
                 fiɛ?
    Answer: ☹

(d) *Question:*   ki: tufia:nũ: *pop music* bura: lagda: fiɛ?
    Answer: ☺

(e) *Question:*   ki: tufia:nũ: pa:lak pani:r pasand fiɛ?
    Answer: soft cheese ☺, but spinach ☹

(f) *Question:*   ki: tufia:nũ: kʰa:ɳa: paka:uɳ da: ʃɔk fiɛ?
    Answer: My wife, cooking ☺. Me, eating ☺.

(g) *Question:*   ki: tufia:nũ: tandu:ri: *chicken* canga: lagda: fiɛ?
    Answer: ☹, I'm a vegetarian.

(h) *Question:*   tusĩ: sigriṭ pĩ:de fio na:?
    Answer: ☹

2 If you have the cassettes, listen to the monologue. Then look at the
following table. Here you will record the speaker's likes and dislikes.
With the list in mind, listen to the recording again. Then fill in the boxes
with **L** for 'likes' and **D** for 'dislikes'.

Panjabi food	
Highly spiced foods	
Cricket	
Football	
Indian film music	
Indian classical music	
Western music	

3 Complete the following dialogue between A and B by supplying A's
questions to which B answers.

A: _____ ?
B: mɛnũː filmãː dekʰaṇ daː ʃɔk ɦɛ.
A: _____ ?
B: náɦĩː jiː. mɛnũː ʃaraːb báɦut buriː lagdiː ɦɛ.
A: _____ ?
B: mɛnũː _classical_ sangiːt pasand ɦɛ, _pop music_ náɦĩː.
A: _____ ?
B: náɦĩː, mɛ̃ _meat_ pasand náɦĩː kardaː.

4 You take a friend to a Panjabi restaurant. Both of you have now read the menu.

(a) _How do you ask your friend what he would like to have?_
(b) He points to a dish called dhansak and asks what's in it. But you don't know either.
   How do you ask the waiter what there is in dhansak?
(c) The waiter says that it has lentils, meat and spices. But your friend is a vegetarian.
   How do you ask the waiter whether they've got vegetarian dhansak?
(d) The waiter says that there is no such thing as a vegetarian dhansak.
   How do you ask your friend whether he would like to have something else?
(e) Your friend chooses shahi panir, but is afraid that it may be too hot.
   How do you ask the waiter whether there are chilli and spices in shahi panir?
(f) The waiter says that shahi panir is a very mild dish.
   How do you then order one dhansak with rice (**cɔl**) _and one shahi panir with naan_ (**naːn**)_?_

5 Mohan Singh Gill is on a visit to the Panjab. There he becomes ill and goes to see a doctor. Their conversation has been translated into English. Can you translate it back into Panjabi?

Gill: Greetings, doctor. My name is Mohan Singh Gill.
Doctor: Greetings, Mr Gill. How are you?.
Gill: Very unwell!
Doctor: What's the matter?
Gill: I have severe headache and stomach ache.
Doctor: Do you have a temperature as well?
Gill: No.

Doctor:	Sore throat?
Gill:	No.
Doctor:	Any other problem (**gall**)?
Gill:	No, nothing else.
Doctor:	Do you smoke or drink?
Gill:	No, I don't smoke or drink.
Doctor:	Well, take this medicine. Have a good rest, and don't do any work today.

5 ਕੱਲ੍ਹ ਨੂੰ ਤੁਸੀਂ ਕੀ ਕਰਨਾ ਹੈ?
What are you going to do tomorrow?

In this unit you will learn to
- talk and ask about your own and other people's plans
- compare people and objects
- talk about visiting places
- use the potential verb form
- use the particles vi:, fii: and tã:

ਗੱਲ ਬਾਤ Dialogues

Dialogue 1 🔲

Surjit Singh Kalsi, who has retired recently, is going on a trip to India. He goes to Baldev Singh Nijjar, a travel agent who knows him well

NIJJAR:	a:o *Kalsi* sá:fiab, beṭʰo. fiukam karo.
KALSI:	menũ: do *return* ṭikṭã: cá:fii:di:ã: ne.
NIJJAR:	a:pṇe lai:?
KALSI:	fiã: ji:.
NIJJAR:	tusĩ: kittʰe ja:ṇa: fie?
KALSI:	dilli:, te aggõ a:gre.
NIJJAR:	kadõ ja:ṇa: fie?
KALSI:	*Christmas* di:ã: cʰuṭṭi:ã: c.
NIJJAR:	agge piccʰe náfĩ:?
KALSI:	náfĩ:. ki: gall fie?
NIJJAR:	*Christmas* di:ã: cʰuṭṭi:ã: c ṭikaṭ máfiingi: fiundi: fie, agge piccʰe sasti:.
KALSI:	tusĩ: máfiingi: sasti: di: cinta: na: karo.
NIJJAR:	ji: báfiut accʰa:.

NIJJAR:	*Come in, Mr Kalsi. What can I do for you?*
KALSI:	*I need two return tickets.*
NIJJAR:	*For yourself?*
KALSI:	*Yes.*
NIJJAR:	*Where are you going?*
KALSI:	*To Delhi, and from there to Agra.*
NIJJAR:	*When are you going?*
KALSI:	*In the Christmas holidays.*
NIJJAR:	*Can't you go before or after that? (Lit.: Before (or) after not?)*
KALSI:	*No. What's the matter?*
NIJJAR:	*The ticket is costly in the Christmas holidays. It's cheap before and after that.*
KALSI:	*Don't worry about its cost. (Lit.: Don't worry about costly and cheap.)*
NIJJAR:	*OK.*

Vocabulary

ja:ɳa:	ਜਾਣਾ	to go
aggõ	ਅੱਗੋਂ	thence, from there
cʰuʈʈi:a: *(f/pl)*	ਛੁੱਟੀਆਂ	holidays
agge	ਅੱਗੇ	before
piccʰe	ਪਿੱਛੇ	after
máɦinga:[ménga:]	ਮਹਿੰਗਾ	costly
sasta:	ਸਸਤਾ	cheap
cinta: *(f)*	ਚਿੰਤਾ	worry

The potential form (intransitive verb)

In Conversation unit 4, we used a form of the verb known as the verbal noun. A verbal noun, though derived from a verb by adding **-ɳa:** or **-aɳ**, functions as a noun. The potential form, which looks and sounds like a verbal noun, is used as a proper verb to describe a planned action, as in

tusĩ:	kittʰe	ja:ɳa:	ɦɛ?
you	where	to go	is

Where are you going? (i.e. Where do you want to go?)

But it does not indicate the time of the action. We shall translate the verbal noun with the English '-ing' form (e.g. 'going') and the potential form with a to-infinitive (e.g. 'to go'). Note that the verb **ja:** has no object. Such a verb is known as an intransitive verb.

The potential form of an intransitive verb always has masculine-singular form.

We shall see later on in the unit that the potential form of a transitive verb can have other number–gender forms as well.

Do not be tempted to call the potential form the future tense form. As we shall see below, the potential form can also refer to a planned action in the past time.

ɦo versus *ɦɛ*

Compare the two sentences

guɽ	**mittʰa:**	**ɦɛ**
brown sugar	sweet	is

The brown sugar is sweet

(i.e. This particular sample of brown sugar is sweet.)

guɽ	**mittʰa:**	**ɦunda:**	**ɦɛ**
brown sugar	sweet	happening	is

Brown sugar is sweet.

(i.e. It is the general quality of brown sugar to be sweet.)

ɦunda: is the imperfective form of the verb **ɦo** ('to become', 'to happen'). When Nijjar says

Christmas	**di:ã:**	**cʰutti:ã:**	**c**	**ţikaţ**	**mãɦiingi:**	**ɦundi:**	**ɦɛ**
Christmas	of	holidays	in	ticket	costly	happening	is

he means that it always happens to be the case that a ticket is costly in the Christmas holidays. He is not talking about any particular ticket. It is important not to confuse the forms of **ɦɛ** and **ɦo**. **ɦɛ** is the only verb in Panjabi that has the present and the past tense forms. No other verb has tense forms. On the other hand, **ɦɛ** does not have any forms other than the present and the past tense forms.

Omission of the postposition *nũ:*

While speaking about the destination of your journey, you may omit the postposition **nũ:**. Instead of saying

mɛ̃	aːgre	nũː	jaːɳaː	ɦɛ
I	Agra	to	to go	is

I am going to Agra

you may simply say

mɛ̃	aːgre	jaːɳaː	ɦɛ.
I	Agra	to go	is.

Note that the masculine singular noun **aːgraː** assumes the oblique form **aːgre** before the postposition. When **nũː** is omitted in such constructions, the oblique form stays on, indicating that the postposition has been omitted.

Dialogue 2

Surjit Kalsi and his wife Nirmal Kaur are staying in a hotel in Agra

SURJIT:	káll ᶠ daː ki: *programme* ɦɛ?
NIRMAL:	mɛnũː kiː pataː? tusĩː dasso.
SURJIT:	canga: pʰir, kállᶠ saverе asĩː *shopping* karniː ɦɛ. dupáɦir daː kʰaːɳaː *Taj Mahal Hotel* c kʰaːɳaː ɦɛ.
NIRMAL:	te ʃaːm nũː kiː karnaː ɦɛ?
SURJIT:	ʃaːm nũː sɛr sapaːʈaː, te panjaːbiː dᶠàːbe c saːg makkiː diː roʈi kʰaːɳĩː ɦɛ.
NIRMAL:	*Taj Mahal* kadõ dekʰɳaː ɦɛ?
SURJIT:	raːt nũː.
NIRMAL:	raːt nũː kiũ?
SURJIT:	caːnaɳi raːt c *Taj Mahal* din naːlõ ziaːda: sóɦaɳaː lagdaː ɦɛ. jivẽ tũː.
NIRMAL:	es umar c ʃaram viː karo. íɦ koi maʃkariːã: karan di: umar ɦɛ?
SURJIT:	náɦĩː, íɦ naːm japaɳ di: umar ɦɛ. tere kol koi: dᶠàram potʰiː ɦɛ?

SURJIT:	*What's tomorrow's programme?*
NIRMAL:	*I don't know. You tell me. (Lit.: What do I know?)*
SURJIT:	*OK then. Tomorrow morning we'll go out shopping. We'll have our lunch in the Taj Mahal Hotel.*
NIRMAL:	*And what are we going to do in the evening?*
SURJIT:	*We'll stroll about in the evening, and eat cooked spinach and corn chapatis in a Panjabi restaurant.*

NIRMAL:	*When are we going to see the Taj Mahal?*
SURJIT:	*At night.*
NIRMAL:	*Why at night?*
SURJIT:	*The Taj Mahal looks more beautiful on a moonlit night than during daytime. Just like you.*
NIRMAL:	*You should be ashamed of yourself at this age. Is this the age for sexy jokes?*
SURJIT:	*No. This is the age for muttering prayers. Do you have a prayer book?*

Vocabulary

kállʱ	ਕੱਲ੍ਹ	tomorrow (but see also p. 90)
savere	ਸਵੇਰੇ	in the morning
dupáɦir [dupér] (*f*)	ਦੁਪਹਿਰ	midday
ʃa:m (*f*)	ਸ਼ਾਮ	evening
sɛr sapa:ʈa: (*m*)	ਸੈਰ ਸਪਾਟਾ	leisurely stroll
ɖʱà:ba: [ʈà:ba:] (*m*)	ਢਾਬਾ	traditional Indian restaurant
sa:g (*m*)	ਸਾਗ	cooked spinach and mustard leaves
makki: (*m*)	ਮੱਕੀ	maize, corn
roʈi: (*f*)	ਰੋਟੀ	chapati, bread
ra:t (*f*)	ਰਾਤ	night
ca:naɳi:	ਚਾਨਣੀ	moonlit
na:lõ	ਨਾਲੋਂ	than
umar (*f*)	ਉਮਰ	age
ʃaram (*f*)	ਸ਼ਰਮ	shame
maʃkari:	ਮਸ਼ਕਰੀ	joke (generally sexy)
na:m (*m*)	ਨਾਮ	name (generally God's)
jap	ਜਪ	to repeat silently, to mutter (a prayer or God's name)
dʱàram [tàram] (*m*)	ਧਰਮ	religion
potʰi: (*f*)	ਪੋਥੀ	book (generally religious)

The potential form (transitive verb)

The potential form of a transitive verb (a verb with an object) agrees with the object in number and gender. This rule applies unless the object is a definite object marked with **nū̃:**, in which case see p. 95.

káll	**savere**	**asĩ:**	shopping	**karni:**	**fiɛ**
			(f/sg)	(f/sg)	(sg)
tomorrow	morning	we	shopping	to do	is

Tomorrow morning, we are going to do shopping (*lit.:* we are to do shopping)

The potential form of the verb is feminine singular because the object 'shopping' is feminine singular in Panjabi. The verb **fiɛ** is not marked for gender. But it does agree with the object in number. Similarly,

(asĩ:)	**dupáfiir**	**da:**	**kʰa:ɳa:**	Taj Mahal Hotel	**c**	**kʰa:ɳa:**	**fiɛ**
			(m/sg)			(m/sg)	(sg)
we	mid-day	of	meal	Taj Mahal Hotel	in	to eat	is

We are going to have our lunch in the Taj Mahal Hotel

(asĩ:)	**panja:bi:**	**dʰà:be**	**c**	**sa:g**
				(m/sg)
we	Panjabi	restaurant	in	cooked spinach

makki: di: roti:	**kʰa:ɳi:**	**fiɛ**
(f/sg)	(f/sg)	
corn chapatis	to eat	is

We are going to eat cooked spinach and corn chapatis in a Panjabi restaurant.

When a verb has more than one object, the verb usually agrees with the last one.

savere

The Panjabi word for 'morning' is **savera:** (m). **savere** is an adverb form meaning 'in the morning'. But you can also say **saver nũ:**. Similarly, you can have

dupáfiir nũ:	or	**dupáfiire**	at midday
ʃa:m nũ:	or	**ʃa:mi:**	in the evening
ra:t nũ:	or	**ra:ti:**	at night

Comparison

Taj Hotel	Manhar Hotel	**na:lõ**	**zia:da:**	**canga:**	**fiɛ**
Taj Hotel	Manhar Hotel	with-from	more	good	is

The Taj Hotel is better than the Manhar Hotel.

You can use **tõ** ('from') in place of **na:lõ**.

If you understand the 'experiencer' constructions in Conversation unit 4, the following sentence should be no problem for you.

cɑːnɑɳiː	rɑːt	c	Taj Mahal	**din**
moonlit	night	in	Taj Mahal	day
nɑːlõ	**ziɑːdɑː**	**sófiɑɳɑː**	**lɑgdɑː**	**ɦɛ.**
with-from	more	beautiful	striking	is

The Taj Mahal looks more beautiful on a moonlit night than during day time.

Dialogue 3 🔳

After seeing the Taj Mahal, the couple are planning to go to see some other places

NIRMAL: ɑsĩː *Mathura Bindraban* de mandar kadõ dekʰɳe ne?

SURJIT: parsõ nũː. kállꜛ nũː *Charanjit* ne dilliːõ ɑːuɳɑː ɦɛ, te parsõ nũː ɑsĩː úɦide nɑːl jɑːɳɑː ɦɛ.

NIRMAL: par úɦine tɑ̃ː cɔtʰ nũː ɑːuɳɑː siː.

SURJIT: ɑːuɳɑː tɑ̃ː úɦine cɔtʰ nũː ɦiː siː, par ɦuɳ úɦidɑː kal nũː ɑːuɳ dɑː *programme* ɦɛ.

NIRMAL: *When are we going to the Mathura Bindraban temples?*

SURJIT: *The day after tomorow. Charanjit is coming tomorrow. We are going with him the day after tomorrow.*

NIRMAL: *But he was coming the day after the day after tomorrow.*

SURJIT: *He was coming the day after the day after tomorrow. But now his programme is to come tomorrow.*

Vocabulary

mandar (*m*)	ਮੰਦਰ	temple
parsõ (*m*)	ਪਰਸੋਂ	day after tomorrow (but see also p. 90)
cɔtʰ (*m*)	ਚੌਥ	day after the day after tomorrow (but see also p. 90)
siː	ਸੀ	was
tɑ̃ː	ਤਾਂ	as for (but see also p. 91)
ɦiː	ਹੀ	only (but see also p. 91)

The Indian concept of time

A language is a part of a country's culture, and a culture embodies the world-view of its people. The linear concept of time – time moving in a single direction from the past, through the present, and into the future – is only one (largely European) view of time. Other cultures may have different views. Note the meanings of the following Panjabi words

ajj	today
káll$^{\hbar}$	yesterday, tomorrow
parsõ	day before yesterday, day after tomorrow
cɔt^h	day before the day before yesterday, day after the day after tomorrow

It appears that it is the present or today or **ajj** which is the temporal point in relation to which the distance of the other days is measured. Whether the other days are in the past or in the future seems unimportant. **káll$^{\hbar}$** is simply a day once removed from today. Whether it is yesterday or tomorrow does not seem to matter. Similarly, **parsõ** is simply a day twice removed from today.

Some speakers add the postposition **nũ:** to mark a future day, as the speakers in Dialogue 3 do. This helps. But this is not a strict rule of Panjabi grammar.

With such a concept of time ingrained in its meaning structure, do not be surprised when you are told that Panjabi grammar does not have the present, past and future tenses of the type you find in European languages.

Use of the agentive postposition *ne*

With the subject of a verb in the potential form, you don't use any postposition if the subject is the first or the second person pronoun. So if the subject is either of the four pronouns **mɛ̃** 'I', **asĩ:** 'we', **tũ:** 'you' (*sg*), **tusĩ:** 'you' (*pl*), you don't add any postposition to it. But if the subject is a noun or a third person pronoun, you have to add the agentive postposition **ne** to it. As with other postpositions, the noun or the pronoun is in the oblique case form.

káll$^{\hbar}$	nũ:	tusĩ:	ki:	karna:	ɦɛ?
tomorrow	to	you	what	to do	is

What are you going to do tomorrow?

mẽ	film	dekʰŋ̣iː	fɛ
I	film	to see	is

I'm going to see a film

tufiaːɖe	bʰàràː	ne	kiː	karnaː	fɛ?
your	brother	(Agt)	what	to do	is

What is your brother (Agt) going to do?

pataː	náfiː	úfine	kiː	karnaː	fɛ
knowledge	not	he (Agt)	what	to do	is

I don't know what he's going to do.

Note that **neː** is not added to **mẽ** and **tus̃iː**, but it is added to **úfi** and **bʰàràː**.

The particles *viː, fiiː* and *tãː*

These words are difficult to translate, but they help organise your speech and give it particular nuances. They are best learnt in actual use.

viː	inclusive particle roughly meaning 'also'
fiiː	exclusive particle roughly meaning 'only'
tãː	rough meaning 'as for' or 'as far as x is concerned'

Study the following examples

menũː	paːlak	viː	cáːfiiːdiː	fɛ
me-to	spinach	also	desirable	is

I would like to have spinach as well (in addition to the other vegetables I'm interested in)

menũː	paːlak	fiiː	cáːfiiːdiː	fɛ
me-to	spinach	only	desirable	is

I would like to have spinach only (and I'm not at all interested in any other vegetables)

menũː	tãː	paːlak	cáːfiiːdiː	fɛ
me-to	as for	spinach	desirable	is

As far as I am concerned, I want spinach (whatever other people may want).

Now an example from Dialogue 3.

aːuŋa	tãː	úfine	cɔtʰ	nũː	fiiː	siː
to come	as for	he (Agt)	day after the day after tomorrow	to	only	was

A really meaningful (but verbose) translation would be:

As for his coming, he certainly was going to come the day after the day after tomorrow.

Past Tense of the verb *fiɛ*

In Conversation unit 2 we came across the present tense forms of the Panjabi verb **fiɛ**. You may have noted that these forms are marked for number and person, but not for gender. Luckily for you, the most widely spoken dialect of Panjabi has only one past tense form of **fiɛ**. This form is **si:**, used with all persons and numbers. The formal written variety of Panjabi has different singular and plural past tense forms of **fiɛ** for different persons. These forms are given on page 228 in the Grammatical summary. If you are learning writing as well, you are advised to use these forms in your writing. But in your speech, you need not use any past tense form of **fiɛ** other than **si:**.

Dialogue 4 🔘🔘

Charanjit Kalsi, Surjit Kalsi's nephew, has arrived to take them to Delhi, and they are now planning what to see there

SURJIT:	dilli: c kífiɽi:ã: kífiɽi:ã: ci:zã: dekʰaɳ va:li:ã: ne?
CHARANJIT:	báfiut sa:ri:ã:, navi:ã: vi: te pura:ɳi:ã: vi:.
SURJIT:	mɛ̃ tã: pura:ɳi:ã: ci:zã: te ima:ratã: nũ: fii: dekʰɳa: fiɛ, te na:le sa:re gurdua:riã: nũ: vi:. mɛnũ: navi:ã: ci:zã: dekʰaɳ da: koi: ʃɔk náfii:.
CHARANJIT:	par kai: navi:ã: ci:zã: vi: báfiut sófiaɳi:ã: ne.
SURJIT:	ťʰi:k fiɛ ka:ka:. par pura:ɳe xia:lã: va:le bande nũ: pura:ɳi:ã: ci:zã: fii: sófiaɳi:ã: lagdi:ã: ne. jivẽ teri: ca:ci:.
NIRMAL:	tufia:nũ: koi: ʃaram fiia: fiɛ jã: náfii̇̃? ífi koi: munɖe de sá:fimaɳe káfiiɳ va:li: gall fiɛ?
SURJIT:	*Charanjit,* dass tũ: a:paɳi: váfiuʈi: nũ: pia:r karda: fiɛ̃?
CHARANJIT::	báfiut.
SURJIT:	pia:r na:l a:pɳi: gʰàr va:li: nũ: cʰeɽna: koi: buri: gall fiɛ?
CHARANJIT:	bilkul náfii̇̃:.
NIRMAL:	tusĩ: ca:ca: bʰatì:ja: dovẽ beʃaram fio.

SURJIT:	*What are the things worth seeing in Delhi?*
CHARANJIT:	*A great many. New as well as old.*
SURJIT:	*As far as I'm concerned, I'm going to see the old things and buildings only. And also all the Sikh temples.*
CHARANJIT:	*But many new things are also beautiful.*
SURJIT:	*You are right, my boy. But an old-fashioned man likes only old things like your aunt.*
NIRMAL:	*Have you no sense of shame? Must you say this thing in front of the boy?*
SURJIT:	*Charanjit, tell me. Do you love your wife?*
CHARANJIT:	*Very much.*
SURJIT:	*Is it bad to lovingly tease your own wife?*
CHARANJIT:	*Not at all.*
NIRMAL:	*You uncle and nephew are both shameless.*

Vocabulary

kíɽi:ã: [kéɽi:ã:] (*f/pl*)	ਕਿਹੜੀਆਂ	which?
dekʰaṇ va:li:ã: (*f/pl*)	ਦੇਖਣ ਵਾਲੀਆਂ	worth seeing
báfiut sa:ri:ã: (*f/pl*)	ਬਹੁਤ ਸਾਰੀਆਂ	a great many
navã:	ਨਵਾਂ	new
pura:ṇa:	ਪੁਰਾਣਾ	old
ima:rat (*f*)	ਇਮਾਰਤ	building
na:le	ਨਾਲੇ	also, in addition
sa:re	ਸਾਰੇ	all
gurdua:ra: (*m*)	ਗੁਰਦੁਆਰਾ	Sikh temple
kai:	ਕਈ	some
sófiaṇa: [sóṇa:]	ਸੋਹਣਾ	beautiful
ka:ka: (*m*)	ਕਾਕਾ	boy
va:la:	ਵਾਲਾ	see p. 95
ca:ca: (*m*)	ਚਾਚਾ	uncle (father's younger brother)
ca:ci: (*f*)	ਚਾਚੀ	aunt (**ca:ca:**'s wife)
ʃaram fiia: (*f*)	ਸ਼ਰਮ ਹਿਆ	sense of shame
a:pṇi:	ਆਪਣੀ	own (see p. 94)
váfiuʈi: [vóʈi:] (*f*)	ਵਹੁਟੀ	wife
gʰar [kàr] va:li: (*f*)	ਘਰ ਵਾਲੀ	wife (see p. 96)
bʰatì:ja: [patì:ja:] (*m*)	ਭਤੀਜਾ	nephew (brother's son)
beʃaram	ਬੇਸ਼ਰਮ	shameless

The use of *aːpŋaː*

aːpŋaː is a possessive adjective literally meaning 'own'. The use of **aːpŋaː** needs careful attention. It is used in two ways.

(1) For emphasis

íꜰi	meri:	aːpŋiː	car	ꜰiɛ
this	my	own	car	is

This is my own car *or* This car is my own.

This use of **aːpŋaː** is quite straightforward and similiar to the English.

(2)   As a substitute for the ordinary possessive pronouns. When something belongs to the subject of the sentence, this relation of possession is indicated by using **aːpŋaː** (or a number–gender variant, i.e. **aːpŋe, aːpŋiː, aːpŋiːãː**) instead of the ordinary possessive adjective. In the following examples, the actual meaning of **aːpŋaː** in the sentence is given in the parentheses. Below each sentence, the possessive adjective which would be used in other types of construction is also given.

mẽ	aːpaŋiː	car	vic	Vancouver	jaːŋaː	siː
I	own (= my)	car	in	Vancouver	to go	was
	(= **meriː**)					

I was to go to Vancouver in my car.

kiː	tusĩː	aːpaŋe	bᵃàraː̀	kol	ráꜰiinde	ꜰio?
Q	you	own (= your)	brother	near	living	are
		(= **tuꜰiaːde**)				

Do you live with your brother?

tũː	aːpaŋiː	váꜰiuʈiː	nũː	piaːr	kardaː	ꜰiẽ?
you	own (= your)	wife	to	love	doing	are
	(= **teriː**)					

Do you love your wife?

But ordinary possessive adjectives must be used when a possession does not belong to the subject.

Ram	ne	kállᵃ	nũː	mere	gᵃàr	aːuŋaː	ꜰiɛ
Ram	(Agt)	tomorrow	to	my	house	to come	is

Ram is coming to my house tomorrow.

The house does not belong to Ram (the subject) but to someone else. So the ordinary possessive adjective **meraː** (in the oblique form **mere**) is used.

Definite object

When the object is definite and is marked with **nū:** the ŋ-form does not agree with it and is in the masculine singular form.

mɛ̃	puraːŋɟiːɑ̃:	imaːratɑ̃:	nū:	fiː	dekʰŋa:	fiɛ
		(*f/pl*)			(*m/sg*)	
I	old	buildings	to	only	to see	is

I am going to see the old buildings only.

Since the old buildings have already been mentioned, they are definite now. This is indicated by adding the postposition **nū:** to the object. The verb does not agree with the object in gender and number (which is feminine plural). Rather, it has the masculine singular form, which is also used when the verb does not agree with anything.

Use of *vaːlaː*

vaːlaː (with its variants **vaːle, vaːliː, vaːliːɑ̃:**) is probably the most versatile grammatical word (postposition) in Panjabi. It is difficult to translate, though 'possessor' is sometimes suggested. So in the English glosses below, 'V' is used instead of translation. Study the following examples.

dekʰaŋ	vaːliːɑ̃:	ciːzɑ̃:
seeing	V	things

things worth seeing

kʰaːŋ	vaːlaː	tel
eating	V	oil

edible oil

cáːfi	vaːlaː:
tea	V

one who sells/supplies tea.

ciʈʈiː	dáːfiɾiː	vaːlaː:	baːbaː:
white	beard	V	old man

old man with a white beard

puraːŋe	xiaːlɑ̃:	vaːle	bande	nū:
old	ideas	V	man	to

to an old-fashioned man

Train	**calaṇ**	**vɑːliː**	**fiɛ**
train	moving	V	is

The train is about to leave

Sometimes the meaning of the whole is more than or different from the sum of its parts

gʰàr	**vɑːliː**
home	V
wife	

kɔɖiːā̃ː	**vɑːlɑː**	**sɑpp**
cowrie shells	V	snake

viper, a treacherous person.

vɑːlɑː is used to convey some other types of meanings too. Speakers of Panjabi use their common sense to find out in what sense it is used. You can do the same!

ਅਭਿਆਸ Exercises

To understand and to speak a language well, you need lots of words (or vocabulary) do deal with different situations you may find yourself in. Also, you need to know how to combine those words meaningfully (grammar). While the number of structures in the grammar of a language is quite limited, the number of words in a language rises to many thousands. And new words are added almost every day. The Conversation units in this book have their own structural limitations and cannot introduce many words. So a section called Word groups (pp. 242–260) has been added to the book. It gives some words grouped according to areas of meaning they generally belong to. Now the time has come for you to be able to look for a suitable word in this section or to find the meaning of a word if you know the area it belongs to.

To do the following exercises you may need to know the meanings of some words you may not have come across before, or you may need to find new words.

1 Look for the meanings of the following words in the area 'Travel and transport' in the section Word groups. One of these words is the name of an animal. Look for the meaning of that word in the area 'Animals and birds'. 🔲

ɦava:i: aɖɖa: ਹਵਾਈ ਅੱਡਾ
ɦava:i: jaɦa:z   ਹਵਾਈ ਜਹਾਜ਼
gʱòɽa: ਘੋੜਾ
rel gaɖɖi: ਰੇਲ ਗੱਡੀ
safar   ਸਫ਼ਰ

If you have the cassette recording, listen to it. Then fill in, in the second column of the following table, the name(s) (in English) of the means of transport used for travel.

London to New Delhi	
New Delhi airport to New Delhi railway station	(1) *or* (2)
New Delhi to Jammu	(1) *or* (2)
Jammu to Srinagar	(1) *or* (2)
Inside Kashmir	(1) *or* (2) *or* (3)

2 Complete the following text by supplying the correct forms of the verbs and the postposition **ne** where needed.

meri: gʱàr va:li: _____ kállʱ nù: kamm te ja: _____ ɦɛ, te mɛ̃ _____ gʱàr ráɦi _____ ɦɛ. mɛ̃ _____ TV te do filmã: dekʰ _____ ne, te úɦinã: filmã: nù: *video te record* vi: kar _____ ɦɛ. mɛ̃ _____ kʰa:ɳa: vi: paka: _____ ɦɛ. ʃa:m nù: mɛ̃ _____ te meri: gʱàr va:li: _____ *John Brook* nù: mil _____ ɦɛ, te úɦide gʱàr asĩ: _____ cá:ɦ pi: _____ ɦɛ. mɛ̃ _____ te *John* _____ *pub* vi: ja: _____ ɦɛ. ra:t da: kʰa:ɳa: asĩ: _____ K2 *Restaurant* c kʰa: _____ ɦɛ. tusi: _____ ate tuɦa:ɖi: gʱàr va:li: _____ kállʱ nù: ki: kar _____ ɦɛ?

3 Supply the correct Panjabi equivalents of the possessive adjectives given within parentheses.

mɛ̃ *(my)* kaːr vic kamm te jãːdaː fiã̃ː. meraː puttar viː mere naːl fiiː *(my)* kaːr vic *school* jã̃ːdaː fiɛ. *(My)* patni: kol *(her own)* kaːr fiɛ. par ajj *(my)* kaːr tʰiːk náfiĩː. mɛ̃ *(my)* patni: di: kaːr vic jaːŋaː fiɛ, te úfine *(her)* bɦaràː de naːl *(his)* kaːr vic jaːŋaː fiɛ. *(My)* puttar ne ajj *(his) school* di: bas vic jaːŋaː fiɛ.

4 At a booking window of Euston railway station in London, a Panjabi woman is having difficulty. Can you help her by acting as an interpreter? (But study the whole exercise very carefully first. You may need to find some suitable Panjabi words from the 'Travel and transport' and 'Numbers' areas of the Word groups section.)

Clerk:	*Where is she going?*
You:	_____ ?
Woman:	**mɛ̃** *Birmingham* **jaːŋaː fiɛ.**
You:	_____ .
Clerk:	*Is she going today?*
You:	_____ ?
Woman:	**fiã̃ː.**
You:	_____ .
Clerk:	*Does she want a single ticket or a return ticket?*
You:	_____ .
Woman:	**mɛ̃ parsõ nũː rel gaɖɖiː c vaːpas viː aːuŋaː fiɛ.**
You:	_____ .
Clerk:	*In that case she should buy a Saver Ticket.*
You:	_____ .
Woman:	**úfi kiː fiundaː fiɛ?**
You:	_____ .
Clerk:	*Please tell her that a Saver Ticket is a very cheap return ticket.*
You:	_____ .
Woman:	**cangaː pʰer menũː ikk** *Saver* **ʈikaʈ dio. kinne daː fiɛ?**
You:	_____ .
Clerk:	*Twenty-two pounds and ninety pence.*
You:	_____ .

6 ਕੱਲ੍ਹ ਤੁਸੀਂ ਕੀ ਕੀਤਾ?

What did you do yesterday?

In this unit you will learn to
- talk about food, health, ailments and medicine in some detail
- talk about past actions
- talk about actions in a sequence
- use the Panjabi constructions appropriate for giving advice
- use the perfective form along with other associated grammatical features

ਗੱਲ ਬਾਤ Dialogues

Dialogue 1

Mohan Lál Joshi is with his doctor, Dr Jagdish Malhotra. Malhotra is a good and conscientious medical practitioner. He carefully studies each patient's medical record before seeing him or her. He also makes his conversation lively with dramatic surprises. But he hates unhealthy life styles and is always sarcastic and blunt with the patients who have them. Joshi is one such patient

JOSHI:	namaste ɖaːkʈar sáːfiab.
MALHOTRA:	namaste *Joshi* sáːfiab. taʃriːf rakʰo. tʰiːk tʰaːk fio naː?
JOSHI:	tʰiːk tʰaːk banda: tufiaːɖe kol kadõ aːũda: fiɛ?
MALHOTRA:	bilkul saɛɛ fiɛ. ajj tufiaːɖe dʰɪɖɖ c piːɽ fiɛ naː?
JOSHI:	fiã: ji:.
MALHOTRA:	cʰaːti: c jalaɳ fiɛ? sir cakraːũda: fiɛ?
JOSHI:	fiã: ji:.
MALHOTRA:	peʃaːb lag ke aːũda: fiɛ?

JOSHI:	ɦɑ̃ː jiː.
MALHOTRA:	kállʰ tuɦɑːnũː ulʈiːɑ̃ː viː ɑːiːɑ̃ː?
JOSHI:	kamaːl ɦɛ! tusĩ̂ː ɖɑːkʈar ɦo jɑ̃ː ɔliːɑː?
MALHOTRA:	*Joshi* sáːɦab, javɑːb dio. savɑːl na: puccʰo.
JOSHI:	ɦɑ̃ː jiː. ɑːiːɑ̃ː.
MALHOTRA:	ɦimm ... ɦimm ...

JOSHI:	*Greetings, doctor.*
MALHOTRA:	*Greetings, Mr Joshi. Please sit down. Aren't you fit and well?*
JOSHI:	*A fit and well person doesn't come to you.* (Lit.: *When does a fit and well person come to you?*)
MALHOTRA:	*Perfectly true. Haven't you got stomach ache today?*
JOSHI:	*Yes.*
MALHOTRA:	*Is there a burning sensation in the chest? Are you feeling giddy?* (Lit.: *Is the head circling?*)
JOSHI:	*Yes.*
MALHOTRA:	*Is urination painful?* (Lit.: *Does urine come painfully?*)
JOSHI:	*Yes.*
MALHOTRA:	*Did you vomit yesterday?* (Lit.: *Did vomits come to you yesterday?*)
JOSHI:	*Amazing! Are you a doctor or a prophet?*
MALHOTRA:	*Mr Joshi, please answer. Don't ask questions.*
JOSHI:	*Yes, I did.* (Lit.: *Yes, (they) came.*)
MALHOTRA:	*Hmm ... hmm ...*

Vocabulary

tʰiːk tʰaːk	ਠੀਕ ਠਾਕ	fit and well, fine
dʱiɖɖ [ûɖɖ] (*m*)	ਢਿੱਡ	stomach
piːɾ (*f*)	ਪੀੜ	pain, ache
cʰaːtiː (*f*)	ਛਾਤੀ	chest
jalaɳ (*f*)	ਜਲਣ	burning sensation
sir cakraː	ਸਿਰ ਚਕਰਾ	to feel giddy
peʃaːb (*m*)	ਪੇਸ਼ਾਬ	urine
lag ke	ਲਗ ਕੇ	painfully
ulʈiː (*f*)	ਉਲਟੀ	vomit
aːiːã̃ː (from ã̃ː 'come')	ਆਈਆਂ	(they) came (*f/pl*)
ɔliːɑː (*m*)	ਔਲੀਆ	prophet

java:b (*m*)	ਜਵਾਬ	answer
dio (from de 'give')	ਦਿਓ	please give
sava:l (*m*)	ਸਵਾਲ	question

Echo words

You have already come across t**ʰi:k**, and you know that it means 'fine', 'healthy', etc. t**ʰi:k t**ʰ**a:k** means more or less the same. But it is less formal and more colloquial. t**ʰa:k** partly sounds like t**ʰi:k** and when it occurs in the company of t**ʰi:k** it has no meaning of its own. This is why it is called an echo word. Its effect is difficult to describe. 'And all that' is a very rough translation of an echo word. So t**ʰi:k t**ʰ**a:k** means 'in good health and all that', i.e. having all the qualities of being in good health. In Dialogue 3, you will find **sia:ŋe bia:ŋe**, 'grown up and all that', i.e. being grown up and having all the qualities of a grown-up person, such as an ability to make rational and sensible decisions, etc. Echo words are different from paired words such as **cá:fi pa:ŋi:** 'tea water'. When two meaningful words which are also somewhat related in meaning are paired, the meaning of the pair as a whole is deliberately vague. **cá:fi pa:ŋi:** means 'light refreshments'. Interestingly enough, tea is not a strictly necessary component of **cá:fi pa:ŋi:**. **bol ca:l** 'speech and physical movement' actually means 'conversational language'.

The perfective form

In the English translation of this dialogue the Panjabi verb form **a:i:ã:** (the stem **a:** plus the feminine plural number–gender affix **-i:ã:**) has been rendered as 'they came'. The English translation is in the past tense. The situation also deals with the past. But still it would be wrong to call **a:i:ã:** a past tense form. (Nearly all the existing Panjabi grammars also make this mistake.) The perfective form simply views an action or situation as completed, without locating it any point in time. The action or the situation is simply viewed as completed. Whether or not it is completed in reality is irrelevant. Also, the time of completion is not indicated by the verb form itself, but by words like **kállʰ** 'yesterday' or by the situation. You can also add **si:**, the past tense form of **fie** if you wish to emphasise the past time. This is done by one of the speakers in Dialogue 2.

We shall come across numerous instances of the use of this form. But do not ever make the mistake of regarding this form as as past tense form, even if in a particular situation it happens to refer to a past action. It can also refer to present and future actions and situations which are regarded or imagined as completed.

Dialogue 2

The medical investigation continues

MALHOTRA: káll^{ɦ} tusĩː gɦàr siː jãː kite gɑe siː?

JOSHI: mɛ̃ viá:ɦ *party* te *Coventry* giɑː siː.

MALHOTRA: ɦimm ... ɦimm ... utt^{h}e tusĩː kiː k^{h}áːd^{ɦ}ɑː piːtɑː?

JOSHI: *chicken, meat,* kabɑːb, macc^{h}iː, c^{h}ole, b^{ɦ}ɑʈùːre, samose, pakɔɽe.

MALHOTRA: p^{h}er tã jɑnɑːb ne váːɦivɑː catpaʈe k^{h}aːɳe c^{h}ake. mircã: vaːliː imliː diː caʈaɳi: naːl. ɦiɛ naː?

JOSHI: ɦiã jiː.

MALHOTRA: tusĩː ʃɑrɑːb viː piːtiː?

JOSHI: rɑjj ke. *beer* te pakkiː donõ piːtiːã.

MALHOTRA: us *party* c mɛ̃ viː siː.

JOSHI: ɦiɛ̃? par mɛ̃ tufiɑːnũː dek^{h}iɑː náɦĩː.

MALHOTRA: tusĩː mɛnũ dek^{h}iɑː zaruːr, par pac^{h}aːɳiɑː náɦĩ. tusĩː naʃe c d^{ɦ}ùtt siːge.

MALHOTRA: *Were you at home yesterday, or did you go anywhere?*

JOSHI: *I went to a wedding in Coventry.*

MALHOTRA: *Hmm ... hmm ... What did you eat and drink there?*

JOSHI: *Chicken, meat, kebabs, fish, curried chickpeas, fried bread, samosas, fritters.*

MALHOTRA: *So Your Excellency relished highly spiced foods. With chilli and tamarind sauce. Isn't it?*

JOSHI: *Yes.*

MALHOTRA: *Did you also drink alcohol?*

JOSHI: *To my heart's content. I drank both beer and the hard stuff.*

MALHOTRA: *I was also there at that party.*

JOSHI: *What! But I didn't see you.*

MALHOTRA: *You* did *see me, but you didn't recognise me. You were dead drunk.*

Vocabulary

kite	ਕਿਤੇ	somewhere, anywhere
gae, gia: (from **ja:** 'go')	ਗਏ, ਗਿਆ	went
viá:fi (*m*)	ਵਿਆਹ	marriage
kʰá:dʰa: [kʰá:da:] (from **kʰa:** 'eat')	ਖਾਧਾ	ate
pi:ta:, pi:ti (from **pi:** 'drink')	ਪੀਤਾ, ਪੀਤੀ	drank
kaba:b (*m*)	ਕਬਾਬ	kebab
maccʰi: (*f*)	ਮੱਛੀ	fish
cʰole (*m/pl*)	ਛੋਲੇ	curried chickpeas
bʰaṭù:re [paṭù:re] (*m/pl*)	ਭਟੂਰੇ	fried bread
samose (*m/pl*)	ਸਮੋਸੇ	samosas
pakɔɾe (*m/pl*)	ਪਕੌੜੇ	spiced fritters
jana:b (*m*)	ਜਨਾਬ	Sir, Your Excellency
vá:fiva: [vá:va:]	ਵਾਹਵਾ	a lot
caṭpata:	ਚਟਪਟਾ	highly spiced
cʰak	ਛਕ	to relish
imli: (*f*)	ਇਮਲੀ	tamarind
caṭaṇi: (*f*)	ਚਟਨੀ	chutney, sauce
dekʰia: (from **dekʰ** 'see')	ਦੇਖਿਆ	saw
zaru:r	ਜ਼ਰੂਰ	certainly
pacʰa:ṇ	ਪਛਾਣ	to recognise
naʃa: (*m*)	ਨਸ਼ਾ	intoxication
naʃe c dʰùtt [tùtt]	ਨਸ਼ੇ 'ਚ ਧੁੱਤ	dead drunk
si:ge (**si:** + **ge**)	ਸੀਗੇ	certainly were

Oblique forms of demonstrative pronouns/adjectives

us	party	**c**	**mẽ**	**vi:**	**si:**
that	party	in	I	also	was

I was also there at that party.

us is the oblique form of the demonstrative adjective **úfi** 'that', because of the presence of the postposition **c**. The other oblique forms of Panjabi pronouns are given in the Grammatical summary, page 223.

Irregular perfective forms

While there are definite rules for the formation of the other verb forms in Panjabi, some Panjabi verbs have irregular perfective forms. Fortunately, there are very few such verbs (about a dozen), and unfortunately these verbs are extremely common. Examples of regular verbs in English are verbs like 'play', 'wash', 'laugh', etc. whose past tense forms are derived by a general rule – adding 'ed'. Examples of irregular verbs are 'go', 'read', 'cut' , 'sleep', etc., which do not follow the general rule.

The perfective forms of all verbs take the normal number–gender affixes given in the Magic square on page 29. But the stem undergoes some unpredictable changes. Perfective forms of important Panjabi verbs are given at the end of the Grammatical summary, pages 234–241. Rules for the derivation of regular perfective forms are also given there. But the best way to learn these forms is to get used to them by practice.

In this dialogue, we used these perfective forms

Verb	*Perfective form*
jɑː 'go'	**gɑe** (*m/pl*)
	giɑː (*m/sg*)
kʰɑː 'eat'	**kʰɑ́ːdʰɑː** (*m/sg*)
piː 'drink'	**piːtɑ** (*m/sg*)
	piːti (*f/sg*)
	piːtiːɑ̃ː (*f/pl*)
cʰɑk 'relish'	**cʰɑke** (*m/pl*)

Agreement of perfective forms

A note of warning is due here. Whether a perfective form should agree with (have the same number–gender affix as) the subject or the object or with neither initially proves to be quite tricky and confusing for learner. The rules are

(1)   If the verb is intransitive the perfective form agrees with the subject.

kɑ́llʰ	**tusĩː**	**kite**	**gɑe**	**siː?**
	(*m/pl*)		(*m/pl*)	
yesterday	you	anywhere	gone	were

Did you go anywhere yesterday?

The verb **jɑː** 'go' has no object. So the verb agrees with the subject in number and gender. The subject is masculine plural. (The plural form is used in respect to a single individual.) Therefore the verb gets the masculine plural affix **-e**. It is notable that we translate **gae** as 'gone', and not as 'went'. In fact, the Panjabi perfective form is closer in meaning to the English past participle form than to the past tense form.

(2)   If the verb is transitive, the perfective form agrees with the object (unless rule (3) applies).

mɛ̃	beer	**te**	**pakki:**	**donõ**	**pi:ti:ɑ̃:**
	(*f/sg*)		(*f/sg*)		(*f/pl*)
I	beer	and	hard stuff	both	drank

I drank both beer and the hard stuff.

A combination of two feminine singular nouns is, of course, feminine plural. So the verb agrees with the feminine plural object (and has the feminine plural affix **-i:ɑ̃:**). It does not agree with the masculine singular subject.

(3)   If the object is marked with the postposition **nũ:** and is thus a definite object, the verb does not agree with anything and has the masculine singular form.

mɛ̃	**tuɦa:nũ:**	**dekʰia:**	**náɦĩ:**
(*m/sg*)	(*m/pl*)		
I	you-to	saw	not

I didn't see you.

As was pointed out in Conversation unit 5, a verb has masculine singular form when it does not agree with anything. In this example, the masculine singular form of the verb should not be taken as agreement with the masculine singular subject. Whatever the number and gender of the subject or the object, the verb will have only this form in this example.

The agreement rules for the perfective form and the potential form are somewhat similar. But there are important differences as well, which can confuse learners. So compare the following contrastive sets of rules very carefully. You will notice that only the first rule differs and that the remaining three are the same.

The perfective form

1 Intransitive verb agrees with the subject.

2 Transitive verb agrees with the non-definite object.

3 If the object is definite and marked with **nǘ:**, the verb does not agree with anything and is in the masculine singular form.

4 When a verb does not agree with a noun subject or a third person subject, (it may or may not agree with the object) the subject is marked with **ne**.

The potential form

1 Intransitive verb does not agree with anything and is in the masculine singular form.

2 Transitive verb agrees with the non-definite object

3 If the object is definite and marked with **nǘ:**, the verb does not agree with anything and is in the masculine singular form.

4 When a verb does not agree with a noun subject or a third person subject, (it may or may not agree with the object) the subject is marked with **ne**.

Now compare the following pairs of sentences.

The perfective form

kuɽi: school   **gai:**
(*f/sg*)   (*f/sg*)
The girl went to school.
(agreement with the subject, no **ne**)

kuɽi: ne samose kʰá:dʰe
(*f/sg*) (*m/pl*) (*m/pl*)
The girl ate samosas.
(agreement with the object, **ne** used with the subject)

The potential form

kuɽi: ne school ja:ŋa: ɦɛ
(*f/sg*)   (*m/sg*)
The girl is to go to school.
(no agreement, **ne** used with the subject)

kuɽi: ne samose kʰá:ŋe ne
(*f/sg*) (*m/pl*) (*m/pl*)
The girl is going to eat samosas.
(agreement with the object, **ne** used with the subject)

The perfective form
kuɽi: ne bɑcciã: nũ: dek^hia (*f/sg*)   (*m/pl*)   (*m/sg*) The girl saw the children. (no agreement, **ne** used with the subject)

The potential form
kuɽi: ne bɑcciã: nũ: dek^hŋɑ (*f/sg*)   (*m/pl*)   (*m/sg*) **ɦɛ** The girl is going to see the children. (no agreement, **ne** used with the subject)

Use of the postposition *ne* with the subject

When the verb does not agree with the subject (it may or may not agree with the object)

(1)   a noun and third person pronoun subject is marked with the agentive postposition **ne**;

(2)   a first person subject (**mẽ** 'I' and **asĩ:** 'we') and a second person subject (**tũ:, tusĩ:** 'you') are not marked with **ne**.

mẽ	**tufiɑ:nũ:**	**dek^hiɑ:**	**náfii:**	
I	you-to	saw	not	
tusĩ:	**menũ:**	**dek^hiɑ:**	**zɑru:r**	
you	me-to	saw	certainly	
tusĩ:	**ʃɑrɑ:b**	**vi:**	**pi:ti:?**	
you	alcohol	also	drank	
jɑnɑ:b		**ne**	**vá:ɦivɑ:**	**cɑʈpɑʈe**
Your Excellency		**ne**	highly	spiced
k^hɑ:ŋe		**c^hɑke**		
foods		relished		

In all these sentences the verb either agrees with the object or does not agree with anything. But **ne** is not added to **mẽ** and **tusĩ:**. It is added to a the noun **jɑnɑ:b**. The postposition **ne** must not be confused with the verb **ne** 'are'.

Tag question with *ɦɛ na:*

In Conversation unit 2 you came across the tag question

tufia:ɖa: nã: ɖa:kʈar jogindar síngʱ fiɛ na:?
Isn't your name Dr Joginder Singh?

In Dialogue 1 you also saw

tʰi:k tʰa:k fio na:?
Aren't you fit and well?

This type of tag question simply involves adding **na:** at the end of the sentence. In its spoken form, the sentence remains a single unbroken whole.

Another type of tag question is formed by adding **fiɛ na:** as a separate sentence. An example is

mircã: va:li: imli: di: caʈaɲi: na:l. fiɛ na:?
With chilli and tamarind sauce. Isn't it?

Fortunately, the form of this type of tag question in Panjabi is always **fiɛ na:**. It does not vary according to the verb of the main sentence, as is the case with English.

Use of *si:ga:*

We came across **fiɛga:** and its variants in Conversation unit 3. **fiɛga:** is formed by adding **fiɛ** 'is' and **ga:**, which is a marker of definiteness. So **fiɛga:** means 'definitely is'. The number–gender variants **fiɛge, fiɛgi:** and **fiɛgi:ã:** are also used, depending on the nature of the subject. Since **si:** means 'was', you can easily guess that **si:ga:** means 'definitely was' or 'certainly was'. Other number–gender variants of **si:ga:** are **si:ge, si:gi:** and **si:gi:ã:**.

tusĩː	naʃe c dʱùtt	si:ge
(*m/pl*)		(*m/pl*)
you	dead drunk	were + ga:

means 'You certainly were dead drunk.'

Dialogue 3 🔘🔘

Now the doctor decides to be blunt with Joshi

MALHOTRA: *Joshi* sá:fiab, tusĩ: sia:ɳe bia:ɳe fio. tusĩ: kiũ a:pɳi: séfiat da: sattia:na:s karde fio?

JOSHI: ma:ʈi:ã: a:datã: náfĩ: jã:di:ã:.

MALHOTRA:	ma:ɽi:ã: a:datã: tufia:nū: kise ɦor ne náɦĩ: pa:i:ã:. tusĩ: xud pa:i:ã:.
JOSHI:	ji: t̪ʰi:k ɦɛ.
MALHOTRA:	jigar tufia:ɖa: xara:b ɦɛ, gurde tufia:ɖe xara:b ne, sá:ɦ di: takli:f tufia:nū: ɦɛ. je tusĩ: akal t̪õ kamm lɛ̃de t̪ã: ajj tusĩ: tandrust ɦunde. tufia:nū: íɦ bi:ma:ri:ã: na: ɦundi:ã:.
JOSHI:	ji: mɛ̃ mannda: ɦã:. galati: meri: a:pɳi: ɦɛ.
MALHOTRA:	dasso ɦuɳ ki: cá:ɦii:da: ɦɛ? ila:j jã: mɔt?
JOSHI:	mɛ̃ sámjʰia: náɦĩ:.
MALHOTRA:	ʃara:b na: pi:ɳ di: sáɦũ kʰa:o:. t̪ã: mɛ̃ ila:j karna: ɦɛ.
JOSHI:	t̪ʰi:k ɦɛ ji: .

MALHOTRA:	*Mr Joshi, you are a grown-up man. Why are you ruining your health?*
JOSHI:	*Bad habits don't go.*
MALHOTRA:	*No one else gave you these bad habits. You yourself are responsible for them. (Lit.: Someone else didn't give you the bad habits. You yourself did.)*
JOSHI:	*Yes, that's true.*
MALHOTRA:	*Your liver is bad. Your kidneys are bad. You have a breathing problem. If you had used any sense (Lit.: If you had taken work from your sense), you would have been perfectly healthy today. You wouldn't have these ailments.*
JOSHI:	*Yes, I agree. It's my fault.*
MALHOTRA:	*Now tell me what you want: treatment or death?*
JOSHI:	*I don't understand.*
MALHOTRA:	*I will start the treatment only if you take a pledge not to drink alcohol. (Lit.: Eat an oath not to drink alcohol. Only then am I going to do the treatment.)*
JOSHI:	*OK.*

Vocabulary

sia:ɳe bia:ɳe	ਸਿਆਣੇ ਬਿਆਣੇ	grown up (see also p. 101)
séɦiat [sét] (*f*)	ਸੇਹਤ	health
sattia:na:s (*m*)	ਸੱਤਿਆਨਾਸ	complete ruin

maːɽaː	ਮਾੜਾ	bad, weak
aːdat (*f*)	ਆਦਤ	habit
kise	ਕਿਸੇ	someone, anyone (see p. 223)
paːiːãː (from **paː** 'put in')	ਪਾਈਆਂ	put in
xud	ਖ਼ੁਦ	yourself (see below)
jigar (*m*)	ਜਿਗਰ	liver
gurdaː (*m*)	ਗੁਰਦਾ	kidney
sáːɦ [sáː] (*m*)	ਸਾਹ	breath
takliːf (*f*)	ਤਕਲੀਫ਼	discomfort, agony
je ... tãː	ਜੇ ... ਤਾਂ	if ... then
akal (*f*)	ਅਕਲ	sense
lɛ̃de (from **lɛ** 'take')	ਲੈਂਦੇ	had taken (see p. 111)
tandrust	ਤੰਦਰੁਸਤ	perfectly healthy
biːmaːriː (*f*)	ਬੀਮਾਰੀ	disease, ailment
mann	ਮੰਨ	to accept, to admit
galati (*f*)	ਗਲਤੀ	mistake, error
ilaːj (*m*)	ਇਲਾਜ	medical treatment
jãː	ਜਾਂ	or
mɔt (*f*)	ਮੌਤ	death
sámjɦia: [sámjiaː]	ਸਮਝਿਆ	understood
sáɦũ [sɔ́̃] (*f*)	ਸਹੁੰ	oath, pledge
sáɦũ kʰaːo	ਸਹੁੰ ਖਾਓ	take an oath

The use of the emphatic pronoun *xud*

tusĩ:	**maːɽiːãː**	**aːdatãː**	**xud**	**paːiːãː**
you	bad	habits	yourself	put in

You yourself developed bad habits

ɖaːkʈar	**ne**	**xud**	**mɛnuː**	**dekʰiaː**
doctor	**ne**	himself	me-to	saw

The doctor himself examined me.

The use of the Panjabi emphatic pronoun **xud** is very similar to the English emphatic pronouns, with the difference that while the form of the English emphatic pronoun varies according to the subject, Panjabi always uses the invariant form **xud**.

Word order, focusing and emphasis

The normal order of words in a Panjabi sentence seems to have been changed in these following sentences

jigar	tufıaːɖaː	xaraːb	ɦɛ
liver	your	bad	is

gurde	tufıaːɖe	xaraːb	ne
kidneys	your	bad	are

sáːɦi	diː	takliːf	tufıaːnũː	ɦɛ
breathing	of	trouble	you-to	is.

In Panjabi you normally say **tufıaːɖaː jigar** and **tufıaːɖe gurde**. If you have the cassette, listen to it carefully. You will note that there is strong stress on **tufıaːɖaː**, **tufıaːɖe** and **tufıaːnũː** in these sentences. In each of these sentences, the speaker first brings an ailment into focus (to the speaker's attention) and then stresses that it is he (the patient) who has it. The order of words in a Panjabi sentence can be altered to create such 'special effects'. Remember that proper stressing of words is very important when you thus manipulate the order of words in a Panjabi sentence.

Another use of the imperfective form

je	tusĩː	akal	tõ	kamm	lɛ̃de
if	you	sense	from	work	taking

tãː	ajj	tusĩː	tandrust		ɦunde
then	today	you	perfectly healthy		happening

If you had used any sense, you would have been perfectly healthy today.

What is notable is that the imperfective form is used to refer to actions that did not take place and to situations that aren't true. The patient did not use his sense and he is not healthy today.

As was pointed out, the imperfective form refers primarily to an incomplete or uncompleted action or situation. By a slight extension of its meaning, it can be used to refer to an ongoing or habitual action or situation as well. Such actions and situations are uncompleted after all. It does not need much mental effort to extend the use of this form to refer to actions and events that did not take place. They are uncompleted actions and events.

mɛ̃ sámjʰia: náfĩ:

This is a useful formula or formulaic expression to use when you wish to say 'I beg your pardon' or 'Sorry, I don't follow you' or 'I don't understand'. A woman should say **mɛ̃ sámjʰi: náfĩ:**.

Dialogue 4 🔲🔲

MALHOTRA:	*Joshi* sá:fiab, mɛnũ: pata: fiɛ. meri:ã: kai: gallã: tufia:nũ: buri:ã: laggi:ã:. par mɛ̃ tufia:ɖa: ɖa:kʈar fiã:. mera: kamm tufia:nũ: ʈʰi:k karna: fiɛ, xuʃ karna: náfĩ:.
JOSHI:	mɛnũ: tufia:ɖi: koi: gall buri: náfĩ: laggi:.
MALHOTRA:	canga: pʰir, páfiilã: tusĩ: ífi do dava:i:ã: lɛɳi:ã:. savere kújʰ kʰa: pi: ke dava:i: lɛɳi:. xa:li: peʈ náfĩ:. agle fiafte a: ke mɛnũ: zaru:r dassaɳa:. koi: fark pia: jã: náfĩ:.
JOSHI:	fior koi: gall?
MALHOTRA:	mirc masa:le tõ parfiez karna:. te ʃara:b nũ: dekʰɳa: vi: náfĩ:.
JOSHI:	ji: ʈʰi:k fiɛ.

MALHOTRA:	*Mr Joshi, I know that you didn't like some of the things I said. But I'm your doctor. My business is to cure you, not to please you.*
JOSHI:	*I didn't dislike anything you said.*
MALHOTRA:	*Well then, first of all you should take these two medicines. In the morning, take the medicine after eating or drinking something, and not on an empty stomach. Do come here next week and tell me whether or not it has made any difference.*
JOSHI:	*Anthing else?*
MALHOTRA:	*Abstain from chilli and spices. Don't even look at alcohol.*
JOSHI:	*OK.*

Vocabulary

xuʃ	ਖ਼ੁਸ਼	happy
páſiilã: [pέlã:]	ਪਹਿਲਾਂ	at first, first of all
xɑ:li:	ਖ਼ਾਲੀ	empty
ke	ਕੇ	(see p. 114)
fark (*m*)	ਫ਼ਰਕ	difference
pia: (from **pɛ** 'fall')	ਪਿਆ	happened
parſiez (*m*)	ਪਰਹੇਜ਼	abstinence

Colloquial pronunciation

The sounds **x**, **f** and **z** were not originally there in Panjabi. They are used in words borrowed from other languages such as Arabic, Persian and English. Many speakers of Panjabi use **kʰ** in place of **x**, **pʰ** in place of **f**, and **j** in place of **z**. So while **x**, **f** and **z** are recommended for your own speech, you are likely to hear some words in this dialogue pronounced differently.

xuʃ	pronounced as	**kʰuʃ**
xɑ:li:	pronounced as	**kʰɑ:li:**
fark	pronounced as	**pʰark**
parſiez	pronounced as	**parſiej**

Perfective form in 'experiencer' sentences

meri:ã:	**kai:**	**gallã:**	**tuſiɑ:nũ:**
		(*f/pl*)	
my	some	things said	you-to
buri:ã:		**laggi:ã:**	
(*f/pl*)		(*f/pl*)	
bad/unpleasant		struck	

You didn't like some of the things I said.

Literally however, the sentence is 'Some of the things I said struck unpleasant to you.' Do not let the English translation mislead you into thinking that 'you' is the subject of the sentence. In Panjabi, **tuſiɑ:nũ:** 'you-to' is simply the experiencer. For all grammatical purposes, it is **meri:ã: kai: gallã:** that is the subject. The verb **lag** in this sentence is intransitive (without an object). Hence it agrees with the real grammatical subject in number and gender.

Use of the potential form to give advice

In some sentences in this dialogue, the potential form is used to give advice, not to refer to future actions as such. (But it can be argued that advice is also a sort of future action.)

páfiilã:	tusĩ:	éfi	do	dava:i:ã:	lɛɳiã:
				(f/pl)	(f/pl)
at first	you	these	two	medicines	to take

First of all, you should take these two medicines

mirc	masa:le	tõ	parfiez	karna:
			(m/sg)	(m/sg)
chilli	spice	from	abstinence	to do

Abstain from chilli and spices

ʃara:b	nũ:	dekʰɳa:	vi:	náfii:
(f/sg)		(m/sg)		
alcohol	to	to see	also	not

Don't even look at alcohol.

In the last sentence, the definite object is marked with **nũ:**. So the verb does not agree with anything. The request form could also be used to give advice. But the use of the potential form is preferred for this purpose.

Actions in a sequence – use of *ke*

ke is the most commonly used verb in Panjabi. It is used when you mention actions or events which occur in a sequence. The verbs are strung together using **ke**, and all the verbs except the last one are in the stem form. A rough translation of **ke** is 'having', as in the following sentences from Dialogue 4.

agle	fiafte	a:	ke	mɛnũ:	dassaɳa:
next	week	come	having	me-to	to tell

Come next week and tell me.

Literally however, the sentence is something like

Having come next week, tell me.

The action of coming and telling are going to be in this particular sequence. So the stem form of the first verb is followed by **ke**, and the second verb is in the appropriate form.

savere	kújⁿ	kʰaː	piː
in the morning	something	eat	drink
ke	**davaːiː**	**leɳiː**	
having	medicine	to take	

In the morning take the medicine after eating or drinking something. (*Lit.:* Having eaten (or) drunk something in the morning, take the medicine.)

There is no grammatical rule governing how many verbs you can string together with the help of **ke**. You can string together as many verbs as your memory (or the air in your lungs!) would allow.

> **mẽ kamre vic jaː ke, kursi te beṭʰ ke, cɑːfi piː ke, xat likʰ ke,** *type* **kar ke, ʃaːm nũː** *post* **kiːte.**

(*Lit.:* I, having gone into the room, having sat on the chair, having taken tea, having written letters, having typed them, posted them in the evening.)

Not until you come to the end of the sentence and see the form of the main verb is it possible to know whether the actions are located in the present or the past or the future time.

Noun + verb sequences as verb equivalents

Panjabi, like other Indian languages, has fewer verbs than English has. Very often the Panjabi equivalent of an English verb will be a noun + verb or adjective + verb sequence. In this unit, we came across

ulṭiː	**aː**	
vomit	come	'to vomit'
tʰiːk	**kar**	
correct	do	'to correct, to cure'
xuʃ	**kar**	
happy	do	'to please'
ilaːj	**kar**	
treatment	do	'to treat'
sattiaːnaːs	**kar**	
ruin	do	'to ruin'

java:b	de	
answer	give	'to answer'

In such case, the noun is regarded as the subject (as in **ulṭi: a:**) or the object of the verb.

ki:	tufia:nũ	ulṭi:ã:	a:i:ã:?
		(*f/pl*)	(*f/pl*)
(Q)	you-to	vomits	came

Did you vomit?

(*Lit.:* Did vomits come to you?) (**ulṭi:ã:** is the grammatical subject)

tusĩ:	mere	sava:l	da:	java:b	na:	ditta:
				(*m/sg*)		(*m/sg*)
you	my	question	of	answer	not	gave

You didn't answer my question.

(*Lit.:* You didn't give the answer of my question.)   (**java:b** is the grammatical object)

The usual rules of verb agreement apply to both these sentences. The word-for-word glosses used in this book are meant to highlight the fact that each language has its own individual grammatical structure. It should be confronted directly and not filtered through the grammatical structure of English or any other language. In Panjabi you do not vomit; rather, a vomit comes to you, or vomits come to you if that happens more than once. You do not answer a question in Panjabi; you give answer of a question. You do not take an oath; you eat an oath. You do not smoke; you drink a cigarette. You do not abstain from something; you do abstinence from something. And so on. Learning a new language does not simply mean learning new sounds, new words and new grammar. It also means learning new ways of thinking.

ਅਭਿਆਸ Exercises

In the following exercises, you may come across some unfamiliar verbs. If that happens, consult the list of verbs in the Grammatical summary in order to know their meanings and grammatical forms.

1 Combine the following pairs of sentences with the help of **ke**. The first one is done for you as an example.

(1) (a) úfinũ: ḍa:kṭar kol ja:ŋa: cá:fii:da: fiɛ,
    (b) ate dava:i: leɳi: cá:fii:di: fiɛ.
        úfinũ: ḍa:kṭar kol ja: ke dava:i: leɳi: cá:fii:di: fiɛ.
(2) (a) úfi mere kol a:ia:,
    (b) ate úfine menũ: ikk gall dassi:.
(3) (a) mera: puttar *library* jã:da: fiɛ.
    (b) uttʰe úfi a:pɳa: *college* da: kamm karda: fiɛ.
(4) (a) bas vic beṭʰo.
    (b) gʰàr ja:o.
(5) (a) tusĩ: kamre vic ja:o.
    (b) uttʰe tusĩ: beṭʰo.
(6) (a) kállfi tusĩ: landan ja:ŋa: fiɛ.
    (b) uttʰe tusĩ: ki: karna: fiɛ?

2 Your friend Wolfgang Schmidt came from Frankfurt, Germany, to attend your birthday party. At the party, he drank too much beer and whisky and ate highly spiced food. At night he became ill and vomited. Now he has headache, stomach ache and a burning sensation in the chest. He also has high temperature and feels giddy. Urination is also painful to him. You take him to your doctor. How do you introduce your friend and answer the doctor's questions?

You: (Introduce your friend and say that he is not feeling well.)
Doctor: ki: takli:f fiɛ?
You: (Describe all the symptoms.)
Doctor: kállfi ífinã: ne ki: kʰá:dfia:?
You: _____ .
Doctor: ífinã: ne ʃara:b vi: pi:ti:?
You: _____ .
Doctor: ki: tufia:ḍe gʰàr c koi: *party* si:?
You: _____ .
Doctor: tufia:ḍe ífi dost kittʰe ráfiinde ne?
You: _____ .

3 If you have the cassettes, listen to the recording. Then fill in (in English) the speaker's schedule for the last week on the following blank page from his diary. 🔊

4 Monday	
5 Tuesday	
6 Wednesday	
7 Thursday	
8 Friday	
9 Saturday	
10 Sunday	

4 Supply the postposition **ne** where necessary in the following sentences. When you add this postposition, the noun or the pronoun to which it is added gets the oblique form. (If you are not sure about the oblique form of a pronoun, consult the relevant part of the Grammatical summary.)

(a) meraː bʱat̃ːjaː *Kirpal* ajj ikk baɽaː ɦiː cangaː kamm kiːtaː.

(b) tuɦiaːɖaː cʰoʈaː bʱaràː itt ʰe kadõ aːuɳaː ɦɛ?

(c) úɦ kállᶠ̃ itt ʰe aːiaː siː, te úɦ kállᶠ̃ nũː pʰir aːuɳaː ɦɛ.

(d) mɛ̃ te meraː dost *Sukhdev* ajj ʃaːm nũː *Dilshad Tandoori* vic kʰaːɳaː kʰaːɳ jaːɳaː ɦɛ. ki: tusĩː saːɖe naːl jaːɳaː cáːɦũde ɦo?

(e) úɦ kuɽiː *Kirpal* nũː aːpɳiː kaːr vic *lift* dittiː. úɦ úɦde naːl kamm kardiː ɦɛ.

(6) mɛ̃ te meriː patniː ajj savere *market* gae. meriː patniː paːlak te ʈamaːʈar xariːde, ate mɛ̃ do kamiːzã̃ː xariːdiːã̃.

5 A computer virus (probably a relative of the one which gobbled up grammatical endings and forms of the verb **ɦɛ** in the passage on page 46) ate up the verb endings and **ke** in the following conversation and left the 'danger sign' ☠ at the site of the damage. Can you supply these verb endings or **ke**, as appropriate, to make the conversation intelligible?

Mr A: kállᶠ̃ tusĩː *Darshan* diː *party* te g☠ siː?

Mr B: ɦã̃ː g☠ siː.

Mr A: *Party* t^hi:k si:?

Mr B: ɦɑ̃: cɑngi: vá:ɦvɑ: si:, pɑr utt^he mɛ̃ cá:ɦ ɦi: pi:ɤ, ʃɑrɑ:b
        náɦĩ:. ʃɑrɑ:b nũ: tɑ̃: mɛ̃ dek^hɤ vi: náɦĩ:. tuɦɑ:nũ: pɑtɑ: ɦi:
        ɦɛ, mɛ̃ *party* c jɑ: ɤ ʃɑrɑ:b náɦĩ: pi:ɤ .

Mr A: utt^he merɑ: dost *Ranjit* tuɦɑ:nũ: milɤ si:?

Mr B: náɦĩ:. pɑr mɛ̃ úɦnũ: milɤ cá:ɦɤ si:. úɦdi:ɑ̃: do c^hoʈi:ɑ̃:
        b^ɦɛŋɑ̃: *party* c ɑ:ɤ si:. úɦde mɑ:tɑ: ji: te pitɑ: ji: vi: ɑ:ɤ si:.
        pɑr *Ranjit* náɦĩ: ɑ:ɤ.

Mr A: úɦ pɑrsõ mɛnũ: ɦɑvɑ:i: ɑɖɖe te milɤ si:. úɦde dost ne
        Canada tõ úɦnũ: milɤ lɑi: ɑ:ɤ si:, te *Ranjit* ne úɦde nɑ:l
        lɑnɖɑn jɑ: ɤ koi: kɑmm kɑrɤ si:. merɑ: xiɑ:l ɦɛ ki *Ranjit*
        ɑ:pɳe us dost de nɑ:l lɑnɖɑn gɤ ɦɛ.

7 ਕੀ ਤੁਸੀਂ ਪੰਜਾਬੀ ਬੋਲ ਸਕਦੇ ਹੋ?

Do you speak Panjabi?

In this unit you will learn to
- talk about your linguistic skills, using the verb **a:**
- talk about your academic interests and plans
- talk about future events
- use the subjunctive verb form
- use the subjunctive + **ga:** form to talk about future events
- use the important auxiliary verbs
- use some compound verb constructions

ਗੱਲ ਬਾਤ Dialogues

Dialogue 1

Manjit Singh Sandhu, a young sociology lecturer in the University of Nottingham in England, is astonished when Anita, a blue-eyed blonde girl and postgraduate student, greets him in Panjabi

SANDHU:	tuɦaːnũ: panjaːbiː aːũdi: ɦɛ?
ANITA:	tʰoɽi: tʰoɽi: aːũdi: ɦɛ.
SANDHU:	tʰoɽi: tʰoɽi: naɦĩ:. tusĩ: baɦut sóɦaɳi: panjaːbi: bolde ɦo. tuɦaːɖi: maːt bʰàːʃa: panjaːbi: ɦɛ jãː angreziː?
ANITA:	mere maːta: ji: angrez ne te pita: ji: panjaːbiː. is lai meri: mã: boli: angrezi: ɦɛ.
SANDHU:	gʰàr vic tusĩ: angrezi: bolde ɦo jãː panjaːbi:?
ANITA:	aːm tɔr te angreziː. par daːdi: ji: panjaːbi: bolde ne. úɦinã: nũ: angrezi: naɦĩ: aːũdi:. maːta: ji: vi: tʰoɽi: tʰoɽi: panjaːbi: bol sakde ne – sirf daːdi: ji: naːl.

SANDHU:	tusĩ: panja:bi: kitt^hõ sikk^hi:?
ANITA:	da:di: ji: tõ. pita: ji: ne vi: mɛnũ: ka:fi: panja:bi: sik^ha:i:.

SANDHU:	*Do you know Panjabi? (Lit.: Is Panjabi coming to you?)*
ANITA:	*A little bit. (Lit.: A little is coming.)*
SANDHU:	*It's not a little bit. You speak Panjabi beautifully. Is your mother tongue Panjabi or English?*
ANITA:	*My mother is English and my father is Panjabi. So my mother tongue is English.*
SANDHU:	*Do you speak English or Panjabi at home?*
ANITA:	*Mostly English. But my grandmother speaks Panjabi. She doesn't know English. Mother can also speak a little bit of Panjabi – only with grandmother.*
SANDHU:	*Where did you learn Panjabi?*
ANITA:	*From grandmother. Father also taught me a lot of Panjabi.*

Vocabulary

a:ũdi: (from **a:** 'come')	ਆਉਂਦੀ	knowledge of a language (see p. 122)
t^hoɽi: (*f/sg*)	ਥੋੜੀ	a little
ma:t b^ɦà:ʃa: [pà:ʃa:] (*f*)	ਮਾਤ ਭਾਸ਼ਾ	mother tongue
angrezi: (*f*)	ਅੰਗ੍ਰੇਜੀ	English (language)
angrez (*m/f*)	ਅੰਗ੍ਰੇਜ਼	English (nationality)
ma:ta: (*f*)	ਮਾਤਾ	mother
pita: (*m*)	ਪਿਤਾ	father
is lai:	ਇਸ ਲਈ	therefore
mã: boli: (*f*)	ਮਾਂ ਬੋਲੀ	mother tongue
a:m tɔr te	ਆਮ ਤੌਰ ਤੇ	generally, mostly
da:di: (*f*)	ਦਾਦੀ	grandmother
sak	ਸਕ	can (see p. 123)
sirf	ਸਿਰਫ਼	only
kitt^hõ	ਕਿੱਥੋਂ	from where
sikk^h	ਸਿੱਖ	to learn
sik^ha:	ਸਿਖਾ	to teach

ma:t bʰà:ʃa: or *mã: boli:*?

In this dialogue, two different expressions **ma:t bʰà:ʃa:** and **mã: boli:**, both meaning 'mother tongue' have been used. **ma:t bʰà:ʃa:** is more formal and is used exclusively by educated Hindus and Sikhs. Educated Muslims generally use the Persian expression **ma:dari: zaba:n**. **mã: boli:** is informal and more colloquial and is used by all types of speakers.

Showing respect to a woman – Panjabi style

You know that in Panjabi you use plural forms to show respect to a single person. This is done in many other languages as well. But Panjabi is probably the only language on earth which shows respect to a woman by using masculine forms for her. So if you want to show respect to a woman, you must use masculine plural forms to refer to her. This is done in

tusĩ:	báɦut	sóɦaɳi:	panja:bi:	bolde	ɦo
				(*m/pl*)	
you	very	beautiful	Panjabi	speaking	are

You speak beautiful Panjabi

par	da:di: ji:	panja:bi:	bolde	ne
			(*m/pl*)	(*pl*)
but	grandmother	Panjabi	speaking	are

But grandmother speaks Panjabi.

The first sentence is addressed to a woman, and the second sentence refers to a woman. The reason for this grammatical peculiarity of Panjabi seems to be historico-cultural. The Panjabi society has traditionally been male-dominated and regards women as being inferior to men. By using masculine grammatical forms for a woman, the speaker seems to say that he or she regards her as equal to a man. This may appear to a be a peculiar and patronising way of showing respect to a woman, and you may find it either amusing or offensive. But since you cannot change the grammar of the language, just accept it.

'Is Panjabi coming to you?'

ki:	tuɦa:nũ:	panja:bi:	a:ũdi:	ɦɛ?
(Q)	you-to	Panjabi	coming	is

Do you know Panjabi?

A more literal rendering of the sentence could be 'Does Panjabi come to you?' or 'Is Panjabi coming to you?' This type of construction is used to talk about skills. Knowing a language, like knowing how to swim, is more a matter of skill than of knowledge. You may also say

menū:	tɑrnɑ:	ɑ:ūdɑ:	fiɛ
me-to	swimming	coming	is

I know how to swim

When you talk about knowledge in the ordinary sense, you use the verb **jɑ:ɳ** 'to know', as in

mɛ̃	tufiɑ:ɖe	pitɑ: ji:	nū:	jɑ:ɳdɑ:	fiɑ̃:
I	your	father	to	knowing	am

I know your father.

Auxiliary verbs in Panjabi

An auxiliary or 'helping' verb is a verb which accompanies another verb (the main verb) and adds to the meaning of the latter. English has auxiliary verbs like 'will', 'shall', 'can', 'could', etc. which play this role in the language. The verb 'will' in

He will go

is an auxiliary verb. It adds to the meaning of the main verb 'go'. But the main verb 'will' in

He is willing to go

is a different verb which simply resembles the helping verb 'will'. The two must not be confused. (They are historically related, but this is irrelevant in modern English grammar.)

The same thing happens in Panjabi. You will come across such resembling and historically related pairs which you must not confuse. In this dialogue, we came across the helping verb **sak**, roughly translatable as 'can'

mɑ:tɑ: ji:	vi:	tʰoɽi: tʰoɽi:	panjɑ:bi:	bol	sakde	ne
mother	also	only a little	Panjabi	speak	can	are

Mother can also speak a little Panjabi.

When **sak** is added, the main verb is in the stem form. It is **sak** which has an imperfective, or perfective or potential or whatever form and also carries the number–gender affix. In Dialogue 4, we have

tusĩ:	meri:	kújʰ	madad	kar	sakde	ɦo?
you	my	some	help	do	can	are

Can you give me some help?

It is important to remember that the main verb is in the invariant stem form and that it is the helping verb which changes its form grammatically.

Repetition of words

Anita repeats the word **tʰoɽi:** in

mɛnũ:	panja:bi:	tʰoɽi:	tʰoɽi:	a:ũdi:	ɦɛ
me-to	Panjabi	little	little	coming	is

to emphasise that she knows only a little of Panjabi.

Dialogue 2 ◖◗

Still amazed at how correctly and fluently Anita (who looks perfectly English) speaks Panjabi, Sandhu is curious to know more about her linguistic skills

SANDHU: tusĩ: panja:bi: páɽʰ likʰ vi: sakde ɦo?

ANITA: ɦa:le cangi: tarʰã: páɽʰ likʰ náɦĩ: sakdi:. mɛ̃ do ku
mafii:niã: tõ panja:bi: páɽʰna: likʰŋa: sikkʰ ráɦi: ɦã:.
mɛ̃ pɛ̃ti: sikkʰ cukki: ɦã:. ɦuŋ mɛ̃ panja:bi: de cʰote
cʰote ʃabad páɽʰ likʰ lɛ̃di: ɦã:. panja:bi: c a:pŋa: nã:
likʰ lɛ̃di: ɦã:.

SANDHU: *Can you also read and write Panjabi?*

ANITA: *I can't read and write it well yet. I've been learning to
read and write Panjabi for about two months. I've
learnt the alphabet. Now I can read and write small
Panjabi words. I can write my name in Panjabi.*

Vocabulary

ɦa:le	ਹਾਲੇ	yet, still
cangi: tarʰã:	ਚੰਗੀ ਤਰਾਂ	well, satisfactorily
ku	ਕੁ	about, nearly
mafii:na: (*m*)	ਮਹੀਨਾ	month

ráfii: [rái:]	ਰਹੀ	helping verb showing continuity (*f/sg*) (see below)
pɛ̃ti: (*f*)	ਪੈਂਤੀ	Panjabi alphabet, thirty-five
cukki:	ਚੁੱਕੀ	helping verb showing completion (*f/sg*) (see p. 126)
ʃabad (*m*)	ਸ਼ਬਦ	word
lɛ̃di:	ਲੈਂਦੀ	helping verb indicating action done for oneself (*f/sg*) (see below)

The helping verbs *ráfii [ré], cukk, lɛ*

It is not always possible to define the meaning of a helping verb precisely. (So translations are not given in the glosses.) But these helping verbs roughly show

ráfii [ré]	continuity of the action or event
cukk	completion of the action or event
lɛ	doing something for oneself

The grammatical behaviour of these helping verbs is like that of **sak**. The main verb is in the invariant stem form and the helping verb undergoes grammatical changes. Study the following examples carefully

ráfii [ré]

munɖa:	**sangi:t**	**sikkʰ**	**ráfia:**	**fiɛ**
(*m/sg*)			(*m/sg*)	(*sg*)
boy	music	learn	**ráfia:**	is

The boy is learning music.

A sentence with the imperfective form **sikkʰda: fiɛ** could also be used to refer to an ongoing (habitual) activity. But you use the sentence with the helping verb **ráfii [ré]** when you wish to emphasise that continuity. Anita says

mɛ̃	**do**	**ku**	**mafii:niã:**	**to**	**panja:bi:**
I	two	about	months	from	Panjabi

páɽʰna:	**likʰna:**	**sikkʰ**	**ráfii:**	**fiã:**
reading	writing	learn	**ráfii:**	am

I have been learning to read and write Panjabi for about two months

to emphasise the fact that her learning is not complete yet and is still going on.

cukk

The meaning of **cukk** is somewhat opposite of **ráfii [ré]**. **cukk** emphasises the completion of an action or event.

mɛ̃	pɛ̃ti:	sikkʰ	cukki:	ɦã:
			(f/sg)	
I	alphabet	learn	**cukki:**	am

I have learnt the Panjabi alphabet.

The speaker is a woman, so the helping verb **cukki:** has the feminine singular form. The literal meaning of **pɛ̃ti:** is 'thirty-five'. The Panjabi alphabet is called **pɛ̃ti:** because it originally (until the close of the nineteenth century) had thirty-five letters. (Now it has forty.)

lɛ

The helping verb **lɛ** is historically related to the main verb **lɛ** 'take'. This helping verb means 'doing something for oneself', i.e. taking the benefit of the action.

mɛ̃	panja:bi:	de	cʰoʈe	cʰoʈe	ʃabad	páṛ̃	lɛ̃di:	ɦã:
I	Panjabi	of	small	small	words	read	**lɛ̃di:**	am

I read only small words of Panjabi (for my own benefit).

Dialogue 3 ●●

What started as a light chat takes a slightly academic turn

SANDHU: tusĩ: kade panja:b gae ɦo?

ANITA: ikk va:ri: gai: si:, jad mɛ̃ cʰoʈi: si:. par mɛnũ: ɦuŋ ya:d náɦĩ:. agle maɦi:ne mɛ̃ pita: ji: na:l pʰir ja: ráɦii: ɦã:.

SANDHU: sɛr karan lai:?

ANITA: ɦã:, mɛ̃ sɛr vi: karã:gi:, te riʃteda:rã: nũ: vi: milã:gi:. kújɦ kʰoj da: kamm vi: karã:gi:.

SANDHU: kʰoj da: kamm?

ANITA: ɦã: ji:, *programme* baṇa: ráɦii: ɦã:. socdi: ɦã: ki *video camera* lɛ calã:, te panja:bi: ɔratã: ba:re *film* baṇa:vã:.

SANDHU: panja:bi: ɔratã: ba:re kiũ?

ANITA:	mɛ̃ xud panjaːbiː ɔrat fiãː. puːriː náfiĩː tãː áddʱiː zaruːr fiãː. mɛ̃ panjaːbiː ɔratãː baːre *thesis* viː likʰ ráfii fiãː. tʰoɽaː jífiaː kamm kar cukkiː fiãː. kújʱ panjaːb jaː ke karãːgiː, te baːki vaːpas aː ke.
SANDHU:	báfiut xuʃiː diː gall fiɛ.

SANDHU:	*Have you ever been to the Panjab?*
ANITA:	*I went there once, when I was a baby* (lit.: *when I was small). But I don't remember that now. Next month, I'm going there again with my father.*
SANDHU:	*For a pleasure trip?*
ANITA:	*Yes, I'll go for pleasure, and also see my relatives. I'll also do some research work.*
SANDHU:	*Research work?*
ANITA:	*Yes, I'm thinking about it. I intend to take a video camera (there) and make a film about Panjabi women.*
SANDHU:	*Why about Panjabi women?*
ANITA:	*I'm myself a Panjabi woman – at least half, if not full. I'm also writing a thesis about Panjabi women. I've already done a little work. I'll do some more work in the Panjab* (lit.: *after going to the Panjab), and I'll do the rest when I come back.*
SANDHU:	*I'm really glad to know this.* (Lit.: *This is a matter of great pleasure.*)

Vocabulary

kade	ਕਦੇ	ever
vaːriː	ਵਾਰੀ	times, turn
ikk vaːriː	ਇੱਕ ਵਾਰੀ	once
jad	ਜਦ	when
yaːd (*f*)	ਯਾਦ	memory
lai	ਲਈ	in order to, for the sake of
karãːgiː	ਕਰਾਂਗੀ	will do (see p. 131)
riʃtedaːr (*m/f*)	ਰਿਸ਼ਤੇਦਾਰ	relative
mil	ਮਿਲ	to meet
kʰoj (*f*)	ਖੋਜ	research, search
banaː	ਬਣਾ	to make
soc	ਸੋਚ	to think

ɔrat (*f*)	ਔਰਤ	woman
baːre	ਬਾਰੇ	about
áddʰaː [**áddaː**]	ਅੱਧਾ	half
jíɦaː, [**jíaː**]	ਜਿਹਾ	like, looking like
tʰoɽaː jíɦaː	ਥੋੜਾ ਜਿਹਾ	a little
baːkiː	ਬਾਕੀ	remaining, rest
vaːpas	ਵਾਪਸ	on return, back

'I don't remember now'

Panjabi uses an 'experiencer' type sentence to express this idea.

mɛnũː	**ɦuṇ**	**yaːd**	**náɦiː**
me-to	now	memory	not

You could add **ɦɛ** 'is' at the end. But do you remember that a negative sentence in Panjabi need not have the present tense form of **ɦɛ**?

gae ɦo and *gaiː siː*

tusĩː	**kade**	**panjaːb**	**gae**	**ɦo?**
			(*m/pl*)	(*pl*)
you	ever	Panjab	gone	are

Have you ever been to the Panjab?

mɛ̃	**ikk**	**vaːriː**	**gaiː**	**siː**
			(*f/sg*)	(*sg*)
I	one	time	gone	was

I went there once.

As has already been pointed out, the Panjabi perfective form is closer in meaning to the English past participle form ('gone' in this case). But the really interesting thing is that both the present tense and the past tense forms of **ɦɛ** (**ɦo** and **siː** respectively) can be used with the perfective form in Panjabi. The first combination indicates a completed action which is relevant to the present situation, as the natural English translation also shows. The second combination emphasises the 'pastness' of the completed action. Now you can see how wrong it is to describe the perfective form as a 'past tense' form, as nearly all the existing Panjabi grammars do.

Referring to immediate future

In English you can say

I am going to the Panjab next month

to refer to the 'immediate future'. You can do the same thing in Panjabi by using the helping verb **ráfii [ré]**, as Anita does

agle	mafii:ne	mɛ̃	pita: ji:	na:l	pʰir	ja:	ráfii:	ﬁã:
next	month	I	father	with	again	go	**ráfii:**	am

Next month, I'm going again with my father.

Compound verbs

You have seen how in Panjabi you can string actions together by joining verbs with **ke**. Very often, you can omit **ke** when there are only two actions and you don't wish to emphasise the sequence of events, as in

mɛ̃	video camera	**lɛ**	calã:
I	video camera	take	may move

I may take the video camera (with me).

The two actions **lɛ** and **cal** are so often performed together in this sequence that the combination has the meaning of a single action now, the action of 'carrying away' or 'taking away'. You take something and then you move away with that thing. This is called 'taking away' in English. The Panjabi verb for the action of 'bringing' is **lia:** (with stress on **a:**). This verb started its life as a combination **lɛ + a:** 'take + come'. After all, the action of bringing does involve getting hold of something (**lɛ**) and then coming (**a:**) with that thing. Panjabi is full of such combinations. But not all combinations (or compound verbs, as we shall call them) are complete fusions of verbs like **lia:**. Most combinations (such as **lɛ cal**) visibly and audibly still have two members.

The subjunctive form

Thankfully, this is the last major verb form we have to deal with. You may find the name a little bit off-putting, but this is the name traditionally used by grammarians. You can remember the name more easily if you keep in mind that this verb form represents the speaker's purely subjective view of an action or event, simply an idea of an action or event, which is viewed as neither completed, nor uncompleted, nor planned, but just a subjective idea of a possibility.

When Anita says

(mɛ̃) socdi: ฀ฉ̃: ki   video camera **lɛ _calã:,_**
I think that   I may take a video camera

te panja:bi: ɔratã: ba:re film _baɳa:vã:_
and may make a film about Panjabi women.

She is simply talking about a possibility, not about definite plans. (The subjunctive verb forms are italicised in the example.)

The subjunctive form is marked for person and number, but not for gender. In other words, endings given in the Magic square are not added to this form. The following table shows the various endings added to the verbs **kar** and **ja:**.

Verbs ending in a consonant

Person	Ending	Example
First		
Singular	-ã:	**karã:**
Plural	-i:e	**kari:e**
Second		
Singular	-ẽ	**karẽ**
Plural	-o	**karo**
Third		
Singular	-e	**kare**
Plural	-an _or_ -aɳ	**karan**

Verbs ending in a vowel

Person	Ending	Example
First		
Singular	-vã:	**ja:vã:**
Plural	-i:e	**ja:i:e**
Second		
Singular	-vẽ _or_ -ẽ	**jaẽ or ja:vẽ**
Plural	-vo _or_ -o	**ja:vo or ja:o**
Third		
Sungular	-ve _or_ -e	**ja:ve or ja:e**
Plural	-ɳ	**ja:ɳ**

The so-called 'future tense' in Panjabi

If you pick up any Panjabi grammar book, you will almost always find 'future tense' forms of verbs. But what is the reality of this 'tense' in Panjabi?

You have come across verb forms like **ɦega:** (**ɦe** + **ga:**) and **si:ga:** (**si:** + **ga:**), and you know that these forms mean 'definitely is' and 'definitely was' respectively. In other words, **ga:** (and its number–gender variants **ge**, **gi:**, **gi:ã:**) is a marker of definiteness. If this **ga:** is added to a subjunctive form, which simply expresses a possibility, the combination will express a definite possibility. And a future event is nothing more than a definite possibility. This is the philosophy of Panjabi grammar.

Now let us look at how all this works. Let us imagine Anita and Manjit Sandhu talking again. We translate a subjunctive form as 'may + verb' and the so-called 'future tense' form by 'will + verb'. The full English translation given below is natural but very free.

ANITA: **mẽ** **panja:b** university **ja:vã:** **jã:** **na:** **ja:vã:?**
                                                (**ja:** + **vã:**)
      I   Panjab   University   may go   or   not   may go
      Should I or shouldn't I go? What do you think?

SANDHU: **je** **ja:o** **tã:** **cangi:** **gall** **ɦoegi:**
                                                 (**ɦo** + **e** + **gi:**)
      if   (you) may go   then   good   thing   (it) will be
      If you go, it'll be good

      (It will definitely be a good thing if the idea of going there is put into practice)

ANITA: **tusĩ:** **ikk** **kamm** **karoge?**
                                      (**kar** + **o** + **ge**)
      you   one   work   will do
      Can I be sure that you will do one thing?

SANDHU: **zaru:r** **karã:ga:.** **dasso**
                  (**kar** + **ã:** + **ga:**)
      certainly   (I) will do   please say (it)
      I will certainly do it. What is it?

There is one little irregularity here. The second person plural subjunctive form of **kar** is **kari:e** (**kar** + **i:e**), as in

je   ɑsĩː   ífi   kamm   kariːe

                      (kar + iːe)

If we do this work.

But if you want to talk about a future action with the subject **ɑsĩː**: 'we', you do not add the plural affix **-iːe** but the singular affix **-ãː**.

ɑsĩː: ífi   kamm   karãːge   (not **kariːege**)

                  (kar + ãː + ge)

We will do this work.

This applies to all the verbs in Panjabi.

Dialogue 4 🔲🔲

A few days later, Anita approaches Sandhu for some help

ANITA: *Sandhu sáːfiab, tusĩː meri: kújⁿ madad kar sakde fio?*

SANDHU: fiãː fiãː zaruːr. dasso.

ANITA: tusĩː *Chandigarh* c kise nũː jaːŋde fio? mɛ̃ panjaːb *University* c kújⁿ din kamm karna: cáːfiũdi: fiãː. par uttʰe ráfiiŋ di: muʃkil fiɛ.

SANDHU: mera: ikk dost uttʰe paʈⁿàːũda: fiɛ. mɛ̃ úfinũː xat likʰ diãːgaː. tusĩː ja: ke úfinũː mil lɛŋaː. tusĩː *Chandigarh* kinne din ʈʰáfiiroge?

ANITA: das din. das *June* tõ víːfi *June* tak.

SANDHU: ʈʰiːk fiɛ. mɛ̃ úfinũː fiuŋe xat likʰ dinda: fiãː. úfi tufiaːɖe ʈʰáfiiran da: intzaːm kar devegaː - *University Women's Hostel* c. fior koi: kamm fiɛ tãː dasso.

ANITA: bas jiː, báfiut báfiut ʃukriːaː.

ANITA: *Mr Sandhu, can you give me some help?*

SANDHU: *Yes, certainly. What can I do for you? (Lit.: Please tell.)*

ANITA: *Do you know anyone in Chandigarh? I wish to work in Panjab University for a few days. But there is a problem of accommodation. (Lit.: difficulty of staying.)*

SANDHU: *A friend of mine teaches there. I'll write to him. You should see him. (Lit.: After going there, you should meet him.). How many days will you stay in Chandigarh?*

ANITA: *Ten days – from the tenth of June to the twentieth.*

| SANDHU: | *OK. I'm going to write to him right now. He will make an arrangement for your stay in the University Women's Hostel. Is there anything else I can do for you? (Lit.: If there is anything else, please tell.)* |
| ANITA: | *That's all. Very many thanks.* |

Vocabulary

madad (*f*)	ਮਦਦ	help
kise	ਕਿਸੇ	oblique form of **koi**: 'any'
ráɦi [ré]	ਰਹਿ	to live, to stay (main verb)
muʃkil (*f*)	ਮੁਸ਼ਕਿਲ	difficulty
muʃkil	ਮੁਸ਼ਕਿਲ	difficult
paɽʱà: [paɽà:]	ਪੜ੍ਹਾ	to teach
xat (*m*)	ਖ਼ਤ	letter
dĩã:ga: (from de'give')	ਦਿਆਂਗਾ	form of the helping verb **de** (see below)
t̪ʰáɦir [t̪ʰér]	ਠਹਿਰ	to stay
das	ਦਸ	ten
din (*m*)	ਦਿਨ	day
víːɦ	ਵੀਹ	twenty
tak	ਤਕ	up to, until
ɦuɳe	ਹੁਣੇ	right now
intzaːm (*m*)	ਇੰਤਜ਼ਾਮ	arrangement
devega: (from de 'give')	ਦੇਵੇਗਾ	form of the helping verb **de** (see below)
bas	ਬਸ	that's all

de as a helping verb

We have already seen that the helping verb **lɛ** roughly means 'doing something for oneself'. We know that this helping verb is historically related to **lɛ** 'take'.

Now the helping verb **de** is historically related to the verb **de** 'give'. So you can easily guess that this helping verb means 'doing something for others' or giving the benefit of an action to someone else.

xat	páɽʱ	lɛ
letter	read	lɛ

would mean 'Read the letter for your own information.' But the only possible meaning of

xat	pár̆ʱ	de
letter	read	**de**

is 'Read the letter aloud so that others may hear.'

cá:fi	pi:	lɛ
tea	drink	**lɛ**

is quite a sensible sentence because you receive the immediate benefit of drinking. But

*cá:fi	pi:	de
tea	drink	**de**

does not seem to make any sense at all. (Grammarians use * to mark an unacceptable sentence.)

Sandhu tells Anita

mɛ̃	úfinũ:	xat	likʰ	diã:ga:
I	him-to	letter	write	**de + ã: + ga:**

I shall write him a letter (for your benefit).

úfi	tufia:ɖe	t̪ʰáfiran	da:	intza:m	kar	devega:
he	your	staying	of	arrangement	do	**de + ve + ga:**

He will make an arrangement for your stay (and as a favour to you).

Instantaneous future

When you wish to say that your are going to do something right now, you can use the imperfective form (thus imagining yourself already in the process). Sandhu says

mɛ̃	úfinũ:	fiuɳe	xat	likʰ	dinda:	fiã:
I	him-to	right now	letter	write	(imperfective form of helping verb **de**)	am

I'm going to write him a letter right now.

fiuɳe is actually **fiuɳ + fii:** 'now only' in a shortened form.

Causative verb forms

You may have noted that verbs in each of following pairs

sikk^h	**sik^{h}ɑː**
to learn	to teach
pɑ́ɽ^ɦ	**pɑɽ^{ɦ}ɑ̀ː**
to read	to teach

are related not only in form but also in meaning. The second member roughly means making someone or helping someone do the action denoted by the first member. Teaching can be looked upon as making someone learn or helping someone learn – in other words, causing an action of learning.

So according to the philosophy of Panjabi grammar, this book cannot teach you Panjabi; it can simply help you learn Panjabi! You, the learner, are going to do all the hard work. This book will help and guide you.

The second member of the pair is called the causative form of the first member. Teaching also means causing someone to learn. In Conversation unit 8 we deal with causative forms. These forms are often used contrastively in Panjabi.

ਅਭਿਆਸ Exercises

1 If you have the cassette recordings, listen to them. Then indicate with a tick (✓) in the appropriate box what the woman speaker can do and what she cannot do. ▮▮

	Can do	Cannot do
Speak English		
Read English		
Write English		
Speak Urdu		
Read Urdu		
Write Urdu		
Speak Panjabi		
Read Panjabi		
Write Panjabi		
Speak German		

2 Match the answers in column B with the questions in column A. If an answer matches more than one question, choose the more appropriate one.

A	B
(a) kiː tufiaːnũː panjaːbiː aːũdiː fiɛ?	(1) *German* te *Urdu* viː.
(b) kiː tufiaːnũː koi fior bʰàːʃaː viː aːũdiː fiɛ?	(2) *School* c.
(c) kiː tufiaːnũː panjaːbiː likʰɳiː viː aːũdiː fiɛ?	(3) fiã̀ː jiː, par mere kol *time* náfiìː.
(d) tusĩː panjaːbiː kittʰe sikkʰ̀ıː?	(4) tʰoɽiː tʰoɽiː aːũdiː fiɛ.
(e) kiː tusĩː koi fior zabaːn viː sikkʰɳaː caːfioge?	(5) sirf aːpɳaː nã̀ː fiiː likʰ sakdaː fiã̀ː.

3 Complete the following sentences by supplying the correct form of the helping verb **de** or **le**. Remember that both these verbs are transitive (i.e. have objects). So be careful about their agreement with the subject or the object or lack of agreement.

(a) mɛnũ̀ː *German* náfiìː aːũdiː. kiː tusĩː ífi xat páɽꜞ _____?

(b) kiː tusĩː ífi dovĕ kitaːbã̀ː páɽꜞ _____ ne?

(c) mɛ̃ ífinã̀ː viccõ ikk kitaːb káll꜠ páɽꜞ _____ siː, ate duːsariː káll꜠ nũ̀ː páɽꜞ _____.

(d) je tusĩː meriː cáːfi baɳaː _____ tã̀ː mɛ̃ aːpɳaː kamm kar _____.

(e) lao, tusĩː cáːfi piː _____, te pʰir meriː kaːr tʰiːk kar _____.

(f) náfiìː, ajj náfiìː. mɛ̃ tufiaːɖi kaːr káll꜠ nũ̀ː tʰiːk kar _____.

(g) mɛ̃ aːpɳe dost nũ̀ː xat likʰ _____, te úfi zaruːr tufiaːnũ̀ː *computer* **de** _____.

(h) je tusĩː mɛnũ̀ː ʈikaʈ **le** _____ tã̀ː mɛ̃ ífi film zaruːr dekʰ _____.

(i) je ɖaːkʈar tufiaːnũ̀ː tʰiːk kar _____ tã̀ː kiː tusĩː meraː kamm kar _____?

(j) meriː kitaːb mez te rakkʰ _____, te aːpɳiː kitaːb mez tõ cukk _____.

4 Supply the missing helping verb (**ráfii**, **cukk** or **sak**) in the following text. All these verbs are intransitive, so verb agreement should be quite straightforward here.

m̃ɛ̃ *Manchester University* vic *Linguistics* ɑte *Computer Science* diː
student fiɑ̃ː. meriː maːdariː zabaːn *French* fiɛ, par m̃ɛ̃ ɑngreziː viː bol,
páɽ̃ʰ ɑte likʰ _____ fiɑ̃ː. mɛnũː zabaːnɑ̃ː sikkʰaɳ daː baɽaː ʃɔk fiɛ. m̃ɛ̃
Europe diːɑ̃ː panj zabaːnɑ̃ː bol _____ fiɑ̃ː. fiuɳ m̃ɛ̃ panjaːbiː ɑte *Hindi*
sikkʰ _____ fiɑ̃ː. mɛnũː panjaːbiː diː pɛ̃tiː báfiut sófiaɳiː lagdiː fiɛ. m̃ɛ̃
pɛ̃tiː sikkʰ _____ fiɑ̃ː, ɑte fiun m̃ɛ̃ panjaːbiː páɽ̃ʰ likʰ viː _____ fiɑ̃ː.
Hindi m̃ɛ̃ tʰoɽiː tʰoɽiː bol fiiː _____ fiɑ̃ː.

5 Complete the following sentences by supplying the correct subjunctive
form, with or without **gaː**, of the verbs given in the brackets.

(a) je tusĩː cáːfiũde fio ki m̃ɛ̃ ʃaraːb naː (piː) tɑ̃ː m̃ɛ̃ ʃaraːb náfiĩː (piː).
(b) tusĩː mɛnũː kújʰ sikʰaːo. mɛnũː pataː náfiĩː lagdaː m̃ɛ̃ ífi kamm kivẽ
(kar).
(c) m̃ɛ̃ kállʰ tufiaːɖiː kitaːb liaː (de)?
(d) je liaː (sak) tɑ̃ː baɽiː cangiː gall (fio).
(e) tufiaːɖaː kiː xiaːl fiɛ? m̃ɛ̃ lanɖan (jaː) jɑ̃ː naː (jaː)?

8 ਇੱਥੇ ਕੀ ਕੀਤਾ ਜਾਂਦਾ ਹੈ?
What is done here?

In this unit you will learn to
- use inter-religious vocabulary
- talk about obligations, using the potential form + **pɛ**
- use some causative verb forms
- use the most common passive construction – perfective form + **ja:**

ਗੱਲ ਬਾਤ Dialogues

Dialogue 1

Akram Khan is talking to his friend Javed Sheikh in the latter's office

AKRAM: *Javed* sá:ɦab, έɦi tufia:ɖa: mez baɽa: sóɦaɳa: ɦɛ.
kitthõ̃ xari:dia: si:?

JAVED: xari:dia: náɦĩ: si:, *order* de ke baɳva:ia: si:.

AKRAM: kitthõ̃? mɛ̃ vi: do mez baɳva:uɳe cá:ɦũda: ɦã:. bilkul
ɛdã: de ɦi:.

JAVED: mere dost di: *furniture factory* ɦɛ, jitthe baɽe vádɦi:a:
kursi:ã: mez baɳde ne. utthe *order* deɳa: paega:.

AKRAM: ki: nã: ɦɛ tufia:ɖe dost da:?

JAVED: *Gurnam Singh Bhamra.* asĩ: ikko *school* c paɽɦà:ũde
si:. ba:d c úɦne paɽɦà:uɳa: chadɖ ke a:pɳa:
xa:nda:ni: ka:roba:r ʃuru: kar lia:.

AKRAM: ki: úɦ xud *furniture* baɳa:ũda: ɦɛ? a:pɳe ɦattɦĩ̃:?

JAVED: náɦĩ:. páɦilã: úɦne *Kenya* tõ a:pɳe ba:p nũ:
mangva:ia:. *Factory* da: sa:ra: kamm úɦde ba:p di:

nigra:ni: c calda: ɦɛ. bá:ɦarala: kamm *Gurnam*
samb^ɦà:lda: ɦɛ, te andarala: kamm úɦida: ba:p. íɦ
bazurg ɦɛ baɽa: ka:ri:gar.

AKRAM: asĩ: káll^ɦ úɦidi: *factory* cali:e?

JAVED: 'zaru:r.

AKRAM: *Mr Javed, your table is beautiful. Where did you buy it from?*

JAVED: *I didn't buy it. I had it made to order.*

AKRAM: *Where from? I would like to order for two tables too. Exactly like this one.*

JAVED: *A friend of mine has a furniture factory, where high quality chairs and tables are made. You'll have to order from there.*

AKRAM: *What's the name of your friend?*

JAVED: *Gurnam Singh Bhamra. We were teaching in the same school. Then he gave up teaching and started his family business.*

AKRAM: *Does he make furniture himself? With his own hands?*

JAVED: *No. He first sent for his father from Kenya. All the work in the factory goes on under his father's supervision. Gurnam takes care of the outside work, and his father the inside work. This old man is a highly skilled craftsman.*

AKRAM: *Shall we go to his factory tomorrow?*

JAVED: *Certainly.*

Vocabulary

baɽa:	ਬੜਾ	very, highly
xari:d	ਖ਼ਰੀਦ	to buy
baṇ	ਬਣ	to become
baṇa:	ਬਣਾ	to make
baṇva:	ਬਣਵਾ	to get made (see p. 141)
ɛdã: da:	ਐਦਾਂ ਦਾ	like this
jitt^he	ਜਿੱਥੇ	where (see p. 159)
paega:	ਪਏਗਾ	will have to (see p. 140)
ikko (ikk + ɦi:)	ਇੱਕੋ	only one
ba:d c	ਬਾਅਦ 'ਚ	later on

cʰaḍḍ	ਛੱਡ	to give up, to abandon
xa:nda:n (*m*)	ਖ਼ਾਨਦਾਨ	family
xa:nda:ni:	ਖ਼ਾਨਦਾਨੀ	ancestral, relating to family
ʃuru:	ਸ਼ੁਰੂ	beginning
ʃuru: kar	ਸ਼ੁਰੂ ਕਰ	to begin
ɦattʰi:	ਹੱਥੀਂ	with hands (see p. 143)
ba:p (*m*)	ਬਾਪ	father
mangva:	ਮੰਗਵਾ	to send for
sa:ra:	ਸਾਰਾ	whole
nigra:ni: (*f*)	ਨਿਗਰਾਨੀ	supervision
bá:ɦarala: [bá:rala̍]	ਬਾਹਰਲਾ	outside
sambʰà:l [sambà:l]	ਸੰਭਾਲ਼	to take care of
andarala:	ਅੰਦਰਲਾ	inside
bazurg (*m/f*)	ਬਜ਼ੁਰਗ	old person (respectful)
ka:ri:gar (*m/f*)	ਕਾਰੀਗਰ	craftsman/craftswoman

Expressing obligation ('will have to')

sa:nū:	uttʰe	order	deṇa:	paega:
us-to	there	order	to give	pɛ + e + ga:
		(*m/sg*)	(*m/sg*)	(*m/sg*)

We'll have to order there.

The combination of the potential form + **pɛ** expresses an obligation or something which must be done. This is an 'experiencer'-type construction because the Panjabi equivalent of the English subject experiences something (a compulsion). Hence **nū:** is used with the person experiencing compulsion. The verb agrees with the object in number and gender. The main verb must be in the potential form. But the helping verb **pɛ** can have any form (imperfective, perfective, potential, subjunctive, or subjunctive + **ga:**), depending upon the meaning the speaker wishes to express. Since the speaker is referring to a future event here, he uses the subjunctive + **ga:** form. Another example is

mɛnū:	roz	uttʰe	tʰandi:	cá:ɦi	pi:ṇi:	pɛ̃di:	ɦɛ
me-to	daily	there	cold	tea	to drink	pɛ	is
			(*f/sg*)	(*f/sg*)	(*f/sg*)	(*f/sg*)	

I have to drink cold tea there every day.

In this example, the helping verb is in the imperfective form because the speaker refers to something which happens again and again.

If the verb has no object or the object is definite (and marked with the postposition **nū:**), the main verb does not agree with anything and is in the masculine singular form.

tuɦɑːnū:	**lanɖan**	**jɑːŋɑː**	**pɛŋɑː**	**ɦɛ**
		(*m/sg*)	(*m/sg*)	
you-to	London	to go	**pɛ**	is

You'll have to go to London.

The helping verb **pɛ** is also in the potential form. The main verb has no object (London is the destination of the journey, not the object of the verb).

Causative forms

Note the meaning of the following three verbs

baŋ	to become
baŋɑː	to make
baŋvɑː	to get something made by someone

It is clear that all the three verb stems come from the same verb root **baŋ**. The difference between a verb root and a verb stem is important in Panjabi grammar. Intricacies of roots and stems cannot be described in this basic level course. But if you wish to learn more Panjabi, you will have to learn them. Briefly, you add an affix to a root to make it a workable stem. The above mentioned stems are derived as follows:

baŋ	=	**baŋ** + zero affix
baŋɑː	=	**baŋ** + ɑː
baŋvɑː	=	**baŋ** + vɑː

It is notable that a non-causative stem **baŋ** has the same spelling and pronunciation as the root **baŋ**. In other words, you do not add an affix (or add a 'zero affix') here. The two 'causative affixes' are difficult to translate. But generally **ɑː** means 'make someone do something', and **vɑː** means 'to get something done by someone'. Study the following examples.

ífi	kaːr	tez	caldi:		fiɛ
this	car	fast	moving		is
			(stem + zero, imperfective)		

This car moves fast

mẽ	kaːr	tez	calaːũda:		fiã:
I	car	fast	driving		am
			(stem + **aː**, imperfective)		

I drive the car fast

mẽ	aːpɳe	puttar	to	kaːr	calvaːi:
					(stem + **vaː**, perfective)
I	own	son	from	car	had driven

I made my son drive the car *or* I had the car driven by my son.

In Panjabi **cal** means 'to move', and **calaː** ('to drive') actually means 'to make something move'. Now you can understand how **páɽʱ** 'to read' and **paɽʱàː** 'to teach' are related, in form as well as meaning.

It is important to remember that the affix -**aː** or -**vaː** is always stressed in such verbs. If the word has a tone, it is given to this affix. Another important thing to remember is that if the root is without a tone, the causative forms are also without a tone. But if the root has a tone (high or low), the causative forms must have the low tone (and never the high tone, whatever tone the root may have). Note the following examples:

cal	**calaː**	**calvaː**
to move	to drive	to get driven

baɳ	**baɳa:**	**baɳva:**
to become	to make	to get made

gʱùmm	**gʱumàː**	**gʱumvàː**
to rotate	to make rotate	to get rotated

páɽʱ	**paɽʱàː**	**paɽʱvàː**
to read	to make read	to get read
	to teach	to get taught

Many verbs have irregular causative forms, which cannot be dealt with here.

With both parts of the body

Some human organs or parts of the body occur in pairs. When you use both the members of such a pair, you refer to this by using a special affix **-ĩ**:

akkʰĩ:	with both eyes
kannĩ:	with both ears
fiattʰĩ:	with both hands
perĩ:	on foot (i.e. with both feet)

For example:

mẽ	**a:pɳi:**	**akkʰĩ:**	**úfinũ:**	**dekʰia:**
I	own	with eyes	him-to	saw

I saw him with my own eyes

Now you should be able understand the meaning of the following sentence without breaking it up.

ki: úfi furniture **a:pɳe fiattʰĩ: baɳa:ũda: fiɛ?**
Does he make furniture with his own hands?

Dialogue 2

Next day, Javed and Akram go to Gurnam Singh's factory. Javed introduces his friend

JAVED:	*Gurnam,* ífi ne mere dost *Akram Khan. Akram* sá:fiab, ífi ne mere dost *Gurnam Singh Bhamra.* kállᶠⁱ asĩ: ífinã: de ba:re fii: gallã: kar ráfie si:.
GURNAM:	milke baɽi: xuʃi: fioi:.
AKRAM:	menũ: vi: baɽi: xuʃi: fioi:. mẽ tufia:ɖi: baɽi: ʃófiarat suɳi: fiɛ. socia: ikk do vádᶠⁱi:a: mez fii: tufia:tʰõ banva: lavã:.
GURNAM:	baɽi: méfiarba:ni:. par ífi kamm mere pita: ji: karde ne. mẽ fiuɳe úfinã: nũ: lia:ũda: fiã:.

(Sardul Singh Bhamra, Gurnam's father, comes in after a few minutes. Javed and Akram both stand up to greet him)

JAVED & AKRAM:	sat sri: aka:l ji:.
SARDUL SINGH:	sat sri: aka:l ji:. bɛtʰo. fiukam karo.

AKRAM:	ɦukam náɦĩː, bazurgvaːr, arz ɦɛ. tuɦaːnũː yaːd ɦoegaː. tusĩː *Javed* sáːɦab laiː ikk mez baɳaːiaː siː. mɛnũː viː bilkul use kism de do mez cáːɦiːde ne. baɳaː dioge?
SARDUL SINGH:	zaruːr baɳaːvã̃ːge. par tinn caːr ɦafte laggaɳge. asĩː káɦli daː kamm náɦĩː karde.
AKRAM:	koi gall náɦĩː. mɛnũː viː koi káːɦli náɦĩː.
JAVED:	*Gurnam, this is my friend Akram Khan.*
	Mr Akram, this is my friend Gurnam Singh Bhamra. We were talking about him yesterday.
GURNAM:	*Pleased to meet you.*
AKRAM:	*I'm also pleased to meet you. I've heard your good reputation. I thought I could have one or two high-quality tables made by you.*
GURNAM:	*That's very kind of you. But it's my father who does this work. I'll bring him right now.*

(Sardul Singh Bhamra, Gurnam's father, comes in after a few minutes. Javed and Akram both stand up to greet him)

JAVED & AKRAM:	*Greetings.*
SARDUL SINGH:	*Greetings. Please sit down. What can I do for you? (Lit.: Please order.)*
AKRAM:	*I wish to make a request, sir. (Lit.: Elderly gentleman, it's not an order. It's a request.) You may remember making a table for Mr Javed. I also wish to have two tables, exactly the same. Will you please make them?*
SARDUL SINGH:	*Certainly. But it will take three or four weeks. We don't work in a hurry.*
AKRAM:	*That's OK. I'm not in a hurry either.*

Vocabulary

ʃóɦarat [ʃórat] (*f*)	ਸ਼ੋਹਰਤ	good reputation
vádʰiːa: [vádiːaː]	ਵਧੀਆ	of high quality
lavã̃ː	ਲਵਾਂ	subjunctive form of **lɛ**
méɦarbaːni: [mérbaːniː] (*f*)	ਮੇਹਰਬਾਨੀ	kindness

bazurgvɑ:r	ਬਜ਼ੁਰਗਵਾਰ	respectful address to an elderly person
fioegɑ: (fio + e + gɑ:)	ਹੋਏਗਾ	will be
use (us + fii:)	ਉਸੇ	that very (see below)
kism (*f*)	ਕਿਸਮ	type
dioge (de + o + ge)	ਦਿਓਗੇ	will do for me
lag	ਲਗ	to take (time)
laggaŋge (lagg + aŋ + ge)	ਲੱਗਣਗੇ	will take
kɑ́:fili: [kɑ́:li:] (*f*)	ਕਾਹਲੀ	hurry, haste

Emphatic forms with *fii:*

We have come across **fii:** before, as an 'exclusive particle' meaning 'only' (as in **menū̃: pɑ:lak fii: cɑ́:fii:di: fie** 'I want only spinach.'). So **fii:** is clearly an 'emphatic particle'. But very often **fii:** becomes fused with the word it is added to, so that it needs some practice to recognise its presence. In the following sentence, the combination **us + fii:** becomes **use**

menū̃: vi:	**bilkul**	**use**	**kism**
me-to also	completely	that very	type
de	**mez**	**cɑ́:fii:de**	**ne**
of	tables	desirable	are

I wish to have tables of exactly the same type.

In Dialogue 4 below, you will find

tinne	all the three

You can add **fii:** to most numbers.

cɑ:re	all the four
panje	all the five

In Dialogue 4, you will find **ifio** ('only this') (some people pronounce it as **ifii:**), which is an emphatic form of **ifi** ('this').

'It will take three or four weeks'

tinn	**cɑ:r**	**fiafte**	**laggaŋge**
			(subjunctive + **gɑ:**)
three	four	weeks	will strike/attach

It will take three or four weeks.

The verb **lag** basically means 'strike' or 'attach'. But it can be used to express many meanings, including passage of time and feeling something (e.g. **menū: ʃaraːb buri: lagdi: fiɛ** 'I hate alcohol').

Dialogue 3

Gurnam is showing Akram the factory

GURNAM: ʃuru: ʃuru: c saːnũ: kai: muʃkilã: aːiːãː. par fiuɳ saːɖa: kamm sófiaɳa: calda: fiɛ. ajj saːɖe kaːme náfiĩ: aːe. úfi *weekend* te cʰuʈʈi: karde ne, te saːɖiːã: maʃiːnã: viː.

AKRAM: ífi tufiaːɖa: *storeroom* fiɛ?

GURNAM: fiã: jiː. ɛtʰe asĩ: lakkaɽ rakkʰde fiãː. saːɖa: *furniture storeroom* vakkʰara: fiɛ ... ɛtʰe lakkaɽ ciːri: jã:di: fiɛ. páfiilã: vaɖɖe aːre te vaɖɖe vaɖɖe ʈukaɽe kaʈʈe jã:de ne. pʰir cʰoʈe aːriã: te loɽ mutabak cʰoʈe ʈukaɽe baɳaːne jã:de ne.

AKRAM: te baːd c?

GURNAM: pʰir mez kursiːã: de vakkʰ vakkʰ fiisse tiaːr kiːte jã:de ne. úfinã: fiissiã: nũ: joɽ ke kursiːã: mez baɳaːne jã:de ne. te axiːr c úfinã: nũ: *polish* kiːta: jã:da: fiɛ.

AKRAM: ífi saːra: kamm kɔɳ karda: fiɛ?

GURNAM: saːɖe kaːme. vɛse tã: úfi saːre fii: cange kaːriːgar ne, par ikk ikk ciːz pita: ji: di: nigraːni: c baɳaːi: jã:di: fiɛ.

AKRAM: maːʃa: allaː! tufiaːɖi: *factory* kaːfi: vaɖɖi: fiɛ.

GURNAM: bas jiː, rabb da: ʃukar fiɛ. saːɖi: daːl roʈi: calli: jã:di: fiɛ, te naːle saːɖe vĩ:fi ku kaːriːgarã: di: viː.

GURNAM: *In the beginning, we had some difficulties. But now our business is going well. Our workers haven't come today. They rest at the weekends. And so do our machines.*

AKRAM: *Is this your storeroom?*

GURNAM: *Yes. Here we store the timber. We have a different furniture storeroom ... The timber is sawn here. First of all, large pieces are cut on the large saw. Then smaller pieces are made on the smaller saws, according to the requirement.*

AKRAM: *Then?*
GURNAM: *The different parts of tables and chairs are prepared.*
            These parts are joined together to make chairs and
            tables. And last of all, they are polished.
AKRAM: *Who does all this work?*
GURNAM: *Our workers. Of course, they are all skilled craftsmen,*
            but every single item is prepared under my father's
            supervision.
AKRAM: *Good Lord! Your factory is quite large.*
GURNAM: *Thank God. We as well as our craftsmen are earning*
            our simple living.

Vocabulary

ka:ma: (*m*)	ਕਾਮਾ	worker
cʰutti: (*f*)	ਛੁੱਟੀ	holiday, rest
lakkaɽ (*f*)	ਲੱਕੜ	wood, timber
vakkʰara:	ਵੱਖਰਾ	separate
vakkʰ	ਵੱਖ	different
ci:r	ਚੀਰ	to saw
jã:di:	ਜਾਂਦੀ	passive auxiliary (see p. 148)
a:ra: (*m*)	ਆਰਾ	saw
ṭukaɽa: (*m*)	ਟੁਕੜਾ	piece
katt	ਕੱਟ	to cut
muta:bak	ਮੁਤਾਬਕ	according to
ɦissa: (*m*)	ਹਿੱਸਾ	portion
tia:r	ਤਿਆਰ	ready
tia:r kar	ਤਿਆਰ ਕਰ	to prepare
joɽ	ਜੋੜ	to join, to assemble
axi:r (*m*)	ਅਖੀਰ	end
axi:r c	ਅਖੀਰ 'ਚ	at the end
vɛse tã:	ਵੈਸੇ ਤਾਂ	otherwise
ma:ʃa: alla:!	ਮਾਸ਼ਾ ਅੱਲਾ!	by God's grace (Muslim)
da:l (*f*)	ਦਾਲ	cooked lentils
da:l roṭi: (*f*) (*idiom*)	ਦਾਲ ਰੋਟੀ	simple living

Passive voice: perfective form + *ja:*

In Panjabi, the most common way of expressing the passive voice sense of an English sentence is to use the helping verb **ja:** with the main verb in the perfective form. In Dialogue 3, you have

ɛtʰe	lakkaɽ	ci:ri:	jã:di:	ɦɛ
	(*f/sg*)	(*f/sg*)	(*f/sg*)	(*sg*)
here	timber	sawn	**ja:** (imperfective)	is
Timber is sawn here				

úfinã:	nũ:	polish	ki:ta:	jã:da:	ɦɛ
them	to	polish	done	**ja:** (imperfective)	is
They are polished. (*Lit.:* Polish is done to them.)					

The verbs agree with the object in number and gender. It is not necessary to mention the performer of the action. But if it is mentioned at all, you add the postposition **tõ** ('from') or **kolõ** ('from near') to it. The helping verb **ja:** can have any form, depending upon the meaning the speaker wishes to convey. But the main verb must be in the perfective form. In more complex cases, other helping verbs like **de** and **lɛ** can come between the main verb and **ja:**.

tufia:ɖi:	ka:r	tʰi:k	karva:	ditti:	gai:	ɦɛ
			(causative stem)	(perfective)		
your	car	correct	got done	**de**	**ja:**	is
Your car has been repaired (for you).						

It is notable that in such cases the main verb is in the stem form (as is always the case when helping verbs **de** and **lɛ** are used). It is the helping verb **de** or **lɛ** that has to be in the perfective form in order to express the passive sense.

You are advised to avoid such complex sentences in the beginning. Just be aware that they exist and that you will need to get to grips with them later on if you wish to go beyond this course.

Repetition of words

ikk ikk ci:z pita: ji: di: nigra:ni: c baɳa:i: jã:di: ɦɛ.
Every single item is prepared under (my) father's supervision.

The speaker repeats the word **ikk** ('one') to mean 'each one'.

ma:ʃa: alla:!

The Muslim speaker in the dialogue above utters this Arabic exclamation, which means 'By God's grace'. All speakers of Panjabi, whatever their religion, believe that pride is a terrible sin which ultimately 'hath a fall'. So whenever they speak of someone's material achievements, or good health or number of children, etc., they would add 'By God's grace.' A Sikh would say **va:ɦiguru: di: kirpa: na:l** ('with God's benevolence'), and a Hindu would use the words **parma:tma di: kirpa: na:l**.

Similarly, if a Muslim speaker hopes to be able to do something worthwhile, he will add **inʃa: alla:** ('God willing') to it. A Hindu speaker would add **parma:tma ne cáɦia: tã:**, and a Sikh would add **va:ɦiguru: ne cáɦia: tã:** ('if it is God's will').

When people belonging to different religions speak with one another, they try to use the common religious vocabulary. In Dialogue 3, the Sikh speaker Gurnam Singh uses the word **rabb** ('God'), which comes from Arabic and is a Muslim word in origin. But it is now used by the Panjabi-speaking Hindus, Sikhs and Christians as well. In Dialogue 4, the Muslim speaker Javed Sheikh uses the word **da:ta:** ('God, the Provider'), which is originally a Sanskrit word from the Hindu religion but is now used by all speakers of Panjabi. The expression **ɦakk ɦala:l di: roʈi:** ('rightfully and honestly earned living') is Islamic in origin but now forms a part of the common Panjabi vocabulary.

Dialogue 4

While Gurnam is showing Akram his factory, Javed is talking to Sardul Singh in the office

JAVED:	*Bhamra sá:ɦab, je bura: na: manno tã: ikk gall puccʰã:?*
SARDUL SINGH:	*zaru:r puccʰo.*
JAVED:	*tuɦa:ɖi: umar ki: ɦɛ?*
SARDUL SINGH:	*sattar sa:l.*
JAVED:	*tusĩ: is umar c vi: ɛna: kamm kivẽ kar lẽde ɦo?*
SARDUL SINGH:	*jana:b, mẽ koi: pár̄ɦia: likʰia: ba:bu: náɦĩ:. mẽ tã: sídd̄ɦa: sa:da: anpár̄ɦ mazdu:r ɦã:. mere guru: da: ɦukam ɦɛ - na:m japo, vanɖ cʰako, kirat karo. mẽ íɦ tinne kamm kari: jã:da: ɦã:. iɦo mera: d̄ɦàram*

fiɛ, ifio mera: i:ma:n fiɛ. mɛnũ: pɛse da: koi: la:lac
náfiĩ:. va:fiiguru: fiakk fiala:l di: roţi: dei: ja:e.
ɛthe kamm karan va:le mere sa:re bacciã: nũ: vi:,
te mɛnũ: vi:. fior mɛnũ: kújfi náfiĩ: cá:fii:da:.

JAVED: tusĩ: bilkul darust farma:ia:. tusĩ: a:pɳa: kamm
kari: jã:de fio, te úfi da:ta: a:pɳa: kamm kari:
jã:da: fiɛ.

JAVED: *Mr Bhmara, may I ask you a question, if you don't
mind?*

SARDUL SINGH: *You certainly can.*

JAVED: *How old are you?*

SARDUL SINGH: *Seventy.*

JAVED: *How are you able to do so much work even at this
age?*

SARDUL SINGH: *Sir, I'm not an educated white-collar man. I'm a
simple and straightforward uneducated labourer.
My Guru's commandment is: Remember God, share
your earnings with others (lit.: eat after sharing),
and do honest work. I go on doing all these three
things. That is my religious faith, and also my moral
principle. I don't run after money. (Lit.: I have no
greed for money.) May God provide an honest wage
– to all my children working here, and to me. I want
nothing else.*

JAVED: *You are absolutely right. (Lit.: You have told the
truth.) You go on doing your work. And the
Provider, goes on doing His work.*

Vocabulary

bura: mann	ਬੁਰਾ ਮੰਨ	to dislike, to mind
sattar	ਸੱਤਰ	seventy
sa:l (*m*)	ਸਾਲ	year (s)
ɛna:	ਐਨਾ	so much
páṛhia: likhia:	ਪੜ੍ਹਿਆ ਲਿਖਿਆ	educated
ba:bu: (*m*)	ਬਾਬੂ	educated white-collar person
síddha:	ਸਿੱਧਾ	straight, straightforward

sa:da:	ਸਾਦਾ	simple
ɑnpáɽ^ĥ [ɑnpáɽ]	ਅਨਪੜ੍ਹ	uneducated
mɑzdu:r (*m/f*)	ਮਜ਼ਦੂਰ	labourer
guru: (*m*)	ਗੁਰੂ	spiritual teacher (Sikhism)
vɑnɖ	ਵੰਡ	to share, to divide
c^hɑk	ਛਕ	to eat
kirɑt (*f*)	ਕਿਰਤ	honest labour
tinne (tinn + ĥi:)	ਤਿੰਨੇ	all the three
kɑri: (kɑr + ĥi:)	ਕਰੀ	go on doing
íĥo/íĥi: (íĥ + ĥi:)	ਇਹੋ	this very
i:mɑ:n (*m*)	ਈਮਾਨ	religious faith (Muslim)
pɛsɑ: (*m*)	ਪੈਸਾ	money
lɑ:lɑc (*m*)	ਲਾਲਚ	greed
ĥɑlɑ:l	ਹਲਾਲ	permitted by religion (Muslim)
ĥɑkk ĥɑlɑ:l (*m*) (*idiom*)	ਹੱਕ ਹਲਾਲ	an honest wage
dei: (de + ĥi:)	ਦੇਈ	go on giving
dɑrust	ਦਰੁਸਤ	correct
fɑrmɑ:	ਫ਼ਰਮਾ	to order, to say (respectful)
dɑ:tɑ: (*m*)	ਦਾਤਾ	provider, God

Another use of the subjunctive form

As was pointed out in Conversation unit 7 the subjunctive form of a Panjabi verb simply represents the idea or the possibility of an action, not an actual action located in time and space or regarded as complete, or incomplete or potential or whatever. So this form is ideal for making suggestions or getting permission. In Dialogue 1, you have

> **ɑsĩ: káll^h úĥdi: factory cɑli:e?**
> Shall we go to his factory tomorrow?

Similarly, in Dialogue 4, you have

> **(je burɑ: nɑ: mɑnno tã:) ikk gɑll pucc^hã:?**
> (If you don't mind), may I ask you a question?

It was pointed out in Conversation unit 4 that **náĥi:** ('not') is actually an emphatic form of **nɑ:**. It is actually **nɑ: + ĥi:**. Now you can easily guess why you cannot use **náfii:** with the subjunctive form. Being emphatic while seeking permission or making a suggestion sounds rather odd. So you cannot use **náfii:** in

*je	mɛ̃	lanḍan	náfii:	jɑːvã:	...
if	I	London	not	go ...	

If I don't go to London, ...

You will have to say

je	mɛ̃	lanḍan	nɑː	jɑːvã:	...

You also know that when you add **-gɑ:** to a subjunctive form, you add an element of some definiteness to the idea of the possibility. After all, the future is nothing more than a somewhat definite possibility. So, **náfii:** which has an emphatic meaning, sounds fine in a sentence in which you use a subjunctive + **gɑ:** form.

mɛ̃	lanḍan	náfii:	jɑːvã:gɑː.

I will not go to London.

No sensible speaker of Panjabi will use **nɑ:** here, which would sound very odd.

*mɛ̃	lanḍan	nɑː	jɑːvã:gɑː.

vanḍ cʰako

The full form of this verb sequence would be

vanḍ ke cʰako
Share (with others) and then eat *or* Eat after sharing (with others).

When two events get associated so closely with each other that they become almost a single action, **ke** is omitted, as in **vanḍ cʰako**. You have already come across the Panjabi verb **liɑ:** ('bring'), which started as **lɛ ke ɑ:** ('take and then come'), then became **lɛ ɑ:**, and finally became a single verb **liɑ:**.

But **liɑ:** still behaves grammatically as **lɛ ke ɑ:** . You know that when a verb is in the perfective form and has an object, it agrees with the object in number and gender (unless the object is definite and has the postposition **nũ:** after it). Also, the subject takes the postposition **ne** in such a sentence. Now the perfective form of **liɑ:** clearly has an object (**kitɑ:b**) in the following sentence.

munɖɑː	kitɑːb	liɑːiɑː
(*m/sg*)	(*f/sg*)	(*m/sg*)
boy	book	brought

The boy brought the book.

But the verb agrees with the subject, which does not have **ne**. The reason simply is that the sentence still behaves as if it were

munɖɑː	kitɑːb	lɛ ke	ɑːiɑː
boy	book	having grasped	came

When verbs are joined with **ke**, only the last verb is marked for number and gender. In this sentence, the last verb is **ɑː**, which is without an object. Hence it agrees with the subject, and the subject does not have **ne**.

How to go on doing something in Panjabi

To express this idea in Panjabi, you add the affix **-iː** (which is a shortened form of **fiiː**) to the main verb and then use the helping verb **jɑː** after it.

tusĩː	ɑːpɳɑː	kamm	kariː	jã̃ːde	fio
			(**kar + iː**)	(**jɑː**, imperfective)	

You go on going your own work.

úfi dɑːtɑː ɑːpɳɑː kamm kariː jã̃ːdɑː fiɛ.
That Provider goes on doing His work.

The helping verb **jɑː** can have any form, depending upon the situation being described. If a helping verb like **réfi** follows, **jɑː** may be in the stem form.

munɖɑː	kamm	kariː	giɑː
		(**kar + i**)	(**jɑː**, perfective)

The boy went on doing the work.

kuɾiːã̃	boliː	jɑː	ráfiiːã̃	ne
	(**bol + iː**)	(**jɑː**, stem)	(perfective form)	

The girls go on talking.

tusĩː dɑrust farmɑːiɑː

The verb **farmɑː** ('to order'), with a stress on the final **ɑː**, which comes from Persian, is used in very formal situations or to refer to the speech of respectable people, saints and prophets, as in

ɦazrat i:sa: ne farma:ia:, 'pese da: la:lac na: karo.'
Lord Jesus said, 'Do not covet wealth.'

So do not use it in ordinary informal situations. (And *never* use it to refer to your own speech!).

ਅਭਿਆਸ Exercises

1 If you have the cassette recording, listen to it and then indicate by ticking in the box given below which of the listed skills and languages are taught in Mrs Gayatri Devi's special school. You may not know the Panjabi words for some of these activities. Now it is your turn to find out from where in the Word groups you can find these Panjabi words. First make a list of these words and then attempt the exercise. ▮▮

Cookery	
Singing	
Instrumental music	
Swimming	
Painting	
Panjabi	
Hindi	
Urdu	
Bengali	
English	

2 The word **ká̃ll̆** is used in each of the sentences in the table given below. Try to judge from the verbs whether this word is used in the sense of 'yesterday' or 'tomorrow' and then tick the correct box.

	Yesterday	Tomorrow
(a) káll^ɦ tusĩː kiː karnaː ɦɛ		
(b) mɛ̃ káll^ɦ landan jaː ke *Ranjit* nũː miliaː.		
(c) tusĩː káll^ɦ *college* náɦĩː jaːŋaː?		
(d) mɛ̃ káll^ɦ íɦi kamm karã̃ː jã̃ː naː?		
(e) jad káll^ɦ aːegaː tã̃ː dekʰã̃ːge.		
(f) tusĩː káll^ɦ *Manchester* jaːŋaː si.		
(g) je káll^ɦ tusĩː *college* jã̃ːde tã̃ː cangiː gall ɦundiː.		
(h) mɛ̃ cáːɦũda: ɦiã̃ː ki tusĩː káll^ɦ uttʰe naː jaːo.		

3 Supply the correct forms of the verbs given in the parentheses. If you see an unfamiliar verb, find out its meaning in the Glossary or the Word groups sections or from the list of verbs in the Grammatical summary.

(a) landan vic báɦut bʰã̃ːʃaːvã̃ː (bol) (jaː) ne.

(b) is *factory* vic angrezi: tõ ilaːvaː panjaːbiː viː (bol) (jaː) ɦɛ.

(c) saːde *restaurant* vic *Asian* kʰaːŋaː viː (pakaː) (jaː) ɦɛ te angrezi: kʰaːŋaː viː.

(d) káll^ɦ *BBC2* te panjaːbiː film *Sassi Punnu* (dikʰaː) (jaː) siː. *(film is feminine)*

(e) agle ɦafte *Urdu* film *Mere Mahboob* (dikʰ) (jaː).

(f) káll^ɦ tuɦaːdiː *party* c ʃaraːb (piː) (jaː). íɦi báɦut ɦiː buriː gall ɦoiː.

(g) tusĩː fikar naː karo. tuɦaːdiː kaːr kújʰ minṭã̃ː vic ɦiː ʈʰik (kar) (de) (jaː).

(h) saːre kaːmiã̃ː nũː ɦukam (de) (jaː) ɦɛ ki is *factory* vic sigriṭ naː (piː) (jaː).

(i) ki *Bajwa* sáːɦab nũː agle somvaːr (dafnaː) (jaː)?

(j) náɦĩː, sikkʰã̃ː nũː (dafnaː) náɦĩː (jaː). úɦnã̃ː daː dáːɦ sanskaːr (kar) (jaː) ɦɛ.

4 Translate into Panjabi:

My wife was not well last week, and I had to cook for the whole family. I don't know how to cook. So I can't say whether or not I cooked well. But my wife and children said that the food was OK. What else could they say?

They had to eat at home. We do not eat in a restaurant. I know that too much chilli and spices are put into the food in Asian restaurants. Spices upset my stomach. Now my wife is OK. My chidren are also happy. Now they won't have to eat tasteless food.

9 ਮੈਨੂੰ ਕੁਝ ਹੋਰ ਵੀ ਕਹਿਣ ਦਿਓ

Let me say something else as well

In this unit you will learn to:
- use some more complex but commonly used grammatical structures

---

In the first eight Conversation units, we have covered practically all the grammatical forms of Panjabi words used by educated speakers of the central variety of the language. But it is equally important to learn how these different forms of words (especially of verbs) are combined to express different varieties of meaning. We have already come across some combinations of the forms of main verbs and helping verbs. In Panjabi and other North Indian languages (including the languages spoken in Pakistan, Bangladesh and Nepal), different forms of main verbs and auxiliary verbs can be combined in hundreds of different ways, each combination expressing a different shade of meaning. It is obviously impossible to deal with all such combinations in this basic-level course. If you decide to learn Panjabi (or any other North Indian language) at an intermediate or advanced level, you will have to learn to use all these combinations. They look and sound complicated at first. But if you know the meanings of the individual members of a combination, the meaning of the whole starts making sense. After all, a Panjabi-speaking child masters all such combinations by the age of nine or ten!

In this unit, we deal with some important and frequently used verb combinations and other grammatical structures which, for reasons of simplicity, could not be dealt with in earlier Units. It is, however, assumed that you have done the first eight Conversation units well and learnt all the grammar and vocabulary presented therein. So in this unit, knowledge of the grammatical points already covered in the earlier units is taken for granted. Also, the grammatical explanations in this unit are quite brief because they are meant only for those learners who are prepared to work hard to learn more Panjabi and are, hopefully, capable of taking charge of their learning by now.

Study the Panjabi examples very carefully and see if you can make any sense of them without reading the grammatical explanation.

Paired conjunctions, pronouns and adverbs

mífinat (*f*)	ਮਿਹਨਤ	hard work
ka:mya:b	ਕਾਮਜਾਬ	successful
cuṇ	ਚੁਣ	to choose
bʰàr	ਭਰ	to fill, to pay
cá:fi (*f*)	ਚਾਹ	desire, will
rá:fi (*m*)	ਰਾਹ	way
dʰànnva:d [tànnva:d] (*m*)	ਧੰਨਵਾਦ	thanks
dʰànnva:di:	ਧੰਨਵਾਦੀ	thankful

ਜਿਹੜਾ ਬੰਦਾ ਮਿਹਨਤ ਕਰੇਗਾ ਉਹ ਕਾਮਜਾਬ ਹੋਏਗਾ
jífira: **banda: mífinat karega:** *ufi* **ka:mya:b fioega:.**
The person who works hard will succeed

ਤੁਸੀਂ *ਜਿਹਨੂੰ* ਚਾਹੋ *ਉਹਨੂੰ* ਚੁਣ ਸਕਦੇ ਹੋ।
tusĩ: *jífinu:* **ca:fio** *ufinũ:* **cuṇ sakde fio.**
You can choose the person you wish to

ਤੁਸੀਂ *ਜਿਸ* ਮੁੰਡੇ ਨੂੰ ਪੈਸੇ ਦਿੱਤੇ ਸੀ *ਉਹ* ਕਿੱਥੇ ਹੈ?
tusĩ: *jis* **munḍe nū: pese ditte si:** *ufi* **kittʰe fiɛ?**
Where is the boy you gave the money to?

ਜਿਹੜਾ ਕਰੇਗਾ ਉਹ ਭਰੇਗਾ।
jífira: **karega:** *ufi* **bʰàrega:.**
He who commits a sin shall have to suffer.
(*Lit.:* He who will do will pay.)

jífira: is what grammarians call a 'relative pronoun', because it relates one part of the sentence to another. **jis** is its oblique form. For forms of this pronoun see page 224 of the Grammatical summary. Some other Panjabi words also behave like relative pronouns. All such relative words in Panjabi start with **j** ਜ.

ਜਿੱਥੇ ਚਾਹ ਉੱਥੇ ਰਾਹ
jitt^he **cá:fi** *utt^he* **rá:fi**
Where there is a will there is a way.

ਜਦ ਕ੍ਰਿਸਮਸ ਆਏਗੀ *ਤਦ*(or *ਤਾਂ*) ਪਾਰਟੀ ਕਰਾਂਗੇ।
jad Christmas **a:egi:** *tad* (*or* *tã:*) party **karã:ge**
When Christmas comes, we shall have a party

ਜੇ ਤੁਸੀਂ ਮੇਰੀ ਮਦਦ ਕਰੋ *ਤਾਂ* ਮੈਂ ਤੁਹਾਡਾ ਬੜਾ ਧੰਨਵਾਦੀ ਹੋਵਾਂਗਾ।
je **tusi̇̃:** **meri:** **madad** **karo** *tã:* **mẽ** **tufia:ɖa:** **baɽa:** **d^hànnva:di:**
fiovã:ga:.
If you help me I shall be very grateful to you.

Use of the helping verb *ja:* to indicate completion of an action

band	ਬੰਦ	closed
mada:ri: (*m*)	ਮਦਾਰੀ	magician
rassa: (*m*)	ਰੱਸਾ	rope
cáɽ^h	ਚੜ੍ਹ	to climb

We have already seen that the helping verb **ja:** when used with a perfective form, conveys the meaning of passive voice. But when **ja:** is used with the stem, it indicates the completion of an activity.

ਸਕੂਲ ਬੰਦ ਹੋ *ਗਿਆ* ਹੈ।
school **band fio** *gia:* **fiɛ**
The school is closed

ਮੈਂ ਆ *ਗਿਆ* ਹਾਂ।
mẽ a: *gia:* **fiã:**
I have arrived

ਮਦਾਰੀ ਰੱਸੇ ਤੇ ਚੜ੍ਹ *ਗਿਆ*।
mada:ri: rasse te cáɽ^h *gia:*
The magician climbed the rope

ਉਹ ਕੱਲ੍ਹ ਮਰ *ਗਿਆ*।
úfi káll^h mar *gia:*
He died yesterday.

Use of the imperfective verb form as an adjective

pariva:r (*m*)	ਪਰਿਵਾਰ	family
sõ	ਸੌਂ	to sleep
vár^ɦ	ਵਰ੍ਹ	to rain
mĩ:ɦ (*m*)	ਮੀਂਹ	rain
ruk	ਰੁਕ	to stop

The imperfective form, like its English equivalent the '-ing' form, can be used as an adjective to refer to someone or something engaged in an ongoing activity. (An example in English would be 'This benefit is for *working* mothers only.')

ਉਹ ਚੰਗਾ *ਖਾਂਦਾ ਪੀਂਦਾ* ਪਰਿਵਾਰ ਹੈ।
úɦ canga: *kʰã̀:da: pĩ:da:* **pariva:r ɦɛ**
That is a prosperous family (*Lit.:* That is a good eating and drinking family)

ਮੈਨੂੰ *ਵਰ੍ਹਦੇ* ਮੀਂਹ 'ਚ ਹੀ ਜਾਣਾ ਪਿਆ।
menū: *vár^ɦde* **mĩ́:ɦ c ɦi: ja:ŋa: pia:**
I had to go in the falling rain

ਬੱਚਾ ਕਹਾਣੀ *ਸੁਣਦਾ ਸੁਣਦਾ* ਸੌਂ ਗਿਆ।
bacca kaɦa:ŋi: *suṇda: suṇda:* **sõ gia:**
The child went to sleep while hearing the story.

Note the repetition of **suṇda:** to emphasise the prolongation of the process.

ਮੈਂ ਗੱਲ *ਕਹਿੰਦਾ ਕਹਿੰਦਾ* ਹੀ ਰੁਕ ਗਿਆ।
mɛ̃ gall *káɦinda: káɦinda:* **ɦi: ruk gia:**
I checked myself from saying something. (*Lit.:* I matter saying saying stopped.)

As we saw in Conversation unit 6, the imperfective form is also used to refer to things which were not done in the past.

Imperfective verb form plus *ráɦi* or *pɛ*

ro	ਰੋ	to cry, weep
cor (*m*)	ਚੋਰ	thief
kutt	ਕੁੱਟ	to beat
ɦar roz	ਹਰ ਰੋਜ਼	daily

We have already seen (in Conversation unit 7) the use of the helping verb **ráfii [ré]** with the stem form of the verb to refer to an ongoing activity. But to focus on or to emphasise an ongoing activity, you use the helping verb **pɛ** with the imperfective form, as in the following two examples

ਬੱਚਾ *ਰੋਂਦਾ ਪਿਆ* ਸੀ।
bacca *rôda: pia:* si:
The child was crying

ਲੋਕ ਚੋਰ ਨੂੰ *ਕੁੱਟਦੇ ਪਏ* ਸਨ।
lok cor nū: *kuṭṭde pae* san
People were beating the thief.

You can emphasise the recurring nature of an event by using the helping verb **ré** with the imperfective form of the verb.

ਮੈਂ ਉੱਥੇ ਹਰ ਰੋਜ਼ *ਜਾਂਦਾ ਰਿਹਾ* ਹਾਂ।
mɛ̃ uttʰe fiar roz *jā:da: rífia:* fiã:
I have been going there daily

ਤੁਸੀਂ ਸਦਾ ਹੀ ਮੇਰੀ ਮਦਦ *ਕਰਦੇ ਰਹੇ* ਹੋ।
tusī: sada: fii: meri: madad *karde ráfie* fio
You have always helped me.

The '-*i*- variety' of the imperfective form

dʰàk	ਢਕ	to cover
mā̃: (*f*)	ਮਾਂ	mother
fiass	ਹੱਸ	to laugh

The **-i-** variety of the imperfective form is derived by first adding an **-i-** to the stem and then adding the usual suffixes of the imperfective form (**-da**, etc.). When you use this form, the subject is not mentioned and the verb either agrees with the object or, if the object is marked with the postposition **nū:**, it is in the masculine singular form. Such sentences generally express some sort of advice or obligation which is thought to be universally applicable.

ਗੁਰਦੁਆਰੇ ਵਿਚ ਸਿਰ ਢਕੀਦਾ ਹੈ।
gurdua:re vic sir *dʰàki:da:* fiɛ.
One should cover one's head in a Sikh temple

ਮਾਂ ਬਾਪ ਦਾ ਹੁਕਮ *ਮੰਨੀਦਾ* ਹੈ।
mã: ba:p da: fiukam *manni:da:* fiɛ
Parents should be obeyed (*Lit.:* Parents' orders should be obeyed)

ਬੱਚਿਆਂ ਨੂੰ *ਕੁੱਟੀਦਾ* ਨਹੀਂ।
bacciã: nũ: *kuṭṭi:da:* náfii:
Children should not be beaten

ਬਹੁਤਾ *ਹੱਸੀਦਾ* ਨਹੀਂ
báfiuta: *fiassi:da:* náfii:
One shouldn't laugh too much.

The verb stems used in these sentences are **dʰàki:** (**dʰàk + i:**), **manni:** (**mann + i:**) and **kuṭṭi:** (**kuṭṭ + i:**). The performer of the action is not mentioned in such sentences and the verb agrees with the object in the first two sentences. The object in the third sentences is marked with **nũ:**, and the fourth sentence has no object. So in these two sentences the verb is in the masculine singular form.

Use of the perfective verb form as an adjective

mar	ਮਰ	to die
kade	ਕਦੇ	ever
tuɽak	ਤੁੜਕ	to fry
mā̃:fi (*m/pl*)	ਮਾਂਹ	black lentils
bʰùnn	ਭੁੰਨ	to roast
kukkaɽ (*m*)	ਕੁੱਕੜ	chicken
fiaḍḍi: (*f*)	ਹੱਡੀ	bone
muɽ	ਮੁੜ	to return

In English the past participle form can be used as an adjective in expressions such as 'broken glass', 'paid workers', 'cooked meat', etc. The Panjabi perfective form of the verb, which is close to the English past participle form in meaning, can be similarly used.

The helping verb **fio** (also in the perfective form) can optionally be used with the perfective form of the main verb in such sentences.

ਮਰਿਆ *(ਹੋਇਆ)* ਬੰਦਾ ਕਦੇ ਵਾਪਸ ਨਹੀਂ ਆ ਸਕਦਾ
maria: (fioia:) banda: kade va:pas náfii: a: sakda:
A dead person can never come back

ਤੁੜਕੀ (ਹੋਈ) ਮਾਂਹ ਦੀ ਦਾਲ ਤੇ *ਭੁੰਨਿਆ (ਹੋਇਆ)* ਕੁੱਕੜ ਛਕੋ।
tuɽki: (ɦoi:) **mā̃:ɦ di: da:l te** *bʰùnnia: (ɦoia:)* **kukkaɽ cʰako**
Enjoy fried black lentils and roasted chicken

ਗੰਗਾ *ਗਈਆਂ* ਹੱਡੀਆਂ ਵੀ ਕਦੇ ਮੁੜੀਆਂ ਨੇ?
ganga: *gai:ā̃:* **ɦaɖɖi:ā̃: vi: kade muɽi:ā̃: ne?**
Lit.: Can the bones which have gone to the Ganges ever come back?

The last sentence is actually a Panjabi proverb used when there is no hope of getting back the money lent or given to someone – just as the ashes and bones of a dead person immersed into the holy river Ganges cannot come back.

Sometimes the perfective form is also used with the helping verb **pɛ**, instead of **ɦo**, to emphasise the sense of 'already done'.

ਚਾਹ ਕੱਪਾਂ ਵਿਚ *ਪਾਈ ਪਈ* ਸੀ।
cá:ɦ kappā̃: vic *pa:i: pai:* **si:**
The tea had (already) been put into the cups

ਖ਼ਤ *ਲਿਖਿਆ ਪਿਆ* ਹੈ।
xat *likʰia: pia:* **ɦɛ**
The letter has (already) been written.

Verbal noun plus *lag* or *lag pɛ*

rok	ਰੋਕ	to stop
imtiɦa:n (*m*)	ਇਮਤਿਹਾਨ	examination
tia:ri: (*f*)	ਤਿਆਰੀ	preparation

The verbal noun (gerund) in the oblique form (i.e. without the final **-a:**) can be used with the helping verb **lag** or with the combination **lag pɛ** to convey the meaning of 'start doing something'.

ਜਦ ਉਹ *ਜਾਣ ਲੱਗਾ* ਤਾਂ ਮੈਂ ਉਹਨੂੰ ਰੋਕ ਲਿਆ।
jad úɦ *ja:ɳ lagga:* **tā̃: mɛ̃ úɦinū̃: rok lia:**
When he started to go, I stopped him

ਕਾਕਾ *ਰੋਣ ਲਗ ਪਿਆ* ਸੀ।
ka:ka: *roɳ lag pia:* **si:**
The baby boy had started crying

ਇਮਤਿਹਾਨ ਦੀ ਤਿਆਰੀ *ਕਰਨ ਲਗ* ਪਓ।
imtiɦa:n di: tia:ri: *karan lag* **pao**
Start preparing for the examination

Use of the gerund plus *de* in the sense of 'allow'

ruk	ਰੁਕ	to stay
ka:nū̃:n (*m*)	ਕਾਨੂੰਨ	law
ji:	ਜੀ	to live

The gerund in such a construction is in the oblique form (i.e. without a final -**a:**), and the person who is to be allowed to do something is marked with the postposition **nū̃:**

> ਮੈਨੂੰ ਕੁਝ ਹੋਰ ਵੀ *ਕਹਿਣ ਦਿਓ* ।
> **mɛnū̃: kújʰ ɦor vi:** *káɦiɳ dio*
> Let me say something else as well

> ਉਹ ਰੁਕਣਾ ਚਾਹੁੰਦੀ ਸੀ, ਪਰ ਮੈਂ ਉਹਨੂੰ *ਜਾਣ ਦਿੱਤਾ* ।
> **úɦ rukɳa: cá:ɦũdi: si:, par mɛ̃ úɦinū̃:** *ja:ɳ ditta:*
> She wanted to stay, but I allowed her to go

> ਕਾਨੂੰਨ ਤੈਨੂੰ *ਮਰਨ* ਨਹੀਂ ਦੇਵੇਗਾ, ਅਤੇ ਮੈਂ ਤੈਨੂੰ *ਜੀਣ* ਨਹੀਂ ਦੇਵਾਂਗਾ ।
> **ka:nū̃:n tɛnū̃:** *maran* **náɦi̇:** *devega:,* **ate mɛ̃ tɛnū̃:** *ji:ɳ* **náɦi̇:** *devã:ga:*
> The law won't allow you to die, and I won't allow you to live.

ਅਭਿਆਸ Exercises

First read the exercises and make a list of the words you do not know or understand. Look up these words in the glossary before attempting the exercises.

1 Complete the following sentences by supplying the correct forms of the Panjabi verbs given in parentheses. A natural English translation of each sentence is provided to help you. The first sentence has been done as an example.

(a) (ਚਲ) ਗੱਡੀ 'ਚੋਂ ਨਹੀਂ (ਉਤਰ)
   (cal) gaɖɖi: cõ náɦi̇: (utar)
   Don't come out of the train while it's moving.

   ਚਲਦੀ ਗੱਡੀ 'ਚੋਂ ਨਹੀਂ *ਉਤਰੀਦਾ*
   caldi: gaɖɖi: cõ náɦi̇: *utari:da:.*

(b) ਉਹ (ਜਾ) (ਜਾ) ਮੈਨੂੰ ਆਪਣੀ ਘੜੀ ਦੇ (ਜਾ)
úfi (ja:) (ja:) menū: a:pɳi: gʱàɽi: de (ja:)
He gave me his watch when he was going.

(c) ਪਹਿਲਾਂ ਆਲੂਆਂ ਨੂੰ ਕੱਟੋ, ਅਤੇ ਫਿਰ (ਕੱਟ) (ਹੋ) ਆਲੂਆਂ ਨੂੰ ਉਬਾਲ (ਲੈ)
páfiilā: a:lu:ā: nū: kaʈʈo, ate pʰir (kaʈʈ) (fio) a:lu:ā: nū: uba:l (lɛ)
Slice the potatoes first, and then boil the sliced potatoes.

(d) ਮੈਨੂੰ ਇਹ ਖ਼ਤ ਪੜ੍ਹ (ਲੈ) (ਦੇ)
menū: ífi xat páɽʰ (lɛ) (de)
Please allow me to read this letter.

(e) ਚਾਚਾ ਜੀ (ਜਾ) ਤਾਂ (ਲਗਾ) ਸੀ, ਪਰ ਮੈਂ ਉਹਨਾਂ ਨੂੰ (ਜਾ) ਨਹੀਂ (ਦੇ)
ca:ca: ji: (ja:) tā: (lag) si:, par mẽ úfinā: nū: (ja:) náfii: (de)
Uncle did start to go, but I stopped him.

(f) ਜਦ ਸੰਗੀਤ ਸ਼ੁਰੂ ਹੋਇਆ ਤਾਂ ਕੁੜੀਆਂ (ਨੱਚ) (ਲਗਾ) (ਪੈ)
jad sangi:t ʃuru: fioia: tā: kuɽi:ā: (nacc) (lag) (pɛ)
When the music started, the girls began to dance.

(g) ਅਸੀਂ ਕਈ ਸਾਲ ਰਾਤ ਦਾ ਖਾਣਾ ਇਸੇ ਰੈਸਟੋਰੈਂਟ ਵਿਚ ਹੀ (ਖਾ) ਰਹੇ) ਹਾਂ
así: kai: sa:l ra:t da: kʰa:ɳa: ise restaurant vic fii: (kʰa:) (ráfii) fiā:
We've been having our dinner in this very restaurant for years.

(h) ਪ੍ਰੋਫੈਸਰ ਸਾਹਬ ਪਹੁੰਚ (ਜਾ) ਸਨ, ਅਤੇ ਉਹ ਲੈਕਚਰ ਸ਼ੁਰੂ (ਕਰ) ਵਾਲੇ ਸਨ
Professor **sá:fiab páfiũc (ja) san, ate úfi** lecture **ʃuru: (kar) va:le san.**
The professor had arrived, and he was about to start the lecture.

(i) ਸਵੇਰ ਦਾ (ਪਕਾ) (ਹੋ) ਖਾਣਾ ਠੰਡਾ (ਹੋ) (ਪੈ) ਸੀ
saver da: (paka:) (fio) kʰa:ɳa: ʈʰanɖa: (fio) (pɛ) si:
The food cooked in the morning had already become cold.

(j) ਬੱਚਿਆਂ ਨੂੰ ਬਾਹਰ ਸੜਕ ਤੇ (ਖੇਡ) ਨਹੀਂ (ਦੇ)
bacciā: nū: bá:fiar saɽak te (kʰeɖ) náfii: (de)
Children shouldn't be allowed to play outside on the road.

10 ਯਾਦਾਂ 'ਚ ਤਾਜ਼ਾ ਨੇ ਸਭ
They're all still fresh in the memory

In this unit, you will find some passages from British Panjabi literature written and published in Britain by writers who were born and brought up in India. These passages are given with the bare minimum of notes and without an English translation. You should work out their meaning.

The purpose of this unit is to help you discover how you can learn more Panjabi from literature and newspapers. You need basically two things – (i) *vocabulary*, i.e. more new words and (ii) *grammar*, i.e. a knowledge of how these words are put together and how they change their form when used in sentences to express different ideas and feelings.

If you wish to go on learning Panjabi at higher levels, you need at least two dictionaries–one from Panjabi to English and the other from English to Panjabi. You will find a number of English–Panjabi dictionaries. *Punjabi University English–Punjabi Dictionary,* published by Punjabi University, Patiala, is quite good and can be carried in a handbag. Another *English–Punjabi Dictionary* prepared by Punjab State University Text-Book Board, Chandigarh, is also very good but is larger in size. There is only one *Punjabi–English Dictionary* which is really useful for you. Its second edition published by Singh Brothers, Amritsar, in 1992 is quite adequate for learners of Panjabi at any level. This dictionary can also be easily carried in a handbag.

Unfortunately, there is currently no good Panjabi grammar prepared exclusively for learners. But you might like to read Gill and Gleason's *A Reference Grammar of Punjabi* (Punjabi University, Patiala, 1969). But this book (first published in 1961) is quite dated now. A recent volume is Tej K. Bhatia's *Punjabi: A Cognitive-descriptive Grammar* (Routledge, 1993). This book is detailed and authoritative but it is meant more for scholars working in the fields of universal grammar and cognitive science than for learners. Also, its transcriptional conventions are different from the ones used in this course.

However, the outline of Panjabi grammar presented in this course ought to be quite adequate for the learners at the basic and intermediate levels, as the study of the following passages will show.

The first passage is taken from Surinder Delhavi's short story ਮਕਾਨ ('House'). The story deals with a young couple struggling to earn enough money to turn their ਮਕਾਨ into a ਘਰ ('home'). The husband has to work over-time because the wife (Daljit) has to stay at home to look after their baby son. One afternoon, she gets bored and finds an excuse to speak to a lodger (Jagdish).

Read the passage with the help of the Vocabulary and the rules of grammar you have learnt and see how much you can understand it. Then read again with the help of the notes and see how the notes help you enhance your understanding. 🔲🔲

1 | ਪੱਪੂ ਰੋਣ ਲੱਗਾ ਸੀ। ਕਿੰਨਾ ਚਿਰ ਉਹ ਪੱਪੂ ਨਾਲ ਖੇਲਦੀ ਰਹੀ ਤੇ ਫਿਰ ਟੈਲੀਵੀਜ਼ਨ ਲਾ ਦਿੱਤਾ। ਕੋਈ ਕੌਮੇਡੀ ਆ ਰਹੀ ਸੀ। ਉਸ ਨੂੰ ਹਾਸਾ ਨਾ ਆਇਆ ਤੇ ਉਹ ਟੈਲੀਵੀਜ਼ਨ ਬੰਦ ਕਰਕੇ ਚਾਹ ਦਾ ਕੱਪ ਬਣਾਉਣ ਲੱਗੀ। ਉਹਦਾ ਦਿਲ ਕੀਤਾ, ਜਗਦੀਸ਼ ਦੀ ਚਿੱਠੀ ਦੇ ਆਵੇ ਨਾਲੇ ਪੁੱਛੇ, "ਭਾ ਜੀ ਚਾਹ ਦਾ ਕੱਪ ਪੀਓਗੇ?" ਪਰ ਉਸ ਨੇ ਇਕ ਹੀ ਕੱਪ ਬਣਾਇਆ ਅਤੇ ਇਕੱਲੀ ਮੇਜ਼ ਤੇ ਬੈਠ ਕੇ ਪੀਣ ਲੱਗੀ।
2 | ਰੋਟੀ ਟੁੱਕ ਦਾ ਵੇਲਾ ਹੋ ਗਿਆ ਸੀ।
3 | ਉਹ ਪਹਿਲੀ ਵੇਰ ਹੌਂਸਲਾ ਕੱਢ ਕੇ ਜਗਦੀਸ਼ ਦੇ ਕਮਰੇ ਵਿਚ ਗਈ। ਸ਼ਾਇਦ ਚਿੱਠੀ ਅਰਜੈਂਟ ਹੋਵੇ। ਉਹਨੇ ਹੌਲੀ ਜਿਹੀ ਦਸਤਕ ਦਿੱਤੀ।
4 | "ਯੈਸ।" ਅੰਦਰੋਂ ਆਵਾਜ਼ ਆਈ।
5 | "ਸੌਰੀ ਭਾ ਜੀ, ਤੁਹਾਡੀ ਚਿੱਠੀ ਸੀ। ਗਲਤੀ ਨਾਲ ਮੈਂ ਆਪਣੀਆਂ ਚਿੱਠੀਆਂ ਨਾਲ ਲੈ ਗਈ।"
6 | "ਕੋਈ ਗੱਲ ਨਹੀਂ ਭਾਬੀ ਜੀ।" ਜਗਦੀਸ਼ ਨੇ ਚਿੱਠੀ ਫੜ ਲਈ। ਦਲਜੀਤ ਦੀਆਂ ਉਂਗਲਾਂ ਦੇ ਪੋਟੇ, ਜਗਦੀਸ਼ ਦੀਆਂ ਉਂਗਲਾਂ ਨਾਲ ਛੋਹੇ ਤਾਂ ਉਹ ਸਾਰੀ ਦੀ ਸਾਰੀ ਕੰਬ ਗਈ।
7 | "ਬੈਣ ਜੀ ਦੀ ਚਿੱਠੀ ਏ?"
8 | "ਨਹੀਂ ਮੇਰੇ ਦੋਸਤ ਦੀ ਏ।"
9 | "ਬੈਣ ਜੀ ਹੁਣਾਂ ਇੰਗਲੈਂਡ ਕਦੋਂ ਆਉਣੈ?"
10 | "ਮੇਰਾ ਹਾਲੇ ਵਿਆਹ ਨਹੀਂ ਹੋਇਆ।"
11 | "ਸੌਰੀ ਭਾ ਜੀ, ਮੈਨੂੰ ਪਤਾ ਨਹੀਂ ਸੀ।"

Vocabulary

ਪੱਪੂ (*m*)	baby boy
ਕੌਮੇਡੀ	comedy
ਹਾਸਾ (*m*)	laughter
ਚਿੱਠੀ (*f*)	letter
ਭਾ (*m*)	brother
ਰੋਟੀ ਟੁੱਕ (*m*)	meal

ਵੇਲਾ (*m*)	time
ਹੌਂਸਲਾ (*m*)	courage
ਸ਼ਾਇਦ	perhaps, maybe
ਕੱਢ	to take out
ਹੌਲੀ ਜਿਹੀ	quite lightly
ਦਸਤਕ (*f*)	knock
ਗਲਤੀ (*f*)	mistake
ਉਂਗਲ (*f*)	finger
ਪੋਟਾ (*m*)	tip
ਛੋਹ	to touch
ਕੰਬ	to tremble
ਹੁਣਾਂ	added to name to show respect
ਆਉਣੈ (ਆਉਂਵਾ + ਹੈ)	is coming, is to come
ਹਾਲੇ	yet, still
ਵਿਆਹ (*m*)	marriage

Notes

1 ਰੋਣ ਲੱਗਾ, ਪੀਣ ਲੱਗੀ, ਬਣਾਉਣ ਲੱਗੀ – gerund (verbal noun) + ਲਗ. The structure is used in the sense of 'began to'. Daljit is trying to prolong all her activities to fill the time available to her in her idle life at home.
ਖੇਲਦੀ ਰਹੀ – imperfective form + ਰਹਿ – to refer to a prolonged activity.
ਲਾ ਦਿੱਤਾ ('switched on') – stem form + auxiliary verb ਦੇ. ਦੇ is actually used to refer to something done for others, but since Daljit has lost all interest in the TV programmes, the use of the auxiliary ਦੇ seems to be more appropriate here.
ਦਿਲ ਕੀਤਾ (*Lit.:* 'heart did') 'had a mind to'.
ਦੇ ਆਵੇ – compound verb ਦੇ + ਆ ('give and come'). ਆਵੇ is ਆ in the subjunctive form, expressing just an idea or a possibility.

2 ਹੋ ਗਿਆ – stem ਹੋ + ਜਾ , indicating the completion of an event. The time for cooking dinner had arrived.

3 ਹੌਂਸਲਾ ਕੱਢ ਕੇ ('having taken out courage'), i.e. taking courage.

4 ਯੈਸ Yes.

5 ਸੌਰੀ Sorry.

6 ਸਾਰੀ ਦੀ ਸਾਰੀ- the whole of her, completely.

7 ਕੰਬ ਗਈ – Stem form ਕੰਬ + ਜਾ, showing the completion of an event. Her whole frame trembled.
ਭੈਣ ਜੀ ('sister') – Jagdish's wife.

9 ਹੁਣਾਂ or ਹੁਰਾਂ can be added to the name of a person (male or female, one or more than one) to show respect.

ਆਉਣੈ . The colloquial Panjabi pronunciation of ਆਉਣਾ ਹੈ. Potential form ਆਉਣਾ + ਹੈ, used for referring to a potential event.

The following passage is a complete short poem by Amarjit Chandan. The poem is simple and straightforward and its effect is immediate. So it needs no special introduction apart from a short comment that it expresses dissatisfaction with the reality of the present and a desire to move into a 'should have been' world.

ਇਸ ਵੇਲੇ

ਅਮਰਜੀਤ ਚੰਦਨ

1	ਇਸ ਵੇਲੇ
	ਮੈਨੂੰ ਕਿਤੇ ਹੋਰ ਹੋਣਾ ਚਾਹੀਦਾ ਸੀ
2	ਜਿਥੇ ਮੈਨੂੰ ਕਿਸੇ ਚੀਜ਼ ਦੀ ਇੰਤਜ਼ਾਰ ਨਾ ਹੁੰਦੀ
3	ਖ਼ਤ ਦੀ
	ਟੈਲੀਫ਼ੋਨ ਦੀ
	ਮੌਤ ਦੀ
4	ਵਗਦੇ ਰਾਹਵਾਂ
	ਚੁਪ ਖੜ੍ਹੇ ਰੁੱਖਾਂ
	ਤੇ ਤੇਰੀਆਂ ਯਾਦਾਂ ਨੇ
	ਮੇਰੇ ਦਿਲ ਅੰਦਰ ਆਲ੍ਹਣਾ ਪਾ ਲਿਆ ਹੈ
5	ਹੁਣ ਬੜੀ ਦੇਰ ਹੋ ਚੁੱਕੀ ਹੈ
6	ਮੈਨੂੰ ਤਾਂ ਕਿਤੇ ਹੋਰ ਹੋਣਾ ਚਾਹੀਦਾ ਸੀ
7	ਜਿਥੋਂ ਮੈਂ ਸੀਟੀ ਵਜਾਉਂਦਾ
8	ਰੇਨਕੋਟ ਤੋਂ ਮੀਂਹ ਦੀਆਂ ਛਿੱਟਾਂ ਝਾੜਦਾ
9	ਤੁਰ ਪੈਂਦਾ ਉਧਰ
10	ਜਿਥੇ ਮੇਰੀ ਉਡੀਕ ਹੋ ਰਹੀ ਹੈ

Vocabulary

ਵੇਲਾ (*m*)	time (moment)
ਇਸ ਵੇਲੇ	at this time
ਕਿਤੇ ਹੋਰ	somewhere else
ਚੀਜ਼ (*f*)	thing
ਇੰਤਜ਼ਾਰ (*f*)	wait
ਵਗ	to flow
ਰਾਹਵਾਂ (*m/pl*)	plural of ਰਾਹ ('way'); ਰਾਹਾਂ is also used
ਚੁਪ	silent
ਖੜ੍ਹ	to stand

ਰੁੱਖ (*m*)	tree
ਯਾਦ (*f*)	memory
ਆਲ੍ਹਣਾ (*m*)	nest
ਪਾ	to put in, to set up
ਦੇਰ (*f*)	time (duration)
ਸੀਟੀ (*f*)	whistle
ਵਜਾ	to play (music)
ਠੰਢਾ	cold
ਰੇਨਕੋਟ (*m*)	raincoat
ਮੀਂਹ (*m*)	rain
ਛਿੱਟ (*f*)	drop
ਝਾੜ	to shake off
ਤੁਰ	to walk
ਓਧਰ	there
ਉਡੀਕ (*f*)	wait
ਉਡੀਕ	to wait

Notes

1 ਹੋਣਾ ਚਾਹੀਦਾ ਸੀ – Gerund form of ਹੋ (means 'being' or 'existence') followed by ਚਾਹੀਦਾ 'desirable' and ਸੀ (showing past time). The whole expression literally means 'my existence should have been'. In more natural English, it means 'I should have been'.

2 ਹੁੰਦੀ. When the imperfective form is used without ਹੈ and and is not functioning as an adjective, it usually refers to an unreal or contrary-to-fact event or to something that did not take place. The whole line means 'where I shouldn't be waiting for anything (such as the ones listed below)'.

3 ਵਗਦੇ ਰਾਹਵਾਂ – 'busy roads' (*lit.*: flowing paths). The imperfective form is used as an adjective.
    ਚੁਪ ਖੜ੍ਹੇ ਰੁੱਖਾਂ – 'trees standing silent'. With the verbs ਖੜ੍ਹ ('stand') and, ਬੈਠ/ਬਹਿ ('sit'), the perfective form is used as an adjective to show the continuing standing or sitting of someone or something. Other examples are ਖੜ੍ਹੀ ਗੱਡੀ 'standing train', ਬੈਠੇ ਬੰਦੇ 'sitting people'.

4 ਆਲ੍ਹਣਾ ਪਾ ਲਿਆ ਹੈ – stem form ਪਾ + auxiliary ਲੈ in the perfective form + ਹੈ showing the present relevance of something that was completed in the past. The expression means something like 'have set up a nest for themselves'.

5 ਬੜੀ ਦੇਰ ਹੋ ਚੁੱਕੀ ਹੈ. The auxiliary ਚੁੱਕ used with the completion of the activity of the verb ਹੋ in the stem form. 'It is already too late.'

7 ਸੀਟੀ ਵਜਾਉਂਦਾ . The imperfective ਵਜਾ is used as an adjective with ਮੈਂ – 'I, blowing a whistle, ...'

8 ਛਿੱਟਾਂ ਝਾੜਦਾ. ਝਾੜਦਾ 'shaking off' is used as an adjective exactly like ਵਜਾਉਂਦਾ.

9 ਤੁਰ ਪੈਂਦਾ . Stem ਤੁਰ + ਪੈ indicated the commencement of an action. But since ਪੈ is in the imperfective form, it refers, in this particular context, to an action that should have started but did not.

10 ਮੇਰੀ ਉਡੀਕ ਹੋ ਰਹੀ ਹੈ . *Lit.:* 'Waiting for me is happening.' Stem ਹੋ + ਰਹਿ + ਹੈ refers to a real ongoing situation.

The following two passages are extracts from Mohinder Gill's poem ਸ਼ਾਮ ('evening'). A snowy and silent evening in England sets the poet musing about a very different type of evening in his native village in the Panjab. The whole effect of the poem is like that of an impressionistic painting. In these extracts, you can experience the typical Indian view of time mentioned in Conversation unit 5. By using the present tense verb form ਨੇ 'are' (in, ਯਾਦਾਂ 'ਚ ਤਾਜ਼ਾ ਨੇ ਸਭ), the poet goes on relating his memories (ਯਾਦਾਂ) to the present time. But then he imaginatively transports himself *inside* those memories, and presents their vivid video images as ongoing or completed or timeless events. Of course, any writer or speaker could do this in any language. (Some English novelists of this century have experimented with this technique of narration.) But this has been something normal, natural and habitual with Indian speakers (especially the uneducated ones) and writers for many centuries. The result is that through lack of use verb forms expressing tense have almost disappeared from Indian languages and verb forms expressing aspect have gained prominence. (For tense and aspect, see the Grammatical summary.) Now only one verb in Panjabi has tense-expressing forms – ਹੈ (present tense) and ਸੀ (past tense). If you read the earlier passages again after reading the following extracts from Gill's poem, you will see that their authors, too, make use of these two forms ਹੈ and ਸੀ simply as 'scene-shifters' in order to move on their video cameras inside the situations in order to present fresh pictures – completed, ongoing or merely possible, etc.

It was pointed out in unit 5 that in Panjabi ਕੱਲ੍ਹ means both 'yesterday' and 'tomorow', ਪਰਸੋਂ means both 'day before yesterday' and 'day after tomorrow', ਚੌਥ means 'day before the day before yesterday' and 'day after the day after tomorrow'. Panjabi also has ਪੰਜੋਥ, and you should now be able to guess what it means. Time is linear and flows from the past through the present into the future only if you imaginatively view it from the *outside*.

If, however, you imaginatively place yourself *inside* the situations you describe and drift along the flow of the narrative, stopping here and there simply to 'look before and after', there is only the present and the non-present. Whether the latter lies behind or ahead is unimportant. Then there is no 'yesterday' and 'tomorrow'; both are simply days 'once removed from today'. The direction in which such a day lies becomes unimportant. A situation becomes fragmented as you explore from the inside its various aspects and facets as completed, ongoing, potential, possible, etc., and you need combinations of aspect-expressing verb forms to represent it. Hence the complicated system of verb combinations in Panjabi and other Indian languages. It may be of interest to you that this view of time is not exclusively Indian. You can see all this in some African languages as well.

If you wish to learn Panjabi or any other Indian language seriously at a higher level, you will have to keep this in mind and avoid making excessive use of ਹੈ and ਸੀ or their equivalents in other Indian languages (as many European learners initially do). Learning the vocabulary and grammar of a new language is necessary but not sufficient. *You should also learn to think like the people whose language you are learning.* You will have to abandon the grand European illusion, reinforced, sadly enough, by some schools of modern philosophy and linguistics, that underneath the diversity of the world languages, there lies only one way of thinking – the European one (of course!).

You may also have noticed that indirect speech is missing from Panjabi. In fact, it is missing from all Indian languages. Indirect speech involves presenting someone's speech from your own present point of view, and thereby making grammatical changes of person and tense and changing words showing time and place. In other words, it means adopting an outside observer's point of view. But the typical Indian style is to adopt an inside participant's point of view, i.e. placing yourself in the position of the speaker whose words you are quoting. Hence, there is only direct, and no indirect, speech. In European languages, you use direct speech to create a special effect of vividness. But there is nothing special about vividness for the people of the Indian subcontinent. It is something normal and usual. Now, however, under the influence of English, some Indian writers have started using indirect speech. Needless to say, this sounds extremely odd. So do not use indirect speech in Panjabi and other Indian languages for at least a hundred years!

Incidentally, if you look at an old and traditional Indian painting, you will find that ancient Indian painters never used perspective as a technique.They adopted a point of view somewhat similar to the one Picasso adopted in some of his greatest paintings. They were excellent artists and paid minute attention to detail. But they did not adopt an outside observer's perspective. Theirs was an inside participant's view until contact with Europeans changed all that.

ਸ਼ਾਮ

ਮਹਿੰਦਰ ਗਿੱਲ

1 | ਸ਼ਾਮ ਦਾ ਘੁਸਮੁਸਾ, ਰਾਹਾਂ ਦੀ ਉਡਦੀ ਧੂੜ, ਘਰਾਂ ਨੂੰ ਪਰਤਦੇ ਡੰਗਰ
2 | ਘੁੰਗਰੂਆਂ ਦੀ ਟਣ ਟਣ, ਸਾਹਾਂ ਦੀ ਫੁੰਕਾਰ, ਖੁਰਾਂ ਦੀ ਠੱਪ ਠੱਪ-
3 | ਯਾਦਾਂ 'ਚ ਤਾਜ਼ਾ ਨੇ ਸਭ ਜਿਉਂ ਕੱਲ੍ਹ ਦੀ ਹੀ ਗੱਲ ਹੋਵੇ।

4 | ਪਿੰਡ ਦੇ ਮੁਖੜੇ 'ਤੇ ਛਾਇਆ ਪਤਲਾ ਧੂੋਂ ਦਾ ਨਕਾਬ
5 | ਪੱਛੋਂ ਦੇ ਅੰਬਰਾਂ ਦੀ ਖੱਡ ਵਿਚ ਡਿਗ ਰਿਹਾ ਸੂਰਜ,
6 | ਸ਼ਾਮ ਦਾ ਘੁਸਮੁਸਾ, ਰਾਹਾਂ ਦੀ ਉਡਦੀ ਧੂੜ, ਘਰਾਂ ਨੂੰ ਪਰਤਦੇ ਡੰਗਰ।

Vocabulary

ਘੁਸਮੁਸਾ (*m*)	twilight
ਉਡ	to fly
ਧੂੜ (*f*)	dust
ਪਰਤ	to return
ਡੰਗਰ (*m/pl*)	cattle
ਘੁੰਗਰੂ (*m/pl*)	little bells
ਟਣ ਟਣ (*f*)	tinkling sound
ਫੁੰਕਾਰ (*f*)	sound of heavy breathing
ਖੁਰ (*m*)	hoof
ਠੱਪ ਠੱਪ (*f*)	sound of hooves
ਯਾਦ (*f*)	memory
ਤਾਜ਼ਾ	fresh
ਜਿਉਂ	as if
ਪਿੰਡ (*m*)	village
ਮੁਖੜਾ (*m*)	face
ਛਾ	spread
ਪਤਲਾ	thin
ਨਕਾਬ (*m*)	veil, mask

ਪੱਛੋਂ (f)	west
ਅੰਬਰ (m)	sky
ਖੱਡ (f)	valley
ਡਿਗ	to fall
ਸੂਰਜ (m)	sun

Notes

1   ਉਤਦੀ ਧੂੜ, ਪਰਤਦੇ ਡੰਗਰ. Imperfective forms of ਉਤ and ਪਰਤ are used as adjectives to give an effect of the prolongation of the activities. The absence of any present tense or past tense form of ਹੈ effectively makes everything timeless.

3   ਜਿਉਂ ਕੱਲ੍ਹ ਦੀ ਹੀ ਗੱਲ ਹੋਵੇ. ਹੋਵੇ is in the subjunctive form. Everything is still fresh in the memory as if it happened only yesterday.

4   ਛਾਇਆ. The perfective form is used here as an adjective to qualify the noun ਨਕਾਬ 'veil'. The thin veil is in a condition of having spread.

5   ਡਿਗ ਰਿਹਾ ਸੂਰਜ. Even ਡਿਗ ਰਿਹਾ is used as an adjective to qualify the noun ਸੂਰਜ. The sun is qualified as being in the continuing process of falling into the 'valley of the west'.

The following passage from the poem is very similar in effect. The present and the past tense forms of **fie** – ਹੈ and ਸੀ – are conspicuously missing except in ਯਾਦਾਂ 'ਚ ਤਾਜ਼ਾ ਨੇ ਸਭ.   ▣

1	ਮੱਝੀਆਂ ਨੂੰ ਉਡੀਕੇ ਸੁਆਣੀ, ਅਤੇ ਮੱਝੀਆਂ ਦਾ ਚਾਰਾ
2	ਧੁੱਪ ਦੀਆਂ ਗਰਮ ਧਾਰਾਂ ਨੂੰ ਉਡੀਕੇ ਸੱਖਣੀ ਬਾਲਟੀ
3	ਯਾਦਾਂ 'ਚ ਤਾਜ਼ਾ ਨੇ ਸਭ ਜਿਉਂ ਕੱਲ੍ਹ ਦੀ ਹੀ ਗੱਲ ਹੋਵੇ।
4	ਨਿੱਕਾ ਮੁੰਡਾ, ਹੱਥ ਵਿਚ ਛਿਟੀ, ਗਿੱਟਿਆਂ ਨੂੰ ਲਿਪਟੀ ਗਰਦ
5	ਘੁੰਗਰੂਆਂ ਦੀ ਟਣ ਟਣ 'ਚ ਗੁਆਚਾ
6	ਸ਼ਾਮ ਦਾ ਘੁਸਮੁਸਾ, ਰਾਹਾਂ ਦੀ ਉਤਦੀ ਧੂੜ, ਘਰਾਂ ਨੂੰ ਪਰਤਦੇ ਡੰਗਰ।

Vocabulary

ਮੱਝੀ (f)	buffalo
ਸੁਆਣੀ (f)	housewife
ਚਾਰਾ (m)	fodder
ਦੁੱਧ (m)	milk
ਗਰਮ	warm, hot
ਧਾਰ (f)	spout

ਸੱਖਣਾ	empty
ਬਾਲਟੀ (*f*)	bucket
ਨਿੱਕਾ	little
ਹੱਥ (*m*)	hand
ਛਿਟੀ (*f*)	stick
ਗਿੱਟਾ (*m*)	ankle
ਲਿਪਟ	to stick to
ਗਰਦ (*f*)	dust
ਗੁਆਚ	to be lost

Notes

1 ਉਡੀਕੇ. The subjunctive form is used to convey the impression of a timeless idea or picture.

4 ਲਿਪਟੀ. The perfective form is used as an adjective to show the continuing effect of a past happening. ਲਿਪਟੀ ਹੋਈ ਗਰਦ 'Dust already clinging' would also have been grammatically correct but would have lengthened the line too much.

5 ਗੁਆਚਾ . Here another perfective form is used as an adjective for the same effect.

Final remarks

Learning a second language, for an adult learner, is quite a strenuous but enjoyable task. If you have been able to understand and enjoy the passages given above, you have used this course well. If you had problems, go back to the earlier units, especially Conversation unit 9. Try to do some more hard work, learn the vocabulary and rules of grammar and do the exercises again.

Also learn how to use *independently* the Word groups section and the Important Panjabi verbs section at the end of the Grammatical summary. These sections should be referred to again and again until you have understood and mastered all the rules and forms of nouns, pronouns and verbs given there. *Above all, learn to think like speakers of Panjabi.*

In the learning process, there comes a stage when the learner has to wean herself or himself off the learning aids devised by others, become an explorer and take charge of her or his own learning. Have you reached that stage?

Best of luck!

ਪਹਿਲਾ ਪਾਠ – ਪੜ੍ਹਾਈ ਲਿਖਾਈ
Script unit 1

We have already pointed out that the symbol for the Panjabi short **a** is invisible. It is wrong to say that this vowel 'has no symbol'. You will realise the significance of this distinction later on. For the present, remember that a Panjabi consonant letter by itself (i.e. without the addition of any visible vowel symbol) may stand for the consonant sound only or for the sound combination consonant + **a**. For example, the consonant letter ਕ can stand for either **k** or **ka**, that is, **k** + **a**. Since a word in Panjabi must have at least one vowel sound, the combination ਕਰ could be pronounced either as **kara** or as **kar**. But a short vowel does not occur at the end of a word in Panjabi (except a few grammatical words). So the only possible pronunciation of ਕਰ is **kar**.

Here we would emphasise once again what we have already said. Never omit the **r** sound in the pronunciation of a Panjabi word if you find it in spelling. ਕਰ is pronounced as **kar**, and not as **ka**, which does not mean anything in Panjabi. It is going to be quite difficult initially to control the English pronunciation habit, but you will have to do it if you wish to speak intelligible Panjabi. If you speak a variety of English in which **r** is pronounced in all the positions (the Scottish variety, for example), then, of course, you will have no problem.

At this stage, you do not have to learn the meanings of the Panjabi words used below, (though you can certainly do this if you want to).

Look at the following combinations carefully and try to read them aloud first before listening to the recordings. You may need to refer to the chart on page 9.

ਕ	+	ਰ	=	ਕਰ		
ka	+	**r**	=	**kar**	do	
ਰ	+	ਸ	=	ਰਸ		
ra	+	**s**	=	**ras**	juice	

ਪ	+	ਰ	=	ਪਰ	
pa	+	r	=	**par**	but

ਲ	+	ੜ	=	ਲੜ	
la	+	ṛ	=	**laṛ**	fight

ਵ	+	ਸ	=	ਵਸ	
va	+	s	=	**vas**	dwell

Combinations of three or more consonant letters should present no problem.

ਸੜਕ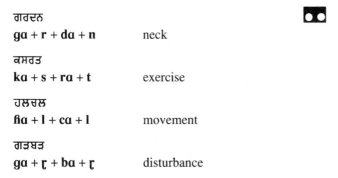
sa + ṛa + k   road

ਗਰਜ
ga + ra + j   thunder

ਸਬਕ
sa + ba + k   lesson

ਚਰਨ
ca + ra + n   holy feet

ਛਤਰ
cʰa + ta + r   canopy

When there is a combination of four consonant letters without any visible vowel symbol, some speakers pronounce the second consonant without **a**. But you may or may not use **a** with the second consonant. For example, you may pronounce ਕਸਰਤ either as **kasrat** or as **kasarat**. Either way, your pronunciation would be acceptable.

ਗਰਦਨ
ga + r + da + n   neck

ਕਸਰਤ
ka + s + ra + t   exercise

ਹਲਚਲ
ɦa + l + ca + l   movement

ਗੜਬੜ
ga + ṛ + ba + ṛ   disturbance

Practice exercise

1 Read aloud the following Panjabi words. (You may use the chart on page 9, but try to read them without transcribing them into the phonetic script.) 📼

ਬਣ   ਛੜ   ਮਰ   ਖ਼ਰਚ   ਫ਼ਰਕ   ਜਨਕ   ਬਰਛ

2 Write the following in Panjabi script.

cʰak, bak, cal, bas, vasaṇ, karan, yarak, jakaṛ, xarc, fasal, ʃarbat, barkat, sardal, pargaṭ, sarvaṇ

ਦੂਸਰਾ ਪਾਠ – ਪੜ੍ਹਾਈ ਲਿਖਾਈ
Script unit 2

In Script unit 1, you learnt how to combine consonant symbols and the invisible symbol for short **a**.

Now let us take up three more vowel symbols (visible ones, this time!)

'	long	**aː**
f	short	**i**
ੀ	long	**iː**

' and ੀ are put after the letter and f is put before the letter.

s + aː	s + iː	s + i
ਸ + '	ਸ + ੀ	f + ਸ
ਸਾ	ਸੀ	ਸਿ

Remember that the symbol for the short **a** is invisible.

Now look at the following examples.

sa + faː	xaː + s	kaː + r
ਸ + ੜਾ	ਖ਼ + ਸ	ਕਾ + ਰ
ਸੜਾ	ਖ਼ਾਸ	ਕਾਰ
page	special	car, work

bʱa + raː		caː + da + r	
ਭ + ਰਾ		ਚਾ + ਦ + ਰ	
ਭਰਾ		ਚਾਦਰ	
brother		sheet	

ma + saː + laː	ka + maː + l
ਮ + ਸਾ + ਲਾ	ਕ + ਮਾ + ਲ
ਮਸਾਲਾ	ਕਮਾਲ
spice	wonder

ka +	ɽa: +	ɦi:		ki: +	ma +	t
ਕ +	ੜਾ +	ਹੀ		ਕੀ +	ਮ +	ਤ
	ਕੜਾਹੀ				ਕੀਮਤ	
	pan				price	

si +	pa: +	ɦi:		bi +	j +	li:
ਸਿ +	ਪਾ +	ਹੀ		ਬਿ +	ਜ +	ਲੀ
	ਸਿਪਾਹੀ				ਬਿਜਲੀ	
	soldier				electricity	

You do not have to learn the meanings of these words at this stage (but you can, if you wish to).

Practice exercises

1 Read aloud the following Panjabi words. (You may refer to the Introduction, but try to resist the temptation to transcribe them.)

ਸਿਹਾਰੀ	ਬਿਹਾਰੀ	ਮਿਸ਼ਰੀ	ਸ਼ਰਾਰਤ	ਕਿਰਪਾਨ	ਸਰਦੀ
ਦਰਜ਼ੀ	ਦਿਮਾਗ਼	ਗ਼ਰੀਬੀ	ਸਾਬਤ	ਛਾਣ	ਠਾਕਰ
ਡਾਕਟਰ	ਬਾਲੀ	ਬਾਲਣ	ਮਾਸਟਰਨੀ	ਲਾਲਚੀ	ਹਾਥੀ

2 Write the following in the Panjabi script. The first group consists of some Indian names.

sarvaṇ ra:m	ɦaki:m sarda:ri: la:l ʃarma:	biɦa:ri:
		la:l varma:
caran da:s	kiran ba:la: mistri:	lata: miʃra:
jamna: da:s	paramji:t sabʰarva:l	kamla: ra:ɳi:

ca:rdi:va:ri:	ba:zi:gar	sargʰi:	sa:kʰi:
ciɽi:	gʰis	karvaṭ	ma:jʰa:
dʰa:sṇa:	dʰa:ga:	sa:ra:	karva:
pita:	ma:ta:		

You have already done four of the ten vowel symbols of the Panjabi script. Here are the remaining six:

˘	˵	ˋ	ˮ
short **u**	long **u:**	**e**	**ɛ**	**o**	**ɔ**

These symbols are used either above or beneath the letters, as shown below:

ਸੁ	ਸੂ	ਸੇ	ਸੈ	ਸੋ	ਸੌ
su	su:	se	sɛ	so	sɔ

Study the following examples carefully.

s	+	u	+	kʰ			
ਸੁ			+	ਖ	=	ਸੁਖ	comfort

s	+	u:	+	r			
ਸੂ			+	ਰ	=	ਸੂਰ	pig

s	+	e	+	k			
ਸੇ			+	ਕ	=	ਸੇਕ	heat

s	+	ɛ	+	r			
ਸੈ			+	ਰ	=	ਸੈਰ	stroll

s	+	o	+	ʈ	+	i:		
ਸੋ			+	ਟੀ			=	ਸੋਟੀ stick

s	+	ɔ			
ਸੌ			=	ਸੌ	hundred

We have not yet dealt with the vowel bearers ੳ, ਅ, ੲ and symbols like ˚,
ˆ, ˇ, but if you have successfully learnt what has been done so far, you
should be able to read and write many of the sentences used in the
dialogues in the conversation units. Look at

namaste	varma:	sa:ɦab,	ki:	ɦa:l	ɦɛ?
ਨਮਸਤੇ	ਵਰਮਾ	ਸਾਹਬ ,	ਕੀ	ਹਾਲ	ਹੈ?

tʰi:k	ɦɛ	ji:
ਠੀਕ	ਹੈ	ਜੀ ।

tuɦa:ɖa: ki: ɦa:l ɦɛ, ɖa:kʈar sa:ɦab?
ਤੁਹਾਡਾ ਕੀ ਹਾਲ ਹੈ, ਡਾਕਟਰ ਸਾਹਬ?

va:ɦiguru: di: kirpa: ɦɛ.
ਵਾਹਿਗੁਰੂ ਦੀ ਕਿਰਪਾ ਹੈ ।

3 Try to read and understand the following passage. (By now, you should
be able to carry on without the help of the chart on page 9, but you can use
it if you get confused.)

ਮੇਰਾ ਘਰ ਮਾਨਚੈਸਟਰ ਵਿਚ ਹੈ, ਯੂਨੀਵਰਸਿਟੀ ਦੇ ਕੋਲ, ਵਿਮਜ਼ਲੋ ਰੋਡ ਤੇ। ਮੇਰੇ ਘਰ ਦੇ ਵਿਚ ਚਾਰ ਕਮਰੇ ਹਨ। ਗਾਰਡਨ ਅਤੇ ਗੈਰਿਜ ਵੀ ਹੈ। ਮੇਰੇ ਘਰ ਦੇ ਕੋਲ ਪਾਰਕ ਹੈ। ਮੇਰੇ ਕੋਲ ਫੋਰਡ ਕੋਰਟੀਨਾ ਕਾਰ ਹੈ, ਪਰ ਮੇਰੇ ਛੋਟੇ ਭਰਾ ਕੋਲ ਮਰਸੀਡੀਜ਼ ਹੈ। ਮੇਰਾ ਭਰਾ ਗਲਾਸਗੋ ਵਿਚ ਬਿਜ਼ਨੈਸਮੈਨ ਹੈ। ਮੇਰੀ ਛੋਟੀ ਭੈਣ ਪਾਰਕ ਹਾਸਪੀਟਲ ਵਿਚ ਨਰਸ ਹੈ।

Can you identify English words (other than names) used in this passage?

4 Read aloud the following sentences. Then check your pronunciation against the recording if you have it.

(a) ਮੇਰੇ ਘਰ ਵਿਚ ਦੋ ਕਮਰੇ ਹਨ।
ਮੇਰੇ ਕਮਰੇ ਵਿਚ ਖਿੜਕੀ ਦੇ ਸਾਹਮਣੇ ਮੇਰੀ ਬੁਕ-ਸ਼ੈਲਫ਼ ਹੈ।
ਮੇਜ਼ ਕੁਰਸੀ ਵੀ ਹਨ।
ਬਾਥਰੂਮ ਨੇੜੇ ਹੀ ਹੈ।
ਬਾਥ ਦੇ ਵਿਚ ਸ਼ਾਵਰ ਵੀ ਹੈ।

(b) ਮੇਰੀ ਕਿਤਾਬ ਮੇਜ਼ ਤੇ ਰਖੋ, ਤੇ ਮੇਜ਼ ਕੁਰਸੀ ਬੂਹੇ ਦੇ ਨੇੜੇ ਰਖੋ।
ਤੁਹਾਡੀ ਕਿਤਾਬ ਮੇਰੇ ਕੋਲ ਹੈ।
ਮੇਰਾ ਕਾਲਾ ਪੈੱਨ ਵੀ ਤੁਹਾਡੇ ਕੋਲ ਹੈ।
ਮੇਰੇ ਕੋਲ ਤੁਹਾਡਾ ਲਾਲ ਪੈੱਨ ਹੈ।

5 Answer the following questions in Panjabi, orally as well as in writing, using the Panjabi script. You have not yet learnt all the symbols of the Panjabi script. You may give imaginary answers.

(a) ਨਮਸਤੇ ਜੀ, ਕੀ ਹਾਲ ਹੈ?
(b) ਤੁਹਾਡਾ ਘਰ ਕਿਥੇ ਹੈ?
(c) ਬਸ ਸਟੇਸ਼ਨ ਕਿਥੇ ਹੈ?
(d) ਖਿੜਕੀ ਦੇ ਸਾਹਮਣੇ ਕੀ ਹੈ?
(e) ਮੇਰਾ ਕਾਲਾ ਪੈੱਨ ਕਿਥੇ ਹੈ?
(f) ਤੁਹਾਡੀ ਜੇਬ ਵਿਚ ਕੀ ਹੈ?

ਤੀਸਰਾ ਪਾਠ – ਪੜ੍ਹਾਈ ਲਿਖਾਈ
Script unit 3

So far, you have been learning the individual letters and symbols of the Panjabi script and some very basic principles of combining them. If you have learnt to distinguish all these individual letters and symbols, you should now be ready to learn the underlying system. This system is based on some principles, which are applied in the order given below:

(1) CV sequences
(2) Nasalised vowels
(3) Homorganic nasals
(4) Long consonants

Do not be daunted by these names! These concepts and categories are really quite simple to use, and they simplify your learning process. You will also find that the Panjabi writing system is extremely ingenious and logical.

CV Sequences

C means a consonant sound and V means a vowel sound. Start dividing a Panjabi word into Cs and Vs and grouping the sounds into CV sequences, starting from the left. An example is

amarji:t

a	m	a	r	j	i:	t
V	C	V	C	C	V	C
V	CV		C	CV		C

It is notable that a V at the beginning must stand alone. If there are two or more adjacent consonants, the furthest right goes with a V and the others stand alone. If there is a C at the end of a word, it also stands alone.

In the Panjabi script,

(a) A CV sequence is represented by a consonant letter plus a vowel symbol;

(b) A lone C is represented by a consonant letter;

(c) A lone V sound is represented by a vowel bearer plus a vowel symbol.

If you have forgotten what a vowel bearer is, have a look at the table on page 9. Remember that the symbol for short **a** is invisible. Of course, this invisible symbol must be added to a vowel bearer if need arises.

But before you start assigning letters and symbols to the Cs and the Vs, keep in mind the other principles given below.

Nasalised vowels

In Panjabi script a nasalised vowel is represented by the addition of one of the following symbols:

or

(called Tippi **ṭippi:**) (called Bindi **bindi:**)

In some Panjabi grammar books you will find a list of rules determining which of the two to choose. But there is only one simple rule: always use Bindi with

θ

and Tippi everywhere else.

Homorganic nasals

Homorganic means 'produced by the same speech organs'. It was already pointed out that within the Consonant square on page 9, all the consonants in a group are homorganic. For example, **t**, **t^h**, **d**, **d^ɦ** and **n** are homorganic because they are all produced by the same organs – the tip of the tongue touching the teeth. Similarly, **k**, **k^h**, **g**, **g^ɦ** and **ŋ** are also homorganic. For the production of all these five consonants, the back of the tongue touches the soft palate. The front of the tongue touches the hard palate for the five homorganic consonants **c**, **c^h**, **j**, **j^ɦ** and **ɲ**. In each of the five groups in the Consonant square, there is a nasal consonant. Thus, we have five nasal consonants in Panjabi – **ŋ**, **ɲ**, **ɳ**, **n** and **m**.

Clusters involving a nasal and a homorganic non-nasal or oral consonant are probably found in all languages, including English and Panjabi. In English, the nasal consonant sound immediately before **k** in the word 'sink' [**siŋk**] is homorganic to the oral consonant **k**. Like **k**, this **ŋ** is pronounced by touching the soft palate with the back of the tongue. Similarly, the nasal consonant in the word 'Ninja' [**niɲjɑ**] is homorganic to the oral consonant **j**. Both are produced by touching the hard palate with the front part of the tongue.

Since **ŋ** and **ɲ** in Panjabi nearly always occur in such clusters as nasal sounds homorganic to the following non-nasal or oral consonants, and rarely as independent nasal consonants (as **ɳ, n** and **m** can in words like **nakk, kamm, pa:ɳi** respectively), the use of the phonetic symbols **ŋ** and **ɲ** has been unnecessary. We have used **n** where **ŋ** and **ɲ** could have been used. But if you pronounce words fluently and effortlessly, you will always pronounce, for example, the word **manja:** as [**maɲja:**]. In anticipation of the **j** sound, the front part of your tongue will go the hard palate, and pronounce the nasal consonant preceding **j** as **ɲ**, even though it is transcribed as **n**. After all, you most probably do pronounce 'sink' as [**siŋk**]. In anticipation of **k**, the back of the tongue goes to the soft palate and you pronounce the letter 'n' as **ŋ** in the process.

In Panjabi script, a homorganic nasal consonant is represented by a Tippi or a Bindi.

Since **ŋ** and **ɲ** almost always occur only as homorganic nasals in the types of clusters mentioned above, and almost never as independent sounds, they are nearly always represented by a Tippi or a Bindi. This means that you may never in your life use the letters ਙ and ਞ. (The author of this book learnt them at the primary school but has not used them since 1950!)

Long consonants

A long (or double) consonant is one which is prolonged. They are not commonly found in English. If you listen to the following words recorded on the cassette, you will understand what a long consonant is. We transcribe it with two letters. It is important to pronounce a long consonant carefully. Now listen to the following words

gada:	mace	**gadda:**	cushion
kala:	art	**kalla:**	lonely
pata:	address	**patta:**	leaf
pati:	husband	**patti:**	small leaf, tea leaves
rasa:	juice	**rassa:**	rope

In short, if a long consonant is not long in your speech, you can be misunderstood.

In our transcription, a long aspirated consonant has only one ^{ɦ} or ^{h}. For example, the long t^h consonant in

patt^{h}ar stone

is transcribed as **tt^h** and not as **t^{h}t^h**, which not only looks odd but is also technically wrong, because the strong breath symbolised by ^{h} comes out only at the end of the comparatively longer 'hold' phase of the consonant.

In Panjabi script, the length of a long consonant (other than that of a nasal) is represented by the symbol

ˇ

(called Addhak)

The word 'Addhak' means 'excessive' . The name explains itself.

In the case of a long nasal consonant, the first half is regarded as a homorganic nasal to the second half and is therefore represented by a Tippi or a Bindi.

Now let us write a few words in Panjabi script. We start with the word we have broken up before into CV sequences.

amarji:t

a	m	a	r	j	i:	t
V	C	V	C	C	V	C

V	CV		CV	C		C

Keeping in mind that the symbol for short **a** in invisible, we can write this word as

a	ma	r	ji:	t
V	CV	C	CV	C
ਅ	ਮ	ਰ	ਜੀ	ਤ

ਅਮਰਜੀਤ

Remember that in this word ਮ is **m** plus the invisible **a**, but ਰ and ਤ are lone consonants without any vowel. The symbol for the initial **a** vowel is invisible, but it must be added to a vowel bearer letter, in this case ਅ.

Use of the vowel bearers

As you know, Panjabi has ten distinct vowel sounds but only three vowel bearer letters. So the vowel symbols are added to the vowel bearer letters as follows:

u	*is added to*	ੳ	*as*	ਉ	ਉਮਰ	**umar**	age
uː	*is added to*	ੳ	*as*	ਊ	ਊਠ	**uːʈʰ**	camel
o	*is added to*	ੳ	*as*	ਓ	ਓਮ	**om**	a name
a	*is added to*	ਅ	*as*	ਅ	ਅਸਲੀ	**asliː**	real
aː	*is added to*	ਅ	*as*	ਆ	ਆਰਾਮ	**aːraːm**	rest
ɛ	*is added to*	ਅ	*as*	ਐ	ਐਸ਼	**ɛʃ**	luxury
ɔ	*is added to*	ਅ	*as*	ਔ	ਔਰਤ	**ɔrat**	woman
i	*is added to*	ੲ	*as*	ਇ	ਇਮਲੀ	**imliː**	tamarind
iː	*is added to*	ੲ	*as*	ਈ	ਈਰਖਾ	**iːrkʰaː**	jealousy
e	*is added to*	ੲ	*as*	ਏ	ਏਕਾ	**ekaː**	unity

You have to be careful about ੳ. ੳ plus ˘ is ੳ, because of the typographical problem of combining the two symbols.

Clearly, you cannot just add any vowel symbol to any vowel bearer letter. If you are interested in why a particular vowel symbol goes with a particular vowel bearer, you have to know how the Panjabi vowels are pronounced. Panjabi vowels can be divided into the following categories.

		Front		Back	
		iː / ਈ			uː / ਊ
High			i / ਇ	u / ਉ	
		e / ਏ			o / ਓ
			a / ਅ		
Low		ɛ / ਐ	aː / ਆ		ɔ / ਔ

The table shows which part of the tongue (front or back) is raised to what height for the production of each Panjabi vowel. Pronounce these vowels one by one and also feel the position of the tongue for each of them. Now you can easily see that symbols for all the high front vowels go with ੲ, those for the high back vowels go with ੳ, and those for the low vowels (irrespective of their front or back position) go with ਅ. Do not forget that the symbol for the short **a** is invisible.

Examples

Study the following examples carefully.

juɑːiː

j	u	ɑː	iː
C	V	V	V

CV	V	V	
ਜੁ	ਆ	ਈ	= ਜੁਆਈ son-in-law

umɑr

u	m	ɑ	r
V	C	V	C

V	CV	C	
ੳੁ	ਮ	ਰ	= ੳੁਮਰ age

kɛ̃ciː

k	ɛ̃	c	iː
C	V (Nasalised V)	C	V

C	V	C	V
ਕ	ੈਂ	ਚ	ੀ
CV		CV	
ਕੈਂ		ਚੀ	= ਕੈਂਚੀ scissors

gũːd

g	ũː	d
C	V (Nasalised V)	C

C	V	C
ਗ	ੂਂ	ਦ
CV		C
ਗੂੰ		ਦ = ਗੂੰਦ glue

kutta:

k	u	tt	ɑ:
C	V	C	V
		(Long C)	

C	V	C	V
ਕ	ੁ	ੱਤ	ਾ
CV		CV	
ਕੁ		ੱਤਾ	= ਕੁੱਤਾ dog

A long consonant is represented by an Addhak placed before it (on the preceding letter). But a long nasal consonant is represented by a Tippi or a Bindi.

kamm

k	ɑ	mm
C	V	C
		(Long nasal C)

CV	C
ਕ	ਂਮ = ਕੰਮ work

unn

u	nn
V	C
	(Long nasal C)

V	C
ਉ	ਂਨ = ਉੱਨ wool

You generally use a Tippi ˚ with ੁ, the symbol for the short vowel sound **u**. But only the Bindi ਂ that can be used with the vowel bearer letter ੳ.

manja:

m	ɑ	n	j	ɑ:
C	V	C	C	V
		(Homorganic nasal C)		

CV	C	CV
ਮ	ਂ	ਜਾ
CV	CCV	
ਮ	ਂਜਾ	= ਮੰਜਾ cot

ungali:

u	n	g	a	l	i:
C	C	C	V	C	V
	(Homorganic nasal C)				

V	C	C	V	C	V
ਉ	ੰ	ਗ		ਲ	ੀ
V	CCV			CV	
ਉ	ੰਗ			ਲੀ	= ਉੰਗਲੀ	finger

You will not find any Panjabi word without a vowel sound (except a weak or reduced form like **c** 'in'), but there are many words in Panjabi which consist of vowel sounds only and have no consonant sound. An example is

a:ia:

a:	i	a:
V	V	V
ਆ	ਇ	ਆ	= ਆਇਆ	He came.

Reading and listening practice

Now you should be able to read the following dialogues from Conversation unit 4. First compare the following text with its phonetic transcription. Then try to read these dialogues slowly and aloud. If you have the cassette recording, rewind and listen to it a few times while silently reading the dialogues in the Panjabi script.

ਅਵਤਾਰ:	ਅੱਛਾ ਸ਼ਰਮਾ ਜੀ, ਸਾਨੂੰ ਇਹ ਦੱਸੋ ਕਿ ਤੁਹਾਡੇ ਕੀ ਕੀ ਸ਼ੌਕ ਨੇ? ਸੰਗੀਤ ਤੋਂ ਇਲਾਵਾ।
ਪ੍ਰੇਮ:	ਮਾਹਲ ਸਾਹਬ, ਸੰਗੀਤ ਮੇਰਾ ਸ਼ੌਕ ਨਹੀਂ, ਕੰਮ ਹੈ, ਕਾਰੋਬਾਰ ਹੈ। ਵੈਸੇ, ਮੇਰੇ ਕਈ ਸ਼ੌਕ ਹੈਨ। ਮੈਨੂੰ ਪੜ੍ਹਨ ਦਾ ਸ਼ੌਕ ਹੈ, ਕਵਿਤਾ 'ਤੇ ਗੀਤ ਲਿਖਣ ਦਾ ਸ਼ੌਕ ਹੈ, ਖਾਣਾ ਪਕਾਉਣ ਦਾ ਸ਼ੌਕ ਹੈ।
ਅਵਤਾਰ:	ਖਾਣਾ ਪਕਾਉਣ ਦਾ?
ਪ੍ਰੇਮ:	ਹਾਂ ਜੀ।
ਅਵਤਾਰ:	ਫੇਰ ਤਾਂ ਤੁਹਾਡੀ ਪਤਨੀ ਬੜੀ ਖ਼ੁਸ਼ਕਿਸਮਤ ਹੈ।
ਪ੍ਰੇਮ:	ਇਹ ਮੈਨੂੰ ਪਤਾ ਨਹੀਂ। ਉਹਨੂੰ ਮੇਰਾ ਖਾਣਾ ਬਹੁਤ ਪਸੰਦ ਹੈ, ਮੇਰਾ ਸੰਗੀਤ ਬਿਲਕੁਲ ਪਸੰਦ ਨਹੀਂ।
ਅਵਤਾਰ:	ਕੀ ਤੁਹਾਡੇ ਧੀਆਂ ਪੁੱਤਰਾਂ ਨੂੰ ਤੁਹਾਡਾ ਸੰਗੀਤ ਪਸੰਦ ਹੈ?
ਪ੍ਰੇਮ:	ਧੀਆਂ ਨੂੰ ਹੈ, ਪੁੱਤਰਾਂ ਨੂੰ ਨਹੀਂ।

ਸਤਵੰਤ:	ਵੀਰ ਜੀ, ਐਹ ਲਓ, ਅਵਤਾਰ ਜੀ ਦੀ ਖ਼ਾਸ ਪਸੰਦ ।
ਪ੍ਰੇਮ:	ਇਹ ਕੀ ਹੈ, ਭਾਬੀ ਜੀ?
ਸਤਵੰਤ:	ਚਿਕਿਨ ਬਿਰਿਆਨੀ ।
ਪ੍ਰੇਮ:	ਨਹੀਂ ਜੀ, ਸ਼ੁਕਰੀਆ । ਮੈਂ ਵੈਜੀਟੇਰੀਅਨ ਹਾਂ ।
ਅਵਤਾਰ:	ਸਤਵੰਤ, ਇਹ ਬੰਦਾ ਸਾਧੂ ਹੈ । ਮੀਟ ਨਹੀਂ ਖਾਂਦਾ, ਸ਼ਰਾਬ ਨਹੀਂ ਪੀਂਦਾ, ਸਿਗਰਿਟ ਨਹੀਂ ਪੀਂਦਾ।
ਸਤਵੰਤ:	ਬਹੁਤ ਚੰਗੀ ਗੱਲ ਹੈ ।
ਅਵਤਾਰ:	ਹੈਂ? ਸਾਧੂ ਹੋਣਾ ਚੰਗੀ ਗੱਲ ਹੈ?
ਸਤਵੰਤ:	ਸਿਗਰਿਟ ਨਾ ਪੀਣਾ ਚੰਗੀ ਗੱਲ ਹੈ । ਬਹੁਤਾ ਨਾ ਬੋਲਣਾ ਵੀ ਚੰਗੀ ਗੱਲ ਹੈ । ਮੂੰਹ ਨੂੰ ਖਾਣਾ ਖਾਣ ਲਈ ਜ਼ਿਆਦਾ ਵਰਤੋ, 'ਤੇ ਬੋਲਣ ਲਈ ਘੱਟ ।

ਚੌਥਾ ਪਾਠ – ਪੜ੍ਹਾਈ ਲਿਖਾਈ
Script unit 4

We have covered all the letters and symbols of the Panjabi script except the following subscript symbols (which are put beneath the letters, or literally 'in the foot of a letter', as speakers of Panjabi say).

੍   ੍   ੍

Of the three symbols ੍ is very commonly used. The other two are going out of fashion and their use is debatable among Panjabi scholars.

Subscript ੍

This symbol is a variant of the letter ਹ but is not pronounced as **ɦ** or **ʰ**. In old Panjabi, it used to represent breathy voice after some voiced sounds (nasal consonants, **r**, **l**, **v** and **ɽ**). For example

ਨ੍ਹ	was pronounced as	**nɦ** or **nʰ**
ਰ੍ਹ	was pronounced as	**rɦ** or **rʰ**
ਲ੍ਹ	was pronounced as	**lɦ** or **lʰ**
ਵ੍ਹ	was pronounced as	**vɦ** or **vʰ**
ੜ੍ਹ	was pronounced as	**ɽɦ** or **ɽʰ**

and so on. This pronunciation has been preserved in some Western Panjabi dialects. But most modern speakers of Panjabi do not pronounce this symbol but use a tone in the word having this symbol. Mostly, it is the high tone, as in

ਵੜ੍ਹਾ	**varʰaː**	[váraː]
ਕੜ੍ਹੀ	**kaɽʰiː**	[káɽiː]
ਬੰਨ੍ਹ	**bannʰ**	[bánn]

You will learn in the next script unit that this symbol can also give the low tone to some words. But the rule of pronunciation for the time being is: Do not pronounce the ੍ symbol and give the word a high tone. In our transcription, we have already marked the high tone in such words.

Subscript ੍ਰ

When the second consonant in a CCV sequence is **r**, this **r** is written as ੍ਰ in the Panjabi script.

Examples:

prem

p	r	e	m
C	C	V	m

CCV	m
ਪ੍ਰੇ	ਮ	= ਪ੍ਰੇਮ love, a name

kriʃan

k	r	i	ʃ	ɑ	n
C	C	V	C	V	C

CCV	CV	C
ਕ੍ਰਿ	ਸ਼	ਨ	= ਕ੍ਰਿਸ਼ਨ a name

pri:tam

p	r	i:	t	ɑ	m
C	C	V	C	V	C

CCV	CV	M
ਪ੍ਰੀ	ਤ	ਮ	= ਪ੍ਰੀਤਮ sweetheart, a name

But many writers have started using the full ਰ in most such words and use the subscript ੍ਰ in names only and in a few 'learned words' which you do not need at this stage. The Sikh greeting **sat sri: ɑkɑ:l**, is written as ਸਤਿ ਸ੍ਰੀ ਅਕਾਲ. The first word of this greeting has an older spelling. But it is now pronounced as **sat**, and not as **sati**.

Subscript ੍ਵ

The use of this symbol is also going out of fashion. But some old-fashioned writers are still using it. It is used exactly like the subscript ੍ਰ i.e. when the second consonant in a CCV sequence is **v**. Examples:

svar

s	v	ɑ	r
C	C	V	C

CCV	C			
ਸ੍	ਰ	=	ਸੁਰ	sound, vowel

svɛ-ji:vani:

s	v	ɛ	–	j	i:	v	ɑ	n	i:
C	C	V		C	V	C	V	C	V

CCV	–	CV	CV	CV
ਸ੍ਵੈ		ਜੀ	ਵ	ਨੀ

ਸ੍ਵੈ	–	ਜੀਵਨੀ
self	–	biography (i.e. autobiography)

ਸੁਰ has retained its old spelling. But everywhere else, most writers have started using a full ਵ. The most common modern spelling of **svɛ-ji:vani:** is ਸਵੈ-ਜੀਵਨੀ.

We have dealt with all the major rules of Panjabi spelling. But you must by now be fully aware of the fact that modern Panjabi spelling represents older pronunciation, which has changed in three important ways in the dialect of Panjabi used in this course.

(1) Some consonant letters (i.e. ਘ, ਝ, ਢ, ਧ and ਭ) do not have any pronunciation of their own. In some positions, they are pronounced as ਕ, ਚ, ਟ, ਤ and ਪ respectively, and in other positions they are pronounced as ਗ, ਜ, ਡ, ਦ and ਬ respectively. Full ਹ is pronounced in some positions but not in others, while the subscript ੍ is not pronounced at all.

(2) Some words having the letter ਹ and symbol for the short **i** (ਿ) or short **u** (ੁ) are pronounced without any **ĥ** sound but with a vowel other than the one shown in spelling.

(3) Nearly all the words in which these letters occur have either of the two tones, low or high.

There are definite rules governing all this. It is always possible to predict pronunciation from spelling. But the converse (predicting spelling from pronunciation) is not always possible.

In Script unit 5, these rules are very briefly described and explained. But a note of warning is due here: these rules are quite technical. So study Script unit 5 only if you are a very dedicated student of the Panjabi script or you are a linguist. The best advice for the rest of you is: when you come across a word whose pronunciation is given within square brackets, e.g. **sáĥura: [sóra:]** ਸਹੁਰਾ 'father-in-law', learn both its pronunciation and its spelling in the Panjabi script. The phonetic transcription is, as has been pointed out time and again, a symbol-for-symbol representation of Panjabi spelling, but with the addition of a tone mark if a tone is there.

Practice exercises

1 Read this restaurant menu and answer the questions which follow:

ਸ਼ੇਰੇ-ਪੰਜਾਬ ਰੈਸਟੋਰੈਂਟ
ਰੇਲਵੇ ਰੋੜ, ਬੈਗਾ

30.7.1994

ਚਿਕਿਨ ਬਿਰਿਆਨੀ	17.50
ਤੰਦੂਰੀ ਚਿਕਿਨ	13.50
ਲੈਮ ਕਬਾਬ	16.50
ਲੈਮ ਰੋਗਨ ਜੋਸ਼	18.50
ਲੈਮ ਕੋਫ਼ਤਾ	14.50
ਚਿਕਿਨ ਭੁਨਾ	14.50
ਪਾਲਕ ਪਨੀਰ	10.50
ਸ਼ਾਹੀ ਪਨੀਰ	12.50
ਪਨੀਰ ਕੋਫ਼ਤਾ	11.50
ਬੈਂਗਣ ਭੜਥਾ	8.50
ਭਿੰਡੀ	7.50

(a) Write down the name and address of the restaurant.
(b) How many vegetarian and how many non-vegetarian dishes are on offer? (**pani:r**, though made from milk, is regarded as vegetarian).
(c) Make a list of the chicken dishes, putting the highest-priced one at the top and the lowest-priced one at the bottom.
(d) Do the same with the lamb dishes.
(e) There are two kofta dishes on the menu. Are they vegetarian or non-vegetarian?
(f) Which of the Panjabi tones is used in the names of the dishes containing aubergine and okra? (You may phonetically transcribe the names.)

2 The astrologer Pandit Sukhchain Lal Prashar believes that certain foods are good or bad for people having a particular zodiac sign (ਰਾਸ਼ੀ). He has recently published the following chart showing what is good (ਚੰਗਾ) and what is bad (ਮਾੜਾ) for each sign.

Even if you do not seriously believe in astrology (ਜੋਤਸ਼), let's combine some innocent fun with reading practice. (The astrologer (ਜੋਤਸ਼ੀ) and the chart are imaginary. So do not take them seriously.)

(a) Find out your own and your partner's or friend's birth signs (ਜਨਮ ਰਾਸ਼ੀ). What are these signs called in English? (Use a newspaper or a magazine to find the English names of the signs.)

(b) Make (in English) a list of the foods which, according to the astrologer, are good and bad for you and your partner or friend. What are the foods you both can have and the foods you both should avoid?

(c) The astrologer seems to have such a strong dislike for one particular food that he thinks that it is bad for everybody. Can you find out what this food is?

(d) By mistake, the astrologer declares one particular food as both good and bad for a particular sign. Can you find out the name of the food and the name of the sign?

੧ **ਮੇਖ** 21ਮਾਰਚ ਤੋਂ 20 ਅਪ੍ਰੈਲ	**ਚੰਗਾ:** ਪਨੀਰ, ਦੁੱਧ, ਮਟਰ, ਸੰਤਰਾ, ਖ਼ਰਬੂਜ਼ਾ, ਭਿੰਡੀ, ਖੀਰਾ, ਟਮਾਟਰ **ਮਾੜਾ:** ਨਾਖ, ਚੌਲ, ਅੰਬ, ਬੈਂਗਣ, ਛੋਲੇ, ਆਲੂ, ਸੇਬ, ਮਿਰਚ, ਆਂਡਾ, ਚਾਹ
੨ **ਬ੍ਰਿਖ** 21ਅਪ੍ਰੈਲ ਤੋਂ 21 ਮਈ	**ਚੰਗਾ:** ਨਿੰਬੂ, ਕੇਲਾ, ਚੌਲ, ਆਲੂ, ਆਤੂ, ਛੋਲੇ, ਮੂਲੀ, ਪੁਦਨਾ, ਧਨੀਆ **ਮਾੜਾ:** ਲਸਣ, ਪਾਲਕ, ਪਨੀਰ, ਗਾਜਰ, ਭਿੰਡੀ, ਬੈਂਗਣ, ਸੇਬ, ਮਸਰ
II **ਮਿਥੁਨ** 22 ਮਈ ਤੋਂ 21 ਜੂਨ	**ਚੰਗਾ:** ਦਹੀਂ, ਪਨੀਰ, ਹਦਵਾਣਾ, ਅੰਬ, ਮਿਰਚ, ਅੰਗੂਰ, ਜੀਰਾ, ਇਮਲੀ **ਮਾੜਾ:** ਚੌਲ, ਘਿਓ, ਭਿੰਡੀ, ਟਮਾਟਰ, ਮਟਰ, ਬੈਂਗਣ, ਮੇਥੀ, ਸੰਤਰਾ, ਆਤੂ
੨ **ਕਰਕ** 22 ਜੂਨ ਤੋਂ 22 ਜੁਲਾਈ	**ਚੰਗਾ:** ਲਸਣ, ਇਮਲੀ, ਨਿੰਬੂ, ਸੇਬ, ਕਣਕ, ਪਿਆਜ਼, ਮੂਲੀ, ਗਾਜਰ **ਮਾੜਾ:** ਬੈਂਗਣ, ਮਾਂਹ, ਰਾਜਮਾਂਹ, ਆਲੂ, ਕੇਲਾ, ਆਤੂ, ਪਨੀਰ, ਦਹੀਂ
੨ **ਸਿੰਘ** 23 ਜੁਲਾਈ ਤੋਂ 23 ਅਗਸਤ	**ਚੰਗਾ:** ਮਾਸ, ਆਂਡਾ, ਮੱਖਣ, ਚੌਲ, ਰਾਜਮਾਂਹ, ਮੱਛੀ, ਮੂੰਗਫਲੀ, ਮਸਰ **ਮਾੜਾ:** ਟਮਾਟਰ, ਖੀਰਾ, ਕੱਦੂ, ਦੁੱਧ, ਪਾਲਕ, ਬੈਂਗਣ, ਗੋਭੀ, ਖ਼ਰਬੂਜ਼ਾ
੨ **ਕੰਨਿਆਂ** 24 ਅਗਸਤ ਤੋਂ 22 ਸਤੰਬਰ	**ਚੰਗਾ:** ਮਾਂਹ, ਮੱਕੀ, ਮਿਰਚ, ਅਦਰਕ, ਧਨੀਆ, ਮੇਥੀ, ਹਦਵਾਣਾ, ਆਤੂ **ਮਾੜਾ:** ਰਾਜਮਾਂਹ, ਬੈਂਗਣ, ਅੰਬ, ਦੁੱਧ, ਲਸਣ, ਗੰਢਾ, ਗਾਜਰ, ਆਲੂ
੨ **ਤੁਲਾ** 23 ਸਤੰਬਰ ਤੋਂ 23 ਅਕਤੂਬਰ	**ਚੰਗਾ:** ਸੇਬ, ਛੋਲੇ, ਪਾਲਕ, ਦੁੱਧ, ਪਿਆਜ਼, ਚੌਲ, ਮੂੰਗਫਲੀ, ਮੇਥੀ, ਖ਼ਰਬੂਜ਼ਾ **ਮਾੜਾ:** ਅੰਗੂਰ, ਕੇਲਾ, ਮੇਥੀ, ਤਰ, ਪਾਲਕ, ਬੈਂਗਣ, ਸੇਬ, ਅਦਰਕ, ਮੂਲੀ
੨ **ਬ੍ਰਿਸ਼ਚਕ** 24 ਅਕਤੂਬਰ ਤੋਂ 22 ਨਵੰਬਰ	**ਚੰਗਾ:** ਕੇਲਾ, ਚੌਲ, ਮਸਰ, ਅੰਬ, ਅੰਗੂਰ, ਰਾਜਮਾਂਹ, ਪਾਲਕ, ਮੇਥੀ, ਆਤੂ **ਮਾੜਾ:** ਲਸਣ, ਛੋਲੇ, ਖੀਰਾ, ਮਿਰਚ, ਇਮਲੀ, ਬੈਂਗਣ, ਸੇਬ, ਮੂਲੀ
੨ **ਧਨ** 23 ਨਵੰਬਰ ਤੋਂ 21 ਦਸੰਬਰ	**ਚੰਗਾ:** ਖ਼ਰਬੂਜ਼ਾ, ਅੰਬ, ਕਣਕ, ਤਰ, ਸੰਤਰਾ, ਮੇਥੀ, ਆਤੂ, ਸੇਬ, ਲਸਣ **ਮਾੜਾ:** ਮਾਸ, ਮੱਛੀ, ਰਾਜਮਾਂਹ, ਮਾਂਹ, ਚੌਲ, ਬੈਂਗਣ, ਨਾਖ, ਹਦਵਾਣਾ
੨ **ਮਕਰ** 22 ਦਸੰਬਰ ਤੋਂ 20 ਜਨਵਰੀ	**ਚੰਗਾ:** ਮੱਛੀ, ਚੌਲ, ਟਮਾਟਰ, ਭਿੰਡੀ, ਇਮਲੀ, ਪਨੀਰ, ਆਤੂ, ਦੁੱਧ, ਕੇਲਾ **ਮਾੜਾ:** ਦਹੀਂ, ਅੰਗੂਰ, ਖੀਰਾ, ਅੰਬ, ਬੈਂਗਣ, ਨਿੰਬੂ, ਸੇਬ, ਨਾਸ਼ਪਾਤੀ
੨ **ਕੁੰਭ** 21 ਜਨਵਰੀ ਤੋਂ 18 ਫ਼ਰਵਰੀ	**ਚੰਗਾ:** ਭਿੰਡੀ, ਖੀਰਾ, ਨਿੰਬੂ, ਮੇਥੀ, ਧਨੀਆ, ਕਣਕ, ਕੇਲਾ, ਅਮਰੂਦ, ਅੰਬ **ਮਾੜਾ:** ਚੌਲ, ਦੁੱਧ, ਪਨੀਰ, ਮਸਰ, ਮਾਂਹ, ਪਾਲਕ, ਬੈਂਗਣ, ਸੰਤਰਾ, ਮੱਖਣ
H **ਮੀਨ** 19 ਫ਼ਰਬਰੀ ਤੋਂ 20 ਮਾਰਚ	**ਚੰਗਾ:** ਦੁੱਧ, ਰਾਜਮਾਂਹ, ਚੌਲ, ਕਾਢੀ, ਪਾਲਕ, ਆਲੂ, ਲਸਣ, ਆਂਡਾ **ਮਾੜਾ:** ਬੈਂਗਣ, ਮੇਥੀ, ਗਾਜਰ, ਕੇਲਾ, ਸੇਬ, ਖ਼ਰਬੂਜ਼ਾ, ਟਮਾਟਰ, ਤਰਬੂਜ਼

ਪੰਜਵਾਂ ਪਾਠ – ਪੜ੍ਹਾਈ ਲਿਖਾਈ
Script unit 5

As already pointed out at the end of Script unit 4, rules of Panjabi spelling and pronunciation given in this unit are quite technical and cannot be dealt with in much detail in this book, which aims at giving a basic knowledge of modern spoken and written Panjabi. But some users of this course may wish to carry on learning spoken and written Panjabi at a higher level. This brief unit is meant for such learners and for those who have some knowledge of technicalities of phonology.

Syllable stress in Panjabi

A spoken word consists of syllables, one of which receives primary stress. For example, the English word 'contradict' has three syllables – con-tra-dict. In other words, you can break this word into these three spoken segments. If you carefully observe your pronunciation of this word, you will notice that you use much more breath force in pronouncing the third syllable '-dict' than you do with the first two syllables. Typically, a stressed syllable in English is louder than an unstressed syllable and has longer vowel sounds. This happens in Panjabi as well. But syllable stress in Panjabi is weaker than in English, and it may be difficult for a speaker of English to perceive.

A syllable in Panjabi has one and only one vowel sound. A word may have only one syllable, which is regarded as a stressed syllable (except in the case of reduced forms of some conjunctions and postpositions – such as **c**, **te**, etc.). If a Panjabi word has a tone (low or high), it is given to the vowel of a stressed syllable only.

Tone and (the former) breathy voiced consonants

Breathy voiced consonants g^h, j^h, $ḍ^h$, d^h and b^h of Old Panjabi are no longer used in many dialects of modern Panjabi, including the one used in this course. Their pronunciation has changed, depending upon their position in the word. But symbols for these consonants (ਘ, ਝ, ਢ, ਧ and ਭ respectively) are still in use. A Panjabi word having any of these symbols invariably has a tone (low or high), which is given to the vowel of the stressed syllable. We shall briefly call such a vowel the stressed vowel or SV. We shall use the abbreviation BVC for a breathy voiced consonant. In order to understand the following rules, you will need to refer to the Consonants chart on page 9. All these five consonants are the 'fourth letters' of their respective group within the Consonant square.

The rules of tone assignment are

(1) If the BVC comes before the SV, the word gets a low tone.
(2) If the BVC comes after the SV, the word gets a high tone.
(3) If the BVC occurs at the beginning of a word, it becomes voiceless unaspirate (or, as far as pronunciation is concerned, the 'fourth letter is pronounced like the first letter').
(4) If the BVC occurs in the middle of or at the end of a word, it becomes voiced unaspirate (or, as far as pronunciation is concerned, the 'fourth letter is pronounced like the third letter').

Now study the following examples carefully. In the phonetic transcript, words are divided into syllables and a stressed syllable is marked with the symbol '.

BVC at the beginning of a word

A BVC at the beginning of a word must necessarily occur before the vowel in the stressed syllable (or the 'stressed vowel' or SV). When a BVC occurs before the SV, the word gets a low tone, which goes with the SV. The BVC in such cases becomes voiceless unaspirate. In other words, as far as pronunciation is concerned, the 'fourth letter is pronounced like the first letter'.

ਘਟਾ	'gʰa ʈa:	[kàʈa:]	dark clouds
ਘਟਾ	gʰa 'ʈa:	[kaʈà:]	to reduce
ਝੰਡਾ	'jʰan ḍa:	[cànḍa:]	flag
ਝੁਕਾ	jʰu 'ka:	[cukà:]	to lower
ਢੋਲ	'ḍʰol	[ʈòl]	drum
ਢਲਵਾ	ḍʰal 'va:	[ʈalvà:]	to get melted
ਧੋ	'ḍʰo	[ʈò]	to wash
ਧੁਆ	dʰu 'a:	[tuà:]	to get washed

| ਭਾਰਤ | 'bʰɑ: rat | [pà:rat] | India |
| ਭਰਾ | bʰɑ 'rɑ: | [parà:] | brother |

BVC in the middle of a word and before the SV 📼

The word gets the low tone, and the BVC becomes voiced unaspirate. As far as pronunciation is concerned, 'the fourth letter is pronounced like the third letter'. For example:

ਸੁਧਾਰ	su 'dʰɑ:r	[sudà:r]	to reform
ਸੰਭਾਲ	sam 'bʰɑ:l	[sambà:l]	care, preservation
ਬੁਝਾ	bu 'jʰɑ:	[bujà:]	to extinguish
ਸੁਝਾਓ	su 'jʰɑ: o	[sujà:o]	suggestion
ਕਢਵਾ	kaɖʰ 'vɑ:	[kaɖvà:]	to get taken out
ਸੰਘਰਸ਼	san 'gʰa raʃ	[sangàraʃ]	struggle

BVC after the SV 📼

If a BVC occurs after the vowel of the stressed syllable (whether the BVC occurs in the middle of a word or at the end makes no difference), the word gets a high tone and the BVC becomes voiced unaspirate. As far as pronunciation is concerned, 'the fourth letter is pronounced like the third letter'.

ਬਾਘ	'bɑ:gʰ	[bá:g]	tiger
ਸਾਂਝਾ	'sâ:jʰɑ:	[sẫ:jà:]	common, shared
ਸਾਧੂ	'sɑ: dʰu:	[sá:du:]	saint, holy man
ਲਾਭ	'lɑ:bʰ	[lá:b]	profit, benefit
ਗੱਭੇ	'ga bbʰe	[gábbe]	in the middle

As has already been pointed out, some dialects of Panjabi still retain the BV consonants. But most of them also have tones. So you may choose to use the BV consonants. But try to use the tones as well.

Tones, ਹ and ੍

The Panjabi dialects show considerable variety in pronouncing ਹ and ੍ . There are variations even within the dialect used in this course. As far as this dialect is concerned, the rules are as follows.

ਹ *at the beginning of a word* 🔘

Pronounce ਹ as ɦ. You may give a low tone to the stressed vowel of the word if you like. If you choose to use the tone, you may omit the ɦ sound. Often an unstressed vowel immediately following ɦ is also omitted. But the omission of the word-initial ɦ in formal educated speech is disliked by some speakers. So do not omit ɦ in such words. The pronunciation marked with * is not recommended for you, though you are likely to hear it.

ਹੱਥ	ɦatt^h	[ɦatt^h] [ɦàtt^h] *[àtt^h]	hand
ਹਿਲਾ	ɦila:	[ɦila:] *[là:]	to shake, to move
ਹੱਕ	ɦakk	[ɦakk] *[ɦàkk] *[àkk]	right
ਹਕੂਮਤ	ɦaku:mat	[ɦaku:mat] *[kù:mat]	government
ਹਕੀਮ	ɦaki:m	[ɦaki:m] *[ɦakì:m] *[kì:m]	physician
ਹਲਵਾਈ	ɦalva:i:	[ɦalva:i:] *[ɦalvà:i:] *[lavà:i:]	confectioner

ਹੱਕ, ਹਕੂਮਤ, ਹਕੀਮ and ਹਲਵਾਈ are Arabic words borrowed by Panjabi, and their 'Panjabi-isation' is regarded as a mark of 'uneducated' speech by some educated speakers of the older generation. So the safest rule for your own speech is: follow the spelling in such words and do not use any tone with the words beginning with ਹ.

ਹ *before the SV in the middle of a word* 🔘

Educated speakers pronounce this ਹ in their formal and careful speech. Some of them give the low tone to the word. Many uneducated speakers (and educated speakers in their informal chat) omit the ɦ sound. The pronunciation marked with * is not recommended.

ਕਹਾਣੀ	ka 'ɦa: ɳi:	[kaɦa:ɳi:] [kaɦà:ɳi:] *[kà:ɳi:]	story
ਸਹਾਰਾ	sa 'ɦa: ra:	[saɦa:ra:] [saɦà:ra:] *[sà:ra:]	support
ਬਹਾਰ	ba 'ɦa:r	[baɦa:r] [baɦà:r] *[bà:r]	spring (season)

The two rules above show that a ਹ before the stressed vowel is quite stable. In all such cases, your pronunciation can follow the spelling.

ਹ *after the SV in the middle of a word* 💿

Educated speakers in their formal and careful speech follow the spelling, i.e. they pronounce ਹ and do not give any tone to the word. But many speakers use the high tone in such a word and do not pronounce ਹ. This pronunciation is the rule for pronouns and postpositions. Remember that you cannot use both ਹ and the high tone in the word.

ਬੂਹਾ	'bu: ɦa:	[bu:ɦa:] [bú:a:]	door
ਚੂਹਾ	'cu: ɦa:	[cu:ɦa:] [cú:a:]	rat
ਰਾਹੀ	'ra: ɦi:	[ra:ɦi:] [rá:i:]	traveller
ਚਾਹੀਦਾ	'ca: ɦi: da:	[ca:ɦi:da:] [cá:i:da:]	desirable
ਬਾਹਰ	'ba: ɦar	[bá:r]	outside (postposition)
ਸਾਹਮਣੇ	'sa:ɦ ma ɳe	[sá:maɳe]	in front of, facing (postposition)
ਉਹਨੂੰ	'uɦ nũ:	[ónũ:]	to him/her (pronoun)
ਉਹਤੋਂ	'uɦ tõ	[ótõ]	from him/her (pronoun)
ਇਹਦਾ	'iɦ da:	[éda:]	his, her, its (pronominal adjective)

Note the pronunciation of the initial vowel letter in the case of pronouns.

ਹ *at the end of a word* 💿

Do not pronounce ਹ and use the high tone.

ਚਾਹ	ca:ɦ	[cá:]	tea, desire
ਵਾਹ!	va:ɦ!	[vá:]	Great!
ਮੀਂਹ	mĩ:ɦ	[mí̃:]	rain
ਮੂੰਹ	mũ:ɦ	[mú̃:]	mouth
ਨੂੰਹ	nũ:ɦ	[nú̃:]	daughter-in-law
ਸੁਆਹ	sua:ɦ	[suá:]	ashes

Words like ਕਹਿਣਾ 💿

Study the spelling and pronunciation of the following words carefully.

ਕਹਿਣਾ	'ka ɦi ŋaː	[kɛ́ŋaː]	saying
ਬਹਿ	'ba ɦi	[bɛ́]	to sit
ਸ਼ਹਿਰ	'ʃa ɦir	[ʃɛ́r]	city
ਜ਼ਹਿਰ	'za ɦir	[zɛ́r]	poison
ਸ਼ਹਿਦ	'ʃa ɦid	[ʃɛ́d]	honey

Since ਹ occurs after the stressed vowel, the word gets a high tone. But something else happens as well. The sequence **aɦi** is replaced by the single vowel sound **ɛ́**.

There is a historical reason for this. The vowel **ɛ** of modern Panjabi was pronounced as **ai** (as a quick glide from **a** to **i**) some centuries ago. At first **ɦ** disappeared and the high tone came. So the pronunciation of the word ਕਹਿਣਾ (**kaɦiŋaː**), for example, became **káiŋaː**. Some time later, **ai** became **ɛ**. This happened to all the Panjabi words having the sequence **aɦi**. Interestingly enough, some dialects of Panjabi still retain the 'quick glide' vowel (linguists use the name diphthong for such a vowel) **ai**. So you are likely to hear, for example, ਕਹਿਣਾ pronounced as **káiŋaː** too.

Words like ਬਹੁਤ 🔘

Study the following examples carefully.

ਬਹੁਤ	'ba ɦut	[bɔ́t]	many, much
ਸਹੁਰਾ	'sa ɦu raː	[sɔ́raː]	father-in-law
ਪਹੁ	'pa ɦu	[pɔ́]	dawn
ਸਹੁੰ	'sa ɦũ	[sɔ̃́]	oath
ਪਹੁੰਚ	'pa ɦũc	[pɔ̃́c]	to reach

The story is similar to the one for the preceding rule. The older pronunciation of modern Panjabi **ɔ** was the glide **au**. At first **ɦ** disappeared and the high tone came. Then the glide vowel **au** became the modern Panjabi **ɔ**. But, again as is the case with **ai**, some Panjabi dialects retain **au**. So you may hear, for example, the word ਬਹੁਤ (**baɦut**) pronounced as [**báut**].

Tones and the subscript ੍ 🔘

The simple rules are:

(1) Do not pronounce the subscript ੍ ;
(2) If the subscript ੍ occurs after the SV, give the word a high tone.
(3) If the subscript ੍ occurs before the SV, give the word a low tone.

Now study the following examples carefully.

High tone

ਪੜ੍ਹ	paɽʱ	[páɽ]	to read
ਪੜ੍ਹਨਾ	paɽʱ na:	[páɽna:]	reading
ਕੜ੍ਹੀ	'ka ɽʱi:	[káɽi:]	curry
ਵਰ੍ਹਾ	'va rʱa:	[vára:]	year
ਬੰਨ੍ਹ	'bannʱ	[bánn]	to bind
ਥੰਮ੍ਹ	'tʰammʱ	[tʰámm]	column
ਬੁੱਲ੍ਹ	'bullʱ	[búll]	lip
ਚੁੱਲ੍ਹਾ	'cullʱa:	[cúlla:]	hearth, stove

Low tone

ਚੜ੍ਹਾਈ	ca 'ɽʱa: i:	[caɽà:i:]	ascent, invasion
ਬੰਨ੍ਹਵਾ	bannʱ 'va:	[bannvà:]	to get bound
ਚੜ੍ਹਵਾ	caɽʱ 'va:	[caɽvà:]	to get raised

Cases with the high tone are more numerous.

Why causative forms cannot have a high tone

In Conversation unit 8 it was pointed out that a causative form in Panjabi is either without a tone or it has the low tone. But it can never have the high tone. The reason should be clear to you now. The last vowel sound of a causative form receives the primary stress. So any consonant which gives rise to the tone (a breathy voiced consonant, or ਹ, or the subscript ੍) must necessarily occur before the stressed vowel. Hence, if a causative form gets a tone, it must be the low tone.

Homophonous and homographic words in Panjabi

When two words with different spelling have the same pronunciation, they are called homophones. Examples from English are 'week' and 'weak'. There can be homophonous sentences as well, such as

The sun's rays meet.
The sons raise meat.

Words or sentences having different pronunciation but the same spelling are called homographic. Examples from English are 'row' (line) and 'row' (fierce quarrel).

Because of changes in Panjabi pronunciation over the past three or four centuries and because of the fact that Panjabi spelling is rather conservative, there are both homophonous and homographic words in Panjabi.

Homophonous words

The causative form of the verb ਝਾੜ ('to dust') is ਝੜਵਾ, and the causative form of the verb ਚਾੜ੍ਹ ('to raise') is ਚੜ੍ਹਵਾ. These causative forms are derived according to the valid rules of Panjabi grammar. Try to find out the pronunciation of ਝੜਵਾ and ਚੜ੍ਹਵਾ in accordance with the rules given above. You will find that both are pronounced as **cɑɽvà:**.

So if you are requested

dɑri:ɑ̃: cɑɽvà: dio

you will have to clarify first whether you should get the carpets dusted (cleaned) –

ਦਰੀਆਂ ਝੜਵਾ ਦਿਓ

or taken upstairs.

ਦਰੀਆਂ ਚੜ੍ਹਵਾ ਦਿਓ

Homographic words

The Panjabi word ਵਰ੍ਹਾ ('year') is stressed on the first syllable and is thus pronounced as **vára:**, with a high tone, according to the rules. But Panjabi also has a verb ਵਰ੍ਹ [**vár**] ('to rain'), whose causative form is also spelled as ਵਰ੍ਹਾ. Since it is the last vowel of a causative form that receives stress, this ਵਰ੍ਹਾ is pronounced with a low tone as [**vɑrà:**]. There is a Panjabi nursery rhyme

ਰੱਬਾ ਰੱਬਾ ਮੀਂਹ ਵਰ੍ਹਾ
ਸਾਡੀ ਕੋਠੀ ਦਾਣੇ ਪਾ
O God! O God! Make the rain fall and fill our granary with foodgrains.

in which ਵਰ੍ਹਾ is pronounced as [**vɑrà:**].

More than one spelling form

The result of homophony is that rules allow some Panjabi words to be spelled in more than one way. Some of these words are

ਉਹਨਾਂ	ਉਨ੍ਹਾਂ	[**únã̀:**] (**nū̃:**)	(to) them
ਇਹਨਾਂ	ਇਨ੍ਹਾਂ	[**ínã̀:**] (**nū̃:**)	(to) them
ਸਾਹਨ	ਸਾਨ੍ਹ	[**sá:n**]	bull
ਕਾਹਨ	ਕਾਨ੍ਹ	[**ká:n**]	a name

| ਕੋਹੜ | ਕੋੜੁ | [kóɾ] | leprosy |
| ਗੁਹੜਾ | ਗੁੜਾ | [gúːɾɑː] | fast (colour) |

You will find each of these (and many other) words spelled in both the ways in Panjabi literature and newspapers. (And you may also come across people who will magisterially declare one of these spellings 'wrong'!) Apply the rules to each of these words and see that both the spellings get the same pronunciation.

There are many other words which could be spelled in two ways, but only one spelling is used. For example:

ਕਾਹਲਾ	* ਕਾਲ੍ਹਾ	[káːlɑː]	impatient
ਮੂਹਰੇ	* ਮੂਰ੍ਹੇ	[múːre]	in front
* ਪੀਹੜੀ	ਪੀੜੀ	[píːɾiː]	generation
ਬਾਹਰ	* ਬਾਰ੍ਹ	[báːr]	outside
ਕੂਹਣੀ	* ਕੂਣ੍ਹੀ	[kúːɳiː]	elbow

The spelling marked with * is not is use.

If you find a chauvinistic Panjabi 'scholar' (and there are thousands in existence) who tells you that 'in Panjabi you write exactly as you speak and speak exactly as you write', listen to him or her quietly and respectfully, and then ignore his/her words of wisdom!

Concluding words

Although Panjabi is one of the major world languages, very little research on its grammatical and phonological structure has taken place. This Unit is extremely sketchy and is intended to stimulate your interest in the spelling and pronunciation system of this language. If you are seriously interested in furthering your knowledge of spoken and written Panjabi, you cannot avoid the issues which have been barely touched upon in this Unit and the issues which could not even be mentioned.

There are more things in Panjabi than are dreamt of in this course!

Exercise 🔲

Read the following Panjabi words aloud. All these words have tone (either high or low). They are also recorded on the cassettes. If you have got the recording, check your pronunciation against it. Otherwise, get it checked by your teacher or a native speaker of Panjabi. The correct pronunciation is also given in the phonetic transcription in the Key to exercises.

ਚੜ੍ਹਾਈ	ascent	ਕਢਵਾ	to get extracted
ਬੜ੍ਹਾਵਾ	encouragement	ਕੂਹਣੀ	elbow
ਕਾਨ੍ਹੜਾ	a Raga melody	ਘੜੀ	clock
ਨਭ੍ਹਿੰਨਵੇਂ	ninety-nine	ਗੁਨਾਹ	sin
ਬਹੁਕਰ	broom	ਸਹਿਨਸ਼ੀਲ	tolerant
ਵਿਆਹ	marriage	ਕਰਾਹੁਣਾ	to moan
ਚਾਹੁੰਦਾ	wanting	ਕਹਿੰਦਾ	saying
ਮਹਿੰ	buffalo	ਮਹਿੰਦੀ	henna
ਸ਼ਹਿਦ	honey	ਪਹੁ	dawn
ਘੜ੍ਹਿਆਲ	large bell	ਝਗੜਾਲੂ	quarrelsome
ਸੰਘਰਸ਼	struggle	ਬਘਿਆੜ	wolf
ਲਾਂਭੇ	elsewhere	ਪਹੁੰਚ	to reach

ਛੇਵਾਂ ਪਾਠ – ਪੜ੍ਹਾਈ ਲਿਖਾਈ
Script unit 6

In this unit, you will find dialogues from the first eight Conversation units in Panjabi script. You can use these dialogues as you like. For example, you can

(1) read these dialogues while listening to the recordings on the cassettes;
(2) compare them with the phonetic transcription;
(3) use them for reading practice;
(4) write sentences in Panjabi script after listening to the recording and then check their correctness by comparing them with the versions printed here.

You can make use of these dialogues in many other ways as well, depending upon your style of learning.

The number before each dialogue indicates the Conversation unit from where the dialogue is taken. For example, Dialogue 5.2 is Dialogue number 2 from Conversation unit 5.

1.1

ਸੋਹਨ ਸਿੰਘ:	ਸਤਿ ਸ੍ਰੀ ਅਕਾਲ ਜੀ।
ਦਰਸ਼ਨ ਸਿੰਘ:	ਸਤਿ ਸ੍ਰੀ ਅਕਾਲ ਜੀ। ਕੀ ਹਾਲ ਹੈ?
ਸੋਹਨ ਸਿੰਘ:	ਠੀਕ ਹੈ ਜੀ, ਤੁਸੀਂ ਦੱਸੋ।
ਦਰਸ਼ਨ ਸਿੰਘ:	ਠੀਕ ਹੈ।

. . .

ਦਰਸ਼ਨ ਸਿੰਘ:	ਅੱਛਾ ਜੀ। ਸਤਿ ਸ੍ਰੀ ਅਕਾਲ।
ਸੋਹਨ ਸਿੰਘ:	ਸਤਿ ਸ੍ਰੀ ਅਕਾਲ।

1.2

ਬਲਦੇਵ ਯਾਦਵ:	ਨਮਸਤੇ ਸ਼ਰਮਾ ਜੀ।
ਅਨਿਲ ਸ਼ਰਮਾ:	ਨਮਸਤੇ ਯਾਦਵ ਸਾਹਬ। ਬੈਠੋ।

ਬਲਦੇਵ ਯਾਦਵ:	ਸ਼ੁਕਰੀਆ ਜੀ।
ਅਨਿਲ ਸ਼ਰਮਾ:	ਕੀ ਹਾਲ ਹੈ?
ਬਲਦੇਵ ਯਾਦਵ:	ਠੀਕ ਹੈ। ਤੁਸੀਂ ਸੁਣਾਓ। ਤੁਹਾਡਾ ਕੀ ਹਾਲ ਹੈ?
ਅਨਿਲ ਸ਼ਰਮਾ:	ਮੇਰਾ ਹਾਲ ਵੀ ਠੀਕ ਹੈ। ਹੁਕਮ ਕਰੋ।
ਬਲਦੇਵ ਯਾਦਵ:	ਹੁਕਮ ਨਹੀਂ ਜੀ। ਬੇਨਤੀ ਹੈ।
	. . .
ਬਲਦੇਵ ਯਾਦਵ:	ਚੰਗਾ ਸ਼ਰਮਾ ਜੀ। ਇਜਾਜ਼ਤ ਦਿਓ। ਨਮਸਤੇ।
ਅਨਿਲ ਸ਼ਰਮਾ:	ਨਮਸਤੇ ਜੀ।

1.3

ਨਜ਼ੀਰ ਹਕ:	ਅੱਸਲਾਮ ਅਲੈਕਮ, ਖ਼ਾਲਿਦ ਸਾਹਬਾ।
ਖ਼ਾਲਿਦ ਰਹਮਾਨ:	ਵਾ ਲੈਕਮ ਅੱਸਲਾਮ, ਨਜ਼ੀਰ ਭਾਈ। ਕੀ ਹਾਲ ਹੈ?
ਨਜ਼ੀਰ ਹਕ:	ਅੱਲਾ ਦਾ ਸ਼ੁਕਰ ਹੈ। ਸਭ ਖ਼ੈਰੀਅਤ ਹੈ ?
ਖ਼ਾਲਿਦ ਰਹਮਾਨ:	ਜੀ ਹਾਂ, ਅੱਲਾ ਦਾ ਸ਼ੁਕਰ ਹੈ। ਤਸ਼ਰੀਫ਼ ਰਖੋ।
ਨਜ਼ੀਰ ਹਕ:	ਜੀ ਨਹੀਂ, ਸ਼ੁਕਰੀਆ। ਖ਼ੁਦਾ ਹਾਫ਼ਿਜ਼।
ਖ਼ਾਲਿਦ ਰਹਮਾਨ:	ਖ਼ੁਦਾ ਹਾਫ਼ਿਜ਼।

2.1

ਰਮੇਸ਼ ਵਰਮਾ:	ਮਾਫ਼ ਕਰਨਾ। ਤੁਹਾਡਾ ਨਾਂ ਡਾਕਟਰ ਜੋਗਿੰਦਰ ਸਿੰਘ ਹੈ ਨਾ?
ਜੋਗਿੰਦਰ ਸਿੰਘ:	ਹਾਂ ਜੀ। ਮੇਰਾ ਨਾਂ ਜੋਗਿੰਦਰ ਸਿੰਘ ਹੈ।
ਰਮੇਸ਼ ਵਰਮਾ:	ਮੇਰਾ ਨਾਂ ਰਮੇਸ਼ ਹੈ।
ਜੋਗਿੰਦਰ ਸਿੰਘ:	ਮਿਲ ਕੇ ਬੜੀ ਖ਼ੁਸ਼ੀ ਹੋਈ। ਤੁਹਾਡਾ ਪੂਰਾ ਨਾਂ ਕੀ ਹੈ?
ਰਮੇਸ਼ ਵਰਮਾ:	ਰਮੇਸ਼ ਵਰਮਾ।
ਜੋਗਿੰਦਰ ਸਿੰਘ:	ਤੁਸੀਂ ਕੀ ਕੰਮ ਕਰਦੇ ਹੋ?
ਰਮੇਸ਼ ਵਰਮਾ:	ਮੈਂ ਅਕਾਊਂਟੈਂਟ ਹਾਂ। ਤੁਸੀਂ ਜੀ ਪੀ ਹੋ ਜਾਂ ਕਨਸਲਟੈਂਟ?
ਜੋਗਿੰਦਰ ਸਿੰਘ:	ਜੀ ਨਹੀਂ। ਮੈਂ ਮੈਡੀਕਲ ਡਾਕਟਰ ਨਹੀਂ। ਮੈਂ ਪੀ ਐੱਚ ਡੀ ਹਾਂ।

2.2

ਮਿਸਿਜ਼ ਸਿੰਘ:	ਕਾਫ਼ੀ ਪੀਓ।
ਮਿਸਿਜ਼ ਵਰਮਾ:	ਜੀ ਨਹੀਂ, ਸ਼ੁਕਰੀਆ। ਮੈਂ ਕਾਫ਼ੀ ਨਹੀਂ ਪੀਂਦੀ।
ਮਿਸਿਜ਼ ਸਿੰਘ:	ਤਾਂ ਚਾਹ ਪੀਓ।
ਮਿਸਿਜ਼ ਵਰਮਾ:	ਸ਼ੁਕਰੀਆ।
ਮਿਸਿਜ਼ ਸਿੰਘ:	ਤੁਹਾਡੇ ਕਿੰਨੇ ਬੱਚੇ ਨੇ?
ਮਿਸਿਜ਼ ਵਰਮਾ:	ਮੇਰੇ ਦੋ ਬੱਚੇ ਨੇ। ਮੁੰਡੇ। ਤੇ ਤੁਹਾਡੇ?
ਮਿਸਿਜ਼ ਸਿੰਘ:	ਤਿੰਨ। ਦੋ ਕੁੜੀਆਂ ਤੇ ਇੱਕ ਮੁੰਡਾ। ਤੁਹਾਡੇ ਬੱਚੇ ਕੰਮ ਕਰਦੇ ਨੇ?
ਮਿਸਿਜ਼ ਵਰਮਾ:	ਜੀ ਨਹੀਂ। ਉਹ ਪੜ੍ਹਦੇ ਨੇ। ਇੱਕ ਹਾਈ ਸਕੂਲ ਜਾਂਦਾ ਹੈ, ਤੇ ਇੱਕ ਪ੍ਰਾਇਮਰੀ ਸਕੂਲ।

2.3

ਜੋਗਿੰਦਰ ਸਿੰਘ:	ਵਰਮਾ ਸਾਹਬ, ਤੁਸੀਂ ਕਿੱਥੇ ਕੰਮ ਕਰਦੇ ਹੋ?
ਰਮੇਸ਼ ਵਰਮਾ:	ਬਰਮਿੰਘਮ 'ਚ। ਸਾਡੀ ਆਪਣੀ ਅਕਾਊਂਟੈਂਸੀ ਫ਼ਰਮ ਹੈ, ਵਰਮਾ ਅਕਾਊਂਟੈਂਟਸ, ਹੈਗਲੀ ਰੋਡ ਤੇ। ਅਸੀਂ ਤਿੰਨ ਸਾਂਝੀਦਾਰ ਹਾਂ, ਮੇਰੇ ਬੜੇ ਭਾਈ ਸਾਹਬ, ਮੈਂ, ਤੇ ਮੇਰਾ ਛੋਟਾ ਭਰਾ। ਸਾਡੀ ਇੱਕ ਭੈਣ ਵੀ ਹੈ। ਉਹ ਡਾਕਟਰ ਹੈ, ਮੈਡੀਕਲ ਡਾਕਟਰ, ਪੀ ਐੱਚ ਡੀ ਨਹੀਂ। ਤੁਸੀਂ ਕਿੱਥੇ ਕੰਮ ਕਰਦੇ ਹੋ?
ਜੋਗਿੰਦਰ ਸਿੰਘ:	ਆਸਟਨ ਯੂਨੀਵਰਸਿਟੀ 'ਚ।

2.4

ਮਿਸਿਜ਼ ਵਰਮਾ:	ਤੁਸੀਂ ਕਿੰਨੇ ਭੈਣ ਭਰਾ ਹੋ?
ਮਿਸਿਜ਼ ਸਿੰਘ:	ਅਸੀਂ ਪੰਜ ਭੈਣ ਭਰਾ ਹਾਂ। ਤਿੰਨ ਭੈਣਾਂ ਤੇ ਦੋ ਭਰਾ। ਤੁਸੀਂ?
ਮਿਸਿਜ਼ ਵਰਮਾ:	ਅਸੀਂ ਚਾਰ ਹਾਂ। ਮੇਰੇ ਤਿੰਨ ਬੜੇ ਭਰਾ ਨੇ।

3.1

ਮੋਹਨ ਸਿੰਘ:	ਸਤਿ ਸ੍ਰੀ ਅਕਾਲ, ਭੈਣ ਜੀ।
ਕੁਲਵੰਤ ਕੌਰ:	ਸਤਿ ਸ੍ਰੀ ਅਕਾਲ, ਭਰਾ ਜੀ। ਕੀ ਹਾਲ ਹੈ?
ਮੋਹਨ ਸਿੰਘ:	ਵਾਹਿਗੁਰੂ ਦੀ ਕਿਰਪਾ ਹੈ। ਦੱਸੋ, ਕੀ ਚਾਹੀਦਾ ਹੈ?
ਕੁਲਵੰਤ ਕੌਰ:	ਤੁਹਾਡੇ ਕੋਲ ਭਿੰਡੀ ਹੈਗੀ ਐ?
ਮੋਹਨ ਸਿੰਘ:	ਹਾਂ ਜੀ, ਹੈਗੀ ਐ। ਕਿੰਨੀ ਚਾਹੀਦੀ ਹੈ?
ਕੁਲਵੰਤ ਕੌਰ:	ਤਿੰਨ ਪੌਂਡ।
ਮੋਹਨ ਸਿੰਘ:	ਹੋਰ ਕੁਝ ਚਾਹੀਦਾ ਹੈ?
ਕੁਲਵੰਤ ਕੌਰ:	ਇੱਕ ਪੌਂਡ ਗਾਜਰਾਂ, ਦੋ ਪੌਂਡ ਬੈਂਗਣ, ਦੋ ਪੌਂਡ ਟਮਾਟਰ।
ਮੋਹਨ ਸਿੰਘ:	ਅੱਜ ਸਾਡੇ ਕੋਲ ਟਮਾਟਰ ਨਹੀਂ।
ਕੁਲਵੰਤ ਕੌਰ:	ਕੋਈ ਗੱਲ ਨਹੀਂ। ਮੈਨੂੰ ਹਰਾ ਧਨੀਆ ਵੀ ਚਾਹੀਦਾ ਹੈ।
ਮੋਹਨ ਸਿੰਘ:	ਹਰੀਆਂ ਮਿਰਚਾਂ ਵੀ ਚਾਹੀਦੀਆਂ ਨੇ?
ਕੁਲਵੰਤ ਕੌਰ:	ਜੀ ਨਹੀਂ।

3.2

ਅਵਤਾਰ ਬਾਸੀ:	ਕਿੱਦਾਂ ਭਾਈਆ ਜੀ? ਠੀਕ ਹੋ ਨਾ?
ਬਿਸ਼ਨ ਦਾਸ:	ਠੀਕ ਕਾਹਦਾ? ਲੱਤਾਂ ਬਾਂਹਾਂ ਚਲਦੀਆਂ ਨਹੀਂ।
ਅਵਤਾਰ ਬਾਸੀ:	ਚਲਦੀਆਂ ਨਹੀਂ? ਬਿਲਕੁਲ ਠੀਕ ਚਲਦੀਆਂ ਨੇ। ਸੋਟੀ ਔਥੇ ਰਖੋ ... ਹਾਂ ਜੀ। ਹੁਣ ਐਥੇ ਲੇਟੋ। ਗੱਦੇ ਤੇ।
ਬਿਸ਼ਨ ਦਾਸ:	ਕਿੱਥੇ?
ਅਵਤਾਰ ਬਾਸੀ:	ਐਥੇ, ਗੱਦੇ ਦੇ ਉੱਤੇ ... ਹਾਂ ਸ਼ਾਬਾਸ਼। ਸੱਜਾ ਪੈਰ ਉੱਤੇ ਚੁੱਕੋ ... ਹਾਂ ਜੀ ... ਠੀਕ। ਹੁਣ ਖੱਬਾ ਪੈਰ ਚੁੱਕੋ ... ਬਹੁਤ ਅੱਛਾ ... ਹੋਰ ਚੁੱਕੋ ... ਹੋਰ ... ਹੋਰ ... ਸ਼ਾਬਾਸ਼ ... ਬਹੁਤ ਅੱਛਾ ... ਹੁਣ ਦੋਵੇਂ ਪੈਰ ਹੇਠਾਂ ਕਰੋ ... ਸ਼ਾਬਾਸ਼ ... ਦੋਵੇਂ ਬਾਂਹਾਂ ਉੱਤੇ ਚੁੱਕੋ।

ਬਿਸ਼ਨ ਦਾਸ:	ਖੱਬੀ ਬਾਂਹ ਦੁਖਦੀ ਹੈ।
ਅਵਤਾਰ ਬਾਸੀ:	ਕੋਈ ਗੱਲ ਨਹੀਂ। ਉੱਤੇ ਚੁੱਕੋ ... ਹੋਰ ਉੱਤੇ ... ਹੋਰ ਉੱਤੇ ... ਸ਼ਾਬਾਸ਼ ... ਬਹੁਤ ਅੱਛਾ ... ਤੁਸੀਂ ਬਿਲਕੁਲ ਠੀਕ ਹੋ ਭਾਈਆ ਜੀ।

3.3

ਜੋਗਿੰਦਰ ਸਿੰਘ:	ਸੱਗੂ ਸਾਹਬ, ਤੁਹਾਡਾ ਕੀ ਖ਼ਿਆਲ ਹੈ? ਕੰਪਿਊਟਰ ਕਿੱਥੇ ਚਾਹੀਦਾ ਹੈ?
ਸੱਗੂ:	ਮੇਰੇ ਖ਼ਿਆਲ 'ਚ ਕੰਪਿਊਟਰ ਖਿੜਕੀ ਦੇ ਸਾਹਮਣੇ ਠੀਕ ਨਹੀਂ।
ਜੋਗਿੰਦਰ ਸਿੰਘ:	ਪਰ ਇਹ ਰੇਡੀਏਟਰ ਦੇ ਕੋਲ ਵੀ ਠੀਕ ਨਹੀਂ।
ਸੱਗੂ:	ਤੁਹਾਡੀ ਗੱਲ ਵੀ ਠੀਕ ਹੈ। ਮੇਰਾ ਖ਼ਿਆਲ ਹੈ ਕਿ ਤੁਸੀਂ ਬੁਕ-ਸ਼ੈਲਫ਼ਾਂ ਕੰਧਾਂ ਦੇ ਨਾਲ ਲਾਓ।
ਜੋਗਿੰਦਰ ਸਿੰਘ:	ਤੇ ਕੰਪਿਊਟਰ?
ਸੱਗੂ:	ਕੰਪਿਊਟਰ ਕਮਰੇ ਦੇ ਗੱਭੇ ਰਖੋ, ਮੇਜ਼ 'ਤੇ।
ਜੋਗਿੰਦਰ ਸਿੰਘ:	ਬੂਹੇ ਦੇ ਕੋਲ ਠੀਕ ਨਹੀਂ?
ਸੱਗੂ:	ਜੀ ਨਹੀਂ।
ਜੋਗਿੰਦਰ ਸਿੰਘ:	ਤੇ ਫ਼ਾਈਲਿੰਗ ਕੈਬਨਿਟ?
ਸੱਗੂ:	ਖੱਬੇ ਪਾਸੇ।
ਜੋਗਿੰਦਰ ਸਿੰਘ:	ਮੇਰੇ ਖੱਬੇ ਪਾਸੇ?
ਸੱਗੂ:	ਜੀ ਨਹੀਂ। *ਮੇਰੇ* ਖੱਬੇ ਪਾਸੇ, ਤੁਹਾਡੇ ਸੱਜੇ ਪਾਸੇ।

3.4

ਮੁਹੰਮਦ ਸ਼ਫ਼ੀ:	ਜ਼ੁਬੈਦਾ ਚਾਹ ਦਾ ਕੱਪ ਲਿਆ। ਤੇ ਇੱਕ ਦੋ ਐਸਪ੍ਰੀਨ ਵੀ।
ਜ਼ੁਬੈਦਾ:	ਕੀ ਗੱਲ? ਤੁਹਾਡੀ ਤਬੀਅਤ ਠੀਕ ਹੈ?
ਮੁਹੰਮਦ ਸ਼ਫ਼ੀ:	ਹਾਂ, ਤਬੀਅਤ ਠੀਕ ਹੈ। ਮਾਮੂਲੀ ਸਿਰ ਦਰਦ ਹੈ।
ਜ਼ੁਬੈਦਾ:	ਹਾਏ ਅੱਲਾ! ਸਿਰ ਦਰਦ ਕਿਉਂ?
ਮੁਹੰਮਦ ਸ਼ਫ਼ੀ:	ਦਰਦ ਅੱਲਾ ਦੇ ਸਿਰ 'ਚ ਨਹੀਂ, ਮੇਰੇ ਸਿਰ 'ਚ ਹੈ। ਜਾ ਚਾਹ ਲਿਆ।

· · ·

ਮੁਹੰਮਦ ਸ਼ਫ਼ੀ:	ਜ਼ੁਬੈਦਾ, ਮੇਰਾ ਪੈੱਨ ਕਿੱਥੇ ਹੈ?
ਜ਼ੁਬੈਦਾ:	ਜੇਬ 'ਚ।
ਮੁਹੰਮਦ ਸ਼ਫ਼ੀ:	ਪਰ ਜੇਬ 'ਚ ਹੈ ਨਹੀਂ।
ਜ਼ੁਬੈਦਾ:	ਕਮੀਜ਼ ਦੀ ਜੇਬ 'ਚ ਨਹੀਂ, ਕੋਟ ਦੀ ਜੇਬ 'ਚ।
ਮੁਹੰਮਦ ਸ਼ਫ਼ੀ:	ਕੋਟ ਕਿੱਥੇ ਹੈ?
ਜ਼ੁਬੈਦਾ:	ਉੱਤੇ, ਬੈੱਡਰੂਮ 'ਚ। ਹੁਣ ਪੁੱਛੋ ਬੈੱਡਰੂਮ ਕਿੱਥੇ ਹੈ। ਜਨਾਬ, ਬੈੱਡਰੂਮ ਘਰ 'ਚ ਹੈ, ਘਰ ਲੰਡਨ 'ਚ ਹੈ, ਲੰਡਨ ਇੰਗਲੈਂਡ 'ਚ ਹੈ।
ਮੁਹੰਮਦ ਸ਼ਫ਼ੀ:	ਇਹ ਕੀ ਮਜ਼ਾਕ ਹੈ?

4.1

ਅਵਤਾਰ ਮਾਹਲ:	ਅੱਛਾ ਸ਼ਰਮਾ ਜੀ, ਸਾਨੂੰ ਇਹ ਦੱਸੋ ਕਿ ਤੁਹਾਡੇ ਕੀ ਕੀ ਸ਼ੌਕ ਨੇ? ਸੰਗੀਤ ਤੋਂ ਇਲਾਵਾ।
ਪ੍ਰੇਮ ਸ਼ਰਮਾ:	ਮਾਹਲ ਸਾਹਬ, ਸੰਗੀਤ ਮੇਰਾ ਸ਼ੌਕ ਨਹੀਂ, ਕੰਮ ਹੈ, ਕਾਰੋਬਾਰ ਹੈ। ਵੈਸੇ, ਮੇਰੇ ਕਈ ਸ਼ੌਕ

ਹੈਨ। ਮੈਨੂੰ ਪੜ੍ਹਨ ਦਾ ਸ਼ੌਕ ਹੈ, ਕਵਿਤਾ   ਤੇ ਗੀਤ ਲਿਖਣ ਦਾ ਸ਼ੌਕ ਹੈ, ਖਾਣਾ ਪਕਾਉਣ ਦਾ ਸ਼ੌਕ ਹੈ।

ਅਵਤਾਰ ਮਾਹਲ:	ਖਾਣਾ ਪਕਾਉਣ ਦਾ?
ਪ੍ਰੇਮ ਸ਼ਰਮਾ:	ਹਾਂ ਜੀ।
ਅਵਤਾਰ ਮਾਹਲ:	ਫੇਰ ਤਾਂ ਤੁਹਾਡੀ ਪਤਨੀ ਬੜੀ ਖ਼ੁਸ਼ਕਿਸਮਤ ਹੈ।
ਪ੍ਰੇਮ ਸ਼ਰਮਾ:	ਇਹ ਮੈਨੂੰ ਪਤਾ ਨਹੀਂ। ਉਹਨੂੰ ਮੇਰਾ ਖਾਣਾ ਬਹੁਤ ਪਸੰਦ ਹੈ, ਮੇਰਾ ਸੰਗੀਤ ਬਿਲਕੁਲ ਪਸੰਦ ਨਹੀਂ।
ਅਵਤਾਰ ਮਾਹਲ:	ਕੀ ਤੁਹਾਡੇ ਧੀਆਂ ਪੁੱਤਰਾਂ ਨੂੰ ਤੁਹਾਡਾ ਸੰਗੀਤ ਪਸੰਦ ਹੈ?
ਪ੍ਰੇਮ ਸ਼ਰਮਾ:	ਧੀਆਂ ਨੂੰ ਹੈ, ਪੁੱਤਰਾਂ ਨੂੰ ਨਹੀਂ।

4.2

ਅਵਤਾਰ ਮਾਹਲ:	ਪ੍ਰੇਮ, ਯਾਰ ਤੇਰੀ ਬੰਸਰੀ ਮੈਨੂੰ ਬੜੀ ਚੰਗੀ ਲਗਦੀ ਹੈ।
ਪ੍ਰੇਮ ਸ਼ਰਮਾ:	ਐਹ ਲੈ, ਫੜ ਬੰਸਰੀ।
ਅਵਤਾਰ ਮਾਹਲ:	ਮੇਰੇ ਕਹਿਣ ਦਾ ਮਤਲਬ ਹੈ, ਮੈਨੂੰ ਇਹਦੀ ਆਵਾਜ਼ ਬੜੀ ਮਿੱਠੀ ਲਗਦੀ ਹੈ। ਪਤਾ ਨਹੀਂ ਕਿਉਂ। ਮੈਨੂੰ ਲਗਦਾ ਹੈ ਕਿ ਇਹ ਆਵਾਜ਼ ਬੰਸਰੀ ਰਾਹੀਂ ਤੇਰੇ ਦਿਲ 'ਚੋਂ ਆਉਂਦੀ ਹੈ।
ਪ੍ਰੇਮ ਸ਼ਰਮਾ:	ਬਿਲਕੁਲ ਸੱਚ। ਤੈਨੂੰ ਸੰਗੀਤ ਦੀ ਚੰਗੀ ਸਮਝ ਹੈ। ਪਰ ਕੀ ਤੈਨੂੰ ਪੱਛਮੀ ਸੰਗੀਤ ਪਸੰਦ ਨਹੀਂ?
ਅਵਤਾਰ ਮਾਹਲ:	ਕਲਾਸੀਕਲ ਸੰਗੀਤ ਠੀਕ ਹੈ, ਪਰ ਮੈਨੂੰ ਮਿਊਜ਼ਿਕ ਮੈਨੂੰ ਬਹੁਤ ਬੁਰਾ ਲਗਦਾ ਹੈ।
ਪ੍ਰੇਮ ਸ਼ਰਮਾ:	ਕਿਉਂ?
ਅਵਤਾਰ ਮਾਹਲ:	ਮੈਂ ਸ਼ੋਰ ਸ਼ਰਾਬਾ ਪਸੰਦ ਨਹੀਂ ਕਰਦਾ। ਮੈਂ ਹਲਕਾ ਭਾਰਤੀ ਸੰਗੀਤ ਪਸੰਦ ਕਰਦਾ ਹਾਂ, ਤੇ ਪੰਜਾਬੀ ਲੋਕ ਗੀਤ ਵੀ।

4.3

ਸਤਵੰਤ ਮਾਹਲ:	ਵੀਰ ਜੀ, ਐਹ ਲਓ, ਅਵਤਾਰ ਜੀ ਦੀ ਖ਼ਾਸ ਪਸੰਦ।
ਪ੍ਰੇਮ ਸ਼ਰਮਾ:	ਇਹ ਕੀ ਹੈ, ਭਾਬੀ ਜੀ?
ਸਤਵੰਤ ਮਾਹਲ:	ਚਿਕਿਨ ਬਿਰਿਆਨੀ।
ਪ੍ਰੇਮ ਸ਼ਰਮਾ:	ਨਹੀਂ ਜੀ, ਸ਼ੁਕਰੀਆ। ਮੈਂ ਵੈਜੀਟੇਰੀਅਨ ਹਾਂ।
ਅਵਤਾਰ ਮਾਹਲ:	ਸਤਵੰਤ, ਇਹ ਬੰਦਾ ਸਾਧੂ ਹੈ। ਮੀਟ ਨਹੀਂ ਖਾਂਦਾ, ਸ਼ਰਾਬ ਨਹੀਂ ਪੀਂਦਾ, ਸਿਗਰਿਟ ਨਹੀਂ ਪੀਂਦਾ।
ਸਤਵੰਤ ਮਾਹਲ:	ਬਹੁਤ ਚੰਗੀ ਗੱਲ ਹੈ।
ਅਵਤਾਰ ਮਾਹਲ:	ਹੈਂ? ਸਾਧੂ ਹੋਣਾ ਚੰਗੀ ਗੱਲ ਹੈ?
ਸਤਵੰਤ ਮਾਹਲ:	ਸਿਗਰਿਟ ਨਾ ਪੀਣਾ ਚੰਗੀ ਗੱਲ ਹੈ। ਬਹੁਤਾ ਨਾ ਬੋਲਣਾ ਵੀ ਚੰਗੀ ਗੱਲ ਹੈ। ਮੂੰਹ ਨੂੰ ਖਾਣਾ ਖਾਣ ਲਈ ਜ਼ਿਆਦਾ ਵਰਤੋ, ਤੇ ਬੋਲਣ ਲਈ ਘੱਟ।

4.4

ਸਤਵੰਤ ਮਾਹਲ:	ਵੀਰ ਜੀ, ਐਹ ਪਾਲਕ ਪਨੀਰ ਕੋਫ਼ਤਾ ਲਓ।
ਪ੍ਰੇਮ ਸ਼ਰਮਾ:	ਇਹਦੇ ਵਿਚ ਕੀ ਹੈ?

ਸਤਵੰਤ ਮਾਹਲ:	ਪਾਲਕ, ਪਨੀਰ, ਘਿਉ, ਮੈਦਾ, ਪਿਆਜ਼, ਅਦਰਕ, ਧਨੀਆ, ਮੇਥੀ, ਮਿਰਚ, ਮਸਾਲਾ।
ਅਵਤਾਰ ਮਾਹਲ:	ਤੇ ਇਕ ਗੁਪਤ ਚੀਜ਼ ਵੀ।
ਪ੍ਰੇਮ ਸ਼ਰਮਾ:	ਗੁਪਤ ਚੀਜ਼ ਕੀ ਹੈ, ਭਾਬੀ ਜੀ?
ਸਤਵੰਤ ਮਾਹਲ:	ਕੁਝ ਨਹੀਂ, ਇਹ ਐਵੇਂ ਛੇੜਦੇ ਨੇ।
ਪ੍ਰੇਮ ਸ਼ਰਮਾ:	ਕਿਉਂ ਬਈ? ਤੈਨੂੰ ਕੀ ਹੱਕ ਹੈ ਮੇਰੀ ਭਰਜਾਈ ਨੂੰ ਛੇੜਨ ਦਾ?
ਅਵਤਾਰ ਮਾਹਲ:	ਮੈਂ ਕਦੋਂ ਛੇੜਦਾ ਹਾਂ? ਖਾਣੇ ਵਿਚ ਇਕ ਗੁਪਤ ਚੀਜ਼ ਹੈਗੀ ਐ - ਪ੍ਰੇਮ।
ਪ੍ਰੇਮ ਸ਼ਰਮਾ:	ਮੈਂ? ਖਾਣੇ ਵਿਚ?
ਅਵਤਾਰ ਮਾਹਲ:	ਨਹੀਂ, ਮੇਰੇ ਕਹਿਣ ਦਾ ਮਤਲਬ ਹੈ - ਪਿਆਰ।
ਸਤਵੰਤ ਮਾਹਲ:	ਚੰਗਾ ਹੁਣ ਬੋਲਣਾ ਬੰਦ ਕਰੋ, ਤੇ ਪ੍ਰੇਮ ਨਾਲ ਖਾਣਾ ਖਾਓ।

4.5

ਅਵਤਾਰ:	ਇਹ ਨੇ ਡਾਕਟਰ ਕੁਰੈਸ਼ੀ, ਤੇ ਇਹ ਨੇ ਮੇਰੇ ਦੋਸਤ ਪ੍ਰੇਮ ਸ਼ਰਮਾ।
ਡਾਕਟਰ:	ਮੈਂ ਜਾਣਦਾ ਹਾਂ। ਮਿਲਕੇ ਬੜੀ ਖ਼ੁਸ਼ੀ ਹੋਈ, ਸ਼ਰਮਾ ਸਾਹਬ।
ਪ੍ਰੇਮ:	ਡਾਕਟਰ ਸਾਹਬ, ਤੁਸੀਂ ਮੈਨੂੰ ਕਿਵੇਂ ਜਾਣਦੇ ਹੋ?
ਡਾਕਟਰ:	ਟੀ ਵੀ ਪ੍ਰੋਗ੍ਰਾਮ ਤੋਂ। ਤੁਹਾਡੀ ਮੋਸੀਕੀ ਕਮਾਲ ਦੀ ਹੈ। ਵਾਹ!
ਪ੍ਰੇਮ:	ਜੀ ਸ਼ੁਕਰੀਆ।
ਡਾਕਟਰ:	ਮੇਰੇ ਲਾਇਕ ਕੋਈ ਖ਼ਿਦਮਤ ਹੈ ਤਾਂ ਹੁਕਮ ਕਰੋ।
ਅਵਤਾਰ:	ਅੱਜ ਇਹਨਾਂ ਦੀ ਤਬੀਅਤ ਠੀਕ ਨਹੀਂ।
ਡਾਕਟਰ:	ਕੀ ਗੱਲ ਹੈ?
ਪ੍ਰੇਮ:	ਮੈਨੂੰ ਥੋੜਾ ਬੁਖ਼ਾਰ ਹੈ, ਸਿਰ ਦਰਦ ਵੀ ਹੈ।
ਡਾਕਟਰ:	ਗਲਾ ਠੀਕ ਹੈ?
ਪ੍ਰੇਮ:	ਜੀ ਨਹੀਂ, ਗਲਾ ਵੀ ਖ਼ਰਾਬ ਹੈ, ਪੇਟ ਦਰਦ ਵੀ ਹੈ।
ਅਵਤਾਰ:	ਡਾਕਟਰ ਸਾਹਬ, ਮੈਨੂੰ ਫ਼ਿਕਰ ਹੈ। ਅਗਲੇ ਹਫ਼ਤੇ ਇਹਨਾਂ ਦਾ ਇਕ ਹੋਰ ਟੀ ਵੀ ਪ੍ਰੋਗ੍ਰਾਮ ਹੈ।
	. . .
ਡਾਕਟਰ:	ਫ਼ਿਕਰ ਦੀ ਕੋਈ ਗੱਲ ਨਹੀਂ। ਮਾਮੂਲੀ ਫ਼ਲੂ ਹੈ। ਸ਼ਰਮਾ ਸਾਹਬ, ਤੁਹਾਨੂੰ ਆਰਾਮ ਦੀ ਲੋੜ ਹੈ, ਦਵਾਈ ਦੀ ਨਹੀਂ।

5.1

ਬਲਦੇਵ ਨਿੱਜਰ:	ਆਓ ਕਲਸੀ ਸਾਹਬ, ਬੈਠੋ। ਹੁਕਮ ਕਰੋ।
ਸੁਰਜੀਤ ਕਲਸੀ:	ਮੈਨੂੰ ਦੋ ਟਿਕਟਾਂ ਚਾਹੀਦੀਆਂ ਨੇ।
ਬਲਦੇਵ ਨਿੱਜਰ:	ਆਪਣੇ ਲਈ?
ਸੁਰਜੀਤ ਕਲਸੀ:	ਹਾਂ ਜੀ।
ਬਲਦੇਵ ਨਿੱਜਰ:	ਤੁਸੀਂ ਕਿੱਥੇ ਜਾਣਾ ਹੈ?
ਸੁਰਜੀਤ ਕਲਸੀ:	ਦਿੱਲੀ, ਤੇ ਅੱਗੋਂ ਆਗਰੇ।
ਬਲਦੇਵ ਨਿੱਜਰ:	ਕਦੋਂ ਜਾਣਾ ਹੈ?
ਸੁਰਜੀਤ ਕਲਸੀ:	ਕ੍ਰਿਸਮਸ ਦੀਆਂ ਛੁੱਟੀਆਂ 'ਚ।
ਬਲਦੇਵ ਨਿੱਜਰ:	ਅੱਗੇ ਪਿੱਛੇ ਨਹੀਂ?

ਸੁਰਜੀਤ ਕਲਸੀ:	ਨਹੀਂ । ਕੀ ਗੱਲ ਹੈ?
ਬਲਦੇਵ ਨਿੰਜਰ:	ਕ੍ਰਿਸਮਸ ਦੀਆਂ ਛੁੱਟੀਆਂ 'ਚ ਟਿਕਟ ਮਹਿੰਗੀ ਹੁੰਦੀ ਹੈ, ਅੱਗੇ ਪਿੱਛੇ ਸਸਤੀ।
ਸੁਰਜੀਤ ਕਲਸੀ:	ਤੁਸੀਂ ਮਹਿੰਗੀ ਸਸਤੀ ਦੀ ਚਿੰਤਾ ਨਾ ਕਰੋ।
ਬਲਦੇਵ ਨਿੰਜਰ:	ਜੀ ਬਹੁਤ ਅੱਛਾ।

5.2

ਸੁਰਜੀਤ ਕਲਸੀ:	ਕੱਲ੍ਹ ਦਾ ਕੀ ਪ੍ਰੋਗ੍ਰਾਮ ਹੈ?
ਨਿਰਮਲ ਕੌਰ:	ਮੈਨੂੰ ਕੀ ਪਤਾ? ਤੁਸੀਂ ਦੱਸੋ।
ਸੁਰਜੀਤ ਕਲਸੀ:	ਚੰਗਾ ਫਿਰ, ਕੱਲ੍ਹ ਸਵੇਰੇ ਅਸੀਂ ਸ਼ੌਪਿੰਗ ਕਰਨੀ ਹੈ। ਦੁਪਹਿਰ ਦਾ ਖਾਣਾ ਤਾਜ ਮਹਲ ਹੋਟਲ 'ਚ ਖਾਣਾ ਹੈ।
ਨਿਰਮਲ ਕੌਰ:	ਤੇ ਸ਼ਾਮ ਨੂੰ ਕੀ ਕਰਨਾ ਹੈ?
ਸੁਰਜੀਤ ਕਲਸੀ:	ਸ਼ਾਮ ਨੂੰ ਸੈਰ ਸਪਾਟਾ, ਤੇ ਪੰਜਾਬੀ ਢਾਬੇ 'ਚ ਸਾਗ ਮੱਕੀ ਦੀ ਰੋਟੀ ਖਾਣੀ ਹੈ।
ਨਿਰਮਲ ਕੌਰ:	ਤਾਜ ਮਹਲ ਕਦੋਂ ਦੇਖਣਾ ਹੈ?
ਸੁਰਜੀਤ ਕਲਸੀ:	ਰਾਤ ਨੂੰ।
ਨਿਰਮਲ ਕੌਰ:	ਰਾਤ ਨੂੰ ਕਿਉਂ?
ਸੁਰਜੀਤ ਕਲਸੀ:	ਚਰਨੀ ਰਾਤ 'ਚ ਤਾਜ ਮਹਲ ਦਿਨ ਨਾਲੋਂ ਜ਼ਿਆਦਾ ਸੋਹਣਾ ਲਗਦਾ ਹੈ। ਜਿਵੇਂ ਤੂੰ
ਨਿਰਮਲ ਕੌਰ:	ਏਸ ਉਮਰ 'ਚ ਸ਼ਰਮ ਵੀ ਕਰੋ। ਇਹ ਕੋਈ ਮਸ਼ਕਰੀਆਂ ਕਰਨ ਦੀ ਉਮਰ ਹੈ?
ਸੁਰਜੀਤ ਕਲਸੀ:	ਨਹੀਂ, ਇਹ ਨਾਮ ਜਪਣ ਦੀ ਉਮਰ ਹੈ। ਤੇਰੇ ਕੋਲ ਕੋਈ ਧਰਮ ਪੋਥੀ ਹੈ?

5.3

ਨਿਰਮਲ ਕੌਰ:	ਅਸੀਂ ਮਥਰਾ ਬਿੰਦਰਾਬਨ ਦੇ ਮੰਦਰ ਕਦੋਂ ਦੇਖਣੇ ਨੇ?
ਸੁਰਜੀਤ ਕਲਸੀ:	ਪਰਸੋਂ ਨੂੰ। ਕੱਲ੍ਹ ਨੂੰ ਚਰਨਜੀਤ ਨੇ ਦਿੱਲੀਓਂ ਆਉਣਾ ਹੈ, ਤੇ ਪਰਸੋਂ ਨੂੰ ਅਸੀਂ ਉਹਦੇ ਨਾਲ ਜਾਣਾ ਹੈ।
ਨਿਰਮਲ ਕੌਰ:	ਪਰ ਉਹਨੇ ਤਾਂ ਚੌਥ ਨੂੰ ਆਉਣਾ ਸੀ।
ਸੁਰਜੀਤ ਕਲਸੀ:	ਆਉਣਾ ਤਾਂ ਉਹਨੇ ਚੌਥ ਨੂੰ ਹੀ ਸੀ, ਪਰ ਹੁਣ ਉਹਦਾ ਕੱਲ੍ਹ ਨੂੰ ਆਉਣ ਦਾ ਪ੍ਰੋਗ੍ਰਾਮ ਹੈ।

5.4

ਸੁਰਜੀਤ ਕਲਸੀ:	ਦਿੱਲੀ 'ਚ ਕਿਹਤੀਆਂ ਕਿਹਤੀਆਂ ਚੀਜ਼ਾਂ ਦੇਖਣ ਵਾਲੀਆਂ ਨੇ?
ਚਰਨਜੀਤ ਕਲਸੀ:	ਬਹੁਤ ਸਾਰੀਆਂ, ਨਵੀਆਂ ਵੀ ਤੇ ਪੁਰਾਣੀਆਂ ਵੀ।
ਸੁਰਜੀਤ ਕਲਸੀ:	ਮੈਂ ਤਾਂ ਪੁਰਾਣੀਆਂ ਚੀਜ਼ਾਂ ਤੇ ਇਮਾਰਤਾਂ ਨੂੰ ਹੀ ਦੇਖਣਾ ਹੈ, ਤੇ ਨਾਲੇ ਸਾਰੇ ਗੁਰਦੁਆਰਿਆਂ ਨੂੰ ਵੀ। ਮੈਨੂੰ ਨਵੀਆਂ ਚੀਜ਼ਾਂ ਦੇਖਣ ਦਾ ਕੋਈ ਸ਼ੌਕ ਨਹੀਂ।
ਚਰਨਜੀਤ ਕਲਸੀ:	ਪਰ ਕਈ ਨਵੀਆਂ ਚੀਜ਼ਾਂ ਵੀ ਬਹੁਤ ਸੋਹਣੀਆਂ ਨੇ।
ਸੁਰਜੀਤ ਕਲਸੀ:	ਠੀਕ ਹੈ ਕਾਕਾ। ਪਰ ਪੁਰਾਣੇ ਖ਼ਿਆਲਾਂ ਵਾਲੇ ਬੰਦੇ ਨੂੰ ਪੁਰਾਣੀਆਂ ਚੀਜ਼ਾਂ ਹੀ ਸੋਹਣੀਆਂ ਲਗਦੀਆਂ ਨੇ । ਜਿਵੇਂ ਤੇਰੀ ਚਾਚੀ।
ਨਿਰਮਲ ਕੌਰ:	ਤੁਹਾਨੂੰ ਕੋਈ ਸ਼ਰਮ ਹਿਆ ਹੈ ਜਾਂ ਨਹੀਂ? ਇਹ ਕੋਈ ਮੁੰਡੇ ਦੇ ਸਾਹਮਣੇ ਕਹਿਨ ਵਾਲੀ ਗੱਲ ਹੈ?
ਸੁਰਜੀਤ ਕਲਸੀ:	ਚਰਨਜੀਤ, ਦੱਸ ਤੂੰ ਆਪਣੀ ਵਹੁਟੀ ਨੂੰ ਪਿਆਰ ਕਰਦਾ ਹੈਂ?
ਚਰਨਜੀਤ ਕਲਸੀ:	ਬਹੁਤ।

ਸੁਰਜੀਤ ਕਲਸੀ:	ਪਿਆਰ ਨਾਲ ਆਪਣੀ ਘਰ ਵਾਲੀ ਨੂੰ ਛੇੜਨਾ ਕੋਈ ਬੁਰੀ ਗੱਲ ਹੈ?
ਚਰਨਜੀਤ ਕਲਸੀ:	ਬਿਲਕੁਲ ਨਹੀਂ।
ਨਿਰਮਲ ਕੌਰ:	ਤੁਸੀਂ ਚਾਚਾ ਭਤੀਜਾ ਦੋਵੇਂ ਬੇਸ਼ਰਮ ਹੋ।

6.1

ਮੋਹਨ ਜੋਸ਼ੀ:	ਨਮਸਤੇ, ਡਾਕਟਰ ਸਾਹਬ।
ਡਾਕਟਰ:	ਨਮਸਤੇ ਜੋਸ਼ੀ ਸਾਹਬਾ। ਤਸ਼ਰੀਫ਼ ਰਖੋ। ਠੀਕ ਠਾਕ ਹੋ ਨਾ?
ਮੋਹਨ ਜੋਸ਼ੀ:	ਠੀਕ ਠਾਕ ਬੰਦਾ ਤੁਹਾਡੇ ਕੋਲ ਕਦੋਂ ਆਉਂਦਾ ਹੈ?
ਡਾਕਟਰ:	ਬਿਲਕੁਲ ਸੱਚ ਹੈ। ਅੱਜ ਤੁਹਾਡੇ ਢਿੱਡ 'ਚ ਪੀੜ ਹੈ ਨਾ?
ਮੋਹਨ ਜੋਸ਼ੀ:	ਹਾਂ ਜੀ।
ਡਾਕਟਰ:	ਛਾਤੀ 'ਚ ਜਲਣ ਹੈ? ਸਿਰ ਚਕਰਾਉਂਦਾ ਹੈ?
ਮੋਹਨ ਜੋਸ਼ੀ:	ਹਾਂ ਜੀ।
ਡਾਕਟਰ:	ਪੇਸ਼ਾਬ ਲਗ ਕੇ ਆਉਂਦਾ ਹੈ?
ਮੋਹਨ ਜੋਸ਼ੀ:	ਹਾਂ ਜੀ।
ਡਾਕਟਰ:	ਕੱਲ੍ਹ ਤੁਹਾਨੂੰ ਉਲਟੀਆਂ ਵੀ ਆਈਆਂ?
ਮੋਹਨ ਜੋਸ਼ੀ:	ਕਮਾਲ ਹੈ! ਤੁਸੀਂ ਡਾਕਟਰ ਹੋ ਜਾਂ ਔਲੀਆ?
ਡਾਕਟਰ:	ਜੋਸ਼ੀ ਸਾਹਬ, ਜਵਾਬ ਦਿਓ। ਸਵਾਲ ਨਾ ਪੁੱਛੋ।
ਮੋਹਨ ਜੋਸ਼ੀ:	ਹਾਂ ਜੀ। ਆਈਆਂ।
ਡਾਕਟਰ:	ਹੂੰ ... ਹੂੰ ...

6.2

ਡਾਕਟਰ:	ਕੱਲ੍ਹ ਤੁਸੀਂ ਘਰ ਸੀ ਜਾਂ ਕਿਤੇ ਗਏ ਸੀ?
ਮੋਹਨ ਜੋਸ਼ੀ:	ਮੈਂ ਵਿਆਹ ਪਾਰਟੀ ਤੇ ਕਾਵੈਂਟਰੀ ਗਿਆ ਸੀ।
ਡਾਕਟਰ:	ਹੂੰ ... ਹੂੰ ... ਉੱਥੇ ਤੁਸੀਂ ਕੀ ਖਾਧਾ ਪੀਤਾ?
ਮੋਹਨ ਜੋਸ਼ੀ:	ਚਿਕਨ, ਮੀਟ, ਕਬਾਬ, ਮੱਛੀ, ਢੋਲੇ, ਭਟੂਰੇ, ਸਮੋਸੇ, ਪਕੌੜੇ।
ਡਾਕਟਰ:	ਫੇਰ ਤਾਂ ਜਨਾਬ ਨੇ ਵਾਹਵਾ ਚਟਪਟੇ ਖਾਣੇ ਛਕੇ। ਮਿਰਚਾਂ ਵਾਲੀ ਇਮਲੀ ਦੀ ਚਟਨੀ ਨਾਲ। ਹੈ ਨਾ?
ਮੋਹਨ ਜੋਸ਼ੀ:	ਹਾਂ ਜੀ।
ਡਾਕਟਰ:	ਤੁਸੀਂ ਸ਼ਰਾਬ ਵੀ ਪੀਤੀ?
ਮੋਹਨ ਜੋਸ਼ੀ:	ਰੱਜ ਕੇ। ਬੀਅਰ ਤੇ ਪੱਕੀ ਦੋਨੋਂ ਪੀਤੀਆਂ।
ਡਾਕਟਰ:	ਉਸ ਪਾਰਟੀ 'ਚ ਮੈਂ ਵੀ ਸੀ।
ਮੋਹਨ ਜੋਸ਼ੀ:	ਹੈਂ? ਪਰ ਮੈਂ ਤੁਹਾਨੂੰ ਦੇਖਿਆ ਨਹੀਂ।
ਡਾਕਟਰ:	ਤੁਸੀਂ ਮੈਨੂੰ ਦੇਖਿਆ ਜ਼ਰੂਰ, ਪਰ ਪਛਾਣਿਆ ਨਹੀਂ। ਤੁਸੀਂ ਨਸ਼ੇ 'ਚ ਧੁੱਤ ਸੀਗੇ।

6.3

ਡਾਕਟਰ:	ਜੋਸ਼ੀ ਸਾਹਬ, ਤੁਸੀਂ ਸਿਆਣੇ ਬਿਆਣੇ ਹੋ। ਤੁਸੀਂ ਕਿਉਂ ਆਪਣੀ ਸੇਹਤ ਦਾ ਸੱਤਿਆਨਾਸ ਕਰਦੇ ਹੋ?
ਮੋਹਨ ਜੋਸ਼ੀ:	ਮਾੜੀਆਂ ਆਦਤਾਂ ਨਹੀਂ ਜਾਂਦੀਆਂ।

ਡਾਕਟਰ:	ਮਾੜੀਆਂ ਆਦਤਾਂ ਤੁਹਾਨੂੰ ਕਿਸੇ ਹੋਰ ਨੇ ਨਹੀਂ ਪਾਈਆਂ। ਤੁਸੀਂ ਖ਼ੁਦ ਪਾਈਆਂ।
ਮੋਹਨ ਜੋਸ਼ੀ:	ਜੀ ਠੀਕ ਹੈ।
ਡਾਕਟਰ:	ਜਿਗਰ ਤੁਹਾਡਾ ਖ਼ਰਾਬ ਹੈ, ਗੁਰਦੇ ਤੁਹਾਡੇ ਖ਼ਰਾਬ ਨੇ, ਸਾਹ ਦੀ ਤਕਲੀਫ਼ ਤੁਹਾਨੂੰ। ਜੇ ਤੁਸੀਂ ਅਕਲ ਤੋਂ ਕੰਮ ਲੈਂਦੇ ਤਾਂ ਅੱਜ ਤੁਸੀਂ ਤੰਦਰੁਸਤ ਹੁੰਦੇ। ਤੁਹਾਨੂੰ ਇਹ ਬੀਮਾਰੀਆਂ ਨਾ ਹੁੰਦੀਆਂ।
ਮੋਹਨ ਜੋਸ਼ੀ:	ਜੀ ਮੈਂ ਮੰਨਦਾ ਹਾਂ। ਗਲਤੀ ਮੇਰੀ ਆਪਣੀ ਹੈ।
ਡਾਕਟਰ:	ਦੱਸੋ ਹੁਣ ਕੀ ਚਾਹੀਦਾ ਹੈ? ਇਲਾਜ ਜਾਂ ਮੌਤ?
ਮੋਹਨ ਜੋਸ਼ੀ:	ਮੈਂ ਸਮਝਿਆ ਨਹੀਂ।
ਡਾਕਟਰ:	ਸ਼ਰਾਬ ਨਾ ਪੀਣ ਦੀ ਸਹੁੰ ਖਾਓ। ਤਾਂ ਮੈਂ ਇਲਾਜ ਕਰਨਾ ਹੈ।
ਮੋਹਨ ਜੋਸ਼ੀ:	ਠੀਕ ਹੈ ਜੀ।

6.4

ਡਾਕਟਰ:	ਜੋਸ਼ੀ ਸਾਹਬ, ਮੈਨੂੰ ਪਤਾ ਹੈ। ਮੇਰੀਆਂ ਕਈ ਗੱਲਾਂ ਤੁਹਾਨੂੰ ਬੁਰੀਆਂ ਲੱਗੀਆਂ। ਪਰ ਮੈਂ ਤੁਹਾਡਾ ਡਾਕਟਰ ਹਾਂ। ਮੇਰਾ ਕੰਮ ਤੁਹਾਨੂੰ ਠੀਕ ਕਰਨਾ ਹੈ, ਖ਼ੁਸ਼ ਕਰਨਾ ਨਹੀਂ।
ਮੋਹਨ ਜੋਸ਼ੀ:	ਮੈਨੂੰ ਤੁਹਾਡੀ ਕੋਈ ਗੱਲ ਬੁਰੀ ਨਹੀਂ ਲੱਗੀ।
ਡਾਕਟਰ:	ਚੰਗਾ ਫਿਰ ਪਹਿਲਾਂ ਤੁਸੀਂ ਇਹ ਦੋ ਦਵਾਈਆਂ ਲੈਣੀਆਂ। ਸਵੇਰੇ ਕੁਝ ਖਾ ਪੀ ਕੇ ਦਵਾਈ ਲੈਣੀ। ਖ਼ਾਲੀ ਪੇਟ ਨਹੀਂ। ਅਗਲੇ ਹਫ਼ਤੇ ਆ ਕੇ ਮੈਨੂੰ ਜ਼ਰੂਰ ਦੱਸਣਾ। ਕੋਈ ਫ਼ਰਕ ਪਿਆ ਜਾਂ ਨਹੀਂ।
ਮੋਹਨ ਜੋਸ਼ੀ:	ਹੋਰ ਕੋਈ ਗੱਲ?
ਡਾਕਟਰ:	ਮਿਰਚ ਮਸਾਲੇ ਤੋਂ ਪਰਹੇਜ਼ ਕਰਨਾ। ਤੇ ਸ਼ਰਾਬ ਨੂੰ ਦੇਖਣਾ ਵੀ ਨਹੀਂ।
ਮੋਹਨ ਜੋਸ਼ੀ:	ਜੀ ਠੀਕ ਹੈ।

7.1

ਮਨਜੀਤ ਸੰਧੂ:	ਤੁਹਾਨੂੰ ਪੰਜਾਬੀ ਆਉਂਦੀ ਹੈ?
ਅਨੀਤਾ:	ਥੋੜੀ ਥੋੜੀ ਆਉਂਦੀ ਹੈ।
ਮਨਜੀਤ ਸੰਧੂ:	ਥੋੜੀ ਥੋੜੀ ਨਹੀਂ। ਤੁਸੀਂ ਬਹੁਤ ਸੋਹਣੀ ਪੰਜਾਬੀ ਬੋਲਦੇ ਹੋ। ਤੁਹਾਡੀ ਮਾਤ ਭਾਸ਼ਾ ਪੰਜਾਬੀ ਹੈ ਜਾਂ ਅੰਗ੍ਰੇਜ਼ੀ?
ਅਨੀਤਾ:	ਮੇਰੇ ਮਾਤਾ ਜੀ ਅੰਗ੍ਰੇਜ਼ ਨੇ ਤੇ ਪਿਤਾ ਜੀ ਪੰਜਾਬੀ। ਇਸ ਲਈ ਮੇਰੀ ਮਾਂ ਬੋਲੀ ਅੰਗ੍ਰੇਜ਼ੀ ਹੈ।
ਮਨਜੀਤ ਸੰਧੂ:	ਘਰ ਵਿਚ ਤੁਸੀਂ ਅੰਗ੍ਰੇਜ਼ੀ ਬੋਲਦੇ ਹੋ ਜਾਂ ਪੰਜਾਬੀ?
ਅਨੀਤਾ:	ਆਮ ਤੌਰ ਤੇ ਅੰਗ੍ਰੇਜ਼ੀ। ਪਰ ਦਾਦੀ ਜੀ ਪੰਜਾਬੀ ਬੋਲਦੇ ਨੇ। ਉਹਨਾਂ ਨੂੰ ਅੰਗ੍ਰੇਜ਼ੀ ਨਹੀਂ ਆਉਂਦੀ। ਮਾਤਾ ਜੀ ਵੀ ਥੋੜੀ ਥੋੜੀ ਪੰਜਾਬੀ ਬੋਲ ਸਕਦੇ ਨੇ - ਸਿਰਫ਼ ਦਾਦੀ ਜੀ ਨਾਲ।
ਮਨਜੀਤ ਸੰਧੂ:	ਤੁਸੀਂ ਪੰਜਾਬੀ ਕਿੱਥੋਂ ਸਿੱਖੀ?
ਅਨੀਤਾ:	ਦਾਦੀ ਜੀ ਤੋਂ। ਪਿਤਾ ਜੀ ਨੇ ਵੀ ਮੈਨੂੰ ਕਾਫ਼ੀ ਪੰਜਾਬੀ ਸਿਖਾਈ।

7.2

ਮਨਜੀਤ ਸੰਧੂ:	ਤੁਸੀਂ ਪੰਜਾਬੀ ਪੜ੍ਹ ਲਿਖ ਵੀ ਸਕਦੇ ਹੋ?
ਅਨੀਤਾ:	ਹਾਲੇ ਚੰਗੀ ਤਰ੍ਹਾਂ ਪੜ੍ਹ ਲਿਖ ਨਹੀਂ ਸਕਦੀ। ਮੈਂ ਦੋ ਕੁ ਮਹੀਨਿਆਂ ਤੋਂ ਪੰਜਾਬੀ ਪੜ੍ਹਨਾ ਲਿਖਣਾ ਸਿੱਖ ਰਹੀ ਹਾਂ। ਮੈਂ ਪੈਂਤੀ ਸਿੱਖ ਚੁੱਕੀ ਹਾਂ। ਹੁਣ ਮੈਂ ਪੰਜਾਬੀ ਦੇ ਛੋਟੇ ਛੋਟੇ ਸ਼ਬਦ ਪੜ੍ਹ ਲਿਖ ਲੈਂਦੀ ਹਾਂ। ਪੰਜਾਬੀ 'ਚ ਆਪਣਾ ਨਾਂ ਲਿਖ ਲੈਂਦੀ ਹਾਂ।

7.3

ਮਨਜੀਤ ਸੰਧੂ:	ਤੁਸੀਂ ਕਦੇ ਪੰਜਾਬ ਗਏ ਹੋ?
ਅਨੀਤਾ:	ਇਕ ਵਾਰੀ ਗਈ ਸੀ, ਜਦ ਮੈਂ ਛੋਟੀ ਸੀ। ਪਰ ਮੈਨੂੰ ਹੁਣ ਯਾਦ ਨਹੀਂ। ਅਗਲੇ ਮਹੀਨੇ ਮੈਂ ਪਿਤਾ ਜੀ ਨਾਲ ਫਿਰ ਜਾ ਰਹੀ ਹਾਂ।
ਮਨਜੀਤ ਸੰਧੂ:	ਸੈਰ ਕਰਨ ਲਈ?
ਅਨੀਤਾ:	ਹਾਂ, ਮੈਂ ਸੈਰ ਵੀ ਕਰਾਂਗੀ, ਤੇ ਰਿਸ਼ਤੇਦਾਰਾਂ ਨੂੰ ਵੀ ਮਿਲਾਂਗੀ। ਕੁਝ ਖੋਜ ਦਾ ਕੰਮ ਵੀ ਕਰਾਂਗੀ।
ਮਨਜੀਤ ਸੰਧੂ:	ਖੋਜ ਦਾ ਕੰਮ?
ਅਨੀਤਾ:	ਹਾਂ ਜੀ, ਪ੍ਰੋਗਰਾਮ ਬਣਾ ਰਹੀ ਹਾਂ। ਸੋਚਦੀ ਹਾਂ ਕਿ ਵੀਡੀਓ ਕੈਮਰਾ ਲੈ ਚਲਾਂ, ਤੇ ਪੰਜਾਬੀ ਔਰਤਾਂ ਬਾਰੇ ਫਿਲਮ ਬਣਾਵਾਂ।
ਮਨਜੀਤ ਸੰਧੂ:	ਪੰਜਾਬੀ ਔਰਤਾਂ ਬਾਰੇ ਕਿਉਂ?
ਅਨੀਤਾ:	ਮੈਂ ਖ਼ੁਦ ਪੰਜਾਬੀ ਔਰਤ ਹਾਂ। ਪੂਰੀ ਨਹੀਂ ਤਾਂ ਅੱਧੀ ਜ਼ਰੂਰ ਹਾਂ। ਮੈਂ ਪੰਜਾਬੀ ਔਰਤਾਂ ਬਾਰੇ ਥੀਸਿਸ ਵੀ ਲਿਖ ਰਹੀ ਹਾਂ। ਥੋੜ੍ਹਾ ਜਿਹਾ ਕੰਮ ਕਰ ਚੁੱਕੀ ਹਾਂ। ਕੁਝ ਪੰਜਾਬ ਜਾ ਕੇ ਕਰਾਂਗੀ, ਤੇ ਬਾਕੀ ਵਾਪਸ ਆ ਕੇ।
ਮਨਜੀਤ ਸੰਧੂ:	ਬਹੁਤ ਖ਼ੁਸ਼ੀ ਦੀ ਗੱਲ ਹੈ।

7.4

ਅਨੀਤਾ:	ਸੰਧੂ ਸਾਹਬ, ਤੁਸੀਂ ਮੇਰੀ ਕੁਝ ਮਦਦ ਕਰ ਸਕਦੇ ਹੋ?
ਮਨਜੀਤ ਸੰਧੂ:	ਹਾਂ ਹਾਂ ਜ਼ਰੂਰ। ਦੱਸੋ।
ਅਨੀਤਾ:	ਤੁਸੀਂ ਚੰਡੀਗੜ੍ਹ 'ਚ ਕਿਸੇ ਨੂੰ ਜਾਣਦੇ ਹੋ? ਮੈਂ ਪੰਜਾਬ ਯੂਨੀਵਰਸਿਟੀ 'ਚ ਕੁਝ ਦਿਨ ਕੰਮ ਕਰਨਾ ਚਾਹੁੰਦੀ ਹਾਂ। ਪਰ ਉਥੇ ਰਹਿਣ ਦੀ ਮੁਸ਼ਕਿਲ ਹੈ।
ਮਨਜੀਤ ਸੰਧੂ:	ਮੇਰਾ ਇਕ ਦੋਸਤ ਉਥੇ ਪੜ੍ਹਾਉਂਦਾ ਹੈ। ਮੈਂ ਉਹਨੂੰ ਖ਼ਤ ਲਿਖ ਦਿਆਂਗਾ। ਤੁਸੀਂ ਜਾ ਕੇ ਉਹਨੂੰ ਮਿਲ ਲੈਣਾ। ਤੁਸੀਂ ਚੰਡੀਗੜ੍ਹ ਕਿੰਨੇ ਦਿਨ ਠਹਿਰੋਗੇ?
ਅਨੀਤਾ:	ਦਸ ਦਿਨ। ਦਸ ਜੂਨ ਤੋਂ ਵੀਹ ਜੂਨ ਤਕ।
ਮਨਜੀਤ ਸੰਧੂ:	ਠੀਕ ਹੈ। ਮੈਂ ਉਹਨੂੰ ਹੁਣੇ ਖ਼ਤ ਲਿਖ ਦਿੰਦਾ ਹਾਂ। ਉਹ ਤੁਹਾਡੇ ਠਹਿਰਨ ਦਾ ਇੰਤਜ਼ਾਮ ਕਰ ਦੇਵੇਗਾ - ਯੂਨੀਵਰਸਿਟੀ ਵਿਮੈੱਨਜ਼ ਹੋਸਟਲ 'ਚ। ਹੋਰ ਕੋਈ ਕੰਮ ਹੈ ਤਾਂ ਦੱਸੋ।
ਅਨੀਤਾ:	ਬਸ ਜੀ, ਬਹੁਤ ਬਹੁਤ ਸ਼ੁਕਰੀਆ।

8.1

ਅਕਰਮ ਖ਼ਾਨ:	ਜਾਵੇਦ ਸਾਹਬ, ਔਹ ਤੁਹਾਡਾ ਮੇਜ਼ ਬੜਾ ਸੋਹਣਾ ਹੈ। ਕਿੱਥੋਂ ਖ਼ਰੀਦਿਆ ਸੀ?
ਜਾਵੇਦ ਸ਼ੇਖ਼:	ਖ਼ਰੀਦਿਆ ਨਹੀਂ ਸੀ, ਆਰਡਰ ਦੇ ਕੇ ਬਣਵਾਇਆ ਸੀ।

ਅਕਰਮ ਖ਼ਾਨ:	ਕਿੱਥੋਂ? ਮੈਂ ਵੀ ਦੋ ਮੇਜ਼ ਬਣਵਾਉਣੇ ਚਾਹੁੰਦਾ ਹਾਂ। ਬਿਲਕੁਲ ਔਂਦਾ ਦੇ ਹੀ।
ਜਾਵੇਦ ਸ਼ੇਖ਼:	ਮੇਰੇ ਦੋਸਤ ਦੀ ਫ਼ਰਨੀਚਰ ਫ਼ੈਕਟਰੀ ਹੈ, ਜਿੱਥੇ ਬੜੇ ਵਧੀਆ ਕੁਰਸੀਆਂ ਮੇਜ਼ ਬਣਦੇ ਨੇ। ਉੱਥੇ ਆਰਡਰ ਦੇਣਾ ਪਏਗਾ।
ਅਕਰਮ ਖ਼ਾਨ:	ਕੀ ਨਾਂ ਹੈ ਤੁਹਾਡੇ ਦੋਸਤ ਦਾ?
ਜਾਵੇਦ ਸ਼ੇਖ਼:	ਗੁਰਨਾਮ ਸਿੰਘ ਭਮਰਾ। ਅਸੀਂ ਇੱਕੋ ਸਕੂਲ 'ਚ ਪੜ੍ਹਾਉਂਦੇ ਸੀ। ਬਾਅਦ 'ਚ ਉਹਨੇ ਪੜ੍ਹਾਉਣਾ ਛੱਡ ਕੇ ਆਪਣਾ ਖ਼ਾਨਦਾਨੀ ਕਾਰੋਬਾਰ ਸ਼ੁਰੂ ਕਰ ਲਿਆ।
ਅਕਰਮ ਖ਼ਾਨ:	ਕੀ ਉਹ ਖ਼ੁਦ ਫ਼ਰਨੀਚਰ ਬਣਾਉਂਦਾ ਹੈ? ਆਪਣੇ ਹੱਥੀਂ?
ਜਾਵੇਦ ਸ਼ੇਖ਼:	ਨਹੀਂ। ਪਹਿਲਾਂ ਉਹਨੇ ਕੀਨੀਆ ਤੋਂ ਆਪਣੇ ਬਾਪ ਨੂੰ ਮੰਗਵਾਇਆ। ਫ਼ੈਕਟਰੀ ਦਾ ਸਾਰਾ ਕੰਮ ਉਹਦੇ ਬਾਪ ਦੀ ਨਿਗਰਾਨੀ 'ਚ ਹੁੰਦਾ ਹੈ। ਬਾਹਰਲਾ ਕੰਮ ਗੁਰਨਾਮ ਸੰਭਾਲਦਾ ਹੈ, ਤੇ ਅੰਦਰਲਾ ਕੰਮ ਉਹਦਾ ਬਾਪ। ਇਹ ਬਜ਼ੁਰਗ ਹੈ ਬੜਾ ਕਾਰੀਗਰ।
ਅਕਰਮ ਖ਼ਾਨ:	ਅਸੀਂ ਕੱਲ੍ਹ ਉਹਦੀ ਫ਼ੈਕਟਰੀ ਚਲੀਏ?
ਜਾਵੇਦ ਸ਼ੇਖ਼:	ਜ਼ਰੂਰ।

8.2

ਜਾਵੇਦ ਸ਼ੇਖ਼:	ਗੁਰਨਾਮ, ਇਹ ਨੇ ਮੇਰੇ ਦੋਸਤ ਅਕਰਮ ਖ਼ਾਨ। ਅਕਰਮ ਸਾਹਬ, ਇਹ ਨੇ ਮੇਰੇ ਦੋਸਤ ਗੁਰਨਾਮ ਸਿੰਘ ਭਮਰਾ। ਕੱਲ੍ਹ ਅਸੀਂ ਇਹਨਾਂ ਦੇ ਬਾਰੇ ਹੀ ਗੱਲਾਂ ਕਰ ਰਹੇ ਸੀ।
ਗੁਰਨਾਮ ਸਿੰਘ:	ਮਿਲਕੇ ਬੜੀ ਖ਼ੁਸ਼ੀ ਹੋਈ।
ਅਕਰਮ ਖ਼ਾਨ:	ਮੈਨੂੰ ਵੀ ਬੜੀ ਖ਼ੁਸ਼ੀ ਹੋਈ। ਮੈਂ ਤੁਹਾਡੀ ਬੜੀ ਸ਼ੋਹਰਤ ਸੁਣੀ ਹੈ। ਸੋਚਿਆ ਇਕ ਦੋ ਵਧੀਆ ਮੇਜ਼ ਹੀ ਤੁਹਾਥੋਂ ਬਣਵਾ ਲਵਾਂ।
ਗੁਰਨਾਮ ਸਿੰਘ:	ਬੜੀ ਮੇਹਰਬਾਨੀ। ਪਰ ਇਹ ਕੰਮ ਮੇਰੇ ਪਿਤਾ ਜੀ ਕਰਦੇ ਨੇ। ਮੈਂ ਹੁਣੇ ਉਹਨਾਂ ਨੂੰ ਲਿਆਉਂਦਾ ਹਾਂ।
	. . .
ਜਾਵੇਦ, ਅਕਰਮ:	ਸਤਿ ਸ੍ਰੀ ਅਕਾਲ ਜੀ।
ਸਰਦੂਲ ਸਿੰਘ:	ਸਤਿ ਸ੍ਰੀ ਅਕਾਲ ਜੀ। ਬੈਠੋ। ਹੁਕਮ ਕਰੋ।
ਅਕਰਮ ਖ਼ਾਨ:	ਹੁਕਮ ਨਹੀਂ, ਬਜ਼ੁਰਗਵਾਰ, ਅਰਜ਼ ਹੈ। ਤੁਹਾਨੂੰ ਯਾਦ ਹੋਏਗਾ, ਤੁਸੀਂ ਜਾਵੇਦ ਸਾਹਬ ਲਈ ਇਕ ਮੇਜ਼ ਬਣਾਇਆ ਸੀ। ਮੈਨੂੰ ਬਿਲਕੁਲ ਉਸੇ ਕਿਸਮ ਦੇ ਦੋ ਮੇਜ਼ ਚਾਹੀਦੇ ਨੇ। ਬਣਾ ਦਿੳਗੇ?
ਸਰਦੂਲ ਸਿੰਘ:	ਜ਼ਰੂਰ ਬਣਾਵਾਂਗੇ। ਪਰ ਤਿੰਨ ਚਾਰ ਹਫ਼ਤੇ ਲਗਣਗੇ। ਅਸੀਂ ਕਾਹਲੀ ਦਾ ਕੰਮ ਨਹੀਂ ਕਰਦੇ।
ਅਕਰਮ ਖ਼ਾਨ:	ਕੋਈ ਗੱਲ ਨਹੀਂ। ਮੈਨੂੰ ਵੀ ਕੋਈ ਕਾਹਲੀ ਨਹੀਂ।

8.3

ਗੁਰਨਾਮ ਸਿੰਘ:	ਸ਼ੁਰੂ ਸ਼ੁਰੂ ਵਿਚ ਸਾਨੂੰ ਕਈ ਮੁਸ਼ਕਿਲਾਂ ਆਈਆਂ। ਪਰ ਹੁਣ ਸਾਡਾ ਕੰਮ ਸੋਹਣਾ ਚਲਦਾ ਹੈ। ਅੱਜ ਸਾਡੇ ਕਾਮੇ ਨਹੀਂ ਆਏ। ਉਹ ਵੀਕਐਂਡ ਤੇ ਛੁੱਟੀ ਕਰਦੇ ਨੇ, ਤੇ ਸਾਡੀਆਂ ਮਸ਼ੀਨਾਂ ਵੀ।
ਅਕਰਮ ਖ਼ਾਨ:	ਇਹ ਤੁਹਾਡਾ ਸਟੋਰ ਰੂਮ ਹੈ?
ਗੁਰਨਾਮ ਸਿੰਘ:	ਹਾਂ ਜੀ। ਐਥੇ ਅਸੀਂ ਲੱਕੜ ਰੱਖਦੇ ਹਾਂ। ਸਾਡਾ ਫ਼ਰਨੀਚਰ ਸਟੋਰ ਰੂਮ ਵੱਖਰਾ ਹੈ। ..... ਐਥੇ ਲੱਕੜ ਚੀਰੀ ਜਾਂਦੀ ਹੈ। ਪਹਿਲਾਂ ਵੱਡੇ ਆਰੇ ਤੇ ਵੱਡੇ ਵੱਡੇ ਟੁਕੜੇ ਕੱਟੇ ਜਾਂਦੇ ਨੇ।

	ਫ਼ਿਰ ਛੋਟੇ ਆਰਿਆਂ ਤੇ ਲੋੜ ਮੁਤਾਬਕ ਛੋਟੇ ਟੁਕੜੇ ਬਣਾਏ ਜਾਂਦੇ ਨੇ।
ਅਕਰਮ ਖ਼ਾਨ:	ਤੇ ਬਾਅਦ 'ਚ?
ਗੁਰਨਾਮ ਸਿੰਘ:	ਫ਼ਿਰ ਮੇਜ਼ ਕੁਰਸੀਆਂ ਦੇ ਵੱਖ ਵੱਖ ਹਿੱਸੇ ਤਿਆਰ ਕੀਤੇ ਜਾਂਦੇ ਨੇ। ਉਹਨਾਂ ਹਿੱਸਿਆਂ ਨੂੰ ਜੋੜ ਕੇ ਕੁਰਸੀਆਂ ਮੇਜ਼ ਬਣਾਏ ਜਾਂਦੇ ਨੇ। ਤੇ ਅਖ਼ੀਰ 'ਚ ਉਹਨਾਂ ਨੂੰ ਪਾਲਿਸ਼ ਕੀਤਾ ਜਾਂਦਾ ਹੈ।
ਅਕਰਮ ਖ਼ਾਨ:	ਇਹ ਸਾਰਾ ਕੰਮ ਕੌਣ ਕਰਦਾ ਹੈ?
ਗੁਰਨਾਮ ਸਿੰਘ:	ਸਾਡੇ ਕਾਮੇ। ਵੈਸੇ ਤਾਂ ਉਹ ਸਾਰੇ ਹੀ ਚੰਗੇ ਕਾਰੀਗਰ ਨੇ, ਪਰ ਇੱਕ ਇੱਕ ਚੀਜ਼ ਪਿਤਾ ਜੀ ਦੀ ਨਿਗਰਾਨੀ 'ਚ ਬਣਾਈ ਜਾਂਦੀ ਹੈ।
ਅਕਰਮ ਖ਼ਾਨ:	ਮਾਸ਼ਾ ਅੱਲਾ! ਤੁਹਾਡੀ ਫ਼ੈਕਟਰੀ ਕਾਫ਼ੀ ਵੱਡੀ ਹੈ।
ਗੁਰਨਾਮ ਸਿੰਘ:	ਬਸ ਜੀ, ਰੱਬ ਦਾ ਸ਼ੁਕਰ ਹੈ। ਸਾਡੀ ਦਾਲ ਰੋਟੀ ਚੱਲੀ ਜਾਂਦੀ ਹੈ, ਤੇ ਨਾਲੇ ਸਾਡੇ ਵੀਹ ਕੁ ਕਾਰੀਗਰਾਂ ਦੀ ਵੀ।

8.4

ਜਾਵੇਦ ਸ਼ੇਖ਼:	ਭਮਰਾ ਸਾਹਬ, ਜੇ ਬੁਰਾ ਨਾ ਮੰਨੋ ਤਾਂ ਇਕ ਗੱਲ ਪੁੱਛਾਂ?
ਸਰਦੂਲ ਸਿੰਘ:	ਜ਼ਰੂਰ ਪੁੱਛੋ।
ਜਾਵੇਦ ਸ਼ੇਖ਼:	ਤੁਹਾਡੀ ਉਮਰ ਕੀ ਹੈ?
ਸਰਦੂਲ ਸਿੰਘ:	ਸੱਤਰ ਸਾਲ।
ਜਾਵੇਦ ਸ਼ੇਖ਼:	ਤੁਸੀ ਇਸ ਉਮਰ ਵਿਚ ਵੀ ਐਨਾ ਕੰਮ ਕਿਵੇਂ ਕਰ ਲੈਂਦੇ ਹੋ?
ਸਰਦੂਲ ਸਿੰਘ:	ਜਨਾਬ, ਮੈਂ ਕੋਈ ਪੜ੍ਹਿਆ ਲਿਖਿਆ ਬਾਬੂ ਨਹੀਂ। ਮੈਂ ਤਾਂ ਸਿੱਧਾ ਸਾਦਾ ਅਨਪੜ੍ਹ ਮਜ਼ਦੂਰ ਹਾਂ। ਮੇਰੇ ਗੁਰੂ ਦਾ ਹੁਕਮ ਹੈ - ਨਾਮ ਜਪੋ, ਵੰਡ ਛਕੋ, ਕਿਰਤ ਕਰੋ। ਮੈਂ ਇਹ ਤਿੰਨੇ ਕੰਮ ਕਰੀ ਜਾਂਦਾ ਹਾਂ। ਇਹੋ ਮੇਰੇ ਧਰਮ ਹੈ, ਇਹੋ ਮੇਰਾ ਈਮਾਨ ਹੈ। ਮੈਨੂੰ ਪੈਸੇ ਦਾ ਕੋਈ ਲਾਲਚ ਨਹੀਂ। ਵਾਹਿਗੁਰੂ ਹੱਕ ਹਲਾਲ ਦੀ ਰੋਟੀ ਦੇਈ ਜਾਏ। ਐਥੇ ਕੰਮ ਕਰਨ ਵਾਲੇ ਮੇਰੇ ਸਾਰੇ ਬੱਚਿਆਂ ਨੂੰ ਵੀ, ਤੇ ਮੈਨੂੰ ਵੀ। ਹੋਰ ਮੈਨੂੰ ਕੁਝ ਨਹੀਂ ਚਾਹੀਦਾ।
ਜਾਵੇਦ ਸ਼ੇਖ਼:	ਤੁਸੀਂ ਬਿਲਕੁਲ ਦਰੁਸਤ ਫ਼ਰਮਾਇਆ। ਤੁਸੀਂ ਆਪਣਾ ਕੰਮ ਕਰੀ ਜਾਂਦੇ ਹੋ, ਤੇ ਉਹ ਦਾਤਾ ਆਪਣਾ ਕੰਮ ਕਰੀ ਜਾਂਦਾ ਹੈ।

Grammatical summary

You may already know that Panjabi, like English and most other European languages, belongs to the Indo-European family of languages. So you can regard Panjabi as a distant cousin of English, which certainly has 'family resemblances' with English and other European languages. If you know a language like French, Italian, Spanish or, especially, Russian, the grammatical system of Panjabi will look familiar to you.

Detailed notes on the relevant aspects of Panjabi grammar appear in the Conversation units. In this section, only an outline summary of the salient features of Panjabi grammar is provided. Use this section in conjunction with and to supplement the more detailed explanations given earlier.

Nouns

A noun in Panjabi, as in English and other Indo-European languages, names persons, places, and concrete or abstract objects.

Gender

A noun in Panjabi is either masculine or feminine. Most male animate beings are masculine and most female animate beings are feminine. But sometimes the sex of an animate being cannot be known or is unimportant. In such cases, grammatical gender is arbitrarily assigned. For example, **kɑ̃:** ਕਾਂ ('crow') and **macchʰar** ਮੱਛਰ ('mosquito') are masculine and **gʰùggi:** ਘੁੱਗੀ ('dove') and **jũ:** ਜੂੰ ('louse') are feminine. As far as objects and place names are concerned, the assignment of grammatical gender is totally arbitrary. There is no reason on earth why **sir** ਸਿਰ ('head'), **a:lu:** ਆਲੂ ('potato'), **pa:ni:** ਪਾਣੀ ('water') and **landan** ਲੰਡਨ ('London') should be masculine and **akkʰ** ਅੱਖ ('eye'), **ga:jar** ਗਾਜਰ ('carrot'), **cá:ɦ** ਚਾਹ ('tea') and **dilli:** ਦਿੱਲੀ ('Delhi') feminine.

A large number of masculine nouns end in **-a:** and a large number of feminine nouns end in **-i:**. But this is not a rule and there are exceptions as well.

Number

Like English, Panjabi uses the singular form of the noun to refer to one person or object and the plural form to refer to more than one person or object. But the Panjabi way of regarding an object as one or more than one may differ from that of English. **paja:ma:** ਪਜਾਮਾ ('pyjamas') and **kẽci:** ਕੈਂਚੀ ('scissors') are singular in Panjabi but plural in English. On the other hand, **cɔl** ਚੌਲ ('rice') and **jɔ** ਜੌਂ ('barley') are singular in English but plural in Panjabi. Interestingly enough, masculine foodgrains in Panjabi are always plural and feminine food grains are always singular.

Direct and oblique forms

Some Panjabi nouns change their form before a postposition (see below). The form of the noun used before a postposition is called the oblique form. The non-oblique form is known as the direct form.

Only masculine nouns have oblique forms which may differ from the direct forms. The rules for the derivation of oblique forms also take into account whether or not the (masculine) noun ends in **-a:**. The following examples illustrate the rules:

(a) Masculine nouns ending in **-a:**

	Direct	*Oblique (before the postposition* **ne**)
Singular	**munɖa:** ਮੁੰਡਾ	**munɖe ne** ਮੁੰਡੇ ਨੇ (**a:** changes into **e**)
Plural	**munɖe** ਮੁੰਡੇ	**munɖiã: ne** ਮੁੰਡਿਆਂ ਨੇ
	(**a:** changes into **e**)	(**a:** changes into **-iã:**)

(b) Masculine nouns not ending in **-a:**

	Direct	*Oblique (before the postposition* **ne**)
Singular	**cor** ਚੋਰ	**cor ne** ਚੋਰ ਨੇ (No change)
Plural	**cor** ਚੋਰ	**corã: ne** ਚੋਰਾਂ ਨੇ
	(No change)	(add **-ã:**)

(c) Feminine nouns

	Direct	Oblique (before the postposition **ne**)
Singular	**kuɽi:**	**kuɽi: ne**
	ਕੁੜੀ	ਕੁੜੀ ਨੇ
Plural	**kuɽi:ɑ̃:**	**kuɽi:ɑ̃: ne**
	ਕੁੜੀਆਂ	ਕੁੜੀਆਂ ਨੇ
	(add -**ɑ̃:**)	(add -**ɑ̃:**)

You can see that the oblique forms of feminine nouns are not different from the direct forms.

Articles

Panjabi has no articles (the equivalents of the English 'a', 'an' and 'the'). But some modern Panjabi writers have started using **ikk** as an equivalent of 'a/an' and **úñ** as an equivalent of 'the' in their formal academic writing.

Pronouns

Pronouns are words used in place of nouns to refer to persons, places, and concrete or abstract objects. Panjabi has the following pronouns.

Personal pronouns

	Direct form	Oblique form with **nū:**	Oblique form with **tõ**
First person			
Singular	**mɛ̃**	**mɛnū:**	**mɛtʰõ**
	ਮੈਂ	ਮੈਨੂੰ	ਮੈਥੋਂ
Plural	**asĩ:**	**sɑ:nū:**	**sɑ:tʰõ**
	ਅਸੀਂ	ਸਾਨੂੰ	ਸਾਥੋਂ
Second Person			
Singular	**tū:**	**tɛnū:**	**tɛtʰõ**
	ਤੂੰ	ਤੈਨੂੰ	ਤੈਥੋਂ
Plural	**tusĩ:**	**tuɦɑ:nū:**	**tuɦɑ:tʰõ**
	ਤੁਸੀਂ	ਤੁਹਾਨੂੰ	ਤੁਹਾਥੋਂ

The third person pronouns of Panjabi are actually demonstratives (the equivalents of the English 'this', 'that', 'these' and 'those'). Hence there is the distinction for nearness (or proximity) and distance.

Demonstrative pronouns

	Direct form	Oblique form with **nū:**	Oblique form with **tõ**
Proximal			
Singular	íɦ	íɦnū:, is nū:	íɦtõ, is tõ
	ਇਹ	ਇਹਨੂੰ , ਇਸ ਨੂੰ	ਇਹਤੋਂ, ਇਸ ਤੋਂ
Plural	íɦ	íɦnã: nū:	íɦnã: tõ
	ਇਹ	ਇਹਨਾਂ ਨੂੰ	ਇਹਨਾਂ ਤੋਂ
Remote			
Singular	úɦ	úɦnū:, us nū:	úɦtõ, us tõ
	ਉਹ	ਉਹਨੂੰ , ਉਸ ਨੂੰ	ਉਹਤੋਂ , ਉਸ ਤੋਂ
Plural	úɦ	úɦnã: nū:	úɦnã: tõ
	ਉਹ	ਉਹਨਾਂ ਨੂੰ	ਉਹਨਾਂ ਤੋਂ

When singular **íɦ** is an adjective, its oblique form is **is**. Similarly, the oblique form of singular adjective **úɦ** is **us**.

Other pronouns

kɔṇ *ਕੌਣ* 'who' (question word)

Singular	kɔṇ	kíɦnū:, kis nū:	kíɦtõ, kis tõ
	ਕੌਣ	ਕਿਹਨੂੰ, ਕਿਸ ਨੂੰ	ਕਿਹਤੋਂ, ਕਿਸ ਤੋਂ
Plural	kɔṇ	kíɦnã: nū:	kíɦnã: tõ
	ਕੌਣ	ਕਿਹਨਾਂ ਨੂੰ	ਕਿਹਨਾਂ ਤੋਂ

koi: *ਕੋਈ* 'any'

	Direct form	Oblique form with **nū:**	Oblique form with **tõ**
Singular	koi:	kise nū:	kise tõ
	ਕੋਈ	ਕਿਸੇ ਨੂੰ	ਕਿਸੇ ਤੋਂ
Plural	koi:		
	ਕੋਈ		

kífiɽaː *ਕਿਹੜਾ* 'which' (masculine)

Singular	**kífiɽaː**	**kífinũː, kis nũː**	**kífitõ, kis tõ**
	ਕਿਹੜਾ	ਕਿਹਨੂੰ, ਕਿਸ ਨੂੰ	ਕਿਹਤੋਂ, ਕਿਸ ਤੋਂ
Plural	**kífiɽe**	**kífinãː nũː**	**kífinãː tõ**
	ਕਿਹੜੇ	ਕਿਹਨਾਂ ਨੂੰ	ਕਿਹਨਾਂ ਤੋਂ

kífiɽiː *ਕਿਹੜੀ* 'which' (feminine)

Singular	**kífiɽiː**	**kífinũː, kis nũː**	**kífitõ, kis tõ**
	ਕਿਹੜੀ	ਕਿਹਨੂੰ, ਕਿਸ ਨੂੰ	ਕਿਹਤੋਂ, ਕਿਸ ਤੋਂ
Plural	**kífiɽiːãː**	**kífinãː nũː**	**kífinãː tõ**
		kífiɽiːãː nũː	**kífiɽiːãː tõ**
	ਕਿਹੜੀਆਂ	ਕਿਹਨਾਂ ਨੂੰ	ਕਿਹਨਾਂ ਤੋਂ
		ਕਿਹੜੀਆਂ ਨੂੰ	ਕਿਹੜੀਆਂ ਤੋਂ

jífiɽaː, jífiɽi: 'who' (relative pronoun)

ਜਿਹੜਾ, ਜਿਹੜੀ

Forms are derived in the same way as those of **kífiɽaː, kífiɽiː**.

Adjectives

Adjectives describe or qualify nouns and pronouns. Unlike the English adjectives but like the Spanish and French adjectives, Panjabi adjectives (or a certain type of Panjabi adjectives; see below) are marked for number and gender and also have oblique forms.

Black and red adjectives

Adjectives in Panjabi, Hindi–Urdu and other North Indian languages can be divided into two classes – the 'black' and the 'red' adjectives. Black adjectives change their form (for number, gender and before a postposition). But red adjectives are always invariant.

It is quite easy to find out the 'colour' of an adjective. If it ends in **-aː**, it is black; otherwise it is red. Indian linguists invented these 'colourful' grammatical terms because the North Indian word **kaːlaː** 'black' is a typical black adjective, and **laːl** 'red' is a typical red adjective!

The following endings are used with black adjectives when they change their form for number and gender. As far as oblique forms are concerned, black adjectives behave like masculine nouns ending in **-aː** or feminine nouns ending in **-iː**. (See page 59.)

	Singular	*Plural*
Masculine	**-a:**	**-e**
feminine	**-i:**	**-i:ã:**

Many forms of verbs also take these endings. (See below.) In Conversation unit 1 we called this table the Magic square.

Possessive adjectives

The Panjabi possessive adjectives (equivalents of the English 'my', 'our', 'your', 'his', 'her', etc.) are grammatically black adjectives. They are given below in the masculine singular form

mera:	ਮੇਰਾ	my
sa:ɖa:	ਸਾਡਾ	our
tera:	ਤੇਰਾ	your (*sg*)
tufia:ɖa:	ਤੁਹਾਡਾ	your (*pl*)
ífida: (*proximal*)	ਇਹਦਾ	his, her, its
ífinã: da: (*proximal*)	ਇਹਨਾਂ ਦਾ	their
úfida: (*remote*)	ਉਹਦਾ	his, her, its
úfinã: da: (*remote*)	ਉਹਨਾਂ ਦਾ	their

Postpositions

The Panjabi equivalents of the English prepositions (such as 'on', 'at', 'in', 'into', etc.) are placed after nouns or pronouns. Hence Panjabi has postpositions.

Simple postpositions

Simple postpositions are one-word postpositions (like the English 'on', 'in', 'from'). Important simple postpositions in Panjabi are

nũ:	ਨੂੰ	to
tõ	ਤੋਂ	from
tɑk	ਤਕ	up to
utte	ਉੱਤੇ	on
vic	ਵਿਚ	'in', into
ne	ਨੇ	agentive marker (see page 107)
va:la:	ਵਾਲਾ	see page 95
da:	ਦਾ	of

da: and **va:la:** change their form like black adjectives.

Compound postpositions

In English, you have compound prepositions like 'in the middle of ', 'in place of ', 'at the top of ', etc., in which a preposition is followed by a noun which in turn is followed by 'of '. The complete phrase or group of words works like a single preposition. This happens in Panjabi as well, except that Panjabi has compound postpositions. The nouns, pronouns and the postposition **da:** involved in such compound postpositions are in the oblique form. For example:

Noun	*compound postposition*
kamre	**de gabbʰe**
ਕਮਰੇ	ਦੇ ਗੱਭੇ
mez	**de utte**
ਮੇਜ਼	ਦੇ ਉੱਤੇ
kʰa:ɳe	**tõ: magrõ**
ਖਾਣੇ	ਤੋਂ ਮਗਰੋਂ

The use of -õ and -ĩː

-õ is often added to nouns to serve the purpose of the postposition **-tõ** ('from'). For example, **gʰàrõ** ਘਰੋਂ and **gʰàr tõ** ਘਰ ਤੋਂ have the same meaning – 'from home'.

-ĩː is added to the names of the body parts which occur in pairs to convey the sense of 'with both'. Examples are **ɦattʰĩː** ਹੱਥੀਂ 'with both hands' and **akkʰĩː** ਅੱਖੀਂ 'with both eyes'.

Question words

The English question words (such as 'who', 'when', 'where', 'why') are also known as 'wh-' words because they all have 'w' and 'h' in them. For the same reason, the Panjabi question words are also known as **k**-words. Important **k**-words in Panjabi are

Pronouns

ki:	ਕੀ	what
kɔɳ	ਕੌਣ	who
kíɦɽa:	ਕਿਹੜਾ	which

Possessive (black) adjectives

kífidɑ:	ਕਿਹਦਾ	whose
kífiɽɑ:	ਕਿਹੜਾ	which

Adverbs

kittʰe	ਕਿੱਥੇ	where
kitʰõ	ਕਿੱਥੋਂ	from where
kɑd	ਕਦ	when
kɑdõ	ਕਦੋਂ	when
kiũ	ਕਿਉਂ	why
kivẽ	ਕਿਵੇਂ	how
kiddɑ̃:	ਕਿੱਦਾਂ	how

Verbs

Since the traditional Indian concept of time is quite different from the European 'unilinear' concept of time (time flowing in a single direction from the past through the present into the future), it would be wrong to expect in Panjabi grammar 'tenses' similar to those found in European languages.

Tense and aspect

Tense is a grammatical category which relates a situation or event to an outside point in time (generally the time of utterance), in relation to which the situation is present or past or future. Tense was important in the grammar of the ancestor languages of Panjabi and other North Indian languages. But now only one verb in Panjabi – fiɛ – is marked for tense. All other verbs are marked for aspect. The grammatical category of aspect marks an event or situation as completed, uncompleted, recurring, potential, etc. without relating it to an outside point in time.

Personal, adjectival and nominal forms

Some verb forms in Panjabi are marked for number and person (first, second and third person). They are called the personal forms. Others are marked for number and gender. They are called adjectival forms because they can also be used as adjectives. There also are forms which function as nouns. They are called the nominal forms.

Personal forms

The verb ਹੈ

ਹੈ is the only verb in Panjabi which is marked for tense (present and past only). Its forms are

Present tense

	Singular	Plural
First person	**hɑ̃:** ਹਾਂ (I) am	**hɑ̃:** ਹਾਂ (We) are
Second person	**hɛ̃** ਹੈਂ (You) are	**ho** ਹੋ (You) are
Third person	**hɛ** ਹੈ (He/she/it) is	**hɑn [ne]** ਹਨ [ਨੇ] (They) are

Past Tense

In formal and written Panjabi, the past tense forms of **ਹੈ** are

	Singular	Plural
First person	**sɑ̃:** ਸਾਂ (I) was	**sɑ̃:** ਸਾਂ (We) were
Second person	**sɛ̃** ਸੈਂ (You) were	**si:** ਸੀ (You) were
Third person	**si:** ਸੀ (He/she/it) was	**sɑn** ਸਨ (They) were

But in the most commonly used colloquial variety of of Panjabi, only **si:** is used for all persons.

Imperative form

This form is used for giving orders and making requests. As in English, the bare stem can be used as an imperative form, which is the third person singular from. **-o** is added to make this form the third person plural. This plural form can be used to make a 'polite' request to one person. There is also another imperative form which expresses a request in the form of a suggestion. This form can be called the suggestive imperative. All these imperative forms of the verb are given below:

Order:	**kar**	do	(*sg*)
Request:	**karo**	Please do	(*pl*)
Suggestion:	**kari:**	Please do	(*sg*)
Suggestion:	**kari:o**	Please do	(*pl*)

Subjunctive form

This form represents the bare idea of an action or event without relating it to any point in time (tense) or indicating its completion, etc. (aspect).

Stems ending in a consonant

Person	Ending	Example
First		
Singular	-ã:	**karã:** ਕਰਾਂ
Plural	-i:e	**kari:e** ਕਰੀਏ
Second		
Singular	-ẽ	**karẽ** ਕਰੇਂ
Plural	-o	**karo** ਕਰੋ
Third		
Singular	-e	**kare** ਕਰੇ
Plural	-an *or* -aṇ	**karan** ਕਰਨ

Stems ending in a vowel

Person	Ending	Example
First		
Singular	-vã:	**ja:vã:** ਜਾਵਾਂ
Plural	-i:e	**ja:i:e** ਜਾਈਏ
Second		
Singular	-vẽ *or* -ẽ	**ja:vẽ** *or* **jaẽ**
		ਜਾਵੇਂ ਜਾਏਂ
Plural	-vo *or* -o	**ja:vo** *or* **ja:o**
		ਜਾਵੋ ਜਾਓ

Person	Ending	Example
Third		
Singular	**-ve** *or* **-e**	**jaːve** *or* **jaːe** ਜਾਵੇ ਜਾਏ
Plural	**-ɳ**	**jaːɳ** ਜਾਣ

When **-gaː** (a personal form – see below) is added to the subjunctive form, the combination refers to a future action or event.

Adjectival forms

The adjectival forms are marked for number and gender, like black adjectives, and they take the same endings (given in the Magic square on page 225).

Imperfective form

This form refers to an action or a situation which is viewed as uncompleted or incomplete. This basic meaning is often extended to cover habitual and recurring situations as well, and to actions or events which could not take place in the past. Very often (and generally in poetry), it is also used to make a situation vivid.

This form is derived by adding **-d-** to the stem and then by adding one of the adjectival number–gender suffixes. If the stem ends in a vowel sound, this vowel is nasalised. With most stems ending in **-aː**, a nasalised **-ū-** is also added before **-d-**. For example:

kardaː ਕਰਦਾ	(kar + d + aː)	(masculine singular)
pĩːde ਪੀਂਦੇ	(piː + nasalisation + d + e)	(masculine plural)
paːūdi ਪਾਉਂਦੀ	(paː + u + nasalisation + d + iː)	(feminine singular)
jãːdiːãː ਜਾਂਦੀਆਂ	(jaː + nasalisation + d + iːãː)	(feminine plural)

There is another form of the imperfective form. It is derived by adding the **d** + suffix to a special form of the stem which ends in **-iː**. When this stem of the verb is used, the subject is not mentioned and the sentence conveys the meaning of some sort of universally applicable obligation or advice.

gurduːre	vic	sir	dʰàkiːdɑ:	fiɛ
ਗੁਰਦੁਆਰੇ	ਵਿਚ	ਸਿਰ	ਢਕੀਦਾ	ਹੈ
Sikh temple	in	head	to cover	is

One should cover one's head in a Sikh temple.

The form **dʰàkiːdɑ:** is drived from the special stem **dʰàkiː: (dʰàk + iː)**. The final **iː** of such a stem is not nasalised before **-d-** with this type of stem.

Perfective form

This form views an action or event as completed or complete, generally, but not necessarily, in the past. So it would be wrong to call it the past tense form (as many Panjabi grammars do). The endings for this form (added to the stem **fiat** in the following table) are

	Singular	*Plural*
Masculine	**-iɑ:** fiaʈiɑ: ਹਟਿਆ	**-e** fiaʈe ਹਟੇ
Feminine	**iː** fiaʈiː ਹਟੀ	**-iːɑ̃:** fiaʈiːɑ̃: ਹਟੀਆਂ

Unfortunately, some Panjabi verbs have irregular perfective forms. While they all take the endings mentioned above, their stems undergo some other changes as well before these endings are added. A list of such irregular verbs is given on page 241.

The perfective form may agree with the subject or the object or may not agree with anything (in which case it is in the masculine singular form). These agreement rules are give on page 104.

Potential form

This form represents an action or event as potential (but with some amount of certainty, and not just as vague idea or possibility, such as the one represented by the subjunctive form). This form is derived by adding **ɳ** or **n** to the stem and then the number–gender suffix. Stems which get a **-u-** before the suffix in the imperfective form get a **-u-** for this form as well. For example:

karna: (kar + n + a:)   (masculine singular)
ਕਰਨਾ

piːɳe	(piː + ɳ + e)	(masculine plural)
ਪੀਣੇ		
paːũɳiː	(pɑː + u + ɳ + iː)	(feminine singular)
ਪਾਉਣੀ		
kʰaːɳiːãː	(kʰɑː + ɳ + iːãː)	(feminine plural)
ਖਾਣੀਆਂ		

The rule governing the choice between **ɳ** and **n** is: use **ɳ ਣ**, except after **ɳ ਣ**, **r ਰ** and **ɾ ੜ** (and **l ਲ**, when you pronounce it as **l̞**), where you use **n ਨ**.

-gaː: -ਗਾ

-gaː: -ਗਾ is not an independent verb form capable of standing alone. It is added to the subjunctive form and to **ɦɛ** and **siː** to convey an idea of definiteness. When it is added to the subjunctive form, the combination refers to a future event. **ɦɛgaː** means 'definitely is' and **siːgaː** means 'definitely was'. The adjectival number–gender affixes are added to **-gaː:** -ਗਾ .

Nominal forms

The nominal forms are derived from verbs but function as nouns.

Gerund or verbal noun

This form is identical to the potential form in spelling and pronunciation. But its grammatical behaviour is that of a masculine singular noun, with the difference that its oblique form is derived not by changing **-aː** into **-e** (as is the case with the masculine singular nouns ending in **-aː**) but by dropping **-aː**. For example:

jaːɳaː	to go
ਜਾਣਾ	
jaːɳ laiː	in order to go
ਜਾਣ ਲਈ	

But some speakers of Panjabi have started using the gerund form like a regular noun, and that they would say

| jaːɳe laiː |
| ਜਾਣੇ ਲਈ |

ke ਕੇ

ke ਕੇ joins a verb in the stem form with another verb in a personal or adjectival or nominal form in order to represent a situation as a series of actions performed in a sequence. There is no grammatical limit on the number of verbs which can be joined in this way. Examples are given on page 114.

Auxiliary verbs or helping verbs

These verbs, when used with other verbs (called the main verbs) add to or modify the meaning of the main verbs. The most commonly used auxiliary verbs in Panjabi are

Auxiliary verb		Meaning
jɑː	ਜਾ	completion
sutt	ਸੁੱਟ	do something vehemently
lɛ	ਲੈ	do something for oneself
de	ਦੇ	do something for others
rakʰ	ਰਖ	do something with concern
cʰadd	ਛੱਡ	do something disinterestedly
cuk	ਚੁਕ	complete something
rɑ́ĥi	ਰਹਿ	continue doing something
sak	ਸਕ	be able to do something
lag	ਲਗ	start doing something
lag pɛ	ਲਗ ਪੈ	start doing something suddenly

Verb sequences

In all the languages spoken in the Indian subcontinent, including Panjabi, there can be long and complicated verb sequences, and the number of such grammatically possible sequences runs into hundreds. You do not have to list all these sequences and learn them one by one. No sensible learner learns an Indian language in this way. (And, of course, no grammarian has so far attempted to list all these possible sequences.) If you know the meanings of the main and auxiliary verbs and their forms in the sequence, it is quite easy to guess the meaning of the sequence as a whole. Some sequences with the main verb **cal** ਚਲ 'move' and forms of **hɛ** ਹੈ 'is', **siː** ਸੀ 'was' and **rɑ́ĥi** ਰਹਿ are given below.

mɛ̃ calda: ɦɑ̃:	ਮੈਂ ਚਲਦਾ ਹਾਂ	I move
mɛ̃ calda: sɑ̃:	ਮੈਂ ਚਲਦਾ ਸਾਂ	I used to move
mɛ̃ calda:	ਮੈਂ ਚਲਦਾ	I'd have moved
mɛ̃ calia: ɦɑ̃:	ਮੈਂ ਚਲਿਆ ਹਾਂ	I have moved *or* I'm going to move right now
mɛ̃ calia: sɑ̃:	ਮੈਂ ਚਲਿਆ ਸਾਂ	I had moved *or* I was going to move right then
mɛ̃ calia:	ਮੈਂ ਚਲਿਆ	I moved
mɛ̃ cal rɪ́ɦia: ɦɑ̃:	ਮੈਂ ਚਲ ਰਿਹਾ ਹਾਂ	I'm moving
mɛ̃ cal rɪ́ɦia: sɑ̃:	ਮੈਂ ਚਲ ਰਿਹਾ ਸਾਂ	I was moving
mɛ̃ calɑ̃:	ਮੈਂ ਚਲਾਂ	I may move
mɛ̃ calɑ̃:ga:	ਮੈਂ ਚਲਾਂਗਾ	I'll move
mɛ̃ cal rɪ́ɦia: ɦovɑ̃:ga:	ਮੈਂ ਚਲ ਰਿਹਾ ਹੋਵਾਂਗਾ	I'll be moving

Word order

The order of words in a Panjabi sentence is not as rigidly fixed as in English. The only rigidly fixed order is that of a noun/pronoun and the postposition. A postposition must come after the noun or the pronoun. But this does not mean that elsewhere you can 'put anything anywhere'. Generally, a verb in Panjabi comes at the end of the sentence, adjectives come before the nouns they qualify and auxiliary verbs follow the main verb. Considerations such as highlighting or emphasising or focusing upon something do considerably affect the order of words in the sentence. But the relevant rules are too complicated for an introductory course such as this (but see p. 111).

Important Panjabi verbs

This section gives some important Panjabi verbs in the gerund (or verbal noun) form, as in Panjabi dictionaries. The gerund form is derived by adding the suffix -ਤਾ or ਨਾ to the stem. ਨਾ is used only after ੜ, ਰ and ੲ (and after ਲ when you pronounce it as ਲ਼).With most stems ending in ਾ (-aː), you insert ੁ (-u-) between the stem and the suffix. An example is ਗਾਉਣਾ (stem ਗਾ plus -ਉਣਾ) but there are a few exceptions like ਜਾਣਾ (ਜਾ plus ਣਾ). (The same thing happens when you add a suffix to derive the imperfective form.)

Verbs are marked as intransitive (*vi*) or transitive (*vt*) or causative (*vc*).

A list of the irregular perfective forms is given separately.

Dictionary order of letters, symbols and markers in Panjabi

The verbs in this section are arranged 'alphabetically' according to the principle followed by some modern Panjabi dictionaries, which is

1   Letters are arranged as they are in the table on page 9, except that

ਸ਼   ਖ਼   ਗ਼   ਜ਼   ਫ਼

are not regarded as different from

ਸ   ਖ   ਗ   ਜ   ਫ   respectively.

But the letters which are printed differently should also be pronounced differently.

2   Subscript ੍ਰ and ੍ਵ are not regarded as different from the 'full' ਰ ਵ respectively.

3   Symbols are arranged in the order given below:
Invisible   ਾ   ਿ   ੀ   ੁ   ੂ   ੇ   ੈ   ੋ   ੌ

4   Other markers (Addhak, Bindi and Tippi) are arranged in this order
ੱ   ਂ   ੰ

Since symbols are added to letters and markers to symbols, the ordering principle seems complex at first but it is really quite simple if you keep in mind the above-mentioned rules. Look at the dictionary order of the following words and you'll see the principle at work:

ਉਮਰ	ਉਠ	ੳਮ	ੳੰਕਾਰ	ਅਨਾਰ	ਆਸ	ਆਂਡਾ	ਔਸ਼
ਔਦਾਂ	ਇਮਲੀ	ਇੰਜਨ	ਈਦ	ਈਨ	ਏਕਤਾ	ਸਪੇਰਾ	ਸਰਾਂ
ਸੱਪ	ਸੰਧ	ਸ਼ਾਹ	ਸਾਂਗਾ	ਸਿਰ	ਸਿੰਘੀ	ਸਿੰਘ	ਸੀਖ
ਸੀਰਾ	ਸ਼ੀਂਹ	ਹਲ	ਹਲਕਾ	ਹੱਕ	ਹੱਲ	ਹਾਕ	ਹਿੱਲ
ਹਿੰਗ	ਹੀਲਾ	ਹੀਂਗ	ਹੁਕਮ	ਹੁੱਕਾ	ਹੁਕ	ਹੁੰਗ	ਹੇਕਾ
ਹੌਂਕਣਾ,	etc.						

The verbs are not given in the phonetic transcription. It is assumed that the learners who wish to advance their knowledge of Panjabi will also learn the Panjabi (Gurmukhi) script.

Verbs

ੳ

ਉੱਠਣਾ (*vi*)	rise
ਉੱਡਣਾ (*vi*)	fly
ਉਡੀਕ (*vt*)	to wait
ਉਤਰ (*vi*)	come down
ਉਤਾਰ (*vt*)	bring down
ਉਬਲਣਾ (*vi*)	boil
ਉਬਾਲਣਾ (*vt*)	boil
ਉਤਨਾ (*vi*)	fly
ਉਲਟਣਾ (*vt*)	reverse

ਅ

ਆਉਣਾ (*vi*)	come
ਆਖਣਾ (*vt*)	say
ਅਟਕਣਾ (*vi*)	stop

ਸ

ਸਕਣਾ (*vi*)	be able to
ਸੱਦਣਾ (*vt*)	invite
ਸੰਭਾਲਣਾ (*vt*)	take care of
ਸਮਝਣਾ (*vi*)	understand
ਸਮਝਾਉਣਾ (*vt*)	persuade
ਸਾਂਭਣਾ (*vt*)	take care of
ਸਿੱਖਣਾ (*vt*)	learn
ਸਿਖਾਉਣਾ (*vc*)	teach
ਸਿਮਰਨਾ (*vt*)	mutter
ਸੁਆਰਨਾ (*vt*)	brush up
ਸੁੱਟਣਾ (*vt*)	throw
ਸੁਣਨਾ (*vi*)	hear
ਸੁਣਾਉਣਾ (*vt*)	tell
ਸੁਲਾਉਣਾ (*vt/vc*)	put to sleep, cause to sleep
ਸੇਕਣਾ (*vt*)	warm

ਸੌਣਾ (*vi*)	sleep

ਹ

ਹੱਸਣਾ (*vi*)	laugh
ਹਟਣਾ (*vi*)	move away
ਹਟਾਉਣਾ (*vt*)	move away
ਹਾਰਨ (*vi*)	lose
ਹਰਾਉਣਾ (*vt*)	defeat
ਹਿੱਲਣਾ (*vi*)	move
ਹਿਲਾਉਣਾ (*vt*)	move
ਹੋਣਾ (*vi*)	be, happen

ਕ

ਕਹਿਣਾ (*vt*)	say
ਕੱਜਣਾ (*vt*)	cover
ਕੱਟਣਾ (*vt*)	cut
ਕੱਢਣਾ (*vt*)	take out
ਕਢਵਾਉਣਾ (*vc*)	cause to take out
ਕੱਤਣਾ (*vt*)	spin
ਕੰਬਣਾ (*vi*)	tremble
ਕਰਨ (*vt*)	do
ਕਰਵਾਉਣਾ (*vc*)	cause to do
ਕੁੱਟਣਾ (*vt*)	beat
ਕੁਤਰਨਾ (*vt*)	cut into small pieces
ਕੁੱਦਣਾ (*vi*)	jump

ਖ

ਖੱਟਣਾ (*vt*)	earn
ਖੜਕਾਉਣਾ (*vt*)	knock at
ਖਰਚਣਾ (*vt*)	spend
ਖੜ੍ਨਾ (*vi*)	stand
ਖਾਣਾ (*vt*)	eat

ਖਿੱਚਣਾ (*vt*)	pull	ਛੱਡਣਾ (*vt*)	give up
ਖਿਲਾਉਣਾ (*vc/vt*)	cause to eat, feed	ਛਾਨਣਾ (*vt*)	sieve
		ਛਾਪਣਾ (*vt*)	print
ਖੇਡਣਾ (*vi/vt*)	play	ਛਿੱਕਣਾ (*vi*)	sneeze
ਖੇਲਣਾ (*vi/vt*)	play	ਛਿੱਲਣਾ (*vt*)	peel
ਖੁੱਲ੍ਹਣਾ (*vi*)	open	ਛੂਹਣਾ (*vt*)	touch
ਖੋਹਲਣਾ (*vt*)	open		

ਜ

ਗ		ਜਪਣਾ (*vt*)	mutter
ਗਾਉਣਾ (*vi/vt*)	sing	ਜੰਮਣਾ (*vi*)	be born
ਗਿਣਨਾ (*vt*)	count	ਜਮਾਉਣਾ (*vt*)	give birth
ਗਿਰਾਉਣਾ (*vt*)	fell	ਜਲਣਾ (*vi*)	burn
ਗੁਆਉਣਾ (*vt*)	lose	ਜਲਾਉਣਾ (*vt*)	burn
ਗੁਆਚਣਾ (*vi*)	become lost	ਜਾਗਣਾ (*vi*)	wake up
ਗੁੰਨ੍ਹਣਾ (*vt*)	knead	ਜਾਣਾ (*vi*)	go
		ਜਾਣਨਾ (*vt*)	know
ਘ		ਜਾਪਣਾ (*vt*)	seem
ਘਲਣਾ (*vt*)	send	ਜਿੱਤਣਾ (*vi/vt*)	win, conquer
ਘੁੱਟਣਾ (*vt*)	hold tightly		
ਘੁੰਮਣਾ (*vi*)	rotate	ਜੀਉਣਾ (*vi*)	live
ਘੇਰਨਾ (*vt*)	surround	ਜੁੜਨਾ (*vi*)	be joined
ਘੋਲਣਾ (*vt*)	dissolve	ਜੋੜਨਾ (*vt*)	join

ਝ

ਚ		ਝਗੜਨਾ (*vi*)	quarrel
ਚਖਣਾ (*vt*)	taste	ਝੜਨਾ (*vi*)	fall off
ਚੱਟਣਾ (*vt*)	lick	ਝਾੜਨਾ (*vt*)	shake off
ਚੱਬਣਾ (*vt*)	munch	ਝਿੜਕਣਾ (*vt*)	rebuke
ਚਬਾਉਣਾ (*vt*)	chew	ਝੁਕਣਾ (*vi*)	bow, bend
ਚਲਣਾ (*vi*)	move	ਝੁਕਾਉਣਾ (*vt*)	bow, bend
ਚਲਾਉਣਾ (*vt*)	drive	ਝੁੱਲਣਾ (*vi*)	blow
ਚੜਨਾ (*vi*)	climb, rise		
ਚੜ੍ਹਾਉਣਾ (*vt*)	raise	**ਟ**	
ਚਾਹੁਣਾ (*vt*)	desire	ਟਕਰਾਉਣਾ (*vi*)	collide
ਚਾੜ੍ਹਨਾ (*vt*)	raise	ਟੰਗਣਾ (*vt*)	hang
ਚੁਨਣਾ (*vt*)	choose	ਟੱਪਣਾ (*vi*)	jump
ਚੀਰਨਾ (*vt*)	saw	ਟਾਲਣਾ (*vt*)	put off
ਚੁੱਕਣਾ (*vt*)	lift, pick up	ਟਿਕਣਾ (*vi*)	stay
ਚੁਰਾਉਣਾ (*vt*)	steal	ਟਿਕਾਉਣਾ (*vt*)	place
		ਟੁੱਟਣਾ (*vi*)	break
ਛ			
ਛਕਣਾ (*vt*)	relish		

ਠ

ਠਹਿਰਨਾ (*vt*)	stay
ਠਹਿਰਾਉਣਾ (*vc*)	cause to stay
ਠਾਰਨਾ (*vt*)	make cool
ਠੋਕਣਾ (*vt*)	beat

ਡ

ਡੱਸਣਾ (*vt*)	sting, bite
ਡੱਕਣਾ (*vt*)	stop
ਡੰਗਣਾ (*vt*)	sting, bite
ਡਟਣਾ (*vi*)	stand firm
ਡਰਨਾ (*vi*)	be afraid
ਡਰਾਉਣਾ (*vt*)	frighten
ਡਾਂਟਣਾ (*vt*)	rebuke
ਡਿਗਣਾ (*vi*)	fall
ਡੇਗਣਾ (*vt*)	bring down
ਡੁੱਬਣਾ (*vi*)	sink
ਡੁਬੋਣਾ (*vt*)	sink
ਡੁੱਲ੍ਹਣਾ (*vi*)	spill
ਡੇਗਣਾ (*vt*)	fell
ਡੋਲ੍ਹਣਾ (*vt*)	shed, spill

ਢ

ਢਹਿਣਾ (*vi*)	fall down
ਢਕਣਾ (*vt*)	cover
ਢਾਹੁਣਾ (*vt*)	fell, demolish
ਢਾਲਣਾ (*vt*)	melt

ਤ

ਤੱਕਣਾ (*vi*)	look
ਤਰਨਾ (*vi*)	swim
ਤਲਣਾ (*vt*)	deep fry
ਤੜਕਣਾ (*vt*)	shallow fry
ਤੜਫਣਾ (*vi*)	writhe in pain
ਤਾਰਨਾ (*vt*)	float
ਤਾੜਨਾ (*vt*)	rebuke
ਤਿਆਗਣਾ (*vt*)	abandon

ਤਿਲ੍ਕਣਾ (*vi*)	slip
ਤੁਰਨਾ (*vi*)	walk, move
ਤੁੜਕਣਾ (*vt*)	shallow fry
ਤੈਰਨਾ (*vi*)	swim
ਤੋੜਨਾ (*vt*)	break

ਥ

ਥੱਕਣਾ (*vi*)	become tired
ਥਕਾਉਣਾ (*vt*)	make tired
ਥਾਪੜਨਾ (*vt*)	tap, pat
ਥੁੱਕਣਾ (*vi*)	spit

ਦ

ਦੱਸਣਾ (*vt*)	tell
ਦੱਫਨਾਉਣਾ (*vt*)	bury (a dead body)
ਦੱਬਣਾ (*vt*)	bury
ਦਬਾਉਣਾ (*vt*)	press
ਦਿਸਣਾ (*vi*)	be visible
ਦਿਖਾਉਣਾ (*vt*)	show
ਦਿਵਾਉਣਾ (*vc*)	cause to be given
ਦੁਹਰਾਉਣਾ (*vt*)	revise
ਦੁਖਣਾ (*vi*)	ache
ਦੁਖਾਉਣਾ (*vt*)	hurt
ਦੇਖਣਾ (*vt*)	see
ਦੇਣਾ (*vt*)	give
ਦੌੜਨਾ (*vi*)	run

ਪ

ਪੱਕਣਾ (*vt*)	push
ਪੜਕਣਾ (*vi*)	palpitate
ਪਾਰਨਾ (*vt*)	resolve
ਧੁਆਉਣਾ (*vc*)	cause to wash
ਧੋਣਾ (*vt*)	wash

ਨ

| ਨੱਸਣਾ (*vi*) | run |

ਨਹਾਉਣਾ (vi)	have a bath	ਪੁਚਾਉਣਾ (vt/vc)	cause to reach
ਨੱਚਣਾ (vi)	dance		
ਨਚੋੜਨਾ (vt)	squeeze	ਪੁੱਜਣਾ (vi)	reach
ਨੱਠਣਾ (vi)	run	ਪੁੱਟਣਾ (vt)	uproot
ਨ੍ਹਾਉਣਾ (vi)	have a bath	ਪੂਜਣਾ (vt)	worship
ਨਾਪਣਾ (vt)	measure		
ਨਬੇੜਨਾ (vt)	finish	**ਫ**	
ਨਿਗਲਣਾ (vt)	swallow	ਫਸਣਾ (vi)	be caught
ਨਿਚੋੜਨਾ (vt)	squeeze	ਫਸਾਉਣਾ (vt)	ensnare, implicate
ਨਿਭਾਉਣਾ (vt)	fulfil	ਫਟਣਾ (vi)	burst
ਪ		ਫਰਮਾਉਣਾ (vt)	order
ਪਹੁੰਚਣਾ (vi)	reach	ਫੜਨਾ (vt)	catch, hold
ਪਹੁੰਚਾਉਣਾ (vc)	cause to reach	ਫੜਵਾਉਣਾ (vc)	cause to catch/hold
ਪਹਿਨਣਾ (vt)	wear	ਫਾੜਨਾ (vt)	tear
ਪਹਿਨਾਉਣਾ (vc)	cause to wear	ਫਿਰਨਾ (vi)	turn
ਪੱਕਣਾ (vi)	ripen	ਫੇਰਨਾ (vt)	turn
ਪਕਾਉਣਾ (vt)	make ripe	ਫੈਲਾਉਣਾ (vt)	spread
ਪਕੜਨਾ (vt)	catch, hold	ਫੁਲਣਾ (vi)	swell
ਪਚਣਾ (vi)	be digested	ਫੁਲਾਉਣਾ (vc)	cause to swell
ਪਚਾਉਣਾ (vt)	digest		
ਪਛਤਾਉਣਾ (vi)	repent	**ਬ**	
ਪਰਖਣਾ (vt)	judge	ਬਹਿਣਾ (vi)	sit
ਪਰਤਣਾ (vt)	turn over	ਬਕਣਾ (vt)	talk incoherently
ਪੜ੍ਹਨਾ (vt)	read	ਬਚਣਾ (vi)	avoid
ਪੜ੍ਹਾਉਣਾ (vt)	teach, make read	ਬਚਾਉਣਾ (vt)	save
ਪੜ੍ਹਵਾਉਣਾ (vc)	get read	ਬੱਝਣਾ (vi)	become bound
ਪਾਉਣਾ (vt)	put in	ਬਣਨਾ (vi)	become
ਪਾਟਣਾ (vi)	get torn	ਬਣਾਉਣਾ (vt)	make
ਪਾੜਨਾ (vt)	tear	ਬਣਵਾਉਣਾ (vc)	cause to make
ਪਿਆਉਣਾ (vc)	cause to drink	ਬਦਲਣਾ (vt)	change
ਪਿਲਾਉਣਾ (vc)	cause to drink	ਬੰਨ੍ਹਣਾ (vt)	bind
ਪੀਸਣਾ (vt)	grind	ਬੰਨ੍ਹਵਾਉਣਾ (vc)	cause to bind
ਪੀਹਣਾ (vt)	grind	ਬਲਣਾ (vi)	burn
ਪੁਆਉਣਾ (vc)	cause to put in	ਬਾਲਣਾ (vt)	burn

ਬਿਗੜਨਾ (*vi*)	be spoiled	ਰਖਵਾਉਣਾ (*vc*)	cause to keep
ਬਿਗਾੜਨਾ (*vt*)	spoil	ਰੰਗਣਾ (*vt*)	dye
ਬਿਠਾਉਣਾ (*vc*)	cause to sit	ਰੰਗਵਾਉਣਾ (*vc*)	cause to dye
ਬੁੱਝਣਾ (*vt*)	guess	ਰਗੜਨਾ (*vt*)	rub
ਬੁਣਨਾ (*vt*)	knit	ਰਟਣਾ (*vt*)	memorise
ਬੁਲਾਉਣਾ (*vt*)	call	ਰਟਾਉਣਾ (*vc*)	cause to
ਬੁਲਵਾਉਣਾ (*vc*)	invite		memorise
ਬੈਠਣਾ (*vi*)	sit	ਰਲਣਾ (*vi*)	mix up
ਬੋਲਣਾ (*vi*)	speak	ਰਲਾਉਣਾ (*vt*)	mix up
		ਰਿੰਨ੍ਹਣਾ (*vt*)	cook
ਭ		ਰੋਣਾ (*vi*)	weep
ਭੱਜਣਾ (*vi*)	become		
	broken	**ਲ**	
ਭੱਜਣਾ (*vi*)	run	ਲਗਣਾ (*vi*)	seem, attach
ਭਜਾਉਣਾ (*vc*)	cause to run	ਲੰਗੜਾਉਣਾ (*vi*)	limp
ਭੰਨਣਾ (*vt*)	break	ਲੰਘਣਾ (*vi*)	pass through
ਭਰਨਾ (*vt*)	fill	ਲੱਭਣਾ (*vt*)	search, find
ਭੁੰਨਣਾ (*vt*)	roast	ਲਮਕਣਾ (*vi*)	be suspended
ਭੁਨਵਾਉਣਾ (*vc*)	cause to roast	ਲੜਨਾ (*vi*)	fight
ਭੇਜਨਾ (*vt*)	send	ਲਾਉਣਾ (*vt*)	fix
ਭੋਗਣਾ (*vt*)	undergo	ਲਾਹੁਣਾ (*vt*)	bring down
		ਲਿਆਉਣਾ (*vt*)	bring
ਮ		ਲਿਖਣਾ (*vt*)	write
ਮੰਨਣਾ (*vi*)	agree	ਲਿਖਵਾਉਣਾ (*vc*)	cause to
ਮਰਨਾ (*vi*)	die		write
ਮਰਵਾਉਣਾ (*vc*)	cause to kill	ਲੁਕਣਾ (*vi*)	be hidden
ਮਾਰਨਾ (*vt*)	kill	ਲੁਕੋਣਾ (*vt*)	hide
ਮਾਪਣਾ (*vt*)	measure	ਲੁੱਟਣਾ (*vt*)	rob
ਮਿਨਣਾ (*vt*)	measure	ਲੈਣਾ (*vt*)	take
ਮਿਲਣਾ (*vi*)	meet		
ਮਿਲਾਉਣਾ (*vt*)	join	**ਵ**	
ਮਿਲਵਾਉਣਾ (*vc*)	cause to meet	ਵਸਣਾ (*vi*)	live
ਮੁਕਣਾ (*vi*)	be finished	ਵੱਜਣਾ (*vi*)	sound
ਮੁੜਨਾ (*vi*)	turn	ਵਜਾਉਣਾ (*vt*)	play (musical
ਮੁੜਵਾਉਣਾ (*vc*)	cause to turn		instrument)
ਮੋੜਨਾ (*vt*)	bend, return	ਵਟਾਉਣਾ (*vt*)	exchange
		ਵੰਡਣਾ (*vt*)	divide
ਰ		ਵੱਢਣਾ (*vt*)	cut
ਰਹਿਣਾ (*vi*)	stay, live	ਵਢਾਉਣਾ (*vc*)	cause to cut
ਰੱਖਣਾ (*vt*)	keep	ਵਰਤਣਾ (*vt*)	use

ਵਰਤਾਉਣਾ (vt)	serve	ਵਿਸਰਨਾ (vi)	be forgotten
ਵਧਣਾ (vi)	increase	ਵਿਖਾਉਣਾ (vt)	show
ਵਧਾਉਣਾ (vt)	increase	ਵਿਚਾਰਨਾ (vt)	think
ਵੜਨਾ (vi)	enter	ਵੇਖਣਾ (vt)	see
ਵਾੜਨਾ (vt)	push in		

Irregular perfective forms

Some Panjabi verbs have irregular perfective forms. These forms do take
the standard number–gender suffixes given in the Magic square on page
225, but the stem undergoes certain changes before a suffix is added.

Stem	*Perfective form (masculine singular)*
ਸੌਂ	ਸੁੱਤਾ
ਕਹਿ	ਕਿਹਾ (other number–gender forms are ਕਹੇ, ਕਹੀ, ਕਹੀਆਂ)
ਕਰ	ਕੀਤਾ (regular ਕਰਿਆ is also used by some speakers)
ਖਾ	ਖਾਧਾ
ਜਾ	ਗਿਆ (other number–gender forms are ਗਏ, ਗਈ, ਗਈਆਂ)
ਦੇ	ਦਿੱਤਾ
ਧੋ	ਧੋਤਾ (regular ਧੋਇਆ is also used by some speakers)
ਨ੍ਹਾ, ਨਹਾ	ਨ੍ਹਾਤਾ (regular ਨਹਾਇਆ is also used by some speakers)
ਪੀ	ਪੀਤਾ
ਬਹਿ	ਬੈਠਾ
ਲੈ	ਲੀਤਾ (but the regular ਲਿਆ, ਲਏ, ਲਈ, ਲਈਆਂ are more common)

Word groups

A few hundred Panjabi words useful for everyday conversation are given below. These words are grouped according to the area of meaning they generally belong to, under the following topic headings:

1. Animals and birds
2. Around the house
3. Body, health and ailments
4. Clothing
5. Family and relations
6. Food and drink
7. Hobbies, interests and spare time
8. Numbers – cardinal, ordinal, fractions, and percentages
9. Religion
10. Time – hours, days, dates, months and years
11. Travel and transport

Nouns are shown as masculine (*m*) or feminine (*f*). Sometimes it is necessary to show their number – singular (*sg*) or plural (*pl*). Adjectives are given in the masculine singular form. As in Panjabi dictionaries, verbs are given in the gerund or verbal noun form.

1 Animals and birds

Animals

animal	**jaːnvar** (*m*)	ਜਾਨਵਰ
	pasuː (*m*)	ਪਸੂ
buffalo	**májjʰ** (*f*)	ਮੱਝ
cat	**billiː** (*f*)	ਬਿੱਲੀ
cattle	**ḍangar** (*m/pl*)	ਡੰਗਰ

cow	**gã:, gau:** (*f*)	ਗਾਂ, ਗਊ
dog	**kutta:** (*m*)	ਕੁੱਤਾ
donkey	**kʰota:, gádʰa:** (*m*)	ਖੋਤਾ, ਗਾਧਾ
goat	**bakkari:** (*f*)	ਬੱਕਰੀ
horse	**gʰòɽa:** (*m*)	ਘੋੜਾ
ox, bullock	**bɔld** (*m*)	ਬੋੱਲਦ
pig	**su:r** (*m*)	ਸੂਰ
sheep	**bʰèɖ** (*f*)	ਭੇਡ

Birds

chicken	**cu:za:** (*m*)	ਚੂਜਾ
duck	**battakʰ** (*f*)	ਬੱਤਖ
goose	**battakʰ** (*f*)	ਬੱਤਖ
hen	**kukɽi:, murgi:** (*f*)	ਕੁਕੜੀ, ਮੁਰਗੀ
rooster	**kukkaɽ, murga:** (*m*)	ਕੁੱਕੜ, ਮੁਰਗਾ
swan	**ɦans** (*m*)	ਹੰਸ

2 Around the house

bathroom	**gusalxa:na:** (*m*)	ਗੁਸਲਖ਼ਾਨਾ
carpet	**dari:** (*f*)	ਦਰੀ
chair	**kursi:** (*f*)	ਕੁਰਸੀ
door	**bu:ɦa:, bú:a:** (*m*)	ਬੂਹਾ,
	darva:za: (*m*)	ਦਰਵਾਜ਼ਾ
floor	**farʃ** (*m*)	ਫ਼ਰਸ਼
glass	**ʃi:ʃa:** (*m*)	ਸ਼ੀਸ਼ਾ
house, home	**gʰàr** (*m*)	ਘਰ
key	**kunji:** (*f*)	ਕੁੰਜੀ,
	ca:bi: (*f*)	ਚਾਬੀ
kitchen	**rasoi:** (*f*)	ਰਸੋਈ
	ba:varci:xa:na: (*m*)	ਬਾਵਰਚੀਖ਼ਾਨਾ
knife	**ca:ku:** (*m*)	ਚਾਕੂ
	cʰuri: (*f*)	ਛੁਰੀ
lock	**jandara:** (*m*)	ਜੰਦਰਾ
	ta:la: (*m*)	ਤਾਲਾ
roof/ceiling	**cʰatt** (*f*)	ਛੱਤ
room	**kamra:** (*m*)	ਕਮਰਾ
table	**mez** (*m*)	ਮੇਜ਼
wall	**kándʰ** (*f*)	ਕੰਧ

| window | **ba:ri:** (*f*) | ਬਾਰੀ, |
| | **kʰiɽki:** (*f*) | ਖਿੜਕੀ |

3 Body, health and ailments

Parts of the body

arm	**bá̃:ɦ** (*f*)	ਬਾਂਹ
back	**pitṭʰ** (*f*)	ਪਿੱਠ
body	**sari:r** (*m*)	ਸਰੀਰ,
	jism (*m*)	ਜਿਸਮ
chest	**cʰa:ti:** (*f*)	ਛਾਤੀ
ear	**kann** (*m*)	ਕੰਨ
eye	**akkʰ** (*f*)	ਅੱਖ
face	**mṹ:ɦ** (*m*)	ਮੂੰਹ
	céɦira: (*m*)	ਚੇਹਰਾ
finger	**ungali:** (*f*)	ਉਂਗਲੀ
	ungal (*f*)	ਉਂਗਲ
foot	**per** (*m*)	ਪੈਰ
hair	**va:l** (*m*)	ਵਾਲ
hand	**ɦattʰ** (*m*)	ਹੱਥ
head	**sir** (*m*)	ਸਿਰ
heart	**dil** (*m*)	ਦਿਲ
leg	**latt** (*f*)	ਲੱਤ
lip	**búllʰ** (*m*)	ਬੁੱਲ੍ਹ
mouth	**mṹ:ɦ** (*m*)	ਮੂੰਹ
neck	**gardan** (*f*)	ਗਾਰਦਨ
	dʰɔ̃ɳ (*f*)	ਧੌਣ
nose	**nakk** (*m*)	ਨੱਕ
stomach	**dʰɪḍḍ** (*m*)	ਢਿੱਡ
	peṭ (*m*)	ਪੇਟ
throat	**gal** (*m*)	ਗਾਲ
	gala: (*m*)	ਗਾਲਾ
tongue	**jĩ:bʰ** (*f*)	ਜੀਭ
	zaba:n (*f*)	ਜ਼ਬਾਨ
tooth	**dand** (*m*)	ਦੰਦ

Health and ailments

ache, pain	**pi:ɽ** (*f*)	ਪੀੜ
	dard (*m*)	ਦਰਦ
ailment	**bi:ma:ri:** (*f*)	ਬੀਮਾਰੀ
breath	**sá:fi** (*m*)	ਸਾਹ
burning sensation	**jalaɳ** (*f*)	ਜਲਣ
common cold	**zuka:m** (*m*)	ਜ਼ੁਕਾਮ
cough	**kʰángfi** (*f*)	ਖੰਘ
feeling breathless	**sá:fi cáɽʰna:**	ਸਾਹ ਚੜੁਨਾ
feeling giddy	**sir cakra:uɳa:**	ਸਿਰ ਚਕਰਾਉਣਾ
health	**séfiat** (*f*)	ਸੇਹਤ
healthy	**tandrust**	ਤੰਦਰੁਸਤ
	tʰi:k tʰa:k	ਠੀਕ ਠਾਕ
high temperature	**ta:p** (*m*)	ਤਾਪ
	buxa:r (*m*)	ਬੁਖ਼ਾਰ
ill	**bi:ma:r**	ਬੀਮਾਰ
illness	**bi:ma:ri:** (*f*)	ਬੀਮਾਰੀ
injury	**saʈʈ** (*f*)	ਸੱਟ

4 Clothing

dress	**kappaɽe** (*m/pl*)	ਕੱਪੜੇ
	puʃa:k (*f/sg*)	ਪੁਸ਼ਾਕ
glasses	**ɛnak** (*f/sg*)	ਐਨਕ
	ɛnakã: (*f/pl*)	ਐਨਕਾਂ
gloves	**dasta:ne** (*m/pl*)	ਦਸਤਾਨੇ
hat	**ʈop** (*m*)	ਟੋਪ
	ʈopi: (*f*)	ਟੋਪੀ
pyjamas	**paja:ma:** (*m/sg*)	ਪਜਾਮਾ
salwar	**salva:r** (*f*)	ਸਲਵਾਰ
shirt	**kami:z** (*f*)	ਕਮੀਜ਼
shorts (traditional)	**kaccʰa:** (*m*)	ਕੱਛਾ
shoes	**jutti:** (*f/sg*)	ਜੁੱਤੀ
	joɽe (*m/pl*)	ਜੋੜੇ
socks	**jura:bã:** (*f/pl*)	ਜੁਰਾਬਾਂ
trousers	**pɛ̃ʈ** (*f/sg*)	ਪੈਂਟ
	patlu:ɳ (*f/sg*)	ਪਤਲੂਣ
turban	**pagg** (*f*)	ਪੱਗ
	pagɽi: (*f*)	ਪਗੜੀ
	dasta:r (*f*)	ਦਸਤਾਰ

5 Family and relations

aunt			
	father's sister	**bʰùːɑː**	ਭੂਆ
		pʰuppʰiː	ਫੁੱਫੀ
	mother's sister	**mɑːsiː**	ਮਾਸੀ
		xɑːlɑː (Muslim)	ਖ਼ਾਲਾ
	father's older brother's wife	**tɑːiː**	ਤਾਈ
	father's younger brother's wife	**cɑːciː**	ਚਾਚੀ
	mother's brother's wife	**mɑːmiː**	ਮਾਮੀ
brother		**bʰɑrɑ̀ː**	ਭਰਾ
		bʰɑ̀ːiː	ਭਾਈ
child			
	male	**bɑccɑː**	ਬੱਚਾ
	female	**bɑcciː**	ਬੱਚੀ
cousin		specify which uncle's or aunt's son or daughter	
daughter		**dʰiː**	ਧੀ
daughter-in-law		**nṹːɦ**	ਨੂੰਹ
		bɑɦiuː	ਬਹੂ
family		**pɑrivɑːr**	ਪਰਿਵਾਰ
		ʈɑbbɑr	ਟੱਬਰ
		xɑːndɑːn	ਖ਼ਾਨਦਾਨ
father		**pitɑː** (Hindu, Sikh)	ਪਿਤਾ
		ɑbbɑː (Muslim)	ਅੱਬਾ
		vɑːlid (Muslim)	ਵਾਲਿਦ
		pio	ਪਿਓ
		bɑːp	ਬਾਪ
		bɑːpuː	ਬਾਪੂ
father-in-law		**sáɦurɑː**	ਸਹੁਰਾ
granddaughter			
	daughter's daughter	**dóɦtiː**	ਦੋਹਤੀ
	son's daughter	**potiː**	ਪੋਤੀ
grandfather			
	father's father	**bɑːbɑː**	ਬਾਬਾ
		dɑːdɑː	ਦਾਦਾ
	mother's father	**nɑːnɑː**	ਨਾਨਾ
grandmother			
	father's mother	**dɑːdiː**	ਦਾਦੀ

mother's mother	**na:ni:**	ਨਾਨੀ
grandson		
daughter's son	**dófita:**	ਦੋਹਤਾ
son's son	**pota:**	ਪੋਤਾ
husband	**pati:** (Hindu, Sikh)	ਪਤੀ
	xa:vind (Muslim)	ਖ਼ਾਵਿੰਦ
	gʰàr va:la:	ਘਰ ਵਾਲਾ
mother	**ma:ta:** (Hindu, Sikh)	ਮਾਤਾ
	ammi: (Muslim)	ਅੰਮੀ
	va:lida: (Muslim)	ਵਾਲਿਦਾ
	mã̀:	ਮਾਂ
mother-in-law	**sass**	ਸੱਸ
nephew		
brother's son	**bʰatì:ja:**	ਭਤੀਜਾ
sister's son	**bʰà:ɳja:**	ਭਾਣਜਾ
	bʰaɳèvã̀:	ਭਣੇਵਾਂ
niece		
brother's daughter	**bʰatì:ji:**	ਭਤੀਜੀ
sister's daughter	**bʰà:ɳji:**	ਭਾਣਜੀ
	bʰaɳèvĩ̀:	ਭਣੇਵੀਂ
relative	**riʃteda:r**	ਰਿਸ਼ਤੇਦਾਰ
sister	**bʰɛ̀ɳ**	ਭੈਣ
son	**puttar**	ਪੁੱਤਰ
	putt	ਪੁੱਤ
son-in-law	**jua:i:**	ਜੁਆਈ
	da:ma:d	ਦਾਮਾਦ
uncle		
father's older brother	**ta:ia:**	ਤਾਇਆ
father's younger brother	**ca:ca:**	ਚਾਚਾ
mother's brother	**ma:ma:**	ਮਾਮਾ
father's sister's husband	**pʰuppʰaɽ**	ਫੁੱਫੜ
mother's sister's husband	**ma:saɽ**	ਮਾਸੜ
	xa:lu: (Muslim)	ਖ਼ਾਲੂ
wife	**patni:** (Hindu, Sikh)	ਪਤਨੀ,
	bi:vi: (Muslim)	ਬੀਵੀ,
	váfiuʈi:	ਵਹੁਟੀ,
	gʰàr va:li:	ਘਰ ਵਾਲੀ

6 Food and drink

Food grains and flours

Words for food grains are either masculine or feminine nouns. Such masculine nouns are always plural and such feminine nouns are always singular.

black beans	**mã́:ɦ** (*m*)	ਮਾਂਹ
chickpeas	**cʰole** (*m*)	ਛੋਲੇ
corn	**makki:** (*f*)	ਮੱਕੀ
flour (wholemeal)	**aːʈaː** (*m*)	ਆਟਾ
flour (refined plain)	**mɛdaː** (*m*)	ਮੈਦਾ
lentils	**masar** (*m*)	ਮਸਰ
kidney beans	**raːjmã́:ɦ** (*m*)	ਰਾਜਮਾਂਹ
rice	**cɔl** (*m*)	ਚੌਲ
split lentils/beans	**daːl** (*f*)	ਦਾਲ
wheat	**kaɳak** (*f*)	ਕਣਕ

Fruits and nuts

apple	**siõ** (*m*)	ਸਿਊਂ
	seb (*m*)	ਸੇਬ
banana	**kelaː** (*m*)	ਕੇਲਾ
fruit	**pʰal** (*m*)	ਫਲ
grapes	**anguːr** (*m*)	ਅੰਗੂਰ
lemon	**nimbu:** (*m*)	ਨਿੰਬੂ
mango	**amb** (*m*)	ਅੰਬ
melon	**xarbuːzaː** (*m*)	ਖ਼ਰਬੂਜ਼ਾ
orange	**santaraː** (*m*)	ਸੰਤਰਾ
peach	**aːɽuː** (*m*)	ਆੜੂ
peanuts	**mũːgpʰaliː** (*f*)	ਮੂੰਗਫਲੀ
pear	**naːkʰ** (*f*)	ਨਾਖ
	naːʃpaːtiː (*f*)	ਨਾਸ਼ਪਾਤੀ
plum	**aːluː buxaːraː** (*m*)	ਆਲੂ ਬੁਖ਼ਾਰਾ
watermelon	**ɦadvaːɳaː** (*m*)	ਹਦਵਾਣਾ
	tarbuːz (*m*)	ਤਰਬੂਜ਼
	matiːraː (*m*)	ਮਤੀਰਾ

Vegetables

aubergine	**bɛ̃gaṇ** (*m*)	ਬੈਂਗਣ
	bata:ū: (*m*)	ਬਤਾਊਂ
cabbage	**band góbʰi:** (*f*)	ਬੰਦ ਗੋਭੀ
carrot	**ga:jar** (*f*)	ਗਾਜਰ
cauliflower	**góbʰi:** (*f*)	ਗੋਭੀ
cucumber	**tar** (*f*)	ਤਰ
	kʰi:ra: (*m*)	ਖੀਰਾ
fenugreek	**metʰi:** (*f*)	ਮੇਥੀ
garlic	**lasaṇ** (*m*)	ਲਸਣ
ginger (fresh)	**adrak** (*m*)	ਅਦਰਕ
mustard (leaves)	**sárʰõ** (*f*)	ਸਰੋਂ
okra	**bʰɪndʒi:** (*f*)	ਭਿੰਡੀ
onion	**pia:z** (*m*)	ਪਿਆਜ਼
	gándʰa: (*m*)	ਗੰਢਾ
peas	**maṭar** (*m/pl*)	ਮਟਰ
potatoes	**a:lu:** (*m*)	ਆਲੂ
radish	**mu:li:** (*f*)	ਮੂਲੀ
spinach	**pa:lak** (*f*)	ਪਾਲਕ
tomato	**ṭama:ṭar** (*m*)	ਟਮਾਟਰ
vegetable	**sabzi:** (*f*)	ਸਬਜ਼ੀ
	bʰà:ji: (*f*)	ਭਾਜੀ

Herbs and spices

black pepper	**ka:li: mirc** (*f*)	ਕਾਲੀ ਮਿਰਚ
chilli	**mirc** (*f*)	ਮਿਰਚ
coriander	**dʰàni:a:** (*m*)	ਧਨੀਆ
cumin	**ji:ra:** (*m*)	ਜੀਰਾ
ginger (dry)	**súndʰ** (*f*)	ਸੁੰਢ
mint	**pu:dana:** (*m*)	ਪੁਦਨਾ
mixed spices	**garam masa:la:** (*m*)	ਗਰਮ ਮਸਾਲਾ
salt	**lu:ṇ** (*m*)	ਲੂਣ
tamarind	**imli:** (*f*)	ਇਮਲੀ
turmeric	**ɦaldi:** (*f*)	ਹਲਦੀ

Miscellaneous

alcoholic drink	**ʃara:b** (*f*)	ਸ਼ਰਾਬ
	da:ru: (*f*)	ਦਾਰੂ

betel leaf	**pa:n** (*m*)	ਪਾਨ
bread	**roʈi:** (*f*)	ਰੋਟੀ
breads (Indian)	**roʈi:** (*f*)	ਰੋਟੀ
	pʰulka: (*m*)	ਫੁਲਕਾ
	capa:ti: (*f*)	ਚਪਾਤੀ
	na:n (*m*)	ਨਾਨ
	pu:ri: (*f*)	ਪੂਰੀ
	parɔ̃ʈʰa: (*m*)	ਪਰੌਂਠਾ
	bʱatù:ra: (*m*)	ਭਟੂਰਾ
butter	**makkʰaɳ** (*m*)	ਮੱਖਣ
buttermilk	**lassi:** (*f*)	ਲੱਸੀ
cheese	**pani:r** (*m*)	ਪਨੀਰ
chicken	**kukkaɽ** (*m*)	ਕੁੱਕੜ
	murga: (*m*)	ਮੁਰਗਾ
cigarette	**sigriʈ** (*m*)	ਸਿਗਾਰਿਟ
	sigaʈ (*m*)	ਸਿਗਟ
coffee	**ka:fi:** (*f*)	ਕਾਫ਼ੀ
cooked lentils	**da:l** (*f*)	ਦਾਲ
curry	**sa:laɳ** (*m*)	ਸਾਲਣ
	salu:ɳa: (*m*)	ਸਲੂਣਾ
egg	**ã:ɖa:** (*m*)	ਆਂਡਾ
meat	**ma:s** (*m*)	ਮਾਸ
	goʃt (*m*)	ਗੋਸ਼ਤ
milk	**dúddʱ** (*m*)	ਦੁੱਧ
mincemeat	**ki:ma:** (*m*)	ਕੀਮਾ
oil	**tel** (*m*)	ਤੇਲ
purified butter (ghee)	**gʱɪo** (*m*)	ਘਿਓ
spinach + mustard leaves (cooked)	**sa:g** (*m*)	ਸਾਗ
sugar	**kʰaɳɖ** (*f*)	ਖੰਡ
	ci:ni: (*f*)	ਚੀਨੀ
	ʃakkar (*f*)	ਸ਼ੱਕਰ
	guɽ (*m*)	ਗੁੜ
sweets	**matʰia:i:** (*f*)	ਮਠਿਆਈ
tobacco	**tama:ku:** (*m*)	ਤਮਾਕੂ
	tama:kʰu: (*m*)	ਤਮਾਖੂ
water	**pa:ɳi:** (*m*)	ਪਾਣੀ
yoghurt	**daɦi:** (*m*)	ਦਹੀਂ

Cooking processes

boiling	**uba:laɳa:**	ਉਬਾਲਣਾ
cooking	**paka:uɳa:**	ਪਕਾਉਣਾ
cutting	**kaṭṭaɳa:**	ਕੱਟਣਾ
frying	**talɳa:**	ਤਲਣਾ
grilling	**sekɳa:**	ਸੇਕਣਾ
grinding	**pí:ɦiɳa:**	ਪੀਹਣਾ
kneading	**gúnnʰaɳa:**	ਗੁੰਨ੍ਹਣਾ
peeling	**cʰillaɳa:**	ਛਿੱਲਣਾ
roasting	**bʱùnnaɳa:**	ਭੁੰਨਣਾ
slitting	**ci:rna:**	ਚੀਰਨਾ
	ci:ra: deɳa:	ਚੀਰਾ ਦੇਣਾ

Tastes

bitter	**kɔɽa:**	ਕੌੜਾ
delicious (tasty)	**sua:d**	ਸੁਆਦ
savoury	**salu:ɳa:**	ਸਲੂਣਾ
	lu:ɳka:	ਲੂਣਕਾ
	namki:n	ਨਮਕੀਨ
sour	**kʰaṭṭa:**	ਖੱਟਾ
spicy	**masa:leda:r**	ਮਸਾਲੇਦਾਰ
	caṭpaṭa	ਚਟਪਟਾ
sweet	**miṭṭʰa:**	ਮਿੱਠਾ
taste	**sua:d**	ਸੁਆਦ
	za:ika:	ਜ਼ਾਇਕਾ
tasteless	**pʰikka:**	ਫਿੱਕਾ
	besua:d	ਬੇਸੁਆਦ

7 Hobbies, interests and spare time

cooking	**kʰa:ɳa: paka:uɳa:**	ਖਾਣਾ ਪਕਾਉਣਾ
dancing	**naccaɳa:**	ਨੱਚਣਾ
gardening	**ba:gva:ni:** (*f*)	ਬਾਗਵਾਨੀ
hobby	**ʃɔk** (*m*)	ਸ਼ੌਕ
literature	**sa:ɦit** (*m*)	ਸਾਹਿਤ
	adab (*m*)	ਅਦਬ
music	**sangi:t** (*m*)	ਸੰਗੀਤ
	mosi:ki: (*f*)	ਮੋਸੀਕੀ

newspaper	**axba:r** (*m/f*)	ਅਖ਼ਬਾਰ
painting	**cittarka:ri:**	ਚਿੱਤਰਕਾਰੀ
	tasvi:rã: bana:una:	ਤਸਵੀਰਾਂ ਬਣਾਉਣਾ
playing (music)	**vaja:una:**	ਵਜਾਉਣਾ
playing (sport)	**kʰedṇa:**	ਖੇਡਣਾ
	kʰelṇa:	ਖੇਲਣਾ
singing	**ga:uṇa:**	ਗਾਉਣਾ
swimming	**tarna:**	ਤਰਨਾ
	terna:	ਤੈਰਨਾ
walking	**gʰùmmaṇa: pʰirna:**	ਘੁੰਮਣਾ ਫਿਰਨਾ
writing	**likʰṇa:**	ਲਿਖਣਾ

8 Numbers

Cardinal numbers

1	**ikk**	ਇੱਕ	24	**cɔvi:**	ਚੌਵੀ
2	**do**	ਦੋ	25	**pánjʰi:, pacci:**	ਪੰਝੀ, ਪੱਚੀ
3	**tinn**	ਤਿੰਨ	26	**cʰabbi:**	ਛੱਬੀ
4	**ca:r**	ਚਾਰ	27	**sata:i:**	ਸਤਾਈ
5	**panj**	ਪੰਜ	28	**aṭʰa:i:**	ਅਠਾਈ
6	**cʰe**	ਛੇ	29	**uṇatti:**	ਉਨੱਤੀ
7	**satt**	ਸੱਤ	30	**tí:ɦ**	ਤੀਹ
8	**aṭṭʰ**	ਅੱਠ	31	**ikatti:**	ਇਕੱਤੀ
9	**nɔ̃**	ਨੌਂ	32	**batti:**	ਬੱਤੀ
10	**das**	ਦਸ	33	**teti:**	ਤੇਤੀ
11	**gia:rã:**	ਗਿਆਰਾਂ	34	**cɔ̃ti:, cɔti:**	ਚੌਂਤੀ, ਚੌਤੀ
12	**ba:rã:**	ਬਾਰਾਂ	35	**pẽti:**	ਪੈਂਤੀ
13	**terã:**	ਤੇਰਾਂ	36	**cʰatti:**	ਛੱਤੀ
14	**cɔdã:**	ਚੌਦਾਂ	37	**sẽti:**	ਸੈਂਤੀ
15	**pandarã:**	ਪੰਦਰਾਂ	38	**aṭʰatti:**	ਅਠੱਤੀ
16	**solã:**	ਸੋਲਾਂ	39	**unta:li:**	ਉਂਤਾਲੀ
17	**sata:rã:**	ਸਤਾਰਾਂ	40	**ca:li:**	ਚਾਲੀ
18	**aṭʰa:rã:**	ਅਠਾਰਾਂ	41	**ikta:li:**	ਇਕਤਾਲੀ
19	**unni:**	ਉਂਨੀ	42	**bata:li, bia:li:**	ਬਤਾਲੀ, ਬਿਆਲੀ
20	**vi:ɦ**	ਵੀਹ	43	**tarta:li:**	ਤਰਤਾਲੀ
21	**ikki:**	ਇੱਕੀ	44	**cut:ali:**	ਚੁਤਾਲੀ
22	**ba:i:**	ਬਾਈ	45	**panta:li:**	ਪੰਤਾਲੀ
23	**tei:**	ਤੇਈ			

46	cʰia:li:,	ਛਿਆਲੀ,	
	cʰata:li:	ਛਤਾਲੀ	
47	santa:li:	ਸੰਤਾਲੀ	
48	aʈʰta:li:	ਅਠਤਾਲੀ	
49	uɳanja:	ਉਣੰਜਾ	
50	panjá:ɦ,	ਪੰਜਾਹ,	
	pajá:ɦ	ਪਜਾਹ	
51	ikvanja:	ਇਕਵੰਜਾ	
52	bavanja:	ਬਵੰਜਾ	
53	tarvanja:	ਤਰਵੰਜਾ	
54	curanja:	ਚੁਰੰਜਾ	
55	pacvanja:	ਪਚਵੰਜਾ	
56	cʰapanja:	ਛਪੰਜਾ	
57	satvanja:	ਸਤਵੰਜਾ	
58	aʈʰvanja:	ਅਠਵੰਜਾ	
59	uɳá:ɦaʈ	ਉਣਾਹਟ	
60	saʈʈʰ	ਸੱਠ	
61	iká:ɦaʈ	ਇਕਾਹਟ	
62	bá:ɦaʈ	ਬਾਹਟ	
63	tréɦaʈ	ਤ੍ਰੇਹਟ	
64	cɔ́ɦaʈ,	ਚੌਹਟ,	
	cɔɦaʈ	ਚੌਹਟ	
65	péɦaʈ	ਪੈਂਹਟ	
66	cʰiá:ɦaʈ	ਛਿਆਹਟ	
67	satá:ɦat	ਸਤਾਹਟ	
68	aʈʰá:ɦaʈ	ਅਠਾਹਟ	
69	uɳ̃ɦàttar	ਉਣਹੱਤਰ	
70	sattar	ਸੱਤਰ	
71	ikɦattar	ਇਕਹੱਤਰ	
72	baɦattar	ਬਹੱਤਰ	
73	tiɦattar	ਤਿਹੱਤਰ	

74	cuɦattar	ਚੁਹੱਤਰ
75	panjɦàttar	ਪੰਜਹੱਤਰ
76	cʰiɦattar	ਛਿਹੱਤਰ
77	satattar	ਸਤੱਤਰ
78	aʈʰattar	ਅਠੱਤਰ
79	uɳa:si:	ਉਣਾਸੀ
80	assi:	ਅੱਸੀ
81	ikia:si:,	ਇਕਿਆਸੀ,
	ika:si:	ਇਕਾਸੀ
82	bia:si:	ਬਿਆਸੀ
83	taria:si:	ਤਰਿਆਸੀ
84	cura:si:	ਚੁਰਾਸੀ
85	panja:si:,	ਪੰਜਾਸੀ,
	paca:si:	ਪਚਾਸੀ
86	cʰia:si:	ਛਿਆਸੀ
87	sata:si:	ਸਤਾਸੀ
88	aʈʰa:si:	ਅਠਾਸੀ
89	uɳa:navẽ	ਉਣਾਨਵੇਂ
90	nabbe, navve	ਨੱਬੇ, ਨੱਵੇ
91	ikiannavẽ,	ਇਕਿਅੰਨਵੇਂ,
	ikannavẽ	ਇਕੰਨਵੇਂ
92	bannavẽ	ਬੰਨਵੇਂ
93	tirianavẽ,	ਤਿਰਿਅੰਨਵੇਂ,
	tarannavẽ	ਤਰੰਨਵੇਂ
94	curannavẽ	ਚੁਰੰਨਵੇਂ
95	pacannavẽ	ਪਚੰਨਵੇਂ
96	cʰiannavẽ	ਛਿਅੰਨਵੇਂ
97	satannavẽ	ਸਤੰਨਵੇਂ
98	aʈʰannavẽ	ਅਠੰਨਵੇਂ
99	naʈɦinnavẽ	ਨੜ੍ਹਿੰਨਵੇਂ
100	sɔ	ਸੌਂ

0	sifar	ਸਿਫ਼ਰ
157	ikk sɔ satvanja:	ਇੱਕ ਸੌ ਸਤਵੰਜਾ
670	cʰe sɔ sattar	ਛੇ ਸੌ ਸੱਤਰ
837	aʈʈʰ sɔ sẽti:	ਅੱਠ ਸੌ ਸੈਂਤੀ
1,000	(ikk) ɦaza:r	(ਇੱਕ) ਹਜ਼ਾਰ
1,213	ikk ɦaza:r do sɔ terã	ਇੱਕ ਹਜ਼ਾਰ ਦੋ ਸੌ ਤੇਰਾਂ

10,000	**das ɦaza:r**	ਦਸ ਹਜ਼ਾਰ
100,000 (a hundred thousand)	**(ikk) lakk^h**	(ਇੱਕ) ਲੱਖ
1,000,000 (a million)	**das lakk^h**	ਦਸ ਲੱਖ
10,000,000 (ten million)	**(ikk) karoɽ**	(ਇੱਕ) ਕਰੋੜ
100,000,000 (a hundred million)	**das karoɽ**	ਦਸ ਕਰੋੜ
1,000,000,000 (a billion)	**(ikk) arab**	(ਇੱਕ) ਅਰਬ

Ordinal numbers

first	**páɦila:**	ਪਹਿਲਾ
second	**du:sara:, du:ja:**	ਦੂਸਰਾ, ਦੂਜਾ
third	**ti:sara:, ti:ju:**	ਤੀਸਰਾ, ਤੀਜਾ
fourth	**cɔt^ha:**	ਚੌਥਾ
fifth	**panjvã:**	ਪੰਜਵਾਂ
sixth	**c^hevã:**	ਛੇਵਾਂ

(Then go on adding **vã:** up to ten. Beyond that, you omit the final **ã:** before adding **vã:**. Some speakers also add the high tone, especialy up to 19.)

eleventh	**giá:r^ɦvã:**	ਗਿਆਰ੍ਹਵਾਂ
twelfth	**bá:r^ɦvã:**	ਬਾਰ੍ਹਵਾਂ
thirty-second	**batti:vã:**	ਬੱਤੀਵਾਂ
seventy-sixth	**c^hiɦattarvã:**	ਛਿਹੱਤਰਵਾਂ
one hundred and tenth	**ikk sɔ dasvã:**	ਇੱਕ ਸੌ ਦਸਵਾਂ
thousandth	**ɦaza:rvã:**	ਹਜ਼ਾਰਵਾਂ
But be careful with		
one hundred and first	**ikk sɔ ikkvã:**	ਇੱਕ ਸੌ ਇੱਕਵਾਂ
	(not * **ikk sɔ páɦila:**)	

Fractions

¼ (a quarter)	**ikk cɔt^ha:i**	ਇੱਕ ਚੌਥਾਈ
½ (half)	**ádd^ha:**	ਅੱਧਾ
¾ (three quarters)	**pɔɳa:**	ਪੌਣਾ
1 ¼	**sava: (ikk)**	ਸਵਾ (ਇੱਕ)
1 ½	**déɽ^ɦ**	ਡੇੜ੍ਹ
1 ¾	**pɔɳe do**	ਪੌਣੇ ਦੋ
	(be careful, not * **pɔɳe ikk**)	
2 ¼	**sava: do**	ਸਵਾ ਦੋ
2 ½	**d^hà:i:**	ਢਾਈ
2 ¾	**pɔɳe tinn**	ਪੌਣੇ ਤਿੰਨ

3 ¼	**sava: tinn**	ਸਵਾ ਤਿੰਨ
3 ½	**sá:dʰe tinn**	ਸਾਢੇ ਤਿੰਨ
3 ¾	**pɔɳe ca:r** (not * **pɔɳe tinn**)	ਪੌਣੇ ਚਾਰ

Then follow the general pattern

number + ¼	**sava:** + number
number + ½	**sá:dʰe** + number
number + ¾	**pɔɳe** + *next* number

Panjabi numerals

Panjabi has its own set of numerals. But they are rarely used these days except in some books on Sikh religion. These numerals are

੧	੨	੩	੪	੫	੬	੭	੮	੯	੦
1	2	3	4	5	6	7	8	9	0

The fundamental principle of the Sikh religion is written as ੧ੴ, which is pronounced as **ikk onka:r** ਇੱਕ ਓੰਕਾਰ. It means 'There is one God'. Since these numerals have been used in the Sikh holy book, they have religious significance for the Sikhs.

9 Religion

ascetic, hermit	**sá:dʰu:** (Hindu, Sikh)	ਸਾਧੂ
	sá:dʰ (Hindu, Sikh)	ਸਾਧ
	faki:r (Muslim)	ਫ਼ਕੀਰ
baptism	**baptisma:** (*m*)	ਬਪਤਿਸਮਾ
Buddhist	**bódʰi:** (*m/f*)	ਬੋਧੀ
burying	**dafna:uɳa:**	ਦਫ਼ਨਾਉਣਾ
	dafan karna:	ਦਫ਼ਨ ਕਰਨਾ
Christian	**i:sa:i:** (*m/f*)	ਈਸਾਈ
church	**girja:** (**gʰàr**) (*m*)	ਗਿਰਜਾ (ਘਰ)
cremation	**dá:ɦ sanska:r** (*m*)	ਦਾਹ ਸੰਸਕਾਰ
	saska:r (*m*)	ਸਸਕਾਰ
devotional song	**bʰàjan** (*m*) (Hindu)	ਭਜਨ
	ʃabad (*m*) (Sikh)	ਸ਼ਬਦ
	na:t (*f*) (Muslim)	ਨਾਤ
God	**i:ʃvar** (Hindu, Sikh)	ਈਸ਼ਵਰ
	parma:tma: (Hindu, Sikh)	ਪਰਮਾਤਮਾ
	bʰagvà:n (Hindu, Sikh)	ਭਗਵਾਨ
	va:ɦiguru: (Sikh)	ਵਾਹਿਗੁਰੂ

	alla: (Muslim)	ਅੱਲਾ
	xuda: (Muslim)	ਖ਼ੁਦਾ
	rabb	ਰੱਬ
heaven	savarag (m) (Hindu, Sikh)	ਸਵਰਗ
	surg (m) (Hindu, Sikh)	ਸੁਰਗ
	jannat (f) (Muslim)	ਜੰਨਤ
hell	narak (m) (Hindu, Sikh)	ਨਰਕ
	dozax (m) (Muslim)	ਦੋਜ਼ਖ਼
	jaɦannum (m) (Muslim)	ਜਹੰਨੁਮ
holy	pavittar (Hindu, Sikh)	ਪਵਿੱਤਰ
	mukaddas (Muslim)	ਮੁਕੱਦਸ
Jesus Christ	i:sa: masi:ɦ	ਈਸਾ ਮਸੀਹ
Jew	yaɦu:di: (m/f)	ਯਹੂਦੀ
mosque	masjid (f)	ਮਸਜਿਦ
	masi:t (f)	ਮਸੀਤ
Muslim	musalma:n	ਮੁਸਲਮਾਨ
prayer	pra:raṯʰana: (f) (Hindu, Sikh)	ਪ੍ਰਾਰਥਨਾ
	arda:s (f) (Sikh)	ਅਰਦਾਸ
	dua: (f) (Muslim)	ਦੁਆ
priest		
Christian	pa:dri: (m)	ਪਾਦਰੀ
Hindu	pandit (m)	ਪੰਡਿਤ
	puja:ri: (m)	ਪੁਜਾਰੀ
	pã:dʰa: (m)	ਪਾਂਧਾ
Sikh	bʰã:i: (m)	ਭਾਈ
	grantʰi: (m)	ਗ੍ਰੰਥੀ
Muslim	mɔlavi: (m)	ਮੌਲਵੀ
	mullã: (m)	ਮੁੱਲਾਂ
	ima:m (m)	ਇਮਾਮ
prophet	pɛgambar (m)	ਪੈਗੰਬਰ
	nabi: (m)	ਨਬੀ
religion	dʰàram (m) (Hindu, Sikh)	ਧਰਮ
	mázɦab (m) (Muslim)	ਮਜ਼ਹਬ
religious	dʰà:rmik	ਧਾਰਮਿਕ
	mazɦabi:	ਮਜ਼ਹਬੀ
sacrifice	bali: (f) (Hindu)	ਬਲੀ
	kurba:ni: (f) (Muslim)	ਕੁਰਬਾਨੀ
saint	sant (m) (Hindu, Sikh)	ਸੰਤ
	darveʃ (m) (Muslim)	ਦਰਵੇਸ਼

Sikh holy book	(**sri:**) (**guru:**) **grant**ʰ **sá:ɦab** (*m*)	(ਸ੍ਰੀ) (ਗੁਰੂ) ਗ੍ਰੰਥ ਸਾਹਬ
sin	**pa:p** (*m*) (Hindu, Sikh)	ਪਾਪ
	guná:ɦ (*m*) (Muslim)	ਗੁਨਾਹ
soul, spirit	**a:tma:** (*f*) (Hindu, Sikh)	ਆਤਮਾ
	rú:ɦ (*f*)	ਰੂਹ
spiritual teacher	**guru:** (*m*) (Hindu, Sikh)	ਗੁਰੂ
	pi:r (*m*) (Muslim)	ਪੀਰ
	murʃid (*m*) (Muslim)	ਮੁਰਸ਼ਿਦ
temple	**mandar** (*m*)	ਮੰਦਰ

10 Time

Hours

o' clock	**vaje** (which you add to the following)	ਵਜੇ
1.15	**sava: (ikk)**	ਸਵਾ
1.30	**ɖéɽ**ʰ	ਡੇਢ
1.45	**pɔɳe do**	ਪੌਨੇ ਦੋ
2.00	**do**	ਦੋ
2.15	**sava: do**	ਸਵਾ ਦੋ
2.30	**ɖʰà:i:**	ਢਾਈ
3.15	**sava: tinn**	ਸਵਾ ਤਿੰਨ
3.30	**sá:ɖʰe tinn**	ਸਾਢੇ ਤਿੰਨ
3.45	**pɔɳe ca:r**	ਪੌਨੇ ਚਾਰ
6.00 am	**saver de c**ʰ**e vaje**	ਸਵੇਰ ਦੇ ਛੇ ਵਜੇ
6.00 pm	**ʃa:m de c**ʰ**e vaje**	ਸ਼ਾਮ ਦੇ ਛੇ ਵਜੇ
at 6.00 pm	**ʃa:m de c**ʰ**e vaje**	ਸ਼ਾਮ ਦੇ ਛੇ ਵਜੇ
35 minutes past 5.00	**panj vajke pẽti: minṭ**	ਪੰਜ ਵਜ ਕੇ ਪੈਂਤੀ ਮਿੰਟ
at 5.35	**panj vajke pẽti: minṭ te**	ਪੰਜ ਵਜ ਕੇ ਪੈਂਤੀ ਮਿੰਟ ਤੇ
10 minutes to 7.00 (i.e. 6.50)	**satt vajaɳ nũ: das minṭ**	ਸੱਤ ਵਜਣ ਨੂੰ ਦਸ ਮਿੰਟ
year	**sa:l** (*m*)	ਸਾਲ
month	**maɦi:na:** (*m*)	ਮਹੀਨਾ
week	**ɦafta:** (*m*)	ਹਫ਼ਤਾ
day	**din** (*m*)	ਦਿਨ

hour	**gʰànṭa:**(*m*)	ਘੰਟਾ
minute	**minṭ** (*m*)	ਮਿੰਟ
second	**sakinṭ** (*m*)	ਸਕਿੰਟ
last week	**picʰale fiafte**	ਪਿਛਲੇ ਹਫ਼ਤੇ
next week	**agle fiafte**	ਅਗਲੇ ਹਫ਼ਤੇ
last month	**picʰale mafii:ne**	ਪਿਛਲੇ ਮਹੀਨੇ
next year	**agle sa:l**	ਅਗਲੇ ਸਾਲ

Times of the day

morning	**saver** (*f*)	ਸਵੇਰ
	savera: (*m*)	ਸਵੇਰਾ
in the morning	**severe**	ਸਵੇਰੇ
	saver nũ:	ਸਵੇਰ ਨੂੰ
midday	**dupáfiir** (*f*)	ਦੁਪਹਿਰ
	dupáfiira: (*m*)	ਦੁਪਹਿਰਾ
at midday	**dupáfiire**	ਦੁਪਹਿਰੇ
	dupáfiir nũ:	ਦੁਪਹਿਰ ਨੂੰ
afternoon	**lɔ́dʰa: vela:** (*m*)	ਲੌਂਢਾ ਵੇਲਾ
in the afternoon	**lɔ́dʰe vele**	ਲੱਢੇ ਵੇਲੇ
time of the sunset	**tirka:lã̃:** (*f/pl*)	ਤਿਰਕਾਲਾਂ
evening	**ʃa:m** (*f*)	ਸ਼ਾਮ
in the evening	**ʃa:mĩ:**	ਸ਼ਾਮੀਂ
	ʃa:m nũ:	ਸ਼ਾਮ ਨੂੰ
night	**ra:t** (*f*)	ਰਾਤ
at night	**ra:t nũ:**	ਰਾਤ ਨੂੰ
	ra:tĩ:	ਰਾਤੀਂ

Days of the week

Names of days marked as 'Muslim' are used exclusively by Muslim speakers and by non-Muslim Panjabi speakers in Pakistan. The names of the days are masculine nouns.

Sunday	**ɛtva:r**	ਐਤਵਾਰ
Monday	**somva:r**	ਸੋਮਵਾਰ
	pi:r (Muslim)	ਪੀਰ
Tuesday	**mangalva:r**	ਮੰਗਲਵਾਰ
Wednesday	**búdʰva:r**	ਬੁਧਵਾਰ
Thursday	**vi:rva:r**	ਵੀਰਵਾਰ
	jumera:t (Muslim)	ਜੁਮੇਰਾਤ

Friday	**ʃukkarvaːr**	ਸ਼ੁੱਕਰਵਾਰ
	jumaː (Muslim)	ਜੁੰਮਾ
Saturday	**cʰaniccʰarvaːr**	ਛਨਿੱਛਰਵਾਰ
	saniccarvaːr	ਸਨਿੱਚਰਵਾਰ
	ɦaftaː (Muslim)	ਹਫ਼ਤਾ

Months

Names of the months of the Western calendar are used in Panjabi but they are pronounced slightly differently. But you can use the English pronunciation. These names of the months are masculine nouns.

11 Travel and transport

aeroplane	**ɦavaːiː jaɦaːz** (*m*)	ਹਵਾਈ ਜਹਾਜ਼
airport	**ɦavaːiː aɖɖaː** (*m*)	ਹਵਾਈ ਅੱਡਾ
bicycle	**saːiːkal** (*m*)	ਸਾਈਕਲ
bus	**bas** (*f*)	ਬਸ
bus station	**bassã: daː aɖɖaː** (*m*)	ਬੱਸਾਂ ਦਾ ਅੱਡਾ
car	**kaːr** (*f*)	ਕਾਰ
fare	**kiraːiaː** (*m*)	ਕਿਰਾਇਆ
(on) foot	**pɛdal**	ਪੈਦਲ
horse carriage	**t̃ãːgaː** (*m*)	ਟਾਂਗਾ
	t̃ãːgaː (*m*)	ਤਾਂਗਾ
	yakkaː (*m*)	ਯੱਕਾ
journey	**safar** (*m*)	ਸਫ਼ਰ
	yaːtraː (*f*)	ਯਾਤਰਾ
passenger	**savaːriː** (*f*)	ਸਵਾਰੀ
road	**saɽak** (*f*)	ਸੜਕ
ticket	**ʈikaʈ** (*m/f*)	ਟਿਕਟ
return ticket	**vaːpasi daː ʈikaʈ** (*m*)	ਵਾਪਸੀ ਦਾ ਟਿਕਟ
	vaːpasi diː ʈikaʈ (*f*)	ਵਾਪਸੀ ਦੀ ਟਿਕਟ
single ticket	**ikk paːse daː ʈikaʈ** (*m*)	ਇਕ ਪਾਸੇ ਦਾ ਟਿਕਟ
	ikk paːse diː ʈikaʈ (*f*)	ਇਕ ਪਾਸੇ ਦੀ ਟਿਕਟ
train	**rel gaɖɖiː** (*f*)	ਰੇਲ ਗੱਡੀ
	rel (*f*)	ਰੇਲ
	gaɖɖiː (*f*)	ਗੱਡੀ

traveller	ya:tri: (*m/f*)	ਯਾਤਰੀ
	ya:tru: (*m/f*)	ਯਾਤਰੂ
	musa:fir (*m/f*)	ਮੁਸਾਫ਼ਿਰ
vehicle	gaḍḍi: (*f*)	ਗੱਡੀ
waiting room	musa:firxa:na: (*m*)	ਮੁਸਾਫ਼ਿਰਖ਼ਾਨਾ
	uḍi:k gʰâr (*m*)	ਉਡੀਕ ਘਰ

Panjabi–English glossary

The Panjabi words used in the Conversation units and Script units are given below in alphabetical order. Generally, the order of letters in the Roman alphabet is used. But long vowels immediately follow their short counterparts, aspirated consonants immediately follow their unaspirated counterparts, and retroflex consonants immediately follow the dentals. As elsewhere in the book, nouns are marked as masculine (*m*) or feminine (*f*).

a aː	ਅ ਆ	
accʰaː	ਅੱਛਾ	good, well
ā́ddʰaː	ਅੱਧਾ	half
adrak (*m*)	ਅਦਰਕ	ginger
agge	ਅੱਗੇ	in front, before
aggõ	ਅੱਗੋਂ	from there, thence
aglaː	ਅਗਲਾ	next
ajj (*m*)	ਅੱਜ	today
akal (*f*)	ਅਕਲ	wisdom, sense
akkʰ (*f*)	ਅੱਖ	eye
allaː (*m*)	ਅੱਲਾ	God (Muslim)
ambar (*m*)	ਅੰਬਰ	sky
andaralaː	ਅੰਦਰਲਾ	inside
anpáɽʰ	ਅਨਪੜ੍ਹ	uneducated
angrez	ਅੰਗ੍ਰੇਜ਼	English nationality
angreziː (*f*)	ਅੰਗ੍ਰੇਜ਼ੀ	English language
arz (*f*)	ਅਰਜ਼	request

asli:	ਅਸਲੀ	real
assala:m alɛkam	ਅੱਸਲਾਮ ਅਲੈਕਮ	Peace be on you (Muslim)
ate	ਅਤੇ	and
axi:r	ਅਖੀਰ	end
ɑ:	ਆ	to come
ɑ:dat (f)	ਆਦਤ	habit
á:lʰaṇa: (m)	ਆਲ੍ਹਣਾ	nest
ɑ:lu: (m)	ਆਲੂ	potato
ɑ:m	ਆਮ	general
ɑ:m tɔr te	ਆਮ ਤੌਰ ਤੇ	generally, mostly
ɑ:pṇɑ:	ਆਪਣਾ	own
ɑ:rɑ: (m)	ਆਰਾ	saw
ɑ:rɑ:m (m)	ਆਰਾਮ	rest
ɑ:vɑ:z (f)	ਆਵਾਜ਼	voice
b bʰ	ਬ ਭ	
bacca: (m)	ਬੱਚਾ	child
bagʰiɑ̀:ṛ (m)	ਬਘਿਆੜ	wolf
bafiɑ:r (f)	ਬਹਾਰ	spring season
báfii	ਬਹਿ	to sit
báfiut	ਬਹੁਤ	very much, highly
báfiut sa:ra: (m)	ਬਹੁਤ ਸਾਰਾ	much, a lot
báfiut sa:ri: (f)	ਬਹੁਤ ਸਾਰੀ	much, a lot
bai: (m)	ਬਈ	informal form of address
band	ਬੰਦ	closed
banda: (m)	ਬੰਦਾ	person
band kar	ਬੰਦ ਕਰ	to stop
bánnʰ	ਬੰਨ੍ਹ	to bind
bannʰvà:	ਬੰਨ੍ਹਵਾ	to get bound
bansari: (f)	ਬੰਸਰੀ	flute
baṇ	ਬਣ	to become
baṇa:	ਬਣਾ	to make
baṇva:	ਬਣਵਾ	to get made
barf (f)	ਬਰਫ਼	snow, ice
bas	ਬਸ	finished, that's all
bas (f)	ਬਸ	bus
bazurg (m/f)	ਬਜ਼ੁਰਗ	old person

bazurgva:r	ਬਜ਼ੁਰਗਵਾਰ	respectful address to an elderly man
ba:bu: (*m*)	ਬਾਬੂ	white collar person
ba:d c	ਬਾਦ 'ਚ	later on
bá:gʱ (*m*)	ਬਾਘ	tiger
bá̃:ɦ (*f*)	ਬਾਂਹ	arm
bá:ɦar	ਬਾਹਰ	outside
bá:ɦarla:	ਬਾਹਰਲਾ	of outside
ba:ki:	ਬਾਕੀ	remaining
ba:laɳ (*m*)	ਬਾਲਣ	fuel
ba:p (*m*)	ਬਾਪ	father
ba:re	ਬਾਰੇ	about
benti: (*f*)	ਬੇਨਤੀ	request
beʃaram	ਬੇਸ਼ਰਮ	shameless
bɛʈʰ	ਬੈਠ	to sit
bɛ̃gaɳ (*m*)	ਬੈਂਗਣ	aubergine
bijli: (*f*)	ਬਿਜਲੀ	electricity
bilkul	ਬਿਲਕੁਲ	completely
billa: (*m*)	ਬਿੱਲਾ	tom cat
billi: (*f*)	ਬਿੱਲੀ	female cat
bi:ma:r	ਬੀਮਾਰ	patient, ill
bi:ma:ri: (*f*)	ਬੀਮਾਰੀ	illness, disease, ailment
biria:ni: (*f*)	ਬਿਰਿਆਨੀ	a rice dish
bol	ਬੋਲ	to speak
bú:ɦa: (*m*)	ਬੂਹਾ	door
bujʱà:	ਬੁਝਾ	to extinguish
búllʱ (*m*)	ਬੁੱਲ੍ਹ	lip
bura:	ਬੁਰਾ	bad, evil, unpleasant
bura: mann	ਬੁਰਾ ਮੰਨ	to dislike, to mind
buxa:r	ਬੁਖ਼ਾਰ	high temperature, fever
bʱà:bi: (*f*)	ਭਾਬੀ	brother's wife, sister-in-law
bʱà:i: (*m*)	ਭਾਈ	brother
bʱàr	ਭਰ	to fill, to pay

bʰarà: (*m*)	ਭਰਾ	brother
bʰarjà:i: (*f*)	ਭਰਜਾਈ	brother's wife, sister-in-law
bʰà:rat (*m*)	ਭਾਰਤ	India
bʰà:rati:	ਭਾਰਤੀ	Indian
bʰà:ʃa: (*f*)	ਭਾਸ਼ਾ	language
bʰat̪î:ja: (*m*)	ਭਤੀਜਾ	nephew (brother's son)
bʰaʈù:ra: (*m*)	ਭਟੂਰਾ	fried bread
bʰèɳ (*f*)	ਭੈਣ	sister
bʰinɖi: (*f*)	ਭਿੰਡੀ	okra
bʰùnn	ਭੁੰਨ	to roast
c cʰ	ਚ ਛ	
cakra:	ਚਕਰਾ	to get puzzled
cal	ਚਲ	to move
canga:	ਚੰਗਾ	good, well
cangi: tarʰã:	ਚੰਗੀ ਤਰਾਂ	well, satisfactorily
caran	ਚਹਨ	holy feet
cáɽʰ	ਚਤੁ	to climb
caɽʰà:i: (*f*)	ਚੜ੍ਹਾਈ	ascent, invasion
caɽʰvà:	ਚੜ੍ਹਵਾ	to get raised
caʈaɳi: (*f*)	ਚਟਣੀ	sauce, chutney
caʈpaʈa:	ਚਟਪਟਾ	spicy
ca:ca: (*m*)	ਚਾਚਾ	uncle (father's younger brother)
ca:ci: (*f*)	ਚਾਚੀ	aunt
ca:dar (*f*)	ਚਾਦਰ	sheet
cá:ɦ (*f*)	ਚਾਹ	desire, tea
ca:naɳi: (*f*)	ਚਾਨਣੀ	moonlight
cinta: (*f*)	ਚਿੰਤਾ	worry
citt̪ʰi: (*f*)	ਚਿੱਠੀ	letter
ci:r	ਚੀਰ	to slice, to saw
ci:z (*f*)	ਚੀਜ਼	thing
cõ	ਚੋਂ	from inside
cor (*m/f*)	ਚੋਰ	thief

cɔtʰ	ਚੌਥ	the fourth day (before or after the present)
cuk	ਚੁਕ	to finish
cukk	ਚੁੱਕ	to lift
cúllʰaː (f)	ਚੁੱਲ੍ਹਾ	stove
cuɳ	ਚੁਣ	to choose
cupp	ਚੁੱਪ	silent
cúːɦaː (f)	ਚੂਹਾ	rat
cʰaḍḍ	ਛੱਡ	to leave, to give up, to abandon
cʰak	ਛਕ	to relish, to eat
cʰatar (m)	ਛਤਰ	canopy
cʰatari: (f)	ਛਤਰੀ	umbrella
cʰaː	ਛਾ	to spread oneself
cʰaːɳ	ਛਾਣ	to filter
cʰaːtiː (f)	ਛਾਤੀ	chest
cʰeɽ	ਛੇੜ	to tease
cʰitt (f)	ਛਿੱਟ	drop
cʰóɦ (f)	ਛੋਹ	touch
cʰole (m/p)	ਛੋਲੇ	curried chickpeas
cʰúːɦ	ਛੂਹ	to touch
cʰuttiː (f)	ਛੁੱਟੀ	holiday, leave
d dʰ	ਦ ਧ	
dard (f)	ਦਰਦ	pain, ache
darust	ਦਰੁਸਤ	correct
darziː (m)	ਦਰਜ਼ੀ	tailor
das	ਦਸ	ten
dass	ਦੱਸ	to say
dastak (f)	ਦਸਤਕ	knock
davaːiː (f)	ਦਵਾਈ	medicine
daː	ਦਾ	of
daːdiː (f)	ਦਾਦੀ	grandmother (father's mother)
dáːɦɽiː (f)	ਦਾਹੜੀ	beard
daːl (f)	ਦਾਲ	cooked lentils
daːl roṭiː (f)	ਦਾਲ ਰੋਟੀ	simple food, simple living

da:ta: (*m*)	ਦਾਤਾ	provider, God
de	ਦੇ	to give
dekʰ	ਦੇਖ	to see
der (*f*)	ਦੇਰ	time, duration
dil (*m*)	ਦਿਲ	heart
dilli: (*f*)	ਦਿੱਲੀ	Delhi
dima:g (*m*)	ਦਿਮਾਗ	brain
din (*m*)	ਦਿਨ	day
do	ਦੋ	two
donõ	ਦੋਨੋਂ	both
dost (*m/f*)	ਦੋਸਤ	friend
dovẽ	ਦੋਵੇਂ	both
dúddⁿ (*m*)	ਦੁੱਧ	milk
dukʰ	ਦੁਖ	to ache
dupáɦir (*f*)	ਦੁਪਹਿਰ	midday
du:ja:	ਦੂਜਾ	second
du:sara:	ਦੂਸਰਾ	second
dⁿàni:a: (*m*)	ਧਨੀਆ	coriander
dⁿànnva:d (*m/s*)	ਧੰਨਵਾਦ	thanks
dⁿànnva:di:	ਧੰਨਵਾਦੀ	thankful
dⁿàram (*m*)	ਧਰਮ	religion (Hindu, Sikh)
dⁿi: (*f*)	ਧੀ	daughter
dⁿò	ਧੋ	to wash
dⁿuà:	ਧੁਆ	to get washed
dⁿù:ã: (*m*)	ਧੂਆਂ	smoke
dⁿù:ɽ (*f*)	ਧੂੜ	dust

ɖ ɖ	ਡ ੜ	
ˌɖangar (*m/pl*)	ਡੰਗਰ	cattle
ɖar (*m*)	ਡਰ	fear
ɖar	ਡਰ	to fear
ɖa:kʈar (*m/f*)	ਡਾਕਟਰ	doctor
ɖig	ਡਿਗ	to fall
ɖⁿàk	ਢਕ	to cover
ɖⁿalvà:	ਢਲਵਾ	to get melted
ɖⁿà:ba: (*m*)	ਢਾਬਾ	traditional Indian restaurant
ɖⁿɪɖɖ (*m*)	ਢਿੱਡ	stomach
ɖⁿòl (*m*)	ਢੋਲ	drum

e ɛ	ਏ ਐ	
eka: (*m*)	ਏਕਾ	unity
ɛdã: ɖa:	ਐਦਾਂ ਦਾ	like this
ɛna:	ਐਨਾ	so much
ɛʃ (*f*)	ਐਸ਼	luxury
ɛvẽ	ਐਵੇਂ	simply, just
f	ਫ਼	
farak (*m*)	ਫ਼ਰਕ	difference
farma:	ਫ਼ਰਮਾ	to order, to say (respectful)
fikar (*m*)	ਫ਼ਿਕਰ	worry
g gʱ	ਗ ਘ	
gábbʱe	ਗੱਭੇ	in the middle/centre
gada: (*f*)	ਗਦਾ	mace
gadda: (*m*)	ਗੱਦਾ	cushion
gáʱu (*m*)	ਗਾਹੁ	attention
gala: (*m*)	ਗਲਾ	throat
gall (*f*)	ਗੱਲ	matter, talk, saying
galti: (*f*)	ਗਲਤੀ	mistake
garaj	ਗਰਜ	to thunder
garam	ਗਰਮ	hot
gardan (*f*)	ਗਰਦਨ	neck
gari:bi: (*f*)	ਗਰੀਬੀ	poverty
gaɽbaɽ (*f*)	ਗੜਬੜ	disturbance
ga:jar (*f*)	ਗਾਜਰ	carrot
gi:t (*m*)	ਗੀਤ	song
guná:ʱ (*m*)	ਗੁਨਾਹ	sin
gupt	ਗੁਪਤ	secret
gurda: (*m*)	ਗੁਰਦਾ	kidney
gurdua:ra: (*m*)	ਗੁਰਦੁਆਰਾ	Sikh temple
guru: (*m*)	ਗੁਰੂ	spiritual teacher (Sikh, Hindu)
guɽ (*m*)	ਗੁੜ	brown sugar
gū:d (*m*)	ਗੂੰਦ	gum, glue
gú:ʱaɽa:	ਗੂਹੜਾ	fast (colour)
gʱàr (*m*)	ਘਰ	home, house
gʱàr va:la: (*m*)	ਘਰ ਵਾਲਾ	husband
gʱàr va:li: (*f*)	ਘਰ ਵਾਲੀ	wife

gʰə̀ɽi: (f)	ਘੜੀ	clock
gʰə̀ʈa (f)	ਘਟਾ	clouds
gʰəʈà:	ਘਟਾ	to lessen, to reduce
gʰə̀ʈʈ	ਘੱਟ	less
gʰʰo (m)	ਘਿਓ	ghee
gʰò̃ɽa: (m)	ਘੋੜਾ	horse
gʰò̃ɽi: (f)	ਘੋੜੀ	mare
gʰùmm	ਘੁੰਮ	to rotate
gʰùngru: (m/pl)	ਘੁੰਗਰੂ	little bells
gʰùsmusa: (m)	ਘੁਸਮੁਸਾ	twilight
ɦ	ਹ	
ɦəd̪d̪i: (f)	ਹੱਡੀ	bone
ɦəfta: (m)	ਹਫ਼ਤਾ	week
ɦəki:m (m)	ਹਕੀਮ	physician
ɦəkk (m)	ਹੱਕ	right
ɦəkk ɦəla:l (m)	ਹੱਕ ਹਲਾਲ	an honest wage
ɦəku:mat (f)	ਹਕੂਮਤ	government
ɦəla:l	ਹਲਾਲ	permitted by religion (Muslim)
ɦəlcal (f)	ਹਲਚਲ	movement
ɦəlka:	ਹਲਕਾ	light
ɦəlva:i: (m)	ਹਲਵਾਈ	confectioner
ɦər roz	ਹਰ ਰੋਜ਼	daily
ɦəra:	ਹਰਾ	green
ɦəss	ਹੱਸ	to laugh
ɦətt̪ʰ (m)	ਹੱਥ	hand
ɦəva:i: əd̪d̪a: (m)	ਹਵਾਈ ਅੱਡਾ	airport
ɦəva:i: jaɦa:z (m)	ਹਵਾਈ ਜਹਾਜ਼	aeroplane
ɦã:	ਹਾਂ	yes
ɦa:e	ਹਾਏ!	oh!
ɦa:l (m)	ਹਾਲ	condition
ɦa:le	ਹਾਲੇ	yet, still
ɦa:sa: (m)	ਹਾਸਾ	laughter
ɦa:t̪ʰi: (m)	ਹਾਥੀ	elephant
ɦeʈʰã:	ਹੇਠਾਂ	below, down
ɦɛ	ਹੈ	is
ɦɛga:	ਹੈਗਾ	definitely is
ɦɛn	ਹੈਨ	definitely are

ɦia: (*f*)	ਹਿਆ	sense of shame
ɦila:	ਹਿਲਾ	to shake, to move
ɦissa: (*m*)	ਹਿੱਸਾ	part, portion
ɦii:	ਹੀ	only
ɦo	ਹੋ	to happen, to be, to become
ɦor	ਹੋਰ	more, else, another
ɦɔ̃sala: (*m*)	ਹੌਂਸਲਾ	courage
ɦukam (*m*)	ਹੁਕਮ	order, commandment
ɦuɳ	ਹੁਣ	now
ɦuɳã:/ɦurã:	ਹੁਣਾਂ/ਹੁਰਾਂ	added to a name to show respect
ɦuɳe	ਹੁਣੇ	right now
i i:	ਇ ਈ	
iɦo/iɦii:	ਇਹੋ/ਇਹੀ	this very
ija:zat (*f*)	ਇਜਾਜ਼ਤ	permission
ikk	ਇੱਕ	one
ikko	ਇੱਕੋ	only one
ikk va:ri:	ਇੱਕ ਵਾਰੀ	once
ila:j (*m*)	ਇਲਾਜ	medical treatment
ila:va:	ਇਲਾਵਾ	in addition
ima:rat (*f*)	ਇਮਾਰਤ	building
imli: (*f*)	ਇਮਲੀ	tamarind
imtiɦa:n (*m*)	ਇਮਤਿਹਾਨ	examination
intza:m (*m*)	ਇੰਤਜ਼ਾਮ	arrangement
intza:r (*f*)	ਇੰਤਜ਼ਾਰ	waiting
is lai: (*f*)	ਇਸ ਲਈ	therefore
itthe	ਇੱਥੇ	here
i:ma:n (*m*)	ਈਮਾਨ	moral principle, religious faith (Muslim)
i:rkha: (*f*)	ਈਰਖਾ	jealousy
j jɦ	ਜ ਝ	
jad	ਜਦ	when
jadõ	ਜਦੋਂ	when
jalaɳ (*f*)	ਜਲਣ	burning sensation
jana:b (*m*)	ਜਨਾਬ	sir, Your/His Excellency
jap	ਜਪ	to mutter (a prayer or God's name)

java:b (*m*)	ਜਵਾਬ	answer
ja:	ਜਾ	to go
jã:	ਜਾਂ	or
ja:ṇ	ਜਾਣ	to know
jeb (*f*)	ਜੇਬ	pocket
je . . . tã:	ਜੇ . . . ਤਾਂ	if . . . then
jigar (*m*)	ਜਿਗਰ	liver
jifia:	ਜਿਹਾ	like, looking like
jitthe	ਜਿੱਥੇ	where
ji:	ਜੀ	to live
ji:van (*m*)	ਜੀਵਨ	life
ji:vani: (*f*)	ਜੀਵਨੀ	biography
joṛ	ਜੋੜ	to join, to assemble
jua:i: (*m*)	ਜੁਆਈ	son-in-law
jʰànda: (*m*)	ਝੰਡਾ	flag
jʰà:ṛ	ਝਾੜ	to shake off
jʰukà:	ਝੁਕਾ	to bow, to lower

k kʰ	ਕ ਖ	
kaba:b (*m*)	ਕਬਾਬ	kebab
kad	ਕਦ	when
kade	ਕਦੇ	when, ever
kadõ	ਕਦੋਂ	when
káḍḍʰ	ਕੱਢ	to take out
kaḍʰvà:	ਕਢਵਾ	to get taken out
kafià:ṇi: (*f*)	ਕਹਾਣੀ	story
káfii	ਕਹਿ	to say
káfiiṇa: (*m*)	ਕਹਿਣਾ	saying
kai:	ਕਈ	some
kala: (*f*)	ਕਲਾ	art
kalla:	ਕੱਲਾ	lonely
kállʰ (*m*)	ਕੱਲ੍ਹ	yesterday, tomorrow
kama:l (*m*)	ਕਮਾਲ	wonder
kamb	ਕੰਬ	to tremble
kami:z (*f*)	ਕਮੀਜ਼	shirt
kamm (*m*)	ਕੰਮ	work
kamra: (*m*)	ਕਮਰਾ	room
kándʰ (*m*)	ਕੰਧ	wall
kann (*m*)	ਕੰਨ	ear

kapp (*m*)	ਕੱਪ	cup
kar	ਕਰ	to do
kará:ĥ	ਕਰਾਹ	to groan
kaɽá:ĥii: (*f*)	ਕੜਾਹੀ	wok, pan
káɽʰi: (*f*)	ਕੜੀ	curry (Panjabi style)
kasrat (*f*)	ਕਸਰਤ	exercise
katt	ਕੱਟ	to cut
kavita: (*f*)	ਕਵਿਤਾ	poem
ka:ĥi: (*f*)	ਕਾਢੀ	coffee
ka:ĥi:	ਕਾਢੀ	enough, a lot
ká:ĥda:	ਕਾਹਦਾ	what sort
ká:ĥla:	ਕਾਹਲਾ	impatient
ká:ĥli: (*f*)	ਕਾਹਲੀ	hurry
ka:ka: (*m*)	ਕਾਕਾ	boy
ka:la:	ਕਾਲਾ	black
ka:ma: (*m*)	ਕਾਮਾ	worker
ka:r (*f*)	ਕਾਰ	car
ka:r (*m*)	ਕਾਰ	work
ka:mya:b	ਕਾਮਯਾਬ	successful
ka:nū̃:n (*m*)	ਕਾਨੂੰਨ	law
ka:ri:gar (*m*)	ਕਾਰੀਗਰ	craftsman
ka:roba:r (*m*)	ਕਾਰੋਬਾਰ	business
kẽci: (*f*)	ਕੈਂਚੀ	scissors
ki	ਕਿ	that
kiddã:	ਕਿੱਦਾਂ	how
kinna:	ਕਿੰਨਾ	how much
kinne	ਕਿੰਨੇ	how many
kirat (*f*)	ਕਿਰਤ	work
kirpa: (*f*)	ਕਿਰਪਾ	kindness, grace
kirpa:n (*f*)	ਕਿਰਪਾਨ	sword
kism (*f*)	ਕਿਸਮ	type
kita:b (*f*)	ਕਿਤਾਬ	book
kite	ਕਿਤੇ	somewhere, maybe
kittʰe	ਕਿੱਥੇ	where
kittʰõ	ਕਿੱਥੋਂ	from where?
kiũ	ਕਿਉਂ	why
kivẽ	ਕਿਵੇਂ	how
ki:	ਕੀ	what
ki:mat (*f*)	ਕੀਮਤ	price

kofta: (*m*)	ਕੋਫ਼ਤਾ	meat or vegetable ball
kóṛʰ (*m*)	ਕੋਹੜ	leprosy
koi:	ਕੋਈ	any, some
kol	ਕੋਲ	near
ku	ਕੁ	about, nearly, approximately
kújʰ	ਕੁਝ	something, anything
kújʰ náffi:	ਕੁਝ ਨਹੀਂ	nothing
kukkaṛ (*m*)	ਕੁੱਕੜ	chicken
kuṛi: (*f*)	ਕੁੜੀ	girl
kursi: (*f*)	ਕੁਰਸੀ	chair
kutta: (*m*)	ਕੁੱਤਾ	dog
kuṭṭ (*f*)	ਕੁੱਟ	beating
kuṭṭ	ਕੁੱਟ	to beat
kú:ɦaɳi: (*f*)	ਕੂਹਣੀ	elbow
kʰabba:	ਖੱਬਾ	left
kʰaḍḍ (*f*)	ਖੱਡ	valley
kʰaṛʰ	ਖੜ੍ਹ	to stand
kʰa:	ਖਾ	to eat
kʰa:ɳa: (*m*)	ਖਾਣਾ	food, meal
kʰeḍ (*f*)	ਖੇਡ	game
kʰeḍ	ਖੇਡ	to play
kʰel (*f*)	ਖੇਲ	game
kʰel	ਖੇਲ	to play
kʰiṛki: (*f*)	ਖਿੜਕੀ	window
kʰoj (*f*)	ਖੋਜ	research
kʰur (*m*)	ਖੁਰ	hoof
l	ਲ	
lag	ਲਗ	to appear, to attach, to strike
lag ke	ਲਗ ਕੇ	painfully
lai:	ਲਈ	in order to, for the sake of
lakkaṛ (*f*)	ਲੱਕੜ	wood, timber
landan (*m*)	ਲੰਡਨ	London
laṛ	ਲੜ	to fight
latt (*f*)	ਲੱਤ	leg
la:	ਲਾ	to fix

lá:bʰ (*m*)	ਲਾਭ	profit, benefit
lá:bʰe	ਲਾਂਭੇ	aside
la:ik	ਲਾਇਕ	befitting, capable
la:l	ਲਾਲ	red
la:lac (*m*)	ਲਾਲਚ	greed
la:laci:	ਲਾਲਚੀ	greedy
leʈ	ਲੇਟ	to lie down
lɛ	ਲੈ	to take
lia:	ਲਿਆ	to bring
likʰ	ਲਿਖ	to write
lok (*m/pl*)	ਲੋਕ	people
lokī: (*m/pl*)	ਲੋਕੀਂ	people
loʈ (*f*)	ਲੋੜ	need
m	ਮ	
maccʰi: (*f*)	ਮੱਛੀ	fish
madad (*f*)	ਮਦਦ	help
mada:ri: (*m*)	ਮਦਾਰੀ	magician
máf̃i (*f*)	ਮਹਿੰ	buffalo
máf̃inga:	ਮਹਿੰਗਾ	costly
mafi:na: (*m*)	ਮਹੀਨਾ	month
makki: (*f*)	ਮੱਕੀ	maize, corn
mandar (*m*)	ਮੰਦਰ	temple
mang	ਮੰਗ	to ask for
mangva:	ਮੰਗਵਾ	to send for
manja: (*m*)	ਮੰਜਾ	cot
mann	ਮੰਨ	to agree, to accept, to admit, to consider
mar	ਮਰ	to die
masa:la: (*m*)	ਮਸਾਲਾ	mixed spices
maʃkari: (*f*)	ਮਸ਼ਕਰੀ	joke (generally sexy)
matlab (*m*)	ਮਤਲਬ	meaning
maza:k (*m*)	ਮਜ਼ਾਕ	joke
mazdu:r (*m*)	ਮਜ਼ਦੂਰ	labourer
ma:dari: zaba:n (*f*)	ਮਾਦਰੀ ਜ਼ਬਾਨ	mother tongue
ma:f kar	ਮਾਫ਼	to forgive, to excuse
mã:fi (*m*)	ਮਾਂਹ	black lentils
ma:mu:li:	ਮਾਮੂਲੀ	ordinary, slight
ma:r	ਮਾਰ	to kill

maːɽaː	ਮਾੜਾ	weak, bad
maːs (*m*)	ਮਾਸ	meat, flesh
maːʃaː alla:	ਮਾਸ਼ਾ ਅੱਲਾ!	By God's grace (Muslim)
maːta (*f*)	ਮਾਤਾ	mother
maːt bʰàːʃa: (*f*)	ਮਾਤ ਭਾਸ਼ਾ	mother tongue
mã: (*f*)	ਮਾਂ	mother
mã: boli: (*f*)	ਮਾਂ ਬੋਲੀ	mother tongue
mefiarba:ni: (*f*)	ਮੇਹਰਬਾਨੀ	kindness
mera:	ਮੇਰਾ	my
metʰi: (*f*)	ਮੇਥੀ	fenugreek
mɛ̃	ਮੈਂ	I
mɛda: (*m*)	ਮੈਦਾ	plain flour
míɦinat (*f*)	ਮਿਹਨਤ	hard work
mil	ਮਿਲ	to meet
mirc (*f*)	ਮਿਰਚ	chilli
miʃri: (*m*)	ਮਿਸ਼ਰੀ	sugar cubes
mittʰa:	ਮਿੱਠਾ	sweet
mɯ́:ɦ (*m*)	ਮੀਂਹ	rain
mosi:ki: (*f*)	ਮੋਸੀਕੀ	music
mɔt (*f*)	ਮੌਤ	death
muccʰ (*f*)	ਮੁੱਛ	moustache
mukʰɽa: (*m*)	ਮੁਖੜਾ	face
munɖa: (*m*)	ਮੁੰਡਾ	boy
muɽ	ਮੁੜ	to return
muʃkil (*f*)	ਮੁਸ਼ਕਿਲ	difficulty
muʃkil	ਮੁਸ਼ਕਿਲ	difficult
muta:bak	ਮੁਤਾਬਕ	according to
mɯ́:ɦ (*m*)	ਮੂੰਹ	mouth, face
mú:fire	ਮੂਹਰੇ	in front
n	ਨ	
nafrat (*f*)	ਨਫ਼ਰਤ	hatred
náɦi:	ਨਹੀਂ	no, not
naka:b (*m*)	ਨਕਾਬ	mask
namaste (ji:)	ਨਮਸਤੇ (ਜੀ)	Hindu greeting
naʃa: (*m*)	ਨਸ਼ਾ	intoxication
navã:	ਨਵਾਂ	new
nã: (*m*)	ਨਾਂ	name

na:l	ਨਾਲ	with, along
na:le	ਨਾਲੇ	in addition, also
na:lõ	ਨਾਲੋਂ	from, than
na:m (*m*)	ਨਾਮ	name (generally God's)
neɾe	ਨੇੜੇ	near
nigra:ni: (*f*)	ਨਿਗਰਾਨੀ	supervision
nű:ɦ (*f*)	ਨੂੰਹ	daughter-in-law
o ɔ	ੳ ਔ	
ɔli:a: (*m*)	ਔਲੀਆ	prophet
ɔrat (*f*)	ਔਰਤ	woman
p pʰ	ਪ ਫ	
paccʰam (*f*)	ਪੱਛਮ	west
paccʰami:	ਪੱਛਮੀ	western
paccʰõ	ਪੱਛੋਂ	west
pacʰa:ɳ (*f*)	ਪਛਾਣ	identity
pacʰa:ɳ	ਪਛਾਣ	to recognise
páɦila:	ਪਹਿਲਾ	first
páɦilã:	ਪਹਿਲਾਂ	first of all, at first
páɦu (*f*)	ਪਹੁ	dawn
páɦũc	ਪਹੁੰਚ	to reach
paka:	ਪਕਾ	to cook
pakɔɾe (*m/pl*)	ਪਕੌੜੇ	fritters
pani:r (*m*)	ਪਨੀਰ	soft cheese
par	ਪਰ	but
parat	ਪਰਤ	to return
parɦez (*m*)	ਪਰਹੇਜ਼	abstinence
pariva:r (*m*)	ਪਰਿਵਾਰ	family
parsõ (*m*)	ਪਰਸੋਂ	day after tomorrow, day before yesterday
páɽʰ	ਪੜ੍ਹ	to read
paɽʰà:	ਪੜ੍ਹਾ	to teach
páɽʰia: likʰia:	ਪੜ੍ਹਿਆ ਲਿਖਿਆ	educated
pasand (*f*)	ਪਸੰਦ	liking
patala:	ਪਤਲਾ	thin
pata: (*m*)	ਪਤਾ	information, knowledge, address

pati: (*m*)	ਪਤੀ	husband
patni: (*f*)	ਪਤਨੀ	wife
patta: (*m*)	ਪੱਤਾ	leaf
patti: (*f*)	ਪੱਤੀ	small leaf, tea leaves
patt^har (*m*)	ਪੱਥਰ	stone
pɑ:	ਪਾ	to put
pɑ:lak (*f*)	ਪਾਲਕ	spinach
pɑ:sɑ: (*m*)	ਪਾਸਾ	side
pɑ:se	ਪਾਸੇ	on the side
pɑ:ʈ^h (*m*)	ਪਾਠ	lesson, reading
peʃɑ:b (*m*)	ਪੇਸ਼ਾਬ	urine
peʈ (*m*)	ਪੇਟ	stomach
pɛ	ਪੈ	to fall, to happen
pɛr (*m*)	ਪੈਰ	foot
pɛsa: (*m*)	ਪੈਸਾ	money
pɛ̃ti: (*f*)	ਪੈਂਤੀ	Panjabi alphabet, thirty-five
piɑ:r (*m*)	ਪਿਆਰ	love
piɑ:z (*m*)	ਪਿਆਜ਼	onion
picc^ha: (*m*)	ਪਿੱਛਾ	back
picc^he	ਪਿੱਛੇ	behind, after
pinɖ (*m*)	ਪਿੰਡ	village
pita: (*m*)	ਪਿਤਾ	father
pi:	ਪੀ	to drink
pi:ɽ (*f*)	ਪੀੜ	pain
pot^hi: (*f*)	ਪੋਥੀ	book (generally religious)
poʈa: (*f*)	ਪੋਟਾ	finger-tip
prem (*m*)	ਪ੍ਰੇਮ	love
pucc^h	ਪੁੱਛ	to ask
purɑ:ɳɑ:	ਪੁਰਾਣਾ	old
putt (*m*)	ਪੁੱਤ	son
puttar (*m*)	ਪੁੱਤਰ	son
pu:rɑ:	ਪੂਰਾ	full
p^haɽ	ਫੜ	to hold, to catch, to grasp
p^her	ਫੇਰ	then; to turn
p^hir	ਫਿਰ	then; to turn

pʰunkaːr (*f*)	ਫੁੰਕਾਰ	breathing sound
r	ਰ	
ráɦi	ਰਹਿ	to stay, to live
ras (*m*)	ਰਸ	juice
rassaː (*m*)	ਰੱਸਾ	rope
ráːɦ (*m*)	ਰਾਹ	way, path
raːɦiː (*m/f*)	ਰਾਹੀ	traveller
raːɦiː	ਰਾਹੀਂ	through
raːt (*f*)	ਰਾਤ	night
rel gaɖɖiː (*f*)	ਰੇਲ ਗੱਡੀ	train
riʃtedaːr (*m/f*)	ਰਿਸ਼ਤੇਦਾਰ	relative
ro	ਰੋ	to cry, to weep
rok	ਰੋਕ	to stop
roʈiː (*f*)	ਰੋਟੀ	bread, chapati
roʈiː ʈukk (*m*)	ਰੋਟੀ ਟੁੱਕ	meal
roz	ਰੋਜ਼	daily
ruk	ਰੁਕ	to stop, to stay
rukkʰ (*m*)	ਰੁੱਖ	tree
s ʃ	ਸ ਸ਼	
sábɦ	ਸਭ	all
sabak (*m*)	ਸਬਕ	lesson
sacc (*m*)	ਸੱਚ	truth
sáɖ̃ɦuː (*m*)	ਸਾਂਢੂ	wife's sister's husband, brother-in-law
safaː (*m*)	ਸਫ਼ਾ	page
safar (*m*)	ਸਫ਼ਰ	journey
saɦaːraː (*m*)	ਸਹਾਰਾ	support
sáɦ̃ũ (*f*)	ਸਹੁੰ	oath
sáɦuraː (*m*)	ਸਹੁਰਾ	father-in-law
sajjaː	ਸੱਜਾ	right (direction)
sak	ਸਕ	be able to
sámajɦ (*f*)	ਸਮਝ	understanding
sámajɦ	ਸਮਝ	to understand
sambɦàːl (*f*)	ਸੰਭਾਲ	care, preservation
sambɦàːl	ਸੰਭਾਲ	to handle, to take care of
samosaː (*m*)	ਸਮੋਸਾ	samosa

sangráfii (*m*)	ਸੰਗ੍ਰਹਿ	collection
sang^ʱàraʃ (*m*)	ਸੰਘਰਸ਼	struggle
sangi:t (*m*)	ਸੰਗੀਤ	music
sardi: (*f*)	ਸਰਦੀ	cold
saɽak (*f*)	ਸੜਕ	road
sasta:	ਸਸਤਾ	cheap
sat sri: aka:l	ਸਤਿ ਸ੍ਰੀ ਅਕਾਲ	Sikh greeting and reply
sattar	ਸੱਤਰ	seventy
sattia:na:s (*m*)	ਸੱਤਿਆਨਾਸ	complete ruin
sava:l (*m*)	ਸਵਾਲ	question
savere	ਸਵੇਰੇ	in the morning
sa:bat	ਸਾਬਤ	whole
sa:da:	ਸਾਦਾ	simple
sá:d^ʱu: (*m*)	ਸਾਧੂ	saint
sa:g (*m*)	ਸਾਗ	cooked spinach
sá:fi (*m*)	ਸਾਹ	breath
sá:fiab (*m*)	ਸਾਹਬ	Mr
sá:fimaɳe	ਸਾਹਮਣੇ	in front of, facing
sá:n (*m*)	ਸਾਹਨ/ਸਾਨ੍ਹ	bull
sá̃:j^ʱa:	ਸਾਂਝਾ	shared, common
sá̃:j^ʱi:da:r (*m/f*)	ਸਾਂਝੀਦਾਰ	partner
sa:l (*m*)	ਸਾਲ	year
sa:r (*m*)	ਸਾਰ	summary
sa:ra:	ਸਾਰਾ	whole
sa:re	ਸਾਰੇ	all
séfiat (*f*)	ਸੇਹਤ	health
sek (*m*)	ਸੇਕ	heat
sɛr (*f*)	ਸੈਰ	stroll
sɛr sapa:ʈa: (*m*)	ਸੈਰ ਸਪਾਟਾ	leisurely stroll
sia:ɳa:	ਸਿਆਣਾ	wise
sia:ɳa: bia:ɳa:	ਸਿਆਣਾ ਬਿਆਣਾ	grown up
sídd^ʱa:	ਸਿੱਧਾ	simple, straight
sikk^h	ਸਿੱਖ	to learn
sik^ha:	ਸਿਖਾ	to teach
sipá:fii: (*m*)	ਸਿਪਾਹੀ	soldier
sir (*m*)	ਸਿਰ	head
sir cakra:	ਸਿਰ ਚਕਰਾ	to feel giddy
sirf	ਸਿਰਫ਼	only

si:	ਸੀ	was
si:ʈi: (f)	ਸੀਟੀ	whistle
soc	ਸੋਚ	to think
sófiɳa:	ਸੋਹਣਾ	beautiful
soʈi: (f)	ਸੋਟੀ	stick
sɔ	ਸੌਂ	hundred
sɔ̃	ਸੌਂ	to sleep
suá:ɦ (f)	ਸੁਆਹ	ashes
sudʰà:r	ਸੁਧਾਰ	to reform
sujʰà:o (m)	ਸੁਝਾਓ	suggestion
sukʰ (m)	ਸੁਖ	comfort
sukʰi:	ਸੁਖੀ	in comfort
suɳ	ਸੁਣ	to hear
suɳa:	ਸੁਣਾ	to tell
su:ci: (f)	ਸੂਚੀ	list
su:r (m)	ਸੂਰ	pig
su:raj (m)	ਸੂਰਜ	sun
svar (f)	ਸੂਰ	sound, vowel
svɛ-ji:vani: (f)	ਸੈ-ਜੀਵਨੀ	autobiography
ʃabad (m)	ਸ਼ਬਦ	word
ʃáɦid (m)	ਸ਼ਹਿਦ	honey
ʃáɦir (m)	ਸ਼ਹਿਰ	city, town
ʃaram (f)	ਸ਼ਰਮ	shame
ʃara:b (f)	ਸ਼ਰਾਬ	alcohol
ʃara:rat (f)	ਸ਼ਰਾਰਤ	mischief
ʃa:ba:ʃ	ਸ਼ਾਬਾਸ਼	well done!
ʃa:m (f)	ਸ਼ਾਮ	evening
ʃóɦarat (f)	ਸ਼ੋਹਰਤ	fame, reputation
ʃor (m)	ਸ਼ੋਰ	noise
ʃor ʃara:ba: (m)	ਸ਼ੋਰ ਸ਼ਰਾਬਾ	loud noise, din, hullabaloo
ʃɔk (m)	ਸ਼ੌਕ	hobby
ʃukri:a: (m)	ਸ਼ੁਕਰੀਆ	thanks
ʃuru: (m)	ਸ਼ੁਰੂ	beginning
ʃuru: kar	ਸ਼ੁਰੂ ਕਰ	to begin
t tʰ	ਤ ਥ	
tabi:at (f)	ਤਬੀਅਤ	health
tak	ਤਕ	up to, until

takli:f (*f*)	ਤਕਲੀਫ਼	discomfort, illness
tandrust	ਤੰਦਰੁਸਤ	healthy
tar	ਤਰ	to swim
tã:	ਤਾਂ	then
ta:za:	ਤਾਜ਼ਾ	fresh
te (shortened form of **ate**)	'ਤੇ	and
te (shortened form of **utte**)	'ਤੇ	on, upon
tɛr	ਤੈਰ	to swim
tia:r	ਤਿਆਰ	ready
tia:ri: (*f*)	ਤਿਆਰੀ	preparation
tia:r kar	ਤਿਆਰ ਕਰ	to prepare
ṭinn	ਤਿੰਨ	three
tõ	ਤੋਂ	from
tõ ila:va:	ਤੋਂ ਇਲਾਵਾ	besides, in addition to
tufia:ɖa:	ਤੁਹਾਡਾ	your (*pl*)
tur	ਤੁਰ	to walk
tuɾak	ਤੁੜਕ	to fry
tusĩ:	ਤੁਸੀਂ	you (*pl*)
tʰámmⁿ (*m*)	ਮ੍	pillar
tʰa:li: (*f*)	ਥਾਲੀ	plate
tʰoɾa:	ਥੋੜਾ	a little, less
ṭ ṭʰ	ਟ ਠ	
ṭama:ṭar (*m*)	ਟਮਾਟਰ	tomato
ṭanṭaṇ (*f*)	ਟਣ ਟਣ	tinkling sound
ṭukaɾa: (*m*)	ਟੁਕੜਾ	piece
ṭʰáfiir	ਠਹਿਰ	to stay
ṭʰanɖa:	ਠੰਡਾ	cold (*adj*)
ṭʰánɖʰa:	ਠੰਢਾ	cold (*adj*)
ṭʰap ṭʰap (*f*)	ਠਪ ਠਪ	sound of hooves
ṭʰi:k	ਠੀਕ	correct; fine
u u:	ਉ ਊ	
uɖɖ	ਉੱਡ	to fly
uɖi:k (*f*)	ਉੜੀਕ	waiting
ulṭi: (*f*)	ਉਲਟੀ	vomit
umar (*f*)	ਉਮਰ	age
ungal (*f*)	ਉਂਗਲ	finger

ungali: (*f*)	ਉੱਗਲੀ	finger
unn (*f*)	ਉੱਨ	wool
uɽ	ਉੜ	to fly
utte	ਉੱਤੇ	on
u:ʈʰ (*m*)	ਊਠ	camel
uttʰe	ਉੱਥੇ	there
v	ਵ	
vádʰi:a:	ਵਧੀਆ	superior, of high quality
vag	ਵਗ	to flow
váɦuʈi: (*f*)	ਵਹੁਟੀ	wife
vaja:	ਵਜਾ	to play (music)
vakkʰ	ਵੱਖ	different
vakkʰara:	ਵੱਖਰਾ	separate, different
vanɖ	ਵੰਡ	to divide, to share
varat	ਵਰਤ	to use
várʰ	ਵਰੵ	to rain
várʰa: (*m*)	ਵਰੵਾ	year
vas	ਵਸ	to live, to dwell
vá:ɦ	ਵਾਹ!	Great!
va:ɦiguru: (*m*)	ਵਾਹਿਗੁਰੁ	God (Sikh)
vá:ɦva:	ਵਾਹਵਾ	excellent, a lot
va:ri: (*f*)	ਵਾਰੀ	times, turn
vela: (*m*)	ਵੇਲਾ	time
vɛse:	ਵੈਸੇ	otherwise
viá:ɦ (*m*)	ਵਿਆਹ	marriage
via:karaɳ (*m*)	ਵਿਆਕਰਨ	grammar
vicc	ਵਿੱਚ	in, inside
vi:	ਵੀ	also
ví:ɦ	ਵੀਹ	twenty
vi:r (*m*)	ਵੀਰ	brother
x	ਖ਼	
xarac (*m*)	ਖ਼ਰਚ	expenses
xara:b	ਖ਼ਰਾਬ	bad
xari:d	ਖ਼ਰੀਦ	to buy
xat (*m*)	ਖ਼ਤ	letter
xa:li:	ਖ਼ਾਲੀ	empty
xa:nda:n (*m*)	ਖ਼ਾਨਦਾਨ	family

xa:nda:ni	ਖ਼ਾਨਦਾਨੀ	of the family
xa:s	ਖ਼ਾਸ	special
xia:l (*m*)	ਖ਼ਿਆਲ	idea, opinion
xidmat (*f*)	ਖ਼ਿਦਮਤ	service
xud	ਖ਼ੁਦ	oneself
xuda: ɦa:fiz	ਖ਼ੁਦਾ ਹਾਫ਼ਿਜ਼!	God protect you (Muslim)
xuʃ	ਖ਼ੁਸ਼	happy
xuʃi: (*f*)	ਖ਼ੁਸ਼ੀ	happiness
xuʃkismat	ਖ਼ੁਸ਼ਕਿਸਮਤ	fortunate, lucky
y	ਯ	
ya:d (*f*)	ਯਾਦ	memory
ya:r (*m*)	ਯਾਰ	friend
z	ਜ਼	
zaba:n (*f*)	ਜ਼ਬਾਨ	tongue, language
záɦir (*m/f*)	ਜ਼ਹਿਰ	poison
zaru:r	ਜ਼ਰੂਰ	certainly, definitely
za:ɦir	ਜ਼ਾਹਿਰ	apparent
zia:da:	ਜ਼ਿਆਦਾ	much, many, more

Key to exercises

Conversation unit 1

1 The speakers are Sikhs. Their names are Mr Gill and Mr Saggoo. **2** (a) sat sri: aka:l. (b) xuda: fia:fiz. (c) t̪ʰi:k fiɛ. (*I'm fine.*) t̪ʰi:k náfĩ:. (*I'm not well.*) (d) va: lɛkam assala:m. (e) arz fiɛ ji:. (f) namaste ji:. (g) fiukam karo. **3** (1) (e), (2) (d), (3) (c), (4) (a), (5) (b) **4** Conversation 1: namaste ji:; mera: fia:l; tusĩ; tufia:ɖa:; mera: Conversation 2: va: lɛkam assala:m; fia:l; da: ʃukar fiɛ; taʃri:f; **5** mera: sir; úfida: kamra:; úfidi: kursi:; tufia:ɖi: kita:b; sa:ɖa: billa:; sa:ɖa: kamra:; mera: gʰòʈa:; tufia:ɖi: akkʰ

Conversation unit 2

1 tufia:ɖa: nã: ki: fiɛ? tusĩ: ki: kamm karde fio? *He doesn't work.* tufia:ɖe kinne bacce ne? *He has four children.* munɖe jã: kuʈi:ã:? *Three boys and one girl.* ki: úfi *school* jã:de ne? *The boys go to school. But the girl is an infant and goes to the nursery.* **2** baʈʈ anvar fiusɛn; 47 Oxford Road, Manchester; Restaurant owner; 74 Victoria Road, Manchester; by car. **3** fiã:, fiã:; mere baʈe; ne; karde ne; fiã:; karda: fiã:; mere; cʰoʈe; ne; fiɛ; fiɛ; mere; cʰoʈe; karde ne; sa:ɖi:; cʰoʈi:; fiɛ; páʈʰdi:; fiɛ; bacce ne; munɖa:; kuʈi:ã:; mere bacce; jã:de ne; baʈi:; kardi: fiɛ; cʰoʈi:; jã:da: fiɛ.

Conversation unit 3

1 F, T, T, T, F, F **2** (a) mere (b) mere (c) mere kol (d) meri:ã (e) mere (f) meri: (g) mere (h) mera: **3** (b) mɛnũ: do pɔ̃ɖ ga:jarã: cá:fii:di:ã ne. (c) mɛnũ: gʰar cá:fiida: fiɛ. (d) mɛnũ: cá:fi da: kapp cá:fii:da: fiɛ. (e) mɛnũ: kuʈi: cá:fii:di: fiɛ, munɖa: náfĩ:. (f) par mere bʰarà: nũ: munɖa: cá:fii:da: fiɛ. (g) mɛnũ: *hotel* vic do kamre cá:fii:de ne. (h) tufia:nũ: ki: cá:fii:da: fiɛ? (i) mɛnũ: *radiator* kʰiʈki: de fieʈʰá: cá:fii:da: fiɛ. **4** sa:ɖe; de; de; vadɖe; kamre; cʰoʈa:; kamra:; cʰoʈe;

kamre; a:pne; de; kamre; vaḍḍa:; kursi:ã:; kánd̃ã:; vaḍḍi:ã; buk-ʃelfã:; ífinã:; buk-ʃelfã:; di:ã:; kita:bã: 5   See the transcript of the dialogue on page 290–291.

Conversation unit 4

1. There can be more than one correct answer. The following answers are suggestions. You do not have to use so-called full sentences. (b) fiã: ji:. canga: lagda: fiɛ. (c) náfĩ: ji:. canga: náfĩ: lagda:. (d) náfĩ:, canga: lagda: fiɛ. (e) pani:r pasand fiɛ, par pa:lak náfĩ:. (f) meri: patni: nũ: paka:uṇ da: fiɛ, mɛnũ: kʰa:ṇ da:. (g) náfĩ: ji:. mɛ̃ *vegetarian* fiã:. (h) náfĩ:. mɛnũ: sigriṭ bafiút bura: layda: fiɛ.   **2**   L, L, D, L, D, L, L   **3**   *Suggested answers:* tufia:nũ: ki: ʃɔk fiɛ? tufia:nũ: ʃara:b cangi: lagdi: fiɛ? ki: tufia:nũ: sangi:t vi: pasand fiɛ? tusĩ: *meat* pasand karde fio? **4**   *Suggested answers:* (a) tufia:nũ: ki: cá:fii:da: fiɛ? (b) d̃ànsak vic ki: fiɛ? (c) ki: tufia:ḍe kol *vegetarian* d̃ànsak fiɛ? (d) tufia:nũ: kújʰ fior cá:fii:da: fiɛ? (e) ʃa:fii: pani:r vic mirc masa:la: fiɛ? (f) ikk d̃ànsak, na:l cɔl; ate ikk ʃa:fii: pani:r, na:l na:n.

5 Suggested translation:

Gill:	sat sri: aka:l da:kṭar sá:fiab. mera: nã: *Mohan Singh Gill* fiɛ.
Doctor:	sat sri: aka:l *Gill* sá:fiab. ki: fia:l fiɛ?
Gill:	báfiut bura:.
Doctor:	ki: gall fiɛ?
Gill:	mɛnũ: (*or* mere) báfiut sir dard te peṭ dard fiɛ.
Doctor:	buxa:r vi: fiɛ?
Gill:	náfĩ: ji:.
Doctor:	gala: xara:b fiɛ?
Gill:	náfĩ:.
Doctor:	fior koi: gall?
Gill:	náfĩ:, fior koi: gall náfĩ:.
Doctor:	tusĩ: sigriṭ jã: ʃara:b pĩ:de fio?
Gill:	náfĩ:, mɛ̃ sigriṭ jã: ʃara:b náfĩ: pĩ:da:
Doctor:	ṭʰi:k fiɛ. éfi dava:i: lao. canga: a:ra:m karo, te ajj koi: kamm na: karo.

Conversation unit 5

1 aeroplane; (1) bus *or* (2) taxi; (1) train *or* (2) aeroplane; (1) bus *or* (2) aeroplane; (1) bus *or* (2) taxi *or* (3) horse **2** ne; jaːŋaː; —; ráɧiŋaː; —; dekʰŋiːãː; karnaː; —; pakaːuŋaː; —; ne; milnaː; —; piːŋiː; —; ne; jaːŋaː; —; kʰaːŋaː; —; ne; karnaː **3** aːpŋiː; meriː; meriː; úɧidi: aːpŋiː; meriː; aːpŋiː; aːpŋe; úɧidiː; mere; aːpŋe **4** . *Suggested translation:* tusĩ: kittʰe jaːŋa: ɧɛ? *She's going to Birmingham.* tusĩ: ajj jaːŋa: ɧɛ? *Yes, she's going today.* tuɧaːnũ: ikk paːse da: tikaɽ cáːɧiːda: ɧɛ jã: vaːpasi: da: vi:? *She's returning by train the day after tomorrow.* tã: tuɧaːnũ: *Saver Ticket* lɛŋa: cáːɧiːda: ɧɛ. *She doesn't know what a Saver Ticket is.* *Saver Ticket* báɧut sasata: vaːpasi: da: ʈikaɽ ɧunda: ɧɛ. *She would like a Saver Ticket. How much is it?* baːi: pɔ̃ɖ te nabbe pɛ̃ns.

Conversation unit 6

1 (2) úɧine mere kol a: ke mɛnũ: ikk gall dassi:. (3) mera: puttar *library* ja: ke aːpŋa: *college* da: kamm karda: ɧɛ. (4) bas vic bɛʈʰ ke gʰàr jaːo. (5) tusĩ: kamre vic ja: ke bɛʈʰo. (6) kállꟼ tusĩ: landan ja: ke ki: karna: ɧɛ?

2 Suggested translation

You:	íɧi ne mere dost *Wolfgang Schmidt.* íɧinã: di: tabiːat ʈʰiːk náɧĩ:..
Doctor:	ki: takliːf ɧɛ?
You:	kállꟼ raːt íɧinã: nũ: ulʈiːã: aːiːã:. ɧuŋ íɧinã: de sir te peɽ c dard ɧɛ. cʰaːti c jalaŋ ɧɛ. buxaːr vi: ɧɛ, te sir vi: cakraːũda: ɧɛ. peʃaːb lag ke aːũda: ɧɛ.
Doctor:	kállꟼ íɧinã: ne ki: kʰáːdꟼaː?
You:	mirc masaːle vaːla: kʰaːŋa: kʰáːdꟼaː.
Doctor:	íɧinã: ne ʃaraːb vi: piːtiː?
You:	*Beer* te *whisky* vi: piːtiː.
Doctor:	ki: tuɧaːɖe gʰàr c koi: *party* si?
You:	ɧã: ji:, meri: *birthday party* si.
Doctor:	tuɧaːɖe íɧi dost kittʰe ráɧinde ne?
You:	*Frankfurt, Germany* c.

3

4 Monday	Went to work. Had dinner in a restaurant. Saw a film at night.
5 Tuesday	Attended a Directors' Meeting in London.
6 Wednesday	Not well. Had headache and temperature. Didn't go to work.
7 Thursday	Phoned the doctor, who came, did a check-up and prescribed a medicine.
8 Friday	Phoned elder brother in the morning. Brother came to see him in the evening and stayed with him for the night.
9 Saturday	Both had a dinner in a restaurant and saw a Panjabi film on the video at night.
10 Sunday	Brother's wife came. She cooked a nice meal. In the evening brother and his wife went back.

4 (a) mere bʱat̀:je *Kirpal* ne ɑjj ikk baɽɑ: ɦi: cɑngɑ: kamm ki:tɑ:. (b) tuɦa:ɖe cʰoʈe bʱarà: ne ittʰe kadõ a:uɳa: ɦɛ? (c) úɦi kállᶠⁱ ittʰe a:ia: si:, te úɦine kállᶠⁱ nũ: pʰir a:uɳa: ɦɛ. (d) mɛ̃ te mere dost *Sukhdev* ne ɑjj ʃa:m nũ: *Dilshad Tandoori* vic kʰa:ɳa: kʰa:ɳ ja:ɳa: ɦɛ. ki: tusĩ: sa:ɖe na:l ja:ɳa: cá:ɦũde ɦo? (e) us kuɽi: ne *Kirpal* nũ: a:pɳi: ka:r vic *lift* ditti:. úɦi úɦide na:l kamm kardi: ɦɛ. (f) mɛ̃ te meri: patni: ɑjj savere *market* gae. meri: patni: ne pa:lak te ʈama:ʈar xari:de, ate mɛ̃ do kami:zã: xari:di:ã:. **5** gae; gia:; pi:ti:; dekʰia:; ke; pĩ:da:; milia:; milna:; cá:ɦũda:; a:i:ã:; a:e; a:ia:; milia:; milaɳ; a:uɳa:; ke; karna:; gia:

Conversation unit 7

1

	Can do	Cannot do
Speak English	✓	
Read English		✓
Write English		✓
Speak Urdu	✓	
Read Urdu	✓	
Write Urdu	✓	
Speak Panjabi		✓
Read Panjabi	✓	
Write Panjabi	✓	
Speak German	✓	

2 (a) (4), (b) (1), (c) (5), (d) (2), (e) (3) 3 (a) dioge (b) lai:ã:
(c) lai:, lavã:ga:/lavã:gi: (d) dio; lavã:ga:/lavã:gi: (e) lao; dio (f) diã:ga:/
diã:gi: (g) diã:ga:/diã:gi:; devega: (h) dio; lavã:ga:/lavã:gi: (i) deve;
dioge (j) dio; lao 4 lĕdi: (*or* sakdi:); lĕdi: (*or* sakdi:); ráfii:; cukki;;
lĕdi: (*or* sakdi:); sakdi: 5 (a) pi:vã:; pi:ã:ga:/pi:ã:gi: (*or* pi:vã:,
pi:vã:ga:, etc.) (b) karã: (c) diã: (*or* devã:) (d) sako; fioegi: (*or* fiovegi:)
(e) ja:vã:; ja:vã:

Conversation unit 8

1 Cookery; Singing; Painting; Panjabi; Hindi; Urdu; English 2 (a)
tomorrow (b) yesterday (c) tomorrow (d) tomorrow (e) tomorrow (f)
yesterday (g) yesterday (h) tomorrow 3 (a) boli:ã:; jã:di:ã: (b) boli:;
jã:di: (c) paka:ia:; jã:da: (d) dikʰa:i:; gai: (e) dikʰa:i:; ja:egi:
(*or* ja:vegi:) (f) pi:ti:; gai: (g) ditti:; ja:egi: (h) ditta:; jã:da:; pi:ta:;
ja:e (*or* ja:ve) (i) dafna:ia:; ja:ega: (j) dafna:ia:; jã:da:; ki:ta:; jã:da:
4 *Suggested translation:* picʰale fiafte meri: patni:; di: tabi:at ʈʰi:k
náfii: si:, ate mɛnũ sa:re xa:nda:n (*or* pariva:r *or* ʈabbar) lai: kʰa:ṇa:
paka:uṇa: pia:. mɛnũ: kʰa:ṇa: paka:uṇa: náfiĩ: a:ũda:. is lai: mɛ̃ ífi náfiĩ:
káfii sakda: ki mɛ̃ cangã: kʰa:ṇa: paka:ia: jã: náfiĩ:. par meri: patni: te
bacciã: ne kífia: ki: kʰa:ṇa: ʈʰi:k si:. úfi fior ki: káfii sakde si:? úfinã: nũ:
kʰa:ṇa: gʰàr kʰa:ṇa: pia:. así: *restaurant* vic kʰa:ṇa: náfiĩ: kʰã:de.
mɛnũ: pata: fiɛ ki *restaurant* vic kʰa:ṇe c bafiút mirc masa:le pa:e jã:de

ne. masa:le mere peʈ nũ: xara:b karde ne. ɦuɳ meri: patni: ʈʰi:k ɦɛ. mere bacce vi: xuʃ ne. ɦuɳ úɦinã: nũ: besua:d kʰa:ɳa: náɦĩ: kʰa:ɳa: paega:.

Conversation unit 9

1 (b) ਉਹ ਜਾਂਦਾ ਜਾਂਦਾ ਮੈਨੂੰ ਆਪਣੀ ਘੜੀ ਦੇ ਗਿਆ úɦi jã:da: jã:da: mɛnũ: a:pɳi: gʰàɽi: de gia:. (c) ਪਹਿਲਾਂ ਆਲੂਆਂ ਨੂੰ ਕੱਟੋ, ਅਤੇ ਫਿਰ ਕੱਟੇ ਹੋਏ ਆਲੂਆਂ ਨੂੰ ਉਬਾਲ ਲਓ páɦilã: a:lu:ã: nũ: kaʈʈo, ate pʰir kaʈʈe ɦoe a:lu:ã: nũ: uba:l lao. (d) ਮੈਨੂੰ ਇਹ ਖ਼ਤ ਪੜੂ ਲੈਣ ਦਿਓ mɛnũ: íɦi xat pàɽʰ leɳ dio. (e) ਚਾਚਾ ਜੀ ਜਾਣ ਤਾਂ ਲੱਗੇ ਸੀ, ਪਰ ਮੈਂ ਉਹਨਾਂ ਨੂੰ ਜਾਣ ਨਹੀਂ ਦਿੱਤਾ ca:ca: ji: ja:ɳ tã: lagge si:, par mɛ̃ úɦinã: nũ: ja:ɳ náɦĩ: ditta:. (f) ਜਦ ਸੰਗੀਤ ਸ਼ੁਰੂ ਹੋਇਆ ਤਾਂ ਕੁੜੀਆਂ ਨੱਚਣ ਲਗ ਪਈਆਂ jad sangi:t ʃuru: ɦoia: tã: kuɽi:ã: naccaɳ lag pai:ã:. (g) ਅਸੀਂ ਕਈ ਸਾਲ ਰਾਤ ਦਾ ਖਾਣਾ ਇਸੇ ਰੈਸਟੋਰੈਂਟ ਵਿਚ ਹੀ ਖਾਂਦੇ ਰਹੇ ਹਾਂ asĩ: kai: sa:l ra:t da: kʰa:ɳa: ise *restaurant* vic ɦi: kʰã:de ráɦe ɦã:. (h) ਪ੍ਰੋਫੈਸਰ ਸਾਹਬ ਪਹੁੰਚ ਗਏ ਸਨ, ਅਤੇ ਉਹ ਲੈਕਚਰ ਸ਼ੁਰੂ ਕਰਨ ਵਾਲੇ ਸਨ *Professor* sá:ɦab páɦũc gae san, ate úɦi *lecture* ʃuru: karan va:le san. (i) ਸਵੇਰ ਦਾ ਪੱਕਿਆ ਹੋਇਆ ਖਾਣਾ ਠੰਡਾ ਹੋਇਆ ਪਿਆ ਸੀ saver da: pakkia: ɦoia: kʰa:ɳa: ʈʰanɖa: ɦoia: pia: si:. (j) ਬੱਚਿਆਂ ਨੂੰ ਬਾਹਰ ਸੜਕ ਤੇ ਖੇਡਣ ਨਹੀਂ ਦੇਈਦਾ baccia̐: nũ: bá:ɦar saɽak te kʰeɖaɳ náɦĩ: deida:.

Script unit 1

1 **baɳ, cʰaɽ, mar, xarc, fark, janak, barf** 2 ਛਕ, ਬਕ, ਚਲ, ਬਸ, ਵਸਣ, ਕਰਨ, ਝਰਕ, ਜਕੜ, ਝਰਚ, ਫ਼ਸਲ, ਸ਼ਰਬਤ, ਬਰਕਤ, ਸਰਦਲ, ਪਰਗਾਟ, ਸਰਵਣ

Script unit 2

ਸਰਵਣ ਰਾਮ, ਹਕੀਮ ਸਰਦਾਰੀ ਲਾਲ ਸ਼ਰਮਾ, ਬਿਹਾਰੀ ਲਾਲ ਵਰਮਾ, ਚਰਨ ਦਾਸ, ਕਿਰਨ ਬਾਲਾ ਮਿਸਤਰੀ, ਲਤਾ ਮਿਸ਼ਰਾ, ਜਮਨਾ ਦਾਸ, ਪਰਮਜੀਤ ਸਬਰਵਾਲ, ਕਮਲਾ ਰਾਣੀ, ਚਾਰਦੀਵਾਰੀ, ਬਾਜ਼ੀਗਰ, ਸਰਘੀ, ਸਾਖੀ ਚਿੜੀ, ਘਿਸ, ਕਰਵਟ, ਮਾਝਾ, ਦਾਸਣਾ, ਧਾਗਾ, ਸਾਰਾ, ਕਰਵਾ, ਪਿਤਾ, ਮਾਤਾ

Script unit 4

1 (a) Shere Panjab Restaurant, Railway Road, Banga. (b) Vegetarian 5, non-vegetarian 6 (c) Chicken biriyani; Chicken bhuna; Tandoori chicken; (d) Lamb rogan josh; Lamb kebab; Lamb kofta (e) One vegetarian and one non-vegetarian (f) Low tone 2 (c) Aubergine (ਬੈਂਗਣ) (d) Apple (ਸੇਬ) for Libra (ਤੁਲਾ)

Script unit 5

1 **caɽà:i:, kaɖvà:, baɽà:va:, kú:ɳi:, ká:naɽa:, kàɽi:, naɽìnnavē, guná:, bókar, sénʃi:l, viá:, karɽʰɳa:, cɔ̃́da:, kḗda:, mɛ̃́, médi:, ʃéd, pó, kaɽià:l, cagɽà:lu:, sangàrʃ, bagià:ɽ, lá:be, pɔ́c**

Listening exercise transcripts

Conversation unit 1

A: sat sriː akaːl jiː.
B: sat sriː akaːl gill sáːɦab. bɛʈʰo.
A: náɦĩː saggu: sáːɦab, ʃukriːaː. mɛnũː ijaːzat dio.

A: ਸਤਿ ਸ੍ਰੀ ਅਕਾਲ ਜੀ।
B: ਸਤਿ ਸ੍ਰੀ ਅਕਾਲ, ਗਿੱਲ ਸਾਹਬ। ਬੈਠੋ।
A: ਨਹੀਂ ਸੱਗੁ ਸਾਹਬ, ਸ਼ੁਕਰੀਆ। ਮੈਨੂੰ ਇਜਾਜ਼ਤ ਦਿਓ।

Conversation unit 2

A: tuɦaːɖaː nãː kiː ɦɛ?
B: anvar ɦusɛn baʈʈ.
A: tusĩː kittʰe ráɦinde ɦo?
B: *Manchester* c.
A: *Manchester* c kitʰe?
B: *47 Oxford Road* te.
A: tusĩː ki kamm karde ɦo?
B: meraː *restaurant* ɦɛ?
A: tuɦaːɖaː *restaurant* kitʰe ɦɛ?
B: *74 Victoria Road* te.
A: tusĩː kamm te kaːr c jãːde ɦo?
B: ɦãː jiː.

A: ਤੁਹਾਡਾ ਨਾਂ ਕੀ ਹੈ?
B: ਅਨਵਰ ਹੁਸੈਨ ਬੱਟ।
A: ਤੁਸੀਂ ਕਿੱਥੇ ਰਹਿੰਦੇ ਹੋ?
B: *Manchester* 'ਚ
A: ਮਾਨਚੈਸਟਰ 'ਚ ਕਿੱਥੇ?
B: *47 Oxford Road* ਤੇ।
A: ਤੁਸੀਂ ਕੀ ਕੰਮ ਕਰਦੇ ਹੋ?
B: ਮੇਰਾ ਰੈਸਟੋਰੈਂਟ ਹੈ।
A: ਤੁਹਾਡਾ ਰੈਸਟੋਰੈਂਟ ਕਿੱਥੇ ਹੈ?
B: *74 Victoria Road* ਤੇ।

A: ਤੁਸੀਂ ਕੰਮ ਤੇ ਕਾਰ 'ਚ ਜਾਂਦੇ ਹੋ?
B: ਹਾਂ ਜੀ।

Conversation unit 3

1

A: malik sá:ɦab, tuɦa:nũ: baɽa: gʰàr cá:ɦi:da: ɦɛ jã: cʰoʈa:?
B: cʰoʈa:. par *terrace house* náɦĩ:. gʰàr de vic canga: *bathroom* vi: cá:ɦi:da: ɦɛ.
A: kinne *bedroom*?
B: tinn.
A: *Garden* agge jã: piccʰe?
B: agge ʈʰi:k ɦɛ.
A: *Garage* vi: cá:ɦi:di: ɦɛ?
B: ɦĩã: ji:.

A: ਮਲਿਕ ਸਾਹਬ, ਤੁਹਾਨੂੰ ਬੜਾ ਘਰ ਚਾਹੀਦਾ ਹੈ ਜਾਂ ਛੋਟਾ?
B: ਛੋਟਾ। ਪਰ ਟੈਰਿਸ ਹਾਊਸ ਨਹੀਂ। ਘਰ ਦੇ ਵਿਚ ਚੰਗਾ ਬਾਥਰੂਮ ਵੀ ਚਾਹੀਦਾ ਹੈ।
A: ਕਿੰਨੇ ਬੈੱਡਰੂਮ?
B: ਤਿੰਨ।
A: ਗਾਰਡਨ ਅੱਗੇ ਚਾਹੀਦਾ ਹੈ ਜਾਂ ਪਿੱਛੇ?
B: ਅੱਗੇ ਠੀਕ ਹੈ।
A: ਗੈਰਿਜ ਵੀ ਚਾਹੀਦੀ ਹੈ?
B: ਹਾਂ ਜੀ।

5

Shopkeeper: namaste ji: ki: ɦa:l ɦɛ?
You: namaste ji:. mera: ɦa:l ʈʰi:k ɦɛ. tuɦa:ɖa: ki: ɦa:l ɦɛ?
Shopkeeper: dasso. ki: cá:ɦi:da: ɦɛ?
You: tuɦa:ɖe kol ajj ɦari:ã: mircã: ɦɛgi:ã: ne?
Shopkeeper: ɦĩã: ji:. kinni:ã: cá:ɦi:di:ã: ne?
You: ikk pɔ̃ɖ. mɛnũ: do pɔ̃ɖ ʈama:ʈar vi: cá:ɦi:de ne.
Shopkeeper: ɛ́ɦi ne ʈama:ʈar.
You: par íɦi ʈama:ʈar la:l náɦĩ:.
Shopkeeper: íɦi ʈama:ʈar ʈʰi:k ne.
You: náɦĩ: mɛnũ: la:l ʈama:ʈar cá:ɦi:de ne.
Shopkeeper: ajj sa:ɖe kol la:l ʈamat:ʈar náɦĩ:.
You: koi: gall náɦĩ:.
Shopkeeper: ɦara: dʰàni:a: lao.
You: ji: náɦĩ: ʃukri:a:. ajj mɛnũ: dʰàni:a: náɦĩ: cá:ɦi:da:

Shopkeeper:	kújʰ ɦor vi: cá:ɦi:da: ɦɛ?
You:	ɦã: ji:. mɛnũ: bʰɪnɖi: vi: cá:ɦi:di: ɦɛ.

ਦੁਕਾਨਦਾਰ:	ਨਮਸਤੇ ਜੀ। ਕੀ ਹਾਲ ਹੈ?
ਤੁਸੀਂ:	ਨਮਸਤੇ ਜੀ। ਮੇਰਾ ਹਾਲ ਠੀਕ ਹੈ। ਤੁਹਾਡਾ ਕੀ ਹਾਲ ਹੈ?
ਦੁਕਾਨਦਾਰ:	ਦੱਸੋ। ਕੀ ਚਾਹੀਦਾ ਹੈ?
ਤੁਸੀਂ:	ਤੁਹਾਡੇ ਕੋਲ ਅੱਜ ਹਰੀਆਂ ਮਿਰਚਾਂ ਹੈਗੀਆਂ ਨੇ?
ਦੁਕਾਨਦਾਰ:	ਹਾਂ ਜੀ। ਕਿੰਨੀਆਂ ਚਾਹੀਦੀਆਂ ਨੇ?
ਤੁਸੀਂ:	ਇੱਕ ਪੌਂਡ। ਮੈਨੂੰ ਦੋ ਪੌਂਡ ਟਮਾਟਰ ਵੀ ਚਾਹੀਦੇ ਨੇ।
ਦੁਕਾਨਦਾਰ:	ਔਹ ਨੇ ਟਮਾਟਰ।
ਤੁਸੀਂ:	ਪਰ ਇਹ ਟਮਾਟਰ ਲਾਲ ਨਹੀਂ।
ਦੁਕਾਨਦਾਰ:	ਇਹ ਟਮਾਟਰ ਠੀਕ ਨੇ।
ਤੁਸੀਂ:	ਨਹੀਂ, ਮੈਨੂੰ ਲਾਲ ਟਮਾਟਰ ਚਾਹੀਦੇ ਨੇ।
ਦੁਕਾਨਦਾਰ:	ਅੱਜ ਸਾਡੇ ਕੋਲ ਲਾਲ ਟਮਾਟਰ ਨਹੀਂ।
ਤੁਸੀਂ:	ਕੋਈ ਗੱਲ ਨਹੀਂ।
ਦੁਕਾਨਦਾਰ:	ਹਰਾ ਧਨੀਆ ਲਓ।
ਤੁਸੀਂ:	ਜੀ ਨਹੀਂ ਸ਼ੁਕਰੀਆ। ਅੱਜ ਮੈਨੂੰ ਧਨੀਆ ਨਹੀਂ ਚਾਹੀਦਾ।
ਦੁਕਾਨਦਾਰ:	ਕੁਝ ਹੋਰ ਵੀ ਚਾਹੀਦਾ ਹੈ?
ਤੁਸੀਂ:	ਹਾਂ ਜੀ। ਮੈਨੂੰ ਭਿੰਡੀ ਵੀ ਚਾਹੀਦੀ ਹੈ।

Conversation unit 4

2

mɛnũ: panja:bi: kʰa:ṇa: kʰa:ṇ da: baɽa: ʃok ɦɛ. mɛ̃ kʰa:ṇe vic báɦut mirc masa:la: pasand karda: ɦã:. mɛnũ: ɦor vi: kai: ci:zã: cangi:ã: lagdi:ã: ne. mɛnũ: *football* báɦut pasand ɦɛ. par *cricket* mɛnũ: buri: lagdi: ɦɛ. mɛnũ: bʰà:rati: *classical* sangi:t canga: lagda: ɦɛ, ate paccʰami: sangi:t vi:. par bʰà:rati: filmi: sangi:t mɛnũ: pasand náɦĩ:.

ਮੈਨੂੰ ਪੰਜਾਬੀ ਖਾਣਾ ਖਾਣ ਦਾ ਬੜਾ ਸ਼ੌਕ ਹੈ। ਮੈਂ ਖਾਣੇ ਵਿਚ ਬਹੁਤ ਮਿਰਚ ਮਸਾਲਾ ਪਸੰਦ ਕਰਦਾ ਹਾਂ। ਮੈਨੂੰ ਹੋਰ ਵੀ ਕਈ ਚੀਜ਼ਾਂ ਚੰਗੀਆਂ ਲਗਦੀਆਂ ਨੇ। ਮੈਨੂੰ ਫੁਟਬਾਲ ਬਹੁਤ ਪਸੰਦ ਹੈ। ਪਰ ਕ੍ਰਿਕੇਟ ਮੈਨੂੰ ਬੁਰੀ ਲਗਦੀ ਹੈ। ਮੈਨੂੰ ਭਾਰਤੀ ਕਲਾਸੀਕਲ ਸੰਗੀਤ ਚੰਗਾ ਲਗਦਾ ਹੈ, ਅਤੇ ਪੱਛਮੀ ਸੰਗੀਤ ਵੀ। ਪਰ ਭਾਰਤੀ ਫ਼ਿਲਮੀ ਸੰਗੀਤ ਮੈਨੂੰ ਪਸੰਦ ਨਹੀਂ।

Conversation unit 5

1

landan tõ kaʃmi:r ja:ṇ lai: -
landan tõ navĩ: dilli: tak da: safar ɦava:i: jaɦa:z vic karo.
navĩ: dilli: de ɦava:i: aɖɖe tõ *railway station* tak *bus* sasti: ɦɛ, ate *taxi* mə́ɦĩngi:.

navĩ: dilli: tõ jammū tak kújʰ ya:tri: rel gaḍḍi: vic jã:de ne, te kújʰ ɦava:i: jaɦa:z vic.

jammū tõ sri:nagar da: bas da: safar báɦiut sóɦaṇa: te sasta: ɦɛ, par ɦava:i: jaɦa:z vi: t̪ʰi:k ɦɛ.

kaʃmi:r vic bas c ja:ṇa: sasta: ɦɛ. *Taxi* báɦiut máɦiingi: ɦɛ. kai: ya:tri:ã: nū: gʰòɽe te ja:ṇ da: ʃok vi: ɦiunda: ɦɛ.

ਲੰਡਨ ਤੋਂ ਕਸ਼ਮੀਰ ਜਾਣ ਲਈ -

ਲੰਡਨ ਤੋਂ ਨਵੀਂ ਦਿੱਲੀ ਤਕ ਦਾ ਸਫ਼ਰ ਹਵਾਈ ਜਹਾਜ਼ ਵਿਚ ਕਰੋ।

ਨਵੀਂ ਦਿੱਲੀ ਦੇ ਹਵਾਈ ਅੱਡੇ ਤੋਂ ਰੇਲਵੇ ਸਟੇਸ਼ਨ ਤਕ ਬਸ ਸਸਤੀ ਹੈ, ਅਤੇ ਟੈਕਸੀ ਮਹਿੰਗੀ।

ਨਵੀਂ ਦਿੱਲੀ ਤੋਂ ਜੰਮੂ ਤਕ ਕੁਝ ਯਾਤਰੀ ਰੇਲ ਗੱਡੀ ਵਿਚ ਜਾਂਦੇ ਨੇ, ਤੇ ਕੁਝ ਹਵਾਈ ਜਹਾਜ਼ ਵਿਚ।

ਜੰਮੂ ਤੋਂ ਸ੍ਰੀਨਗਰ ਤਕ ਬਸ ਦਾ ਸਫ਼ਰ ਬਹੁਤ ਹੀ ਸੋਹਣਾ ਤੇ ਸਸਤਾ ਹੈ, ਪਰ ਹਵਾਈ ਜਹਾਜ਼ ਵੀ ਠੀਕ ਹੈ।

ਕਸ਼ਮੀਰ ਵਿਚ ਬਸ 'ਚ ਜਾਣਾ ਸਸਤਾ ਹੈ। ਟੈਕਸੀ ਬਹੁਤ ਮਹਿੰਗੀ ਹੈ। ਕਈ ਯਾਤਰੀਆਂ ਨੂੰ ਘੋੜੇ ਤੇ ਜਾਣ ਦਾ ਸ਼ੌਕ ਵੀ ਹੁੰਦਾ ਹੈ।

Conversation unit 6

3

somva:r:	mɛ̃ kamm te gia:. ʃa:m da: kʰa:ṇa: *restaurant* c kʰá:d̪ʰa:, te ra:t nū: film dekʰi:.
mangalva:r:	*Dirctor's meeting* vic landan gia:.
búd̪ʰva:r:	mɛ̃ t̪ʰi:k náɦĩ: si:. sir dard ate buxa:r si:. mɛ̃ kamm te náɦĩ: gia:.
vi:rvanr:	ḍa:ktar nū: phone ki:ta:. úɦine gʰàr a: ke mɛnū: dekʰia: te dava:i: ditti:.
ʃukkarva:r:	mɛ̃ savere bʰà:i: sá:ɦab nū: *phone* ki:ta:. úɦi ʃa:m nū: mera: ɦa:l dekʰaṇ a:e. ra:t úɦi mere kol raɦe.
saniccarva:r:	ʃa:m da: kʰa:ṇa: asĩ: *restaurant* vic kʰá:d̪ʰa:. ra:t nū: *video* te panja:bi: *film* dekʰi:.
ɛtva:r:	bʰà:bi: ji: a:e. úɦinã: ne báɦiut sóɦaṇa: kʰa:ṇa: paka:ia:. bʰà:i: sá:ɦab ate bʰà:bi: ji: ʃa:m nū: gae.

ਸੋਮਵਾਰ:	ਮੈਂ ਕੰਮ ਤੇ ਗਿਆ। ਸ਼ਾਮ ਦਾ ਖਾਣਾ ਰੈਸਟੋਰੈਂਟ 'ਚ ਖਾਧਾ, ਤੇ ਰਾਤ ਨੂੰ ਫ਼ਿਲਮ ਦੇਖੀ।
ਮੰਗਲਵਾਰ:	ਡਾਇਰੈਕਟਰਜ਼ ਮੀਟਿੰਗ ਵਿਚ ਲੰਡਨ ਗਿਆ।
ਬੁਧਵਾਰ:	ਮੈਂ ਠੀਕ ਨਹੀਂ ਸੀ। ਸਿਰ ਦਰਦ ਅਤੇ ਬੁਖਾਰ ਸੀ। ਮੈਂ ਕੰਮ ਤੇ ਨਹੀਂ ਗਿਆ।
ਵੀਰਵਾਰ:	ਡਾਕਟਰ ਨੂੰ ਫ਼ੋਨ ਕੀਤਾ। ਉਹਨੇ ਘਰ ਆ ਕੇ ਮੈਨੂੰ ਦੇਖਿਆ ਤੇ ਦਵਾਈ ਦਿੱਤੀ।
ਸ਼ੁੱਕਰਵਾਰ:	ਮੈ ਸਵੇਰੇ ਭਾਈ ਸਾਹਬ ਨੂੰ ਫ਼ੋਨ ਕੀਤਾ। ਉਹ ਸ਼ਾਮ ਨੂੰ ਮੇਰੇ ਹਾਲ ਦੇਖਣ ਆਏ। ਰਾਤ ਉਹ ਮੇਰੇ ਕੋਲ ਰਹੇ।
ਸਨਿੱਚਰਵਾਰ:	ਸ਼ਾਮ ਦਾ ਖਾਣਾ ਅਸੀਂ ਰੈਸਟੋਰੈਂਟ ਵਿਚ ਖਾਧਾ। ਰਾਤ ਨੂੰ ਵੀਡੀਓ ਤੇ ਪੰਜਾਬੀ ਫ਼ਿਲਮ ਦੇਖੀ।

ਐਤਵਾਰ: ਭਾਬੀ ਜੀ ਆਏ। ਉਹਨਾਂ ਨੇ ਬਹੁਤ ਸੋਹਣਾ ਖਾਣਾ ਪਕਾਇਆ। ਭਾਈ ਸਾਹਬ ਅਤੇ
            ਭਾਬੀ ਜੀ ਸ਼ਾਮ ਨੂੰ ਗਏ।

Conversation unit 7

1

A: *Mrs Khan*, tuɦaːnũː kinniː̃ãː zabaːnãː aːũdiːã̃ ne?

B: tinn. meriː maːdariː zabaːn panjaːbiː ɦɛ. par *school* c mɛ̃ urduː
    sikkʰiː. mɛ̃ urduː páɽ̃ʰ likʰ viː sakdiː ɦã̃ː.

A: te panjaːbiːː?

B: bol ɦiː sakdiː ɦãː.

A: tuɦaːnũː angreziː viː aːũdiː ɦɛ?

B: angreziː mɛ̃ tʰoɽiː tʰoɽiː bol sakdiː ɦãː. páɽ̃ʰ likʰ náɦĩ̃ː sakdiːː.

A: ਮਿਸਿਜ਼ ਖ਼ਾਨ, ਤੁਹਾਨੂੰ ਕਿੰਨੀਆਂ ਜ਼ਬਾਨਾਂ ਆਉਂਦੀਆਂ ਨੇ?

B: ਤਿੰਨ। ਮੇਰੀ ਮਾਦਰੀ ਜ਼ਬਾਨ ਪੰਜਾਬੀ ਹੈ। ਪਰ ਸਕੂਲ 'ਚ ਮੈਂ ਉਰਦੂ ਸਿੱਖੀ। ਮੈਂ ਉਰਦੂ ਪੜ੍ਹ ਲਿਖ ਵੀ
    ਸਕਦੀ ਹਾਂ।

A: ਤੇ ਪੰਜਾਬੀ?

B: ਸਿਰਫ਼ ਬੋਲ ਹੀ ਸਕਦੀ ਹਾਂ।

A: ਤੁਹਾਨੂੰ ਅੰਗਰੇਜ਼ੀ ਵੀ ਆਉਂਦੀ ਹੈ?

B: ਅੰਗਰੇਜ਼ੀ ਮੈਂ ਥੋੜੀ ਥੋੜੀ ਬੋਲ ਸਕਦੀ ਹਾਂ। ਪਰ ਪੜ੍ਹ ਲਿਖ ਨਹੀਂ ਸਕਦੀ।

Conversation unit 8

1

A: *Gayatri Devi* jiːː, tuɦaːɖe *school* vic kiː kiː sikʰaːiaː jãːdaː ɦɛ?

B: *Chauhan* sáːɦab, saːɖe *school* c panj bʰaːʃaːvã̃ paɽàːiːã̃ jãːdiːã̃
    ne – panjaːbiːː, gujaraːtiːː, ɦindiːː, urduːː, te angreziːː.

A: tusĩ̃ː ɦor kiː kiː sikʰaːũde ɦo?

B: kʰaːɳa pakaːuɳaːː, gaːuɳaːː, sitaːr vajaːuɳaːː, bʰãngaɽa *dance*,
    gárbʰaː   *dance*, te cittarkaːri. agle saːl asĩ̃ː bangaːliː viː
    sikʰaːvã̃ːge.

A: ਗਾਯਤ੍ਰੀ ਦੇਵੀ ਜੀ, ਤੁਹਾਡੇ ਸਕੂਲ ਵਿਚ ਕੀ ਕੀ ਸਿਖਾਇਆ ਜਾਂਦਾ ਹੈ?

B: ਚੌਹਾਨ ਸਾਹਬ, ਸਾਡੇ ਸਕੂਲ 'ਚ ਪੰਜ ਭਾਸ਼ਾਵਾਂ ਪੜ੍ਹਾਈਆਂ ਜਾਂਦੀਆਂ ਨੇ - ਪੰਜਾਬੀ, ਗੁਜਰਾਤੀ, ਹਿੰਦੀ,
    ਉਰਦੂ, ਤੇ ਅੰਗਰੇਜ਼ੀ।

A: ਤੁਸੀਂ ਹੋਰ ਕੀ ਕੀ ਸਿਖਾਉਂਦੇ ਹੋ?

B: ਖਾਣਾ ਪਕਾਉਣਾ, ਗਾਉਣਾ, ਸਿਤਾਰ ਵਜਾਉਣਾ, ਭੰਗੜਾ ਡਾਂਸ, ਗਰਭਾ ਡਾਂਸ, ਤੇ ਚਿੱਤਰਕਾਰੀ। ਅਗਲੇ
    ਸਾਲ ਅਸੀਂ ਬੰਗਾਲੀ ਵੀ ਸਿਖਾਵਾਂਗੇ।

Index

The numbers refer to the Conversation units in the book. Panjabi words are given in **bold type**, using characters from the International Phonetic Alphabet.

adjectives 3
  black 3
  oblique forms 3
  paired 8
  possessive 1, 4, 5
  red 3
adverbs 3
agentive postposition **ne** 5, 6
agreement
  of adjectives 3
  lack of 5, 6
  fiɛ 2
  imperfective verb form 2
  perfective verb form 6
  potential verb form 5
  si: 5
  subjunctive verb forms 7
ambiguous sentences 4
auxiliary verbs 7
  cukk 7, 10
  de 7, 9, 10
  ja: 8, 9, 10
  lɛ 7, 10
  ráfii 7, 10
  sak 7
  passive auxiliary 8
  a: 7

reference to skills 7
a:pŋa: 5
black adjectives 3
causative verb forms 7, 8
ca:fii:da: 3, 10
comparision 5
  use of **tõ** and **na:lõ** 5
compound verbs 7
conjunctions (paired) 9
cukk (helping verb) 7, 10
de (helping verb) 7, 10
definite object 4
  with **nũ:** 4, 5
echo words 6
experiencer 4
  omission of 4
focus and emphasis 6
future time (referring to) 7
gender 1
  respectful use of masculine gender 7
gerund 4
  used with **lag** and **lag pɛ** 9
habitual actions
  use of the imperfective form 2
fiatʰi:, etc.
  use of the 'instrumental dual'

form
have 2, 8
fiɛ 2, 5
  contrasted with **fio** 5
  omission in negative
    sentences 2
  past tense 5
  present tense 2
fiɛ naː 6
fiɛgaː 3
helping verbs (see auxiliary verbs)
fiiː
  emphatic use 8
  particle 5
fio 5
  auxiliary verb 9
  contrasted with **fiɛ** 5
  used with perfective form 9
immediate future 7
  use of **ráfii** 7, 9
imperfective verb form 2
  use as adjective 9, 10
  agreement 2
  'contrary to fact' use 6, 10
  -i- variety 9
  reference to instantaneous
    future 7
  used with **ráfii** 9
instantaneous future 7
  use of the imperfective
    form 2, 6, 9
jaː
  auxiliary verb 9, 10
  passive auxiliary 8
jaːŋ 7
  contrasted with **aː** 7
ke 6, 10
  sequence of actions 6
kiː 4

in yes/no questions 4
lag 4
  helping verb 9, 10
  used with gerund 9
  used with imperfective form 10
  used with **pɛ** 9
lɛ (helping verb) 7, 10
náfiiː 8
  contrasted with **naː** 8
naːlõ 5
  making comparision 5
ne (agentive postposition) 5, 6
noun + verb as verb equivalent 6
nũː 4
  marker of a definite object 5
  omission of 5
number–gender affixes 1
  with adjectives 1
  with verb forms 2, 5, 6, 7, 8
obligation 8
  use of **pɛ** 8
oblique forms 3
  adjectives 3
  nouns 3
  pronouns 6
paired conjunctions, pronouns,
  adverbs 9
particles **fiiː**, **viː**, **tãː** 5
pasand 4
  pasand fiɛ 4
  pasand kar 4
pɛ (auxiliary verb) 9
  used with **lag** 9
perfective verb form 6
  used as adjective 6, 9, 10
  agreement 6
  used with **fio** 9
plural 1
  nouns 2

pronouns 2
   respectful use 1
polite forms 1
possessions
   inseparable 2
   separable 3
possessive adjectives 1
postposition 3
   compound 3
   simple 3
   strong and weak forms 3
postpositional phrases 3
   chained 3
   simple 3
potential verb form 5
   use as adjective 6
   giving advice 6
   agreement 5
   used with **fiɛ** 10
pronouns
   demonstrative 1
   emphatic 6
   paired 9
   personal 1
ráfii (helping verb) 7
   used with imperfective
      form 7, 9, 10

red adjectives 3
repetition of words 4, 7, 8
sɑk (auxiliary verb) 7
siːgɑ: 6
SOV word-order 2
subjunctive verb form 7
   agreement 7
   making suggestions 8
   seeking permission 8
   subjunctive + **gɑ:** 7
tag questions
   with **fiɛ nɑ:** 6
   with **nɑ:** 2
tɑ̃: 5
time 5
   Indian (bidirectional)
   concept 5
tõ 5
   use for making comparision 5
vɑːlɑ: 5
verb combinations 9
verbal noun (see gerund)
vi: 5
word order 1–10
   focus and emphasis 6
xud 6
yes/no questions 1, 4